D0084661

EMERGING MINDS

EMERGING MINDS

The Process of Change in Children's Thinking

ROBERT S. SIEGLER

New York Oxford
OXFORD UNIVERSITY PRESS
1996

Oxford University Press

Oxford New York
Athens Auckland Bangkok Bogota Bombay
Buenos Aires Calcutta Cape Town Dar es Salaam
Delhi Florence Hong Kong Istanbul Karachi
Kuala Lumpur Madras Madrid Melbourne
Mexico City Nairobi Paris Singapore
Taipei Tokyo Toronto

and associated companies in
Berlin Ibadan

Published by Oxford University Press, Inc.,
198 Madison Avenue, New York, New York 10016

Library of Congress Cataloging-in-Publication Data
Siegler, Robert S.
Emerging Minds : the process of change
in children's thinking / Robert S. Siegler.
p. cm.
Includes bibliographical references and index.
ISBN 0-19-507787-3
1. Cognition in children. 2. Cognitive styles in children.
3. Human information processing in children. I. Title.
BF723.C5S53 1996
155.4'13—dc20 95-42099

1 3 5 7 9 8 6 4 2
Printed in the United States of America
on acid-free paper

Preface

Every intellectual discipline is an attempt to answer a few basic questions. For developmental psychology, one of these questions, perhaps *the* basic question, is "How does change occur?" My goal in writing this book is to focus attention directly on this issue of how change occurs, and in particular, to focus attention on how changes occur in children's thinking.

The book includes a critique of traditional ways of viewing cognitive-developmental change, a proposed alternative framework, and illustrations of the benefits that the alternative framework can bring. The critique begins with the observation that for many years, those interested in cognitive development have followed an implicit metaphor: cognitive development as a staircase. Within this metaphor, children's thinking is depicted as being at a given level for a prolonged period of time, then undergoing a sudden upward movement, then being at the new, higher level for another prolonged period of time, and so on. This approach has helped create many dramatic and memorable depictions of children's thinking. However, it has not helped us understand change, and may well have hindered our efforts to do so. The research approaches that have stemmed from this metaphor tell us about differences between younger and older children, but not about how children get from here to there.

An alternative framework, which I believe is both more consistent with empirical data and more helpful in understanding change, is based on an analogy to biological evolution. In both evolutionary and cognitive developmental contexts, adaptive change seems to require mechanisms for producing new variants (species or ideas), mechanisms that select among the varying forms available at any given time, and mechanisms that lead to the more successful forms becoming increasingly prevalent over time. This analogy leads to such assumptions as that children will generally think about given phenomena in a variety of ways, rather than only having a single understanding; that they will choose adaptively among these alternative understandings; and that their thinking will change continuously and become increasingly adaptive over time. These assumptions prove to have large implications for the questions we ask about children's thinking, the methods we use to study it, and the mechanisms that we propose to account for changes in it.

After describing the framework for conceptualizing cognitive development, I examine its usefulness for understanding changes in children's thinking in a variety of domains: problem solving, conceptual understanding, reasoning, planning, remembering, and producing and comprehending language, among them. The changes involve varied age groups engaging in diverse activities: infants choosing strategies for locomoting up and down ramps; toddlers searching for hidden objects and choosing which words to say and how to say them; preschoolers trying to understand conservation and class inclusion; elementary school children trying to solve mathematics problems individually and in collaboration with peers; and adolescents and adults reasoning about morality, fairness, and scientific experimentation. The effort to understand change processes also makes use of a wide range of methods, including trial-by-trial assessments of strategy use, microgenetic designs that intensively examine children's changing competence as it changes, and computer simulations of the mechanisms that produce changes in children's thinking.

Cognitive developmental change is a complex phenomenon, and no single approach can reveal all of its secrets. I believe, however, that the present approach can reveal some of them.

Pittsburgh, Pennsylvania R. S.
February 1996

Acknowledgments

This book has benefitted from the generosity of many friends. The first to read and comment on it were colleagues at Carnegie Mellon who attended a seminar I organized in the winter of 1995. They read through the book one chapter per week, offering extensive and insightful comments about each of them. The regulars at the seminar were Karen Adolph, Martha Alibali, Sharon Carver, Melissa Ipollito, Patrick Lemaire, Marsha Lovett, Yuko Munakata, Bethany Rittle, Chris Schunn, Alice Siegler, and Doug Thompson. Numerous others attended when their schedules permitted. So dedicated were members of the seminar that several of them even sent extensive e-mail comments on particular chapters when they were out of town or otherwise unavailable for a meeting.

When I had incorporated the comments of seminar members, I next sought the reactions of four colleagues at other universities. Shari Ellis, John Flavell, Kevin Miller, and Bob Sternberg each read the entire book and made numerous incisive and constructive suggestions regarding it. Their suggestions covered everything from typos and grammatical errors to the deepest mysteries of cognitive development. The care with which they read the manuscript, and the thoughtfulness of their ideas for improving it, exceeded any reasonable expectation.

The ideas expressed in the book also reflect the perspectives of colleagues at Carnegie Mellon with whom I have had the good fortune to collaborate on research over the past decade. Especially large contributions to my thinking have been made by Kevin Crowley, Shari Ellis, Eric Jenkins, Kate McGilly, Chris Shipley, and Jeff Shrager. Special thanks are due to Dave Klahr, who has helped shape my thinking on any number of the issues discussed in the book, and whose friendship and collegiality over the past 21 years have been invaluable to my development, both personal and professional.

Many other institutions and individuals have contributed to the project in all kinds of ways. Generous financial support has been provided for the research by the National Institutes of Health and by the Spencer, Mellon, and McDonnell Foundations. Carnegie Mellon has been a friendly, supportive environment throughout the time I have been here. Lily Dalton, Kathy Dennler, and Alice Siegler all played essential roles in conducting and analyzing most of the research studies on which I am an author. Theresa Treasure added skilled and enthusiastic secretarial support, helping especially in creation of figures and tables and in locating references. My wife Alice and children, Todd, Beth, and Aaron have endured patiently and with good humor the many times that I was preoccupied with the book or the research within it. Beth also provided useful comments on several chapters from the perspective of an intelligent person who was unfamiliar with the field. Last but far from least is Joan Bossert, my editor at Oxford University Press, who has enthusiastically supported the project from its outset and provided help at critical moments.

It is tempting to try to thank the innumerable others who also have made major contributions to the book, but it is impossible to know either where to begin or where to end.

Contents

EMERGING MINDS

1

Whose Children Are We Talking About?

My children have never looked much like those described in most theories of cognitive development. I don't mean that they are generally deviant or that they perform abnormally on conservation or class inclusion tasks. They generally seem more or less normal, and on the few occasions when I have presented tasks from the cognitive developmental literature, they have acted pretty much like the children described in the articles.

Where my children are altogether different from the theoretical descriptions is in the variability of their thinking. Cognitive developmental theories generally depict age and thought as proceeding in a 1:1 relation. At an early age, children think in one way; at a later age, they think in another way; at a still later age, they think in a third way. Such descriptions are so pervasive that they begin to feel like reality. Young children are said to form thematic concepts; somewhat older ones to form chain concepts; yet older ones to form true concepts. The reasoning of young children is said to be preoperational; that of somewhat older ones concrete operational; that of yet older ones formal operational. Young children are said to have one theory of mind; somewhat older ones a different, more inclusive theory; yet older ones a more advanced theory still.

The story is the same with characterizations of performance on specific tasks. In descriptions of the development of the concept of living things, 3- and 4-year-olds are said to think that anything that moves is alive, 5- to 8-year-olds that animals—and only animals—are alive, and older children that plants as well as animals are alive. In descriptions of the development of addition skill, kindergartners are said to count from one; first through third graders to count from the larger addend; fourth graders and older children to retrieve answers from memory. In descriptions of the development of serial recall strategies, 5-year-olds are said not to rehearse; 8-year-olds to rehearse in a simple way; 11-year-olds to rehearse in a more elaborate way.

My children's thinking has never looked as neat and clean as these 1:1 characterizations of the relation between age and thought. Each child seems to have diverse ways of thinking about almost everything. As a 4-year-old, my older son explicitly asked whether plants were alive; when I wondered why he asked, he told me that they grew but they didn't move. When she started to add, my daughter would sometimes retrieve an answer from memory and 5 minutes later count fingers to solve the same problem. When he started calling friends on the phone, my younger son would, after looking up a phone number, sometimes write the number on a piece of paper, other times rehearse it aloud, and other times just try to remember it.

My children's concepts, theories, and reasoning also vary widely. Listening to them talk at the dinner table reveals a remarkable range of ideas, ranging from insightful to incoherent. The same child will first make a clever and penetrating argument, only to buttress the position with a second argument so feeble that it undermines the positive impression created by the first. If our family is at all representative, it seems likely that children's thinking is far more variable than suggested by traditional theories of cognitive development.

This variability implies a second way in which my children's behavior differs from that described in most theories of cognitive development: Unlike the depictions of children within the theories, they must constantly choose what to do. When children are depicted as only having a single way of representing a situation, thinking about a concept, or solving a problem, there are no choices to be made. They are, in a sense, the slaves of their cognitive structures. In contrast, if they possess multiple ways of performing these cognitive activities, then they must choose which one to use in each situation. This is not to say that all, or even most, of the choices involve conscious evaluation of the advantages and disadvantages of alternative courses of action. A great many are made without any apparent conscious consideration. Nonetheless, choices are constantly being made. Each time children try to remember an unfamiliar phone number or solve an arithmetic problem, they must choose how to do so. They also must decide whether to try to argue their way out of cleaning their room or to just do it, whether they should study in advance for the next quiz or cram at the last minute, whether to write a paper on a computer or by hand, whether to talk to a friend about a conflict or to let the passage of time blur the disagreement, and so on. Note that none of these decisions closely resembles the type of problems studied in the field known as "decision making." The "decision-making problems" typically studied within this field are only a small (and I suspect rather unrepresentative) subset of the situations in which children and adults must decide what to do.

My children also dramatically diverge from most theories of cognitive development in a third respect: the omnipresence of change in their behavior. Most theories of cognitive development relegate change to an occasional, and underspecified, role. For example, within stage theories, transitions tend to be brief, rather mysterious episodes during which children ascend from one stable way of viewing the world to a different, more advanced way. Within such approaches, as Flavell (1971) remarked, "the individual spends virtually all his childhood years 'being' rather than 'becoming'" (pp. 426–427). Such depictions are far from unique to stage theories. Regardless of whether the approach describes cognitive development in terms of stages, rules, strategies, or theories; regardless of whether its content centers on problem solving, memory, or conceptual understanding; regardless of whether the children being described are infants, preschoolers, school age children, or adolescents; both classic and contemporary theories typically place static states at center stage and place change processes either in the wings or offstage altogether.

This makes the theories very different from my own children, who almost never stay still, either literally or metaphorically. They are continually acquiring new concepts, skills, strategies, and frameworks for thinking about the world. The changes were most dramatic early in their lives, when almost every day would bring a milestone. However, they have continued at a high rate throughout childhood and adolescence.

For example, in the last few years, all three children have earned money in a variety of ways, ranging from setting up lemonade stands to delivering newspapers to baby-sitting to buying and selling baseball, football, and hockey cards. Their understanding of these activities, and of more general economic issues, has changed continually as they have engaged in them. From running the lemonade stands, they have learned the importance of choosing a good location, not pricing the product too high, offering discounts for large purchases, and agreeing in advance among themselves how to divide profits. From delivering newspapers, they have learned about the importance of timeliness and reliability, the hidden costs involved in having to go to customers to collect money, and the proper mix of politeness and threats needed to motivate deadbeats to pay their bills. From baby-sitting, they have learned the usefulness of establishing a competitive advantage (in this case by developing a box of special toys and activities to bring to the children for whom they sit), the need to insist on being paid the agreed-upon rate (people have a strangely asymmetric tendency to misrecall the hourly fee), and the advisability of simply refusing to render future services for people who have not lived up to past agreements. From playing the sports cards market, they have learned the importance of acting on new information before the crowd does, of the difference between local and national markets, of the premium commanded by goods of the highest quality, and of the difference between what a book or magazine says something is worth and what people will actually pay for it. These activities have also been instructive about a host of noneconomic issues such as discrimination (parents often prefer girls as baby-sitters), about the value of inside information (professional sports card dealers know about future price increases before others do, and sometimes inform favored customers about impending changes), and about word of mouth (baby-sitting jobs often originate with the recommendations of satisfied customers or other baby-sitters). All of these realizations derive from the children's economic activities, a very small aspect of their lives; many other aspects have, no doubt, led to more numerous and profound changes.

The Mystery of the Immaculate Transition

Suppose that I am right in believing that most theories of cognitive development depict children's thinking as less variable, less demanding of choice, and less dynamic than it really is. Maybe these are mere peccadilloes rather than fundamental flaws. After all, might not the gains in simplicity, elegance, and memorability of the theories outweigh the loss in accuracy and completeness entailed in understating the variability and need for choices in children's thinking? And might not the initial focus on static states be a necessary first step toward understanding change?

If this were 1960, 1970, or even 1980, such arguments might be persuasive. As more and more research has been conducted, however, the arguments have become less and less compelling. Simply put, the accumulation of such descriptions has not advanced us very quickly toward what I consider the deepest goal of theories of cognitive development: *to understand the process of change in children's thinking*.

The way in which focusing on static states limits understanding of change has often been recognized, and has been the subject of a number of insightful discussions (Flavell, 1984; Miller, 1989; Sternberg, 1984). To the degree that describing these static states becomes a goal in itself, it diverts attention from the elusive problem of how changes occur. Saying that we cannot understand change until we have better descriptions of thinking at particular points in development also provides an excuse for all seasons, a justification for avoiding the difficult issues involved in hypothesizing and testing mechanisms that could produce the changes.

The way in which underestimating the variability in children's thinking has hindered attempts to understand change is less obvious and has rarely been discussed explicitly. It may, however, be at least as large an impediment to progress. Portraying children's thinking as monolithic at each point in the developmental sequence has the effect of segregating change from the ebb and flow of everyday cognitive activity. It makes change a rare, almost exotic event that demands an exceptional explanation. If children of a given age have for several years consistently thought of a problem in a particular way, why should they suddenly start thinking about the problem in a different way? The process is especially mysterious because the kinds of problems that play central roles within many theories—for example, questions about conservation, balance scales, and purple taxicabs—are ones that children rarely if ever encounter or think about outside the laboratory. Thus, it is unlikely to be negative feedback or direct instruction that leads to the change. This leaves us with a paradox: If children have a single concept of x for a protracted period of time, and no external stimulus tells them that anything is wrong with thinking about x in that way, why would they start thinking about it differently? Put more succinctly: What is the cause of such immaculate transitions?

The problem is exacerbated by the large qualitative changes that are often hypothesized to mark successive steps in the developmental sequence. Such depictions make for an appealing story in classroom lectures and textbooks, but also make it difficult to understand how children could ever bridge the gap. Viewing changes in terms of leaps from one understanding to a qualitatively different one may subtly discourage investigators from even trying to account for them. It is hard to imagine mechanisms that would allow a child who initially possessed only holistic concepts to form analytic ones, that would allow a child who could form only sensorimotor representations to form representational ones, or that would allow a child to restructure a psychologically based theory of biology into a biologically based one. Trying to understand change is inherently challenging and complex. However, in our efforts to describe development as cleanly and dramatically as possible, we may inadvertently have made the task harder than it needs to be.

If there were strong empirical basis for believing that the fundamental changes in children's thinking occur at a few particular times, the problems entailed by underestimating the variability of children's thinking and overestimating the magnitude of the few changes that are recognized might be justified as convenient simplifications. As the database in the field has expanded, however, the assumption of domain-general stage changes has become increasingly untenable. Important changes have been documented at every age. As a result, labeling certain times as the critical transition periods has come to seem completely arbitrary. What constitutes the critical change for cognitive development as a whole: the vocabulary explosion that begins between 18 and 24 months (McCarthy, 1954), the differentiation of categories that occurs between 24 and 30 months (Mandler, Bauer, & McDonough, 1991), the change in understanding of symbolic representations that occurs between 30 and 36 months (DeLoache, 1987), or the change in understanding of the mind that occurs between 36 and 48 months (Wellman, 1990)? It seems likely that the more we know, the less sense it will make to single out some periods as the key transitions in cognitive development as a whole and other periods as ones of stability. Instead, we will want to recognize that all of development is a transition period, with children always thinking in multiple ways, rather than just one.

From this perspective, it is no accident that recent approaches that have emphasized the goal of explaining change, notably dynamical systems approaches (Thelen & Smith, 1994; Thelen & Ulrich, 1991; van Geert, 1991; van der Maas & Molenaar, 1992), connectionist approaches (Changeux & Dehaene, 1989; MacWhinney & Leinbach, 1991; McClelland, 1995; Shultz et al., 1995), symbolic self-modifying systems approaches (Halford, 1995; Klahr, 1992; Simon & Klahr 1995), and some neo-Piagetian approaches (Acredolo & O'Connor, 1990; Karmiloff-Smith, 1992; Kuhn, 1995) all have emphasized both the variability of thought and the continuity of the underlying process of change. Such approaches continue to be in the minority, however. The large majority of research on cognitive development continues to focus on identifying *the* way in which children think about a given topic at a given age and leaves issues regarding change to the future.

Why Do We Have These Problems?

If change is the dominant reality in cognitive development, why have so many efforts been made to divide development into discrete periods punctuated by brief transitions? Oyama (1985) placed this issue in an interesting perspective. She suggested that much of psychology is aimed at identifying *essences*. Are people at their core aggressive or peaceful, selfish or altruistic, rational or irrational? Is their behavior essentially determined by nature or nurture, heredity or environment, genes or culture?

In the context of developmental research, the goal of such efforts has been to identify the essence at each age. For example, what is the nature of 5-year-olds' thinking, and how does it differ from the thinking of 8-year-olds? The goal has generated many attempts to label the fundamental difference. The 5-year-olds' thinking is said to be "egocentric," "associative," "preconceptual," "wholistic," "undifferentiated," "thematic," and so on. The 8-year-olds' thinking is given an entirely different set of labels, intended both to identify its essence and to distinguish it clearly from its predecessor.

Years of accumulated research, however, have thrown into doubt the existence of such essences. Regardless of the particular essence that has been postulated, exceptions abound. Furthermore, the attempt to identify such essences may have led to a focus on confirming or disconfirming the essence and to a neglect of the specifics of thinking that do not fit neatly into the hypothesized mold. Such exceptions may be critical to the change process precisely *because* they do not fit neatly into the mold.

Oyama's critique has an interesting implication for understanding cognitive development: The separation of stable states from transition periods may result from our attempt to define essences rather than from any underlying reality. Attempting to isolate the essence of thinking at different ages may have led to inaccurate descriptions of children's thinking at particular ages and discouraged serious theorizing about mechanisms (because of the seeming impossibility of describing in detail mechanisms that would accomplish the transition from one essence to another).

These criticisms of theories that posit 1:1 relations between age and thought should not be taken as dismissing their contributions. Attempts to support and refute them have led to impressive demonstrations of both early competence and later incompetence, stimulated creation of increasingly sensitive methods to demonstrate that infants and young children "have" or do not "have" the competence in question, and generally led to an increasingly rich database about development. Rather, the intent of the critique is to question basic assumptions about the nature of cognitive development and to advance to center stage a terribly important issue about which most current theories have little to say—the issue of how change occurs.

The three issues introduced so far—the variability of children's thinking, the need for children to choose among alternative ways of thinking, and the omnipresence of changes in their thinking—are the focus of the remainder of this chapter (and of the book as a whole). In particular, the remaining sections of the chapter examine in more detail how major theories of cognitive development have dealt with these issues, how their inattention to variability and choice have interfered with understanding of change, and how modern evolutionary theory provides a natural framework for thinking about cognitive change in more fruitful ways.

Variability

Fields of psychology are defined in large part by the sources of variability they emphasize. Personality psychology emphasizes variability attributable to individual differences; comparative psychology emphasizes variability attributable to species differences; social psychology emphasizes variability attributable to interpersonal influences; cross-cultural psychology emphasizes variability due to cultural differences; and so on. Researchers within each field typically describe themselves as interactionists, and many do study interactions among sources of variability. For example, a good number of personality researchers study interactions between individual and situational characteristics (e.g., Carver & Scheier, 1992). Nonetheless, the type of variability that receives the most attention is in large part what defines each field.

Within developmental psychology, variability among age groups is the main focus of attention. The attempt to document such variability is the touchstone of most research in the field. As if obeying the dictum from graduate research methods courses, "maximize variability between groups, minimize variability within groups," most theories of cognitive development have depicted children of varying ages as thinking in dramatically different ways and have relegated to the background variability within each age group. This can be seen in the following brief and oversimplified characterizations of how a number of well-known theories depict age-related changes in thinking. The descriptions do not do justice to the complexity of the theorists' visions, but they should at least be recognizable.

As with so much in the field of cognitive development, Piaget's theory is a good place to start. Piaget depicted children's understanding of various concepts as a sequence of increasingly adequate understandings that reflected their general level of thought and reasoning. For example, 4- to 6-year-olds are described as being unable to understand the conservation concept (Piaget, 1952a). This leads them to think of conservation problems in terms of single static dimensions: relative amount of liquid is equated with relative height of the liquid columns, relative number of objects is equated with relative length of the rows of objects, relative length of objects is equated with relative endpoint in the direction that one of the objects was moved, and so on. After thinking of conservation in this way for several years, children are said to enter into a brief transitional period, marked by cognitive conflict. Following this transition, they arrive at the next, higher, steady state–concrete operational reasoning. At this point, they understand the logic that leads to conservation of number, amount, length, and so on.

Similar characterizations are offered for changes in thinking that occur in other developmental periods. For example, infants younger than 9 months are viewed as not understanding that objects have a permanent existence, as not being able to imitate the actions of other people, and of generally being unable to form enduring representations of objects and events (Piaget, 1952b). Preoperational children, in contrast, possess all of these competencies. Similarly, concrete operations stage children are viewed as unable to understand ratios and proportions, combinatorial possibilities, and chance and probability, whereas formal operations stage children are viewed as having such understanding (Inhelder & Piaget, 1958).

Piaget (e.g., 1967/1971) did hypothesize greater variability of thinking during brief transitional periods and viewed this variability as critical to cognitive change. He also recognized that even during periods of general equilibrium, the cognitive structures continually changed in small ways through the processes of assimilation and accommodation. Despite being the quintessential stage theorist, he also was far more sensitive than almost all of his successors to the importance of explaining change, and made a greater effort to do so. Nonetheless, the dominant impression of children's thinking that emerges from his work is that at almost all times, a child of a given age will think of a given problem in a certain way, one that reflects the child's cognitive structure at that time.

This impression was buttressed by subsequent stage theories of cognitive development. For example, Bruner, Olver, and Greenfield (1966) hypothesized a stage progression of alternative representational forms. Children were said first to generate enactive representations, in which concepts are represented through perception and action; then to generate ikonic representations, in which mental images play a dominant role; and then to generate symbolic representations in which abstract relations are foremost. Thus, 4- and 5-year-olds' difficulty on liquid quantity conservation problems was ascribed to their representation emphasizing ikonic rather than symbolic relations.

Kohlberg's (1969) theory of moral development also posited a 1:1 relation between children's developmental status and their reasoning. Kohlberg hypothesized that children progress through six stages of moral reasoning, which could be grouped into three broad classes: preconventional, conventional, and postconventional. Children at a given level of moral development would reason in accord with one or another of these modes of reasoning. All children would begin with the Stage 1 approach (punishment and obedience orientation), and would move through the subsequent stages in an invariant order. How far children progressed was influenced by the culture in which they lived, by their local environments, by individual differences in intellect and personality, and by a host of other factors. At each age, however, the child would be in a particular stage of moral reasoning and would reason about moral issues in a way consistent with that stage.

Piaget's, Bruner's, and Kohlberg's theories, empirical findings, epistemological stances, and sets of psychological issues constitute a rich legacy for everyone interested in development. Not surprisingly, different inheritors have maintained and built upon different parts of the legacies. However, almost all have adhered to the tradition of describing children of a particular age as thinking in a particular way and children of a different age as thinking in a different way. This can be seen by considering three of the most influential current approaches to cognitive development: neo-Piagetian, theory-based, and information-processing approaches.

Case's (1985) theory of intellectual development is probably *the* prototypic neo-Piagetian approach. Like Piaget's theory, it includes four age-linked stages: sensorimotor, representational, logical, and formal operations. These correspond to qualitatively distinct ways of representing the world; for example, in the representational operations stage, children cannot represent transformations, but in the logical operations stage, they can. Also as in Piaget's theory, the transition periods between stages are far briefer than the periods during which children are "in" a stage (though there also is considerable development within each stage), and the mechanisms that produce the changes are less fully described than performance within each stage. Case hypothesizes that between-stage changes occur when working memory capacity for the particular type of representation reaches four units. This is a highly specific claim, but it remains unclear why or how attaining four units of working memory capacity within one type of representation should allow formation of a different type of representation.

Carey's (1985) depiction of the development of a theory of biology is a good representative of approaches emphasizing theories, constraints, principles, and other high-order but domain-specific constructs (e.g., Carey, 1985; R. Gelman & Gallistel, 1978; S. Gelman, 1988; Wellman, 1990). Carey suggested that 4- and 5-year-olds have a merged behavioral/psychological theory of biology, whereas older children, such as 10-year-olds, have distinct theories of biology and psychology. In particular, the younger children are said to think about living things in terms of characteristic features, such as movement, whereas the older ones are said to think about the living things in terms of biological essences.

Those adopting an information-processing approach, myself included, also have often depicted development in terms of young children using one approach, somewhat older children a different approach, and yet older children a third approach (e.g., Klahr, 1984; Siegler, 1983; Sternberg, 1985). For example, 5- and 6-year-olds have been said not to use rehearsal and organizational strategies, 8- and 9-year-olds to use simple versions of these strategies, and 11- and 12-year-olds to use sophisticated versions of the strategies (e.g., Naus & Ornstein, 1983).

Such descriptions of developmental sequences have a number of virtues. They are simple, straightforward, and memorable. They call attention to the order in which changes occur, clearly an important aspect of development. They have none of the maddening character of "some people, in some situations, it all depends" that characterize so many psychological descriptions. They are testable; those wishing to disconfirm the hypothesized developmental sequence need only demonstrate that children of a given age think in ways different from those that are described.

Unfortunately, they also have proved to be inconsistent with a great deal of data. Furthermore, the way in which they are inconsistent with the data has created a serious dilemma.

One type of inconsistency involves demonstrations of early competence. Many such demonstrations have been stimulated by Piaget's theory. Contrary to theoretical predictions, 4- and 5-year-olds show understanding of conservation, class inclusion, transitivity, and other "concrete operational concepts" in some situations (e.g., Bryant & Trabasso, 1971; Markman & Siebert, 1976; McGarrigle & Donaldson, 1974). Theoretically irrelevant variables such as the presence of memory aids, the wording of questions, and the particular stimulus materials turn out to influence thinking and reasoning a great deal. These findings of greater early competence than envisioned within Piaget's theory have not been limited to the preoperational period. Children as young as 2 weeks are capable of imitating behaviors that they have seen (Meltzoff & Moore, 1983). Infants as young as 4 months show evidence of understanding that objects do not cease to exist when the child cannot see them (Baillargeon, 1987, 1993). Five-month-olds can remember for at least 24 hours attributes of objects they have encountered (Strauss & Cohen, 1978).

Similar findings can be cited for all of the hypothesized developmental sequences described above. Children as young as 1 year are not limited to enactive concepts; they can form symbolic ones as well (Bauer & Mandler, 1989). Early elementary school age children reason about moral issues in terms of universal values as well as whether they will be rewarded or punished (Turiel, 1983). In domains in which children's knowledge exceeds that of adults, the children's working memory capacity also is often greater (e.g., Chi & Koeske, 1983). Preschoolers utilize specifically biological information, not just psychological information, for drawing inferences about biological properties when the task presentation indicates that biological beliefs are the relevant ones (S. Gelman, 1988; Keil, 1989). Five- and six-year-olds often use the same types of rehearsal strategies for serial recall as older children do (McGilly & Siegler, 1989).

These findings of early competence pose a dilemma. On the one hand, statements of the form "Children of age *N* cannot understand *X*" generally have proved to be wrong. Under some circumstances, infants and young children display impressive reasoning, conceptual understanding, and problem-solving strategies. In a sense, they "have" the competencies they were thought to lack. On the other hand, the new data do not make the old disappear. Even if children "have" the competencies, they clearly lack something that makes them fail on tasks that older children and adults solve with ease. Demonstrations of early competence do not end the discussion; they only begin it. After all, it is the same cognitive system that is generating the successes in some contexts and the failures in others. The problem has often been described (e.g., Braine, 1959; Brown, 1976; Flavell, 1985), but no compelling solution has been forthcoming.

How can we reconcile children's competence with their incompetence? I believe that one important step is to recognize the variability of thinking within individual children (and adults). Each of us has a variety of ways of thinking about particular concepts, a variety of ways of reasoning about particular issues, a variety of strategies applicable to solving particular problems. Some are more adequate, others less so. Some fit well in one situation, others in another. Until we move beyond attempts to characterize *the* way that children of a given age think, and recognize the variability of their thinking, we will continually be surprised when young children do better (or older children worse) than theoretical descriptions of their competence predict. We will continue to be reduced to vague references to "task demands," "misunderstanding of instructions," "horizontal decalage," "unnatural contexts," and "external factors" to explain the discrepancies between theoretical characterizations and empirical findings. Worse yet, our descriptions will continue to be inaccurate and incomplete and to miss much of the dynamic character of children's thinking.

This critique does not imply that we should stop trying to identify early competencies. Rather, the implication is that we should change our interpretation of what the demonstrations of early competence mean. Instead of concluding that they indicate that the child "really has" the competence in question, and discarding previous studies as insufficiently sensitive to register the child's knowledge, we should conclude that both types of demonstrations are meaningful. In particular, they reveal that the infant or young child possesses multiple ways of thinking, of varying degrees of sophistication, and that much of what changes in development is the range of situations in which they rely on each one. The issues that then emerge involve the factors that determine the prevalence of different ways of thinking at any one time, the processes that lead to changes in frequency of reliance on each way of thinking over time, and the processes through which children add new ways of thinking to their repertoires.

One response to this perspective might be to think, "Perhaps there is more variability than usually recognized early in development, but with increasing competence, shouldn't children and adults come to use a single, mature approach?" This is likely the case on some tasks; children who from ages 3 to 5 reason about Piaget's (1952a) classic number conservation problem in multiple ways (Church & Goldin-Meadow, 1986; Siegler, 1995) eventually come to reason about it consistently in terms of the type of transformation that was performed.

On the other hand, it is also true, as noted by Eleanor Gibson (1994), that in many cases, "the dawning of potential new affordances brings greater variation of behavioral strategies . . . learning in development need not lead to automaticity and 'habit' but rather to potentially greater variability and selectivity" (p. 74). To cite a specific instance, college students who have taken more than five physics courses reason in a greater variety of ways, both correct and incorrect, about simple force and kinetic energy problems than do students who have only taken one or two physics courses (Maloney & Siegler, 1993). Even on tasks such as single-digit addition, in which intuition might suggest that everyone comes to consistently use the single approach of retrieving the answer from memory, detailed analyses indicate that college students use multiple strategies (LeFevre, Sadesky, & Bisanz, 1996). Thus, it is unclear whether cognitive variability in general increases or decreases with increasing competence. What is clear is that great cognitive variability exists early in learning, late in learning, and at all points in-between—if not on every task, at least on many.

This critique, like that made by advocates of domain-specific approaches to development (e.g., Carey, 1985; Chi, 1978; Feldman, 1986), is based on the belief that cognitive development is too varied to allow meaningful generalizations of the form "Children's thinking at age *N* is like ———". However, it goes beyond the domain specificity critique to argue that there is a great deal of variability of thinking within each domain as well as between domains, and that this variability is generally present even within a given individual's thinking about a given task within a domain. Thus, in the present view, variability is a basic property of human thought.

Choice

What difference does it make whether children know and use multiple cognitive approaches, rather than just one? The import can be illustrated in the context of problem-solving strategies. Strategies for solving problems differ in their accuracy, in how long they take to execute, in their demands on processing resources, and in the range of problems to which they apply. These varying advantages and disadvantages allow children who choose strategies wisely to adapt to the demands of changing circumstances. However, the advantages accrue only if the choices are wise. Randomly assigning strategies to situations would be no better than only using a single strategy (and could easily be worse).

How then do children decide what to do? The question has been given some attention in a number of theories of cognitive development. Such constructs as Flavell's (1979) metacognition, Sternberg's (1985) metacomponents, and Case's (1985) executive processes have all been motivated, at least in part, by the goal of explaining how children decide what to do.

Despite the numerousness of these constructs, understanding of their operation has been slow in coming. In general, they only hint at the cognitive processes through which choices are made. They serve more as place holders that indicate that there is something important to be explained than as clearly described mechanisms that produce choices among alternative conceptions or strategies.

An important commonality among the constructs is that all envision choice as an explicit, mindful, top-down process. Within the classic view of metacognition, for example, strategy choices depend on explicit knowledge of strategies, cognitive capacities, and problem characteristics. Thus, a child might reason, "This is a hard problem, too hard to solve without doing *X*, I'd better do *X*." Such a view of how metacognition directs strategy choices is evident in Kuhn's (1988) statement:

> In order to select a strategy as the appropriate one to apply in solving a particular problem, the individual must understand the strategy, understand the problem, and understand how the problem and strategy intersect or map onto one another. (p. 237)

This statement paints an appealingly thoughtful and rational portrait of children's thinking. However, metacognition seems less promising as a general explanation of children's choice processes than it once did. Empirical research has revealed relatively modest correlations between metacognitive knowledge and strategic performance (Cavanaugh & Perlmutter, 1982; Schneider & Pressley, 1989). Theoretically, the construct has remained quite underdeveloped, despite 15 years of use. How exactly does metacognitive knowledge lead to strategy choices? Do people make explicit judgments about their intellectual capacities, available strategies, and task demands every time they face a task they could perform in two or more ways? If not, how do they decide on which tasks to do so? Do they consider every strategy that might be applicable, or only a subset of them? If only a subset, how do they decide which ones? How do people determine their cognitive capacity on a novel task, and how do they determine what strategies are applicable to that task? Specifying how metacognition would actually operate to produce strategy choices is much more complex than it at first appears.

There also appears to be a mismatch between the relatively sophisticated strategy choices that very young children often make and such children's apparent lack of explicit metacognitive knowledge. For example, when 1 1/2-year-olds in a laboratory saw an experimenter hide objects that they later needed to find, they named and pointed to the objects more than when the objects were visible (DeLoache, 1984). DeLoache reached the reasonable conclusion that the toddlers used labeling and pointing to keep alive a memory trace under conditions in which it might otherwise fade, but not under conditions in which fading of the trace would not prevent retrieval of the object. But how did the 1 1/2-year-olds arrive at this conclusion? Did they possess sufficient knowledge of their memory capacities, the effectiveness of alternative strategies, and task demands to decide that their memory traces might fade if they did not name or point at the hidden object?

Just as deep-rooted beliefs about essences support the assumption of a 1:1 correspondence between age and mode of thought, similarly deep-rooted beliefs regarding agency and the relation between cognition and action support traditional views of choice. We experience the world in large part as agents who act upon objects and other people. The very words we use to describe the relevant psychological processes—for example, "I decided to do *X*, so I . . ."—imply an inner self that reaches a conclusion that then guides further action. The inner self bears more than a passing resemblance to the much maligned homunculus. Thinking of choice as requiring a chooser is very much part of our naive psychology, and in this respect, naive psychology is not so different from much of scientific psychology.

A central thesis of this book is that many choices are made not through any specific choice module, or rational consideration of advantages and disadvantages of alternative actions, but rather through the ongoing interaction of strategies, associative knowledge, and problem-solving experience. The choices often are at least as much attributable to "mindless" processes that are part of the basic cognitive architecture as to more "mindful" ones (cf. Langer, 1989 for a similar view). From this perspective, processing units of a large variety of types compete with each other for use. The more useful combinations, in terms of predicting and understanding the world as well as in terms of gaining reinforcements, are chosen increasingly often. Studies of animals and adult humans, as well as of children, indicate that competition and choice are pervasive processes, present at all levels of analysis of the cognitive system: the neural level (Coles, Gratton, Bashore, Eriksen, & Donchin, 1985; Greenough, Black, & Wallace, 1987; LeVay, Wiesel, & Hubel, 1980); the level of elementary information processes (Abrams & Balotta, 1991; Gillilund & Shiffrin, 1984; Seidenberg & McClelland, 1989); and the level of higher cognitive processes such as analogy, concept formation, and question answering (Gentner, 1989; Holland, Holyoak, Nisbett, & Thagard, 1986; Reder, 1987). It also underlies contemporary models of adult cognition, both connectionist (McClelland, 1995), and symbolic (Anderson, 1990). Ignoring such competitive processes, like ignoring variability, may produce simpler theories of how children choose what to do, but also theories that are narrower, less accurate, and more divorced from what is known about cognition in general.

Change

Over the past 20 years, developmentalists interested in change repeatedly have made two points: Understanding change is very important, but current understanding of it is very limited. The following comments are representative:

> As a final point, we concentrated on "what develops" in keeping with the title of the volume. However, we would like to point out that an equally important question is how development occurs. . . . Considerable progress has been made in mapping what develops, but there has been far less attention paid to what mechanisms underlie this progression. (Brown & DeLoache, 1978, p. 31)

> There are two fundamental questions in developmental psychology. First, what are the psychological states individuals pass through at different points in their development? Second, what are the mechanisms of development by which individuals pass from one state to another? A strong case could be made that the second question is the more basic one. . . . [Yet] I doubt that as much as 1 percent of our developmental literature addresses the question of the mechanisms by which developmental changes are effected. (Sternberg, 1984, p. vii)

> A third common weakness of developmental theories is the lack of an adequate account of mechanisms of development. (Miller, 1993, p. 437)

There is no shortage of constructs hypothesized to produce change: maturation; readiness; differentiation and integration; assimilation, accommodation, and equilibration; zone of proximal development, conceptual restructuring; social scaffolding, and so on. As with constructs regarding choice, however, they have served more as place holders, indicating that there is something important to be explained, than as well-specified mechanisms. Klahr's (1982) critique of the Piagetian constructs intended to explain change applies in spirit to other hypothesized change mechanisms as well:

> For 40 years now, we have had *assimilation* and *accommodation*, the mysterious and shadowy forces of *equilibration*, the "Batman and Robin" of the developmental processes. What are they? How do they operate? Why is it after all this time, we know no more about them than when they first sprang upon the scene? (p. 80)

We usually attribute our impoverished understanding of change mechanisms to the inherent complexity of understanding change. This attribution is undoubtedly correct to some extent. However, I believe that there is also another reason. Our efforts to characterize thinking at particular points in development in as simple and dramatic a way as possible have handicapped our attempts to understand how change occurs. More specifically, our difficulty in understanding change seems in large part attributable to our failing to acknowledge the omnipresence of variability and choice in children's thinking.

Why should variability and choice be central for understanding change? I first became interested in this issue in the context of writing a review paper on mechanisms of cognitive development (Siegler, 1989b). The criteria that I adopted for choosing which mechanisms to discuss were that the mechanisms be important in a wide variety of domains and over a wide range of ages, that they as a group include a variety of types and levels of change, and that there exist at least one relatively well-worked-out model of how each mechanism might operate. The mechanisms that met these criteria—synaptogenesis, associative competition, encoding, analogy, and strategy choice—seemed an extremely varied group.

Despite this initial impression of diversity, I became aware while writing the review that the relatively well-worked-out models of how each mechanism operated had a core similarity. All contained some means of producing variation, some means of selecting adaptively among the variants, and some means that led to the most useful variants being used increasingly often. This similarity may have been due to similarities in the thinking of the people who developed the models, rather than similarities in the mechanisms they were modeling. Alternatively, the similarity may have reflected an unconscious preference of my own that led me to single out these particular models. Nonetheless, it also seemed possible that nature was trying to tell us something, that there was good reason for cognitive developmental change mechanisms consistently to include processes that produce variability, adaptive selection, and inheritance.

Variability, selection, and inheritance seem necessary to allow organisms to meet the twin goals of learning and performing. If an organism always acts in the same way, it has no opportunity to learn whether some other behavior would yield better outcomes. Always acting in the same way in a given situation can be effective if the environment is stable, and the behavior well adapted to it. However, if circumstances change, the lack of variability will be a serious drawback. Thus, variability is important for promoting change because it provides opportunities to learn which activities are most effective in achieving goals. Adaptive selection among the varying entities is important because it allows organisms to perform effectively at any given time, through using effective approaches disproportionately often. Inheritance of the lessons gained through using each approach in the past is critical for learning, in the sense that increasingly comprehensive databases allow choices to become increasingly adaptive over time.

If this interpretation of cognitive-developmental change is reminiscent of Darwin's theory of the evolution of species, the reminiscence is not coincidental. I believe that as a high-level analogy, evolutionary theory provides a useful framework for thinking about developmental change. At a global level, evolution is the product of interactions among mechanisms that produce variability (genetic mutation, genetic recombination, chromosomal alterations, etc.), mechanisms that select among the varying entities (environmental pressures and self-regulatory processes), and mechanisms that preserve the lessons of the past (the genome). These mechanisms allow species to adapt to constantly changing environmental conditions without prescience about the future environment.

Individuals face the same need to balance stability and change as do species. To perform efficiently, we need to select effectively among the approaches we know. We also need to maintain behaviors that have been effective in the past. Knowledge, memory, and habit are some of the terms we use to allude to such stabilizing processes in the context of behavior. However, we cannot blindly repeat behaviors that at one time were the most effective. As internal capabilities and external demands change, so must our actions.

This need to adapt to changing competence, as well as changing external circumstances, can be seen in the context of skiing. The sharp turns needed to slalom down a hill can be accomplished in a variety of ways. A beginning skier may read about or be instructed in a number of these. Trying several of them will almost always lead to the conclusion that the easiest ones, those that include the widest berths and the most gradual turns, are the best ones to use. The others will simply be too difficult, causing falls, collisions, and other mishaps. However, the situation will change. As the skier becomes more accomplished, the more difficult, but potentially faster and more efficient, turns will become feasible and will be chosen increasingly often. The same type of turn that previously led to the worst outcomes will now lead to the best. Thus, there is a change in the relative value of different strategies, as well as in how well each can be executed.

This example illustrates why variability is so critical to change. If the skier decided once and for all that one turn was the best, the other turns would never again be tried, and the potential for improvement would be limited to better execution of the initial approach. More advanced approaches would be tried only if there were some outside intervention, such as a later lesson in which such a turn was suggested, or if the person had a metacognitive insight of the form "Hmm, I'm a better skier than I used to be, this other turn that I tried before might work now, maybe I should try it again." The natural variability of behavior provides an alternative pathway. Without ever explicitly analyzing the situation, the skier will produce numerous variants of the basic turn. Some will produce more efficient and elegant turns than others. This variability provides a path through which change can occur, even in the absence of explicit instruction or rational analysis.

This example also underscores the importance of selection within the change process. Different skiing turns have varying advantages and disadvantages. Jumping and lifting both skis off the ground can be faster than lifting one ski or just leaning, but it also is more likely to lead to a fall, even for a strong skier. As in cognitive domains, effective changes require not only variability in activity, but appropriate selection among the varying forms.

The remainder of this book is an attempt to illustrate how thinking in terms of variability, choice, and change can help us better understand cognitive development. Chapter 2 examines how thinking in these terms has contributed to an understanding of mechanisms underlying biological evolution and how it is beginning to contribute to an understanding of mechanisms underlying cognitive evolution. Chapters 3 and 4 document the pervasive variability that is present within children's thinking and how that variability changes with age and experience. Chapter 5 focuses on the adaptiveness of the choices children make among alternative ways of thinking. Chapter 6 presents a formal model of how even young children can choose so adaptively and how the choices change with increasing knowledge. Chapter 7 examines how children generate new ways of thinking. Chapter 8 summarizes the main arguments in the book and examines implications of the general approach for the assumptions we make about cognitive development, the questions we ask about it, the methods we employ to study it, the mechanisms we propose to explain it, and the metaphors we use to think about it.

2

Evolution and Cognitive Development

The central argument of this chapter is that *concepts that have helped biologists understand the evolution of species can also help cognitive developmentalists understand the growth of children's thinking*. This argument rests on four main points, corresponding to the four main sections of the chapter. The first point is that current theories of cognitive development are limited by lack of understanding of change mechanisms. The second point is that the problem of explaining the evolution of species has important commonalities with the problem of explaining changes in children's thinking. The third point is that explanations emphasizing variation, self-regulation, adaptive change, and inheritance have proved useful in understanding biological evolution. The fourth point is that these same concepts are implicitly present in a number of the most promising mechanisms that have been proposed to account for cognitive-developmental change, and that it may be generally useful to try to understand cognitive-developmental change in terms of them. The rest of this chapter elaborates these themes.

Limitations of Current Theories of Cognitive Development

At present, there is no dominant theory of cognitive development. The limitations of the major theories in the area—Piagetian, neo-Piagetian, Vygotskian, information processing, social learning, ethological, and neo-nativistic—are sufficiently large and apparent that none of them can claim the adherence of anything like a majority of investigators. In all likelihood, the greatest number of developmentalists see themselves as eclectic, borrowing concepts from many theories, but not being entirely comfortable with any one of them.

After reviewing current theories of development, Miller (1993) concluded that they share three weaknesses: overly narrow scope, uncertain ecological validity, and inadequate accounts of developmental mechanisms. Of these, the inadequate accounts of developmental mechanisms seems the fundamental limitation. A better understanding of mechanisms would contribute to overcoming the other two problems; it would expand the range of phenomena that could be understood as products of the same underlying mechanisms, and these would likely include everyday as well as laboratory phenomena. The converse does not seem likely: The vast accumulation of data we already possess has generated only limited progress in understanding mechanisms, and it is difficult to see how a broader range of data and/or more ecologically valid data would change the situation much. Thus, the single advance that I believe would contribute most to a better understanding of development is a better account of the mechanisms that produce change.

This is not a new problem. The classic theories of Piaget, Bruner, and Vygotsky, as well as more recent neo-Piagetian, information processing, and neo-nativist theories, have all included much more description of what children's thinking is like at different ages than detailed accounts of the mechanisms that produce the changes. As Flavell (1984) commented, "Serious theorizing about basic mechanisms of cognitive growth has actually never been a popular pastime, now or in the past. It is rare indeed to encounter a substantive treatment of the problem in the annual flood of articles, chapters, and books on cognitive development" (p. 189).

A large part of the problem seems to be confusion concerning what types of mechanisms are needed to account for development. For example, there has been a long, often vituperative, argument about whether large scale and small scale change are produced by the same mechanisms. Asking whether cognitive change in childhood is primarily due to "learning" or to "development" is one common framing of the issue (e.g., Liben, 1987). Analysis of the confused nature of this "learning vs. development" debate illustrates just why theoretical progress depends so critically on more detailed specification of mechanisms than is currently available.

Much of the confusion seems to stem from failures to distinguish differences in linguistic use from differences in hypothesized mechanisms. At the level of linguistic use, changes that are labeled "learning" differ from ones labeled "development" along at least five dimensions: temporal duration, breadth of impact, inter-individual variability, known precursors, and timing within the lifespan. Cognitive changes occurring over short time periods usually are termed "learning," whereas those occurring over longer periods are typically termed "development." Cognitive changes of limited scope are most often termed "learning," whereas broad changes tend to be termed "development." Cognitive changes whose existence or timing vary among individuals are generally termed "learning," whereas those whose existence and timing are highly consistent across individuals more frequently are termed "development." Cognitive changes with known precursors are generally ascribed to "learning," whereas changes whose precursors are unknown are attributed to "development." Cognitive changes in early and middle adulthood are almost always termed "learning," whereas those in childhood sometimes are termed "learning" and sometimes "development."

These linguistic distinctions are useful in explicating some of the considerations that lead us to apply one label or the other to particular intellectual changes. However, they are only tangentially related to the issue at the heart of the learning/development distinction: whether the mechanisms producing the changes are the same or different. Regardless of whether two changes occur over short or long periods, in children or adults, universally or variably, with known or unknown precursors, or on a large or small scale, they could be produced by either the same or different mechanisms.

An example may help illustrate this point. Consider regularity detection, postulated as a key cognitive mechanism by Klahr (1992), as well as by many others. Both children and adults induce trivial as well as profound regularities. Some regularities, such as that larger things are usually heavier, are induced very quickly; inducing others, such as that torque equals mass times distance, take much longer. Some regularities, such as that pouring water does not affect the amount of water, are learned by most children at relatively similar ages; others, such as the rules governing placements of knives and forks around a plate, are learned by different people at different times, if at all. Some, such as the tendency for bigger objects to be heavier, have many applications; others, such as "to predict which side of a balance scale will go down, multiply the weight and the distance on each side, and pick the side with the larger product" are of quite narrow usefulness. In sum, the linguistic considerations that lead us to call one change "learning" and another "development" are at best loosely linked to the cognitive mechanisms through which the changes occur.

How, then, can we determine the relation between mechanisms that produce changes we call learning and mechanisms that produce changes we call development? Ideally, we could compare a variety of mechanisms hypothesized to account for short-term and long-term changes, small-scale and large-scale changes, and so on and establish their dimensions of similarity and difference. Unfortunately, there are few well-worked-out cognitive change mechanisms to compare. Worse, I have not encountered a single well-worked-out mechanism hypothesized to generate large-scale, long-term changes. Without such detailed mechanistic accounts, issues regarding the relation of learning and development are impossible to resolve (as the round-and-round nature of the learning/development debate so well illustrates).

Commonalities in the Problems Posed in Explaining Cognitive Development and Biological Evolution

When faced with such an impasse, one useful strategy is to look to neighboring scientific fields that have successfully faced similar problems. For those interested in psychological development, the field of biology provides a particularly promising source of ideas and positive examples regarding change mechanisms. Biologists have had to face many of the same issues as developmental psychologists: How to account for long- and short-term change; for both diversity and unities; for the generation of qualitative novelties as well as continuous, quantitative change; and for self-regulatory processes that allow adaptation to varied circumstances but still constrain development sufficiently for it to stay on course. Biologists' success in meeting these challenges is inspiring. Exciting theoretical progress has been made in understanding the mechanisms that produce and direct change. Valuable practical applications have followed. In part, this is attributable to technological innovations such as electron microscopes and recombinant DNA technology. Another large part of the progress, however, is due to the power of the central concepts in the field.

Among the subareas of biology, the study of evolution seems especially relevant to those interested in development. The fundamental question in the two fields is the same: How does change occur? In both cases, perhaps the greatest challenge is accounting simultaneously for large- and small-scale change. In biology, the issue takes the form of how to account simultaneously for both *macroevolution* (large-scale changes in organisms, such as the origin of novel designs, occurring over very long time periods) and *microevolution* (changes over generations in relative frequencies of genes within a population). In psychology, the issue takes the form of how to account simultaneously for both development and learning. A number of key concepts within evolutionary biology—variation, self-regulation, inheritance, and adaptive change—also seem useful for thinking about cognitive development.

To avoid false impressions, I should clarify early-on the senses in which I believe analogies to evolutionary biology are useful for understanding cognitive development and the senses in which I view their value as questionable. First, consider three commonly drawn classes of analogies between evolution and development that do not seem very useful to me: approaches emphasizing the search for ultimate origins, the search for historical parallels, and the search for epistemological universals. Although each of these analogies has appealing aspects, each has serious drawbacks as well.

Perhaps the most common use of evolutionary analogies involves the *search for ultimate origins*: how people came to be moral, honest, altruistic, homosexual, aggressive, jealous, loyal, conscious, artistic, religious, and so on (Buss, 1991; Charlesworth, 1986; Cosmides & Tooby, 1987; Symons, 1992). These are fascinating questions, but ones that probably will never yield compelling answers. The brand of evolutionary psychology devoted to addressing such questions involves analysis of "the selection pressures that humans and their ancestors have faced over thousands of generations" (DeKay & Buss, 1992, p. 185). But where is the detailed evidence regarding the environments of a million or two million years ago to come from? Evidence from archaeology and anthropology seems totally inadequate to conduct such analyses with enough precision to engender confidence in whatever conclusions are drawn. There are always reasons that explain why human evolution should have taken the path it did—and equally compelling reasons to explain completely different paths, had they occurred. How hard would it be for this type of evolutionary theory to explain the absence of homosexuality, loyalty, or altruism in humankind? For this reason, the search for ultimate origins often reduces to speculation about the function that a behavior might have served in hypothetical environments of the distant past. Given the difficulty of identifying the advantages and disadvantages of a behavior in the here and now, and given our inherently fragmentary knowledge of environments of the distant past, this type of analysis seems unlikely to lead to firmly grounded understanding (though it is fun).

A second use of evolutionary analogies emphasizes the *search for parallels*—parallels between change within an individual lifetime and change over historical or evolutionary time. The slogan "ontogeny recapitulates phylogeny" is one example of such analogies. Similar analogies between change within an individual lifetime and change over evolutionary time can be found in many classic theories of cognitive development, such as those of Baldwin, Piaget, Werner, and Vygotsky (Morss, 1990).

The problem in drawing such parallels between development and evolution again is in deciding whether similarities between the two "have a common causal basis or represent striking but superficial analogies" (Gould, 1984; p. 233). The dangers of mistaking the two types of parallels are all too evident in cases of scientists equating the thinking of children with that of "primitive peoples" and women. Even superficially compelling parallels often prove to be more superficial than compelling. For example, Morss (1990) noted that the large majority of parallels drawn by Piaget, Vygotsky, and Werner between evolution and cognitive development fit better the Aristotelian and Lamarckian accounts of evolution than the Darwinian one.

A straightforward reason for the slipperiness of these analogies involves a fundamental difference between the specific mechanisms operating in developmental and in evolutionary contexts. A key difference is in the mechanisms that produce variability: Genetic mutation, the ultimate source of biological variability, is a random process, whereas the generation of new ideas is constrained by existing knowledge and is far from random (Gelman, Meck, & Merkin, 1986; Keil, 1989; Siegler & Crowley, 1994). This difference in the generation of variability leads to children's cognitive development being directional in a way that the evolution of species is not.

Attempts to bridge or blur differences in the specific mechanisms that produce cognitive and evolutionary change have led to confusion regarding developmental mechanisms. One prominent example is Piaget's (1975) phenocopy theory. Piaget postulated that development involves "the replacement of the exogenous variation by an endogenous variation of analogous morphology" (p. 810). Within this theory, "a new genotype, actually imitating the preceding phenotype, will be genetically fixed, once having achieved a certain threshold or 'selective plateau' " (Piaget, 1975, p. 810). Piaget specifically claimed that this was not a Lamarckian theory, but the basis for his disclaimer is not obvious. Further, given that the genotype is fixed at conception, and given that mutations are generated randomly, "the genotype actually imitating the preceding phenotype" cannot be right, either within a lifetime or over generations. The problem is not unique to Piaget; for example, the "Baldwin effect," the idea that acquired characteristics can become hereditary, reflects an essentially identical view (Baldwin, 1895). The problem seems inherent in attempting to map the directionless mechanisms that produce evolutionary changes onto the directional processes that produce cognitive change within an individual lifetime.

A third use of evolutionary theory that I would like to distinguish from the present one (though the distinction is less categorical) involves use of the evolutionary analogy to justify blind-variation-and-selective-retention (BVSR) models of the growth of knowledge (e.g., Campbell, 1960; 1974). Such analogies are often referred to as "*evolutionary epistemology*" (Cziko, 1995). This approach has a number of aspects in common with the present perspective, but strives for a level of specificity in the analogy that, depending on the particular version, is either clearly incorrect when applied to human cognition or impossible to evaluate. The present discussion focuses on Donald Campbell's version of evolutionary epistemology, because it is both the best articulated and the best known of this class of approaches.

Like the present approach, Campbell's BVSR model assumes mechanisms for generating variation, mechanisms for selecting among the variants, and mechanisms for differentially preserving the selected variants. The main difference is Campbell's claim that the mechanisms that generate variation are blind. The meaning of this claim has varied over time and sometimes at different places within a single article. In some contexts, the claim seems indistinguishable from the view that variations are generated randomly. For example, Campbell (1974) claimed that variations generated after incorrect trials do not make use of the direction of error of the previous trial and cannot be considered corrections of previous outcomes. This description is inconsistent with the boundedly rational behavior and rapid adaptation to feedback that people exhibit even in novel situations (Newell & Simon, 1972). To deal with this problem, Campbell (1974) went on to posit a "substitute process carrying on the blind search at another level," and to suggest that behavior may emerge only after being filtered through "feedback circuits selecting partially adequate variations, providing information to the effect 'you're getting warm,' etc." (p. 421).

There are several problems with this latter account. Most important, it does not seem disconfirmable. How would we know if such feedback systems did not exist or if the variations that they cull are blindly generated? Second, it is unclear how, even if such a system existed, it could operate in real time. People often respond to novel circumstances in sensible ways within a few seconds. How could a variation generator blindly produce huge numbers of alternatives, subject them to the internal feedback circuits, and choose a plausible one so quickly? And if the blind variation system is in fact constrained in the alternatives it generates, how could it be distinguished from a variation generating system that was not blind? In sum, evolutionary epistemology, in particular Campbell's version of it, has a number of appealing features, but one troubling assumption—that the variation generating mechanism must be blind. (For related, and more detailed critiques of Campbell's BVSR approach, see Perkins, 1994.)

What level of analogy between evolution and development, then, is both justified and useful? It seems to me that the most revealing, least misleading analogy is that between *the functions that must be accomplished to produce evolutionary and developmental change*. The details of the mechanisms that accomplish these functions clearly differ, but in both evolutionary and developmental change, there must be mechanisms that produce variation, mechanisms that select among the variations, and mechanisms that produce adaptive change through greater future use of variants that have produced successful outcomes in the past. (See Changeux & Dehaene, 1989, and Edelman, 1987, who, from neuroscience perspectives, reached very similar conclusions regarding the best use of Darwinian analogies for understanding learning and development.)

This functional analogy is important because it directs our attention to critical empirical issues that otherwise are often overlooked in the study of psychological development: the types of variability that are present at any one time, the properties and determinants of the choices that are made, and the changes that occur over time both in which variants are present and in which choices are made. The analogy also serves the useful function of directing our attention to the mechanisms that generate the varying thoughts and behaviors, the mechanisms that select among them, and the mechanisms through which the changes occur. Further, although the particulars of the mechanisms differ, the better-worked-out evolutionary mechanisms illustrate basic forms that developmental mechanisms may take. They also illustrate the multiple, interacting levels at which such mechanisms must function within complex living systems.

For these reasons, a better understanding of evolutionary mechanisms seems likely to enrich our understanding of cognitive development. The two remaining sections of this chapter focus on ideas regarding biological evolution that seem useful for understanding cognitive development, and ideas about cognitive developmental mechanisms that in important ways parallel the ideas regarding biological evolution.

Central Ideas for Understanding Biological Evolution

The study of evolution is of fundamental importance within modern biology. As the author of one popular, college-level biology textbook wrote, "Evolution, the transformation of life on Earth from its earliest beginnings to its apparently unending diversity today, is the one biological theme that ties together all others" (Campbell, 1991, p. 11).

Within evolutionary biology, four ideas are central: variation, self-regulation, adaptive change, and inheritance. A central argument of this book is that these ideas also are crucial for understanding cognitive development. In evaluating this argument, it is useful to have some knowledge of the history of thinking about biological evolution. For many centuries, theories of biological evolution closely resembled current theories of cognitive development. Just as current theories of cognitive development are based on the premise that children's thinking at each age has a certain essence, early theories of biology were based on the premise that species had distinct essences. Just as current theories of cognitive development postulate that successive ways of thinking are strictly ordered from lowest to highest, so did early evolutionary theories postulate an ordering of species from lowest to highest. And just as current theories of cognitive development postulate that new ways of thinking emerge in sudden spurts at widely spaced intervals, so did early theories depict species evolution. The greatest flowering of the field of evolutionary biology did not begin until it abandoned this approach in favor of one that emphasized processes of variation, self-regulation, adaptation, and inheritance. The same may someday be said about the field of cognitive development.

Pre-Darwinian Views of Evolution

Darwin was not the first to hypothesize that life evolved gradually from prior forms. Several classical Greek philosophers also propounded this view. However, the philosophers whose thinking most profoundly influenced the subsequent history of Western thought, Plato and Aristotle, held views sharply at odds with any belief in evolution. Plato viewed the organisms on earth as embodiments of idealized essences that had always existed. This perspective eliminated any reason for evolution, because any change could only be away from the unchanging, idealized form. Aristotle's views were antagonistic to evolutionary thinking in a different way. He believed that all species could be ordered from simplest to most complex, on what was later termed the *scala naturae*. This scale provided a fixed ordering of organisms, which has been likened to a ladder with a different species on each rung. In the Middle Ages, the Church incorporated these Platonic and Aristotelian ideas into a broader world view of an unchanging universe, created by God, as described in Genesis. There were challenges to this view, for example when Tycho Brahe in 1572 observed a nova and correctly concluded that he had witnessed the creation of a new star. However, theologians rebutted Brahe's conclusion by arguing that the new star had always been there and simply had not been noticed. This argument prevailed at the time.

Several developments during the 18th Century undermined these foundational assumptions and created a more hospitable environment for evolutionary ideas. One was the rise of paleontology. The fossil record told a clear story of different species appearing in different strata; the older the strata, the less similar the fossils to modern plants and animals. This evidence did not lead Cuvier, the individual most identified with the founding of paleontology, to anything like a Darwinian view. His interpretation was that a succession of catastrophes separated the different strata, with new plants and animals being created following each catastrophe. Cuvier's data did not lead everyone to his conclusions, however.

One who drew a different conclusion was the Scottish geologist James Hutton. He argued that the profound changes in the earth's surface arose not through catastrophes but rather through the accumulation of gradual, continuously operating processes. This argument, together with subsequent developments in geology, led Darwin and others to the idea that the earth might be far older than the 6,000 years inferred from biblical statements. The revised estimate was critically important for beliefs concerning the causes of the differences in the fossils at different depths within the earth's crust. If the earth was extremely old, then gradual but continuously operating processes could plausibly have generated the profound changes in life forms evident in the fossil record.

Another development working in the same direction was scientists' increasing appreciation of the remarkable degree to which life on earth is adapted to the environment. Again, however, such observations did not immediately lead to evolutionary interpretations. Instead, they were used initially to support existing world views. For example, the philosopher and theologian William Paley saw the fit between organisms and environments as evidence for the existence of God. In his book *Natural Theology*, Paley (1802) noted that if someone who knew nothing of watches found one lying on the ground, studied it enough to understand its workings, and then wondered how it came to be, the watch's complexity and precise ability to achieve its purpose would demonstrate that it could not have arisen by chance. The watch implied a watchmaker. By the same logic, Paley argued, the adaptedness of organisms to their environments implied a grand designer, God, who created everything in the world for the benefit of all.

Again, however, others drew radically different conclusions from this evidence. One of the best known of these alternative views was propounded by Lamarck in a book published in 1809, the year Darwin was born. Lamarck posited that life arose spontaneously from inanimate matter, and that complexity and improved adaptation arose through a process of responding to "felt needs." In particular, the changes occurred through a mechanism of use and disuse, whereby frequently used organs of living things became larger and stronger, and through a mechanism of inheritance of acquired characteristics, whereby capacities gained in an organism's lifetime were passed on to the organism's descendants. Lamarck's views are frequently ridiculed today, but neither his contemporaries nor Darwin himself could offer a better alternative about mechanisms of inheritance. Such superior alternatives became possible only with increased understanding of genetics.

The ideas of Lamarck and other evolutionary theorists of the early 19th century gained some adherents in their day. However, the prevailing ideology through the middle of the century remained true to the natural theology notions of a fixed set of living forms, each fitted perfectly to its environment.

The Darwinian Revolution

On November 24, 1859, Charles Darwin published *On the Origins of Species by Means of Natural Selection*. The book made two basic points. First, species were not specially created in their present form; they evolved from earlier forms. Second, the main mechanism that produced these new species was natural selection, which occurred through the interaction of organisms and their environments. More specifically, new species arose from ancestral forms through the accumulation of adaptations to different or changing environments.

Darwin's argument for these conclusions involved five key facts and three inferences (Mayr, 1982). The facts were that species generally have sufficient fertility that their population size would increase exponentially if all newborn individuals lived long enough to reproduce; that instead of this exponential increase, most populations tend to be relatively stable; that resources are limited; that individuals within a population vary extensively; and that much of the variation is heritable. From these facts, Darwin drew three main inferences: that there must be a struggle for survival, with only some newborn individuals surviving to reproduce; that heredity must influence the likelihood of this survival; and that organisms with inherited characteristics that allow them to live long enough to reproduce must become more numerous over time.

Darwin's position regarding the facts of evolution was accepted quite quickly, but his inferences were slower to prevail. Lacking knowledge of genetics, Darwin could not convincingly explain how variations arose nor how favorable variations were preserved through heredity. Mendel was a contemporary of Darwin's, but neither Darwin nor other scientists of the time realized the importance of Mendel's findings for the inferences Darwin had drawn regarding the sources of variability and inheritance.

Ironically, when Mendel's research was rediscovered near the end of the 19th century, it was initially viewed by many as partially refuting Darwinian theory. Darwin focused on *polygenic traits* (traits that vary continuously because they are influenced by many separate genes, such as running speed). Mendel, on the other hand, focused on traits influenced by single genes in a dichotomous fashion, such as whether a flower is purple or white. Several scientists initially interpreted Mendel's findings as meaning that evolution occurred in large jumps, caused by genetic mutations, rather than as the accumulation of small changes described by Darwin. It was not until the advent of population genetics in the 1930s that the importance of quantitative variation and the extensiveness of genetic variation within populations became recognized, thus allowing reconciliation of Darwinian and Mendelian concepts and observations.

Working out the genetic basis of variation and inheritance allowed formulation of the *Neo-Darwinian synthesis* in the late 1930s and early 1940s. Three assumptions were central within it: that inheritance at the level of individual genes is *particulate* (discrete) rather than continuous; that the effects of mutations occur on a continuum from small to large, with such mutations the ultimate source of both microevolution and macroevolution; and that all adaptive evolutionary change is produced by natural selection acting on abundant naturally occurring variation. Although much subsequent debate has focused on whether additional principles are needed to account for macroevolution, the three basic assumptions of the synthesis have not come into serious dispute.

A key implication of this synthesis is that there is no essence to a species. Instead, each individual is recognized as having a highly heterogeneous genotype (with genotypes of different individuals also varying considerably). Changes occur in the distribution of genes within populations, rather than in the presence or absence of any one special gene definitional for the species. The synthesis also ended several fruitless debates, among them debates over whether drastically different life forms can emerge in a single generation (they can't), whether acquired characteristics are inherited (they aren't), and whether there is a built-in drive toward progress (there isn't).

Contemporary Evolutionary Thinking

The Neo-Darwinian synthesis has endured for more than a half century, suggesting many fruitful questions and issues. The reason for its longevity is that it has provided the base for a fascinating field in which rapid progress has been made toward understanding how change occurs at multiple levels. Four concepts that play key roles within the synthesis, and within contemporary evolutionary biology, also seem directly relevant for understanding cognitive development: variation, self-regulation, adaptive change, and inheritance. These concepts are discussed in this section in the context of evolutionary biology; they are discussed in the next section in the context of cognitive development.

Variability

Biological change depends on there being ample variability on which natural selection can operate. Such variability is evident at every biological level: genes, chromosomes, proteins, cells, tissues, organs, organisms, populations, and ecologies. However, the importance of this variability was not always recognized within evolutionary biology; Mayr (1988) observed that it was not generally understood until the late 1930s, 80 years after publication of *The Origins of Species*.

Analyses of biological variability hold three particularly important lessons for understanding cognitive development: the sheer amount of variability, the constrained nature of variability, and the adaptive advantages of variability. Studies using *electrophoresis* (a method for separating proteins that differ in electric charge), have revealed the sheer amount of variability at the genetic level. Both in *drosophila* (fruit flies) and in humans, such studies indicate that the genotypes of two randomly selected individuals within a species differ on average at about 25% of *loci* (locations on the chromosome) (Campbell, 1991). The mechanism ultimately responsible for this variability is mutation. Mutations are not extremely numerous, about one or two per *gamete* (a mature sperm or egg) on average. Further, the large majority of mutations have little if any effect, and most that do have effects are harmful. Nonetheless, over vast stretches of time, they have been the ultimate source of the tremendous diversity of life on earth.

On a generation-to-generation level, however, it is *recombination* (the combining of genes from the two parents) rather than mutation that is the main source of genetic variability. So important is recombination that some have concluded that "the primary role of sex is more subtle than straightforward: it is the creation of genetic diversity among offspring" (Lumsden & Wilson, 1981, p. 28). Not everyone would go quite this far, but creating genetic diversity is clearly an important function of sexual reproduction.

Among the most valuable features of recombination is that it produces *constrained variability*. The constraints are imposed by spatially contiguous genes on a chromosome tending to be involved in related functions and also tending to move together through *meiosis* (the cell division process that produces sperm and eggs) and fertilization. *Crossing-over* (the recombining of corresponding genetic material on the sperm and the egg) leads to fragments of genetic material on the original gamete breaking linkages, thus leading to new combinations within the offspring. The frequency of genes being separated during crossing-over increases with the distance between the segments of genetic material. Thus, if functionally-related genes are close together on the chromosome, as they often are, they will usually stay together in the next generation. This preserves functions that are critical for adapting to the current environment, while still allowing considerable variability to be introduced, which may be critical for adapting to future environments.

Other evolutionary processes also produce constrained variability and thus help balance the need for adaptation to the current environment and the potential to adapt to different circumstances in the future. *Diploidy*, the presence of two *alleles* (forms of a gene) at most loci, allows the survival of recessive genes that are unfavorable in the present environment but that might prove adaptive in a different one. The cost is minimized especially effectively with uncommon recessive genes, which are rarely expressed in the phenotype.

A third finding regarding biological variability with interesting implications for psychological development is that variability per se can be advantageous for functioning. Quite often, *heterozygosity* (presence of different alleles at a given location on the chromosome) itself confers adaptive advantage. One example is the advantage conferred by the recessive gene that, if expressed, leads to sickle-cell anemia, but that when paired with a dominant gene confers resistance to malaria. Similarly, crossbreeding different types of relatively inbred corn plants often produces offspring that are healthier than either parent. This hybrid vigor appears to be produced by reduction in the number of homozygous harmful recessive genes, and by *heterozygote advantage*, the phenomenon by which variability at a gene site as such is advantageous.

In the psychological context, there may be an analogous phenomenon of *heterocognitive advantage*, a phenomenon in which cognitive variability as such is advantageous. Memory, learning, and understanding all seem likely to benefit from being able to reach the same conclusion via several different lines of reasoning, or from knowing multiple strategies that generate the same answer. Consistent with this hypothesis, children who on pretests display a greater number of ways of thinking about a given phenomenon subsequently learn more than children whose initial thinking is less variable (Alibali & Goldin-Meadow, 1993; Church & Goldin-Meadow, 1986; Graham & Perry, 1993; Siegler, 1995).

Taking a similar perspective, investigators who study the Japanese educational system have hypothesized that part of this system's success in mathematics instruction is due to its explicitly encouraging students to think about problems in multiple ways. For example, Stigler and Perry (1988) noted that Japanese teachers emphasize extended consideration of a single math problem, identification of alternative ways of thinking about the problem, and evaluation of the advantages and disadvantages of each way of thinking. Stigler and Perry suggested that such instruction increases the coherence of the lesson. From the present perspective, it also may tap into the more general phenomenon of heterocognitive advantage, enabling students to better learn subsequent material because their existing knowledge is more interconnected and accessible.

Self-Regulation

With enhanced appreciation of intra-individual genetic variability has come enhanced appreciation of the ubiquitous need for the biological system to control its own workings—for example, to select which genes to turn on and off at which times. Only a small percentage of genes appear to be structural, that is, used for the manufacture of protein. The large majority have other functions, among which regulation seems particularly prominent.

Three lessons from analyses of biological self-regulation that seem especially important for understanding behavioral development are the special importance of self-regulation in governing development, the presence of regulatory mechanisms for directing development of the whole organism as well as more specific developments, and the need to consider multiple hierarchical levels to fully understand the regulatory process.

First consider the special importance of self-regulation in governing development. The influence is felt from life's beginning to its end. The zygote is *totipotent* (capable of giving rise to any type of cell). With increasing numbers of cell divisions, this flexibility narrows; later-formed cells are increasingly constrained in the types of cells to which they can lead. The reason is that with repeated cell divisions, each cell acquires features that allow it to perform some specialized functions but preclude it from performing others.

How do cells achieve this differentiation? Because all cells include the same genes, the difference must come in regulatory processes switching different genes in different cells on and off at different times. The process can be illustrated by considering how cells in the lens of the eye come to produce crystallin, a type of protein produced by no other cell, but one that allows the lens to transmit and focus light. The regulatory event that leads to this specialized function is contact of the relevant lens cells with retinal cells. These retinal cells produce chemical signals that result in the lens cell transcribing messenger RNA molecules that code for production of crystallin. With the relevant genes turned on, the lens cells begin to produce crystallin, eventually devoting 80% of their capacity for protein synthesis to its manufacture.

A second lesson from biology that is relevant to thinking about psychological development is that self-regulation is present at the level of the whole organism as well as at the level of particular cells and genes. This is evident in recent discoveries concerning *homeotic genes* (sets of genes that control the general body plan). For example, such homeotic genes determine the relative position of the head, body, and legs. A mutation of even one homeotic gene can lead to legs growing out of the head of a fruitfly.

These homeotic genes are present in all organisms from yeast to humans. They also are surprisingly similar in different animals. For example, although fruit flies and frogs have been evolutionarily separate for hundreds of millions of years, they share in common 59 of the 60 amino acids in a *homeobox* (a contiguous group of homeotic genes) that helps control the overall body plan (Campbell, 1991). Human and fruit fly homeoboxes are sufficiently similar that placing one of the four known human homeoboxes in a fruit fly embryo allows a normal fruit fly head to develop. This stability over vast stretches of time attests to the fundamental nature of such self-regulatory functions in governing development. It also raises the issue of whether analogous homeotic systems might not govern the broad pattern of cognitive development as well, predisposing the cognitive system to develop in certain general directions.

The aging process itself, and indirectly the life span, also seems to be under the control of regulatory genes. Each type of cell undergoes a characteristic number of divisions in an organism's lifetime (70 to 100 in most types of human cells). When an embryonic cell is removed from the body and cultured in an artificial medium, it still undergoes the characteristic number of divisions. The pattern holds true even if the cell undergoes some of its divisions, then is frozen in liquid nitrogen so that it does not divide further, and later is thawed so that it can divide again. *Telomeres* (repeating sequences of nucleotide bases located at the tips of chromosomes), seem to play an important role in the regulatory process. Ordinarily, they act like bookends, holding the rest of the chromosome in place and protecting it from harm. However, with each cell division, the telomeres become shorter. When they become quite short, the genetic material between them becomes warped, sticky, and likely to attach in twisted configurations to other chromosomes. This leads to cell death. Such findings suggest that aging and death, like development in infancy and childhood, are ultimately attributable to self-regulatory mechanisms.

As suggested by the above examples, a third key characteristic of these self-regulatory mechanisms is that they are hierarchical. Control processes within biological systems generally involve several levels of organization. Consider the roles of genes, enzymes, and the cellular environment in regulating the manufacture of the amino acid *tryptophan*. When tryptophan concentration within the cell falls below a certain level, the enzyme *RNA polymerase* begins to be manufactured. RNA polymerase activates structural genes needed for tryptophan manufacture, resulting in more tryptophan being produced. This increases the cellular concentration of tryptophan, which shuts off the structural genes, which shuts off manufacture of RNA polymerase. As this example illustrates, genes, enzymes, and cellular environment are mutually regulating. Again, comparable mutual self-regulation among different aspects of the developing cognitive system seems likely.

Biologists' analyses of self-regulation generally consider three levels: a focal level, a higher level, and a lower level (Grene, 1987). For example, if the focal level is the reproductive characteristics of the organism, then the lower level is the organism's genome, and the higher level is the local population of the species. As the tryptophan example illustrates, bidirectional influences are the rule. It seems likely that in psychology as well, attaining a deep understanding of self-regulation will require understanding influences from above and below, as well as knowledge of the level of direct interest. For example, fully understanding children's use of a strategy will require understanding not only that strategy's characteristics, but also the strategy's place within the total set of strategies that children might use on the task (higher level knowledge) and the content knowledge that determines the ease of use of the strategy in the particular context (lower level knowledge).

Adaptive and Nonadaptive Change

As with variation and self-regulation, important lessons regarding behavioral change may be derived from progress in understanding biological change mechanisms. Three lessons that seem especially applicable to cognitive development involve the pervasiveness of nonadaptive as well as adaptive change, the fact that changes derive from a number of different mechanisms rather than from one or two essential ones, and the fact that particular changes tend to involve a mix of innate predispositions and encounters with particular environmental conditions.

With regard to the first point, biological change can be dichotomized into two main types: adaptive and nonadaptive. Some biologists believe that all (relatively enduring) changes have adaptive value, but most believe that there is a great deal of neutral change, change that has little if any impact on adaptation (Campbell, 1991). The change that led to each human having distinctive fingerprints is one example of a change with no obvious adaptive value.

Changes whose adaptive value is approximately neutral can have a number of sources, among them *genetic drift* (changes in the gene pool due to chance patterns of differential reproduction), *founder effects* (changes due to a small subpopulation being cut off from the main population, which leads to idiosyncracies of the genes of the founders heavily influencing the genomes of descendants), and *assortative mating* (the tendency of individuals to mate with individuals with whom they share phenotypic characteristics).

Such neutral changes at the biological level raise the issue of how often new, but not necessarily better, ways of thinking are introduced in the course of cognitive development. For example, young children tend to believe that sheer effort is the main determinant of cognitive performance, whereas older children more often believe that ability is foremost (Stipek, 1984). The older children's belief may be more accurate, but, as Bjorklund and Green (1992) have suggested, the young children's total belief in effort may be useful in helping them persist in trying to learn. Thus, overall, it is not clear which way of thinking is more useful. Similarly, to the extent that there are broad changes in cognitive style, they may represent another instance of neutral change, in the sense that each type of processing is best suited for certain types of learning. For example, holistic processing of language input may be best suited for learning the phonology of a new language, whereas a more analytic approach may be more useful for learning mathematical formulas. The relative prevalence of such neutral cognitive changes has not received much attention, but seems likely to be fairly high. Having some idea of their prevalence, relative to that of changes that are unambiguous improvements over previous ways of thinking, could lead to a better estimate of the types of constraints operating on change mechanisms.

Regardless of its degree of prevalence, adaptive change plays a particularly important role in evolution, as it does in cognitive development. Adaptation is perhaps the single central organizing idea in modern evolutionary theory (Lewontin, 1978). This is true despite the concept being almost as difficult to define in biological as in psychological contexts. Much of the difficulty in the biological context comes in defining the ecological niche to which the organism is adapting. Such niches cannot be described without describing the organism that lives in the niche, because the organism determines which dimensions of the environment are relevant to adaptation, helps create the environment in which it lives, and in some cases chooses where to live. The acquisition of lungs, wings, opposable thumbs, and other evolutionary novelties all profoundly changed organisms' adaptive potential and thus changed which aspects of the environment were relevant to their adaptation.

People's behavioral flexibility leads to the difficulty of defining adaptive behavior and adaptive change being at least as great in the psychological realm as in the biological realm. The relevant environment is hugely multidimensional. It is not the same for people from different cultures or for people from different groups within a single culture. Individuals within a given group also actively choose environments in ways that allow them to maximize their strengths and minimize their weaknesses (Scarr, 1992). Further, people, even more than other organisms, help create the environments to which they adapt, and are constantly changing them. Despite the difficulty in defining adaptation, however, the idea that the environment sets challenges that organisms meet in distinctive ways is fundamental for understanding both evolution and psychological development. It is so fundamental that it is hard to imagine a vibrant science in either area in which adaptation is not assigned a central role.

How is adaptation achieved at the biological level? A particularly instructive and well-worked-out case involves the functioning of the immune system, in which an explicitly evolutionary model has proved extremely useful in understanding changes within an individual's lifetime (Deary, 1988). This model also illustrates particularly well the interaction of species-general innate predispositions and individual organisms' responses to their experience.

Just as the cognitive system must adapt to the physical and social environments, so the immune system must adapt to the chemical environment. Specifically, the immune system scans the chemical environment and responds to incoming stimuli on the basis of prior experiences, many of them from years or even decades earlier. In a sense, the immune system must remember a large variety of *antigens* (foreign substances, such as toxins or microorganisms, that are introduced into the body) and learn from experience which *antibodies* (proteins that neutralize the antigens) to produce in response. It must also recognize its own structures and not produce antibodies to attack them. The system is immensely selective, recognizing and responding distinctively to "thousands, probably millions" of different antigens (Campbell, 1991, p. 855).

How the immune system meets these challenges remained a mystery until the formulation of an explicitly evolutionary model (Burnet, 1970; Jerne, 1955). This model began with the observation that there is great spontaneously occurring variability in the population of *lymphocytes* (white blood cells) that produce immune responses. Hundreds of thousands of subpopulations of such lymphocytes are present, with each type of cell competent at recognizing a specific antigen and at producing a specific antibody to neutralize it. The lymphocyte recognizes its antigen through a receptor for the antigen that is present on the cell's surface. Some lymphocyte cells of each type are present even if the organism has never been exposed to the relevant antigen.

The first exposure to a given antigen produces a relatively slow and limited response; subsequent exposures to it produce faster, more powerful responses. This "learning" is due to each exposure to the antigen triggering not only antibody release from effector cells, but also the creation of memory cells, which help create both additional effector cells and additional memory cells. The effector cells ordinarily live for only a few days, but the memory cells can survive for decades. In some cases, such as mumps and chicken pox, the memory cells built through exposure to the disease confer liftetime immunity against it. Thus, the immune process, by increasing the production of antibody cells that have been useful in the past, allows the organism to adapt to a vast array of challenges from the chemical environment.

This evolutionary account of immune system functioning is among the major success stories in modern biological theory (Deary, 1988). It is supported by a large amount of evidence, has generated numerous successful predictions regarding how the immune system operates (Ada & Nissal, 1987), and is one source of the belief that evolutionary accounts may be useful in a wide variety of domains (Cziko, 1995).

Inheritance

For variation and selection to have a long-term effect, a mechanism for differentially preserving the successful variants must be present. As noted above, this was a central stumbling block for Darwin's initial formulation of evolutionary theory. Only with advances in genetics did it become possible to account for how the effects of natural selection could be preserved across generations. The above sections provide several illustrations of how genetic inheritance influences the production of variation, self-regulation, and adaptation at the species and physiological systems level. Genetics textbooks provide numerous others.

Genetic inheritance also influences psychological development by providing an innate kernel of general and specific learning propensities that affect every aspect of human behavior. Whether the topic is perception, language, or understanding of basic concepts such as time, space, and causality, infants demonstrate impressive competence that is difficult to explain solely in terms of the general purpose learning mechanisms that also are present (cf. Carey & Gelman, 1991). Instead, it appears that humans come to the world prepared to code environmental input in useful ways and to learn many lessons, both specific and general, with minimal exposure to relevant stimuli.

Genetic inheritance is not the only mechanism that allows psychological development to benefit from the experience of past generations. Culture and socialization also are powerful mechanisms of inheritance. Like the biological inheritance, this social inheritance greatly increases the rate at which people can learn and enables them to benefit from the experience of past generations.

Microevolution and Macroevolution

These advances in understanding of variability, self-regulation, adaptive change, and inheritance have allowed considerably more sophisticated discussion of the relation between biological microevolution and macroevolution than previously possible. In particular, they have led to intriguing analyses of whether the mechanisms that produce microevolution are sufficient also to produce macroevolution. The following examples provide a hint of what a better understanding of mechanisms might also bring to the learning-development debate.

Microevolutionary Mechanisms

The main causes of microevolution were described above in the section on adaptive and nonadaptive change: natural selection, genetic drift, founder effects, mutation, and assortative mating. Of these, only natural selection directly produces adaptive change. However, the other microevolutionary processes also contribute to macroevolution, though under more restricted circumstances.

The indirect but important contribution to microevolution that is made by factors other than natural selection was well illustrated in Darwin's observations of the Galapagos Islands. In large populations, genetic drift and founder effects only slightly affect adaptation. In small, isolated populations, however, they can exert large influences. The Galapagos Islands were sufficiently close together to allow occasional transfer of a plant or animal across islands, but sufficiently far apart to prevent large scale transfer of species between them. This circumstance maximized founder effects, because idiosyncracies of the genotypes of a few founders of the new population would greatly influence the gene pool of their descendants. Magnifying the effect, differences in local environments would lead to different selection pressures on the new group. The combination of founder effects and different selection pressures can lead to quite rapid speciation (by evolutionary standards), as the distribution of alleles in the new group becomes less and less like those typical of the original population.

Mutations are another microevolutionary mechanism that can give rise to new species. This is especially likely when the mutations involve genes that regulate development. For example, regulatory genes determine the relative growth rates of various parts of the body. Even small changes in these growth rates can profoundly influence the adult form of the animal, and can lead to production of new types of animals. Human evolution may have been critically influenced by such a mutation. In general, humans and chimpanzees seem more similar as fetuses than as adults. However, the human brain develops for a considerably longer time, and the mature human skull retains the shape that human and chimpanzee skulls share in the fetal period. This has led to speculation that mutation of a gene regulating growth of the skull and the brain was involved in the evolution of humans as a distinct species (Campbell, 1991). More generally, there is no question that at the level of species, microevolutionary processes contribute greatly to macroevolution.

Other Contributors to Macroevolution

Recognizing the contribution of microevolutionary mechanisms to macroevolution does not imply that macroevolution can be explained entirely in terms of such mechanisms or reduced to them. A variety of other types of events also play important roles, in particular, ones that open up new adaptive possibilities. These are critical for understanding the uneven pace of evolutionary change—long periods of relatively slow change, punctuated by shorter periods of more rapid change.

Many macroevolutionary changes are set in motion by changes in the external environment that interact with biological systems, rather than by changes within the biological systems themselves. This is exemplified by the profound evolutionary changes produced by continental drift. In a particularly important episode that occurred about 250 million years ago, continental drift brought all the continents together into one land mass (*Pangaea*). Competition from previously separated species and the disappearance of habitats in shallow coastal waters led to mass extinction; by some estimates, 90% of previously existing species disappeared. However, these extinctions opened niches for other species, which proliferated during this period. And the breakup of Pangaea, about 180 million years ago, again led to profound evolutionary change, creating separate evolutionary trends within what had been single species.

The contribution of chance to macroevolution also should not be underestimated. Exactly one primate species (*Purgatorius*) is known to have survived the mass extinctions of 65 million years ago. No dinosaur species did. How different subsequent evolutionary history might have been had one dinosaur species and no primate species survived! Yet it is hard to imagine any scientific principle that would have foreordained that out of the great many previously existing dinosaur and primate species, the one survivor would be a primate.

Finally, some biological changes that make large contributions to macroevolution could be classified as either the cumulation of microevolutionary changes or as distinctly macroevolutionary. The developments that led to flight provide such a case. From one perspective, wings are homologous to reptilian forelegs, feathers are homologous to reptilian scales, and the two developed through a series of small changes that at first had adaptive consequences other than flight and that eventually made flight possible. This account stresses the role of microevolutionary processes. On the other hand, those who view macroevolutionary change as involving distinct mechanisms emphasize the possibility that regulatory processes may have allowed at least some of the changes to occur in relatively large jumps, rather than as the accretion of innumerable small changes. Gaps in the fossil record, and the subjectivity of saying whether a development that occurs over a period of 10,000 or 100,000 years is a "sudden" change, have prevented resolution of the debate.

Though these issues about macroevolution are far from resolved, the discussion has been constrained in important ways. No one argues that microevolutionary mechanisms are irrelevant to macroevolutionary change. No one argues that a single genetic change instantaneously gives rise to an evolutionary novelty. No one argues that all macroevolutionary change proceeds at the same pace; the existence of relatively rapid, as well as very gradual, change is universally acknowledged. The contrast with the lack of constraint on the learning-development debate within psychology is striking. There, an incredibly wide range of positions are espoused, ranging from development and learning being identical, to their being produced by altogether different mechanisms. It often seems that the only limit on the range of the debate is the range of the debaters' hunches.

The differing roles of change mechanisms in the debates are equally striking. Disagreements about macroevolution focus primarily on the relative importance of particular mechanisms. Some investigators highlight the role of genetic drift in creating evolutionary novelties within small, isolated, subpopulations. Others argue for the centrality of regulatory genes as a way in which large structural and functional changes can emerge relatively quickly. Yet others focus on the roles of external events, such as continental drift and climatic change. And yet others emphasize that the gradual changes in gene pools produced by microevolutionary processes are the ultimate source of change. All agree, however, that each of these mechanisms plays a role. Better understanding of cognitive mechanisms might result in similarly useful constraints on views of behavioral change and thus in more fruitful discussions of the relation between learning and development.

Lessons from Evolutionary Biology: A Summary

Evolutionary biologists address many questions that parallel the basic issues regarding cognitive development. They have achieved considerable success by emphasizing the variability that exists at multiple, hierarchically organized levels; the ways in which regulatory mechanisms constrain variability and govern the organism's general functioning; the contributions of both adaptive and nonadaptive processes to evolutionary change; and the role of inheritance in making adaptive change possible.

Most important, emphasizing variability, self-regulation, change, and inheritance has allowed biologists to make considerable progress in understanding the mechanisms that produce evolution. Focusing on the sources of variability has led to discoveries regarding linkages of genes on chromosomes; the importance of diploidy in preserving variants that are disadvantageous in one environment but that may be advantageous in another; and the phenomenon of heterozygote advantage, where variability per se conveys benefits. Focusing on self-regulation has shown how both top-down and bottom-up processes regulate production of amino acids such as tryptophan, thus allowing adaptation to changing environmental and organismic circumstances; how high-level mechanisms such as homeoboxes operate in invariant ways across very different organisms to keep general development on track; and how the life span itself is regulated by the number of cell divisions and its effects on telomeres. Focusing on change has shown how microevolutionary processes contribute not only to relatively short-term changes but also to longer term ones, how organisms both choose among environments and help create them, and how changes in the external environment often set in motion organismic changes. Finally, focusing on inheritance stimulated creation of the immensely productive and exciting field of genetics, as well as allowing an understanding of how species can adapt over time to changing environments.

These insights from the study of biological evolution have also proved useful for understanding biological changes within an individual lifetime. The use of evolutionary principles to understand immune system functioning is an especially compelling case. Focusing on variability, self-regulation, adaptive change, and inheritance allowed great progress to be made in understanding the complex workings of this system.

But can the same concepts that have aided understanding of biological evolution help us understand cognitive development? As discussed in the next section, there is reason to think they can.

Central Concepts for Understanding Cognitive-Developmental Change

This section focuses on some of the best specified cognitive-developmental change mechanisms. I have two main goals in describing them. The first is to make clear the commonalities among these superficially diverse mechanisms. The second is to make clear the resemblance between the functions they serve and the functions served by mechanisms of biological evolution.

Synaptogenesis

The density of synapses within numerous parts of the brain follows a distinctive developmental course, in which there is initial overproduction and later pruning of connections. Synaptic connections are produced in especially great numbers during the late prenatal and early postnatal periods. For example, Huttenlocher (1979) found that the average number of synaptic connections in the third layer of the middle frontal gyrus grew from 10,000 to 100,000 between birth and 12 months of age. The density of synapses increased until age 2, after which it gradually decreased to adult levels. These adult levels were reached by about age 7 years; from age 6 months to age 7 years, synaptic density in the children's brains exceeded adult levels.

Greenough, Black, and Wallace (1987) suggested that the initial overproduction of synapses is genetically regulated, but that which ones are pruned depends on experience. Normal experience at the normal time results in neural activity that maintains typical connections; abnormal experience, or lack of experience at the usual time, results in atypical patterns of pruning and therefore in atypical connections. This would allow both efficient learning in normal environments and reasonable adaptation in abnormal environments. In particular, the genes provide a rough outline of the eventual form of the process, thus allowing rapid acquisition under usual circumstances. Unusual environments or physical deficiencies, however, lead to unusual neural activity, which creates alternative neural organizations that are adaptive given the unusual circumstances.

Evidence for this account comes from studies of young cats and monkeys who had one eye sewed shut for particular periods of time, thus manipulating the ages during which visual input was received by that eye (Wiesel & Hubel, 1965). Restricting visual input during an early sensitive period resulted in severe visual impairment when the eye was later reopened. The reason had to do with the pruning of each eye's terminal fields of axons. In normal development, axon fields from both eyes are pruned equally from the visual cortex columns that are usually dominated by the other eye. However, in the visually deprived animals, terminal fields of the deprived eye were cut back from a larger area, and those from the nondeprived eye from a smaller area, than usual. The abnormal experience led to neurons from the nondeprived eye winning competitions that these neurons are predisposed to lose when both eyes receive typical input early in development.

Synaptic changes also are related to cognitive changes. In one demonstration, Turner and Greenough (1985) contrasted the neural structures of rats raised in small, empty cages with those of rats housed in large cages filled with diverse objects. The rats raised in the stimulating environments formed 20% to 25% more synapses per neuron in the upper visual cortex. In a related study, presenting rats with novel tasks resulted in their forming new synapses within 10 to 15 minutes at sites within the brain that had been involved in intense processing activity (Chang & Greenough, 1984). As with the above-described studies of visual development, such learning appears to involve initially producing more synapses than will be maintained, with maintenance dependent on whether the synapses are involved in subsequent processing (Greenough et al., 1987).

Advances in understanding of synaptogenesis have led to new perspectives on classic problems in cognitive development. In one such case, Goldman-Rakic (1987) suggested that early synaptic overproduction is critical to the development of ability to solve A-not-B object-permanence and delayed-response problems. With both monkey and human infants, ability to perform these tasks follows soon after the age at which synaptic density first exceeds adult levels, roughly age 2 months in monkeys and 6 months in humans. This synaptic overproduction affects the prefrontal cortex and a number of areas to which the prefrontal cortex is strongly connected. These areas are believed to be critical for performing visuo-spatial memory tasks, such as object permanence (Rakic, Bourgeois, Eckenhoff, Zecevic, & Goldman-Rakic, 1986). Further, surgically produced lesions in the prefrontal cortex resulted in adult rhesus monkeys showing the same pattern of performance as infant humans and monkeys: consistent success when the object was hidden at the previously rewarded location, and near-chance performance when the location was changed (Diamond, 1985). Similar-size lesions in a different part of the brain, the parietal lobe, did not produce comparable interference on these tasks.

Goldman-Rakic (1987) theorized that the high density of synapses in the prefrontal cortex and connected areas is needed for infant monkeys and humans to initially form enduring representations capable of overcoming associative habits. She noted that the lesioned monkeys did not show perseverative errors with delay periods below 2 seconds. However, at all delays equal to or greater than 2 seconds, when working-memory representations would presumably be necessary for success, the lesions seriously disrupted performance. Delays of 2 seconds had almost as large an adverse effect as delays of 10. Overall, the monkeys with prefrontal lesions appeared unable to use working-memory representations to regulate their performance so as to transcend the effects of the previous reinforcement pattern.

This example is not the only one in which synaptic overproduction (relative to adult norms) and subsequent pruning has been hypothesized to contribute to early development. Brody's (1981) explanation of changes in short-term cued recall between 8 and 16 months; Fox, Kagan, and Weiskopf's (1979) explanation of object permanence, stranger distress, and separation anxiety; and Fischer's (1987) explanation of complex means-ends variation in actions, use of single words, and general stage transitions in infancy have also emphasized the contribution of synaptogenesis to cognitive development.

Changeux and Dehaene (1989) proposed a "selectionist" framework for conceptualizing cognitive development in general. Within this explicitly Darwinian model, variability is a fundamental property of brain development, and is hypothesized to have many sources. Among the most important are genes that code for overproduction of synapses early in development; fluctuations in the chemical gradients that guide growth cones and their trailing neurons to their destinations during prenatal and early postnatal development; and spontaneous activity of "prerepresentations" within the brain. This last process involves the correlated firing of groups of neurons that through both exposure to environmental stimuli and internal activity come to represent percepts, concepts, and more general knowledge. The extent of variability produced by these sources is constrained by the "genetic envelope," which regulates the connections that the developing system can form.

The selection process is governed largely by use. Connections that frequently participate in brain activity are strengthened; connections that do not are pruned. Selection pressure from the immediately higher level of neural organization plays an important role in determining which prerepresentations stabilize to become full-fledged representations. Quality of the match between prerepresentations and environmental stimulation also is important in the selection process. Given this emphasis on variation, selection, and inheritance, and the extensive explicit theorizing about the mechanisms through which these functions are achieved, it is no wonder that Changeux and Dehaene (1989), like Edelman (1987), refer to their approach as "mental Darwinism."

Associative Competition

The evolutionary analogy is also apparent in models of associative competition. Some of the best-worked-out ideas about how associative competition might operate have been developed in the context of connectionist models. These models emphasize distributed representations, parallel processing, and interactions among large numbers of simple processing units. Most current models of this type involve an input level, one or more hidden levels, and an output level. Each level contains a number of discrete processing units.

A model of how children acquire the German language's system of definite articles (MacWhinney, Leinbach, Taraban, & McDonald, 1989) illustrates how such models of associative competition can advance understanding of cognitive development. These definite articles are the multiple terms that in German serve the function that the single word *the* serves in English. The task was of interest precisely because the German article system is so complex. Which article should be used to modify a given noun depends on a number of features of the noun being modified, including its gender (masculine, feminine, or neuter), its number (singular or plural), and its role within the sentence (subject, possessor, direct object, or indirect object). Making the learning task even more difficult, assignment of nouns to gender is often nonintuitive. For example, the word for *fork* is feminine, the word for *spoon* is masculine, and the word for *knife* is neuter.

The MacWhinney et al. model, however, demonstrated that despite previous claims to the contrary (e.g., Maratsos, 1982), the phonological and semantic cues provided by German nouns are sufficient for children to learn their language's modifier system. A connectionist system that did not possess any specifically syntactic information was shown to be sufficient to acquire the German article system, and to acquire it in a way that closely paralleled children's acquisition process.

The model included three levels: An *input level*, several *hidden levels*, and an *output level*. As in other connectionist models, learning was achieved through a cycle of the system (a) being presented initial input (in this case, a noun in a certain context), (b) projecting the most likely output on the basis of the strengths of its various connections, and (c) adjusting the strengths of connections between units so that connections that suggested the correct answer were strengthened and connections that suggested the wrong answer were weakened. In particular, after each trial, connection strengths were adjusted to reflect the cumulative frequency with which combinations of nouns' features had been associated with use of each article. Thus, the very large number of connections among units and the diverse connection strengths linking them formed a pool of variations; adaptive change occurred through differential strengthening of connections that were associated with successful outcomes; the connection strengths produced by past processing experience represented an inheritance that preserved the lessons of that previous experience; and the system as a whole regulated itself in a way that reflected the input it received.

When presented the 100 most common German nouns in proportion to their frequency of use within the language and given feedback regarding which article was correct, the connectionist model demonstrated impressive learning. It chose the correct article for 98% of the nouns in the original set, when these nouns were presented in familiar contexts. It also chose the correct article for 92% of the nouns when they were presented in unfamiliar contexts, despite the noun's often taking a different article in the new context than it had in the previously encountered ones. Especially impressive, the simulation proved able to make "educated guesses" about which article would accompany entirely unfamilar nouns; it was correct on 61% of novel nouns, versus the 17% that would have been expected by random guessing among the six possible articles.

The simulation's learning also paralleled that of children in the types of errors it generated. Like children, the simulation initially overgeneralized the feminine form. It also made many of the same specific errors that characterize children's speech, and took the longest time to master the same article-noun combinations.

Overall, this and other connectionist simulations of language development (Marchman & Callan, 1995; MacWhinny & Chang, in press; Plunkett & Sinha, 1991) illustrate the potential for explaining language development of models that produce variability through having large numbers of connections and varying connection strengths, that produce adaptive change through differential strengthening of connections that contribute to successful outcomes, and that produce inheritance through altered connection strengths preserving the lessons of past experience. The approach also has proved useful in modeling other aspects of cognitive development, such as problem solving (McClelland, 1995; Shultz et al., 1995), reading (Seidenberg & McClelland, 1989), and causal reasoning (Shultz et al., 1995).

Encoding

Encoding is a process by which information is represented in a particular situation. In almost any context, some information is encoded and used to operate on the environment, other information is encoded but not used to guide behavior, and yet other information is not encoded. When existing strategies fail, information that has been encoded but not used provides a kind of reserve capital for constructing new, potentially superior approaches. For example, if a child in a conservation experiment judges which glass has more water by differences in height of the columns of water, but also encodes differences in cross-sectional area, that child is in a better position to learn that pouring does not change the amount of water. Improved encoding has been found to be critical for a variety of kinds of developments, including improvements in scientific reasoning, transitive inference, insightful problem solving, reading, and skill in interpersonal interactions (Davidson, 1986; Dodge, Pettit, McCloskey, & Brown, 1986; Lorsbach & Gray, 1985; Siegler, 1976; Sternberg & Rifkin, 1979).

How might new encodings arise? The genetic algorithm model (Holland, Holyoak, Nisbett, & Thagard, 1986), based on an explicit analogy to biological evolution, illustrates one potential way. Within this model, a learner's knowledge is represented as a set of rules. Each rule is a condition-action pairing, much like a production in a production system. Within a rule, a string of 1's, 0's, and neutral values on the condition side indicates the rule's encoding of the environment. Another string of 1's, 0's, and neutral values on the action side indicates what changes occur when that rule fires. Each rule also has a strength, which determines its probability of firing when several rules are applicable. Rule strengths change as a function of how often the rule is used and how consistently its use is followed by attainment of the system's goal.

The genetic algorithm is explicitly aimed at serving the functions of variability, self-regulation, adaptive change, and inheritance. New variations (encodings and rules) are produced through a process modeled on genetic recombination. Periodically, two rules with different condition sides but identical action sides are selected to be "parents." For example, the two selected rules might be 110—>010 and 001—>010. New rules are produced by making a cut at an arbitrary point in the condition side of each parent, combining the part of the condition to the left of one cut with the part of the condition to the right of the other cut, and linking that new condition side to the action side of the parent productions. In the above example, making a cut between the second and third symbol on the condition side of each parent rule gives rise to the rules 111—>010 and 000—>010. The actual codings of the system are much longer than three symbols; since new rules are produced by making a single cut within the condition side of each parent, nearby symbols tend to move together, just as they do in genetic recombination. By producing new encodings, the genetic algorithm allows the system to determine whether considering the new combination of variables yields better predictions of the outcome of interest than do existing combinations alone.

Selection of the rules that will "reproduce" reflects their relative strengths. In particular, the probability of a given rule's being chosen to be a parent is proportional to its strength relative to that of alternative rules. This assures that rules more closely linked with goal attainment more often contribute to new encodings. It also assures that other rules have some chance of doing so, which keeps the system's variability from becoming too small.

Retention of the most advantageous rules is accomplished through newly formed rules always replacing the weakest of the existing rules. Over "generations," this inheritance leads to increasingly effective adaptation to the environment.

The genetic algorithm has proved useful not only in providing theoretical accounts of learning mechanisms, but also in yielding practical applications. One of the most useful of these involves a computer model that detects gas pipeline leaks (Goldberg, 1983, described in Holland et al., 1986). This model began with a randomly generated set of encodings and rules. Each hour, it received input concerning ingoing and outgoing flow of gas, ingoing and outgoing pressure of gas, and changes in pressure of gas, date, time, and temperature. The goals were to deliver gas at the minimum pressure needed to meet demand and to locate any leaks that were present in the pipeline. New encodings and rules were formed via the genetic algorithm.

Despite the initial random generation of rules (and encodings), the system progressed to near optimal performance in detecting leaks and in compensating for them by sending additional gas through that part of the pipeline. It eliminated useless rules, restricted the range of overly general rules, and produced new rules that were more useful than any of the initially existing ones. For example, it eventually produced a rule that included the information "If ingoing and outgoing pressure are low, and the rate of change in pressure is very negative, then send a 'leak' message." This rule gained considerable strength once it was generated, because the simultaneous presence of the three encoded conditions was very predictive of actual leaks. The model demonstrates how varying rules, adaptive choices among the varying rules, and selective preservation of the more advantageous rules can lead to an effective self-regulating system.

Analogy

Analogies can lead to cognitive progress because they allow novel situations to be interpreted in terms of better understood ones. They often are especially helpful in problem solving. For example, people are more likely to solve Duncker's famous X-ray problem (focusing separate X-rays at the location of a tumor) if they have already learned the solution to a parallel problem in which an attacking army must divide into separate units and travel from different directions to converge at the enemy's location (Gick & Holyoak, 1980). Children as young as 1 to 3 years have been found to solve new problems more effectively if they have previously solved analogous problems (Brown, 1990).

Gentner's (1989; Falkenhainer, Forbus, & Gentner, 1986) structure-mapping engine provides a detailed account of how people draw analogies. The model's focus is on how people establish correspondences between a base domain and a target. Its central idea is that people try to form analogies in which the system of relations in the less known domain resembles the system of relations in the better known one. The objects being related need not have any particular resemblance; instead, the key is the similarity of the corresponding relations in the two circumstances.

The model works by identifying the objects and structures of the better known domain and matching them to the objects and structures of the less known situation. Matches between specific objects and specific relations within the two representations lead the simulation to generate a large variety of potential analogies between them. Rules assign evidence scores to these local matches. One rule is to increase the evidence score if corresponding relations in the base and target have the same name. Another is to increase the score for a given local match if the relation immediately higher in each hierarchy also matches. This leads the simulation to choose analogies that match the base situation on a greater number of hierarchical levels. These analogies are assigned higher preference in future evaluations of analogies, thus preserving the lessons of past experience.

This structure-mapping model has proved useful for understanding how analogical reasoning develops. Falkenhainer et al. (1986) described three variants of the structure-mapping engine: one that operated solely on matches between objects in the two situations, one that operated solely on matches between relations in the two situations, and one that used both. These alternative versions generated output that differed in ways similar to the differences in the analogical reasoning of children of different ages. Gentner and Toupin (1986) found that 4- to 6-year-olds saw situations as analogous only when corresponding objects were similar. Their behavior was like that of the object-matching simulation. In contrast, 8- to 10-year-olds did not require such similarities between objects to draw the analogies; parallel sets of relations were sufficient for them to do so. Thus, their performance was more like that of the programs that relied on relations.

These models of synaptogenesis, associative competition, encoding, and analogy are far from the only ones that have at their core the functional evolutionary analogy. A number of classic psychological models, drawn from diverse theoretical perspectives, embody the same basic structure. Thorndike's model of trial and error and Skinner's model of operant conditioning are based on free operants producing variability, reinforcement contingencies providing a basis for selecting among the responses, and reinforced responses becoming increasingly frequent. Newell, Shaw, and Simon's (1958) generate and test model is based on varying operators being generated from within the problem space, and problem solving experience selecting among them those that should be used to solve such problems. Anderson's (1991) rational analysis of categorization assumes that people generate numerous potential categorizations, that the ones that best fit the structure of the world are chosen most often, and that learning leads to their being used increasingly. The ideas of Brunswik (1955), Changeux and Dehaene (1989), Edelman (1987), Gibson (1994), Keil (1989), and Miller, Galanter, and Pribram (1960) also fit this functional evolutionary analogy, some quite explicitly. For example, Gibson (1994) wrote, "Evolution requires variation and selection. So does ontogenetic development. Both are essential for learning to occur" (p. 75). I can only agree.

Conclusions

Analyses of cognitive development may benefit from consideration of lessons learned in the study of biological evolution. Evolutionary biologists have had to face many of the same issues as cognitive developmentalists. The issue of how changes occur is at the heart of both disciplines. They are also united by a number of more specific issues: how to account for diversity as well as commonalities; how to account for qualitative novelties as well as continuous, incremental change; how to account for self-regulation and adaptation to changing circumstances; and the degree to which long-term changes arise from the same mechanisms as short-term ones.

Psychologists have drawn a variety of analogies to species-level evolution, most of which go in different directions than the one that I am drawing. The analogy that I find the most revealing and least misleading involves the functions that must be accomplished to produce the two types of changes. In both evolutionary and cognitive-developmental contexts, change seems to require self-regulating systems that include mechanisms that produce variation, mechanisms that select among the variants at any given time, and mechanisms that preserve the lessons of past experience. The specifics of these mechanisms clearly differ between evolutionary and psychological domains, but the functions that they serve seem to be the same.

Examining the history of thinking about species-level evolution reveals that early thinking in the field had certain commonalities with current thinking about cognitive development. For example, Aristotle conceptualized relations among species in terms of a *scala naturae,* a kind of ladder along which all species could be ordered from the simplest to the most complex. Even after discoveries in paleontology and geology provided evidence against this conception, it persisted for many years. When Darwin published *The Origins of Species*, his position regarding the facts of evolution was accepted quite quickly, but his view that natural selection was the primary mechanism was much slower to prevail. Only when advances in genetics indicated how the genome preserved favorable variations was evolutionary theory fully accepted. Current thinking about cognitive development involves its own *scala naturae*, a sequence of steps through which children progress on their way to mature competence. Understanding mechanisms that produce changes and stability in children's thinking could play the same role in advancing the field of cognitive development as understanding of genetics played in advancing evolutionary biology.

Current evolutionary thinking assigns central roles to variability, self-regulation, change, and inheritance. Studies document the enormous variability that exists at every biological level, from genes to ecologies. The production of this variability is constrained in a variety of ways, so that although the ultimate mechanism that produces variation, genetic mutation, is random, the variants that are generated are quite constrained. Self-regulative processes operate at a variety of levels, from molecules that turn on and off specific genes at specific times to homeoboxes that regulate the body plan of the entire organism. Evolutionary theorists have identified a number of mechanisms that contribute to species-level change: genetic drift, bottleneck and founder effects, assortative mating, and environmental selection. Finally, advances in genetics have profoundly increased understanding of the mechanisms of inheritance, as well as all of the other evolutionary functions.

Breakthroughs in understanding the immune system provide a concrete instance of how understanding of changes within an individual's lifetime can benefit from application of these evolutionary concepts. Thinking about the immune system within an evolutionary framework has facilitated recognition of the immense, spontaneously occurring variability that exists in the population of white blood cells that produce immune responses. It also has promoted discoveries regarding the self-regulation and adaptive change that occurs through exposure to an antigen giving rise to increased number of cells that react to that antigen, and of the inheritance produced by memory cells that still react to the antibody decades later. The hope is that thinking of cognitive development within a framework that emphasizes how the system produces variability, self-regulation, change, and inheritance will give rise to similar progress.

Analysis of some of the best specified cognitive-developmental change mechanisms provides reason to believe that this hope will be fulfilled. The models involve widely varying content domains and levels of analysis: synaptogenesis, associative competition, encoding, and analogical reasoning. They also have been used to explain developments that occur at very different ages: infancy, the toddler period, and later childhood. Despite these differences, the well-worked-out models all include processes for generating variation, self-regulation, adaptive change, and inheritance. Thus, there is reason to hypothesize that one unity among otherwise diverse cognitive-developmental change mechanisms is that they all serve these evolutionary functions.

3

Cognitive Variability: The Ubiquity of Multiplicity

No one doubts that immense variability exists at the neural level. Even when the identical stimulus is presented repeatedly within a single experimental session, the response of an individual neuron varies from trial to trial. Similarly, with low-level cognitive processes such as association, there is no disagreement concerning the existence of competing units. Models of associative memory, both symbolic (e.g., Gillilund & Shiffrin, 1984) and subsymbolic (e.g., Seidenberg & McClelland, 1990), are predicated on the assumptions that stimuli have multiple associations and that these varying associations influence the way in which we remember.

Higher level cognition, however, has been treated differently. Many models are universalist: Everyone is depicted as proceeding in the same way when relevant stimuli are presented. Other models are comparative; they hypothesize different ways of thinking among groups defined on the basis of such characteristics as age, expertise, or aptitudes, but hypothesize a single consistent kind of reasoning within each group. Thus, 8-year-olds might be depicted as performing in one way and 5-year-olds in another, experts in one way and novices in another, people with high spatial ability in one way and those with low spatial ability in another, and so on. The finest differentiations that are typically made within these comparative approaches examine individual differences within people of a single age; for example, reflective 8-year-olds are described as taking a long time but answering accurately on the Matching Familar Figures Test, and impulsive 8-year-olds are described as answering more quickly but less accurately (Kogan, 1983).

The main purpose of this chapter is to summarize the rapidly growing body of research suggesting that variability is actually a pervasive reality in high-level, as well as low-level, cognition. To place this work in context, however, it seems useful first to briefly consider some prominent examples of universalist and comparative models of cognition and then to consider why they might be proposed and widely accepted even if thinking is far more variable than they depict it as being.

Alternative Approaches to Cognitive Variability

Universalist Approaches

A great deal of cognitive research has been devoted to identifying *the* processing approach that people use on a particular task. This universalist approach has led to many influential models and theories. These include models of language processing (Carpenter & Just, 1975; Glucksberg & Keysar, 1990), spatial processing (Cooper & Shepard, 1973), inductive and deductive reasoning (Anderson, 1983; Guyote & Sternberg, 1981; Holyoak, Koh, & Nisbett, 1989; Johnson-Laird, Byrne, & Tabossi, 1989), judgment and decision making (Kahneman & Tversky, 1982; Tversky, Sattath, & Slovic, 1988), scientific reasoning (McCloskey, 1983; Proffitt, Kaiser, & Whelan, 1990), and many other types of tasks.

Such models are parsimonious and represent a logical place to start in trying to characterize the cognitive processes through which people draw inferences, reach decisions, reason, and solve problems. However, because the models are based on data averaged over subjects, they run the risk of not accurately reflecting what any individual is doing. Sidman (1952) and Estes (1956) were among the earliest to warn of this danger. They noted that continuous group learning curves can mask discontinuous individual learning. Even if each individual in a sample progresses from 0% to 100% correct performance in a single trial, the percent correct for the group can still take on the S-shape often used to infer that learning over trials is continuous (Figure 3.1). On the basis of this and similar evidence, Newell (1973) formulated his "Second Injunction of Psychological Experimentation": *Never average over methods.* In particular, he advocated careful experimental analyses of each subject's performance so that "we can settle what method he did indeed use" (p. 296).

The point made by Sidman, Estes, and Newell has been quite widely accepted, at least theoretically. I suspect that few researchers believe that all individuals perform higher level cognitive tasks in the same way, even if their models depict them as doing so. One response to this conflict has been to study, and sometimes model, between-subject variability in thinking.

Comparative Approaches

A common approach to between-subject variability is to specify two or more processing approaches that could be used on a task and to hypothesize that one group of people uses one approach and a different group a different approach. This *comparative paradigm* is a dominant strategy in studies of cognitive development—younger children are often said to think in one way, older children in another. The basic research strategy has become quite common among investigators in other areas of psychology as well.

Students of individual differences have been in the forefront of those documenting the use of different approaches by different people. In many such studies, people who are high in some ability are viewed as using one strategy and people lower in that ability another. For example, in several of the above-cited

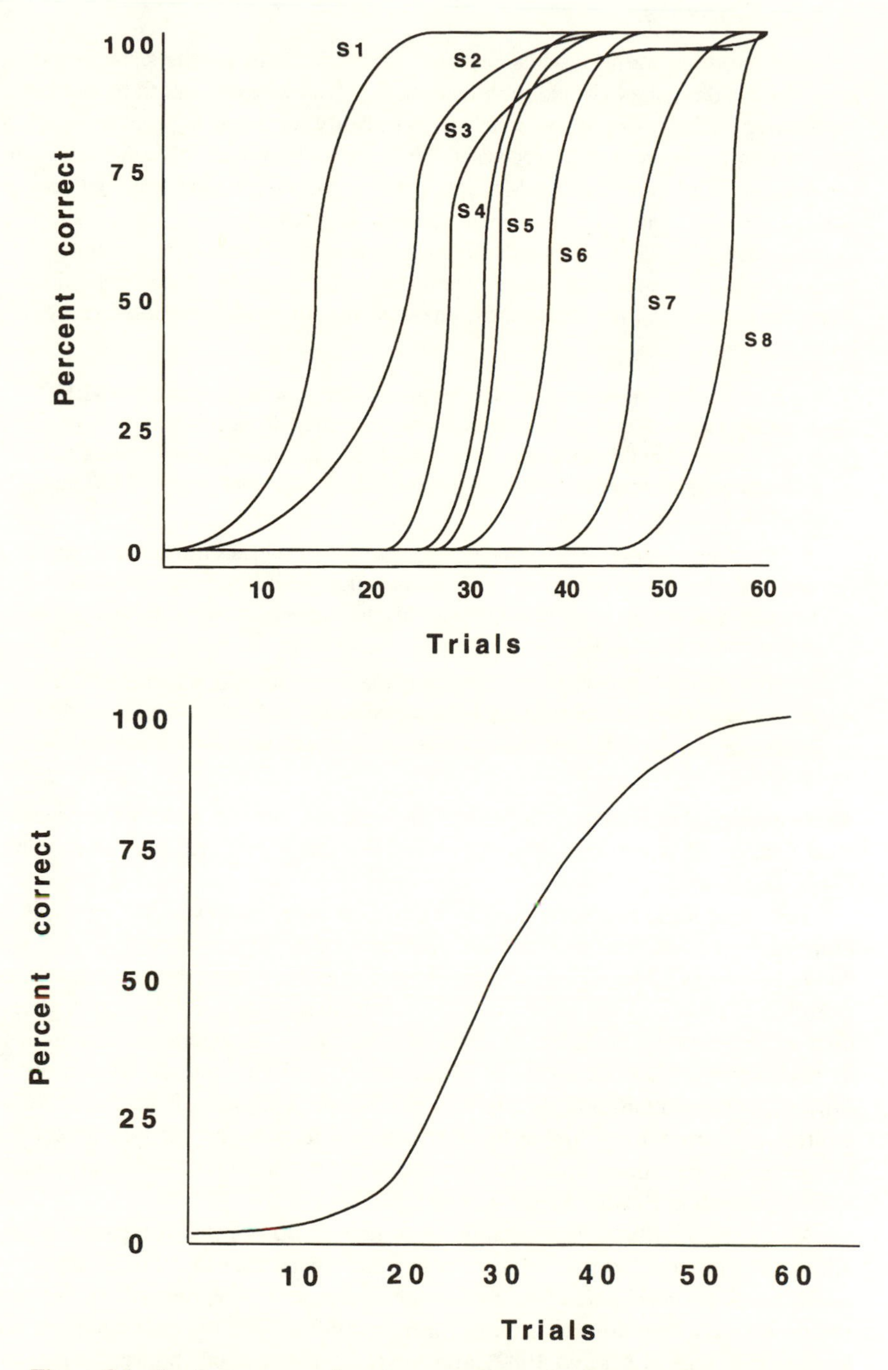

Figure 3.1. Continuous group learning curves can arise from averaging discontinuous individual learning patterns. Top graph shows eight hypothetical subjects, each of whom moved rapidly from inaccurate to accurate performance during a learning procedure. Bottom graph shows the continuous learning curve generated by averaging their performance.

domains in which initial models depicted everyone as using the same strategy, later models described people high in spatial ability as using spatially demanding strategies and people lower in spatial ability as using approaches with a greater emphasis on verbal processes. These include models of language comprehension (Mathews, Hunt, & McCleod, 1980), spatial problem solving (Cooper & Regan, 1982; Egan & Grimes-Farrow, 1982; Just & Carpenter, 1985; Kyllonen, Lohman, & Snow, 1984), and deductive reasoning (Sternberg & Weil, 1980). The findings and accompanying models from these studies raise fundamental doubts about the accuracy of the universalist one-size-fits-all models, as noted in the following comments:

> Discussion of the appropriate models for psycholinguistic tasks is usually couched in general terms (i.e., "What models apply to people?") Our results can be seen as a reminder that this approach is too simplistic. The same ostensibly linguistic task can be approached in radically different ways by different people. (MacLeod, Hunt, & Mathews, 1978, p. 506)
>
> The factor analysis methodology assumes that all subjects use the same general processes and structures on a test. This assumption is incorrect, and its violation may account for many of the confusions in the psychometric literature. (Just & Carpenter, 1985, p. 168)
>
> Too often psychologists set out to study *the* way that a task is performed, and miss one of the most interesting and general aspects of human cognitive performance: that there is more than one way to skin a cat. (Farah & Kosslyn, 1982, p. 164)

These empirical studies and theoretical arguments represent exactly the types of modification of traditional approaches envisioned in the critiques of Sidman, Estes, and Newell.

The same logic has been used in numerous other contexts. For example, a number of studies of expertise have contrasted the "expert strategy" with the "novice strategy." Mental calculation experts have been described as calculating from left to right and novices from right to left (Staszewski, 1988), expert physicists as representing problems in terms of qualitative characteristics and novices as representing them in terms of equations (Chi, Feltovich, & Glaser, 1981; Larkin, McDermott, Simon, & Simon, 1980; Simon & Simon, 1978), expert headwaiters as formulating hierarchical representations with multiple levels for remembering restaurant orders and novices as representing the orders at a single level (Ericsson & Polson, 1988), and so on.

Many cross-cultural investigations also have followed this comparative paradigm. For example, schooled Moroccans have been said to rehearse on serial recall tasks but unschooled Moroccans not to rehearse (Wagner, 1978), Western children to ask questions to acquire information but West African children not to do so (Greenfield & Lave, 1982), and Australian aboriginal children to use spatial strategies but urban children verbal ones to recall the locations of objects (Kearins, 1981).

Similar logic is common within "noncognitive" areas, such as the study of personality. For example, mastery-oriented individuals are depicted as persisting in the face of adversity, whereas helpless individuals are said to give up (Dweck & Leggett, 1988), sex-typed individuals are depicted as organizing information in terms of gender whereas androgynous individuals are said to rely less on this categorization (Bem, 1981), and optimists are said to persist in attempts to reduce the discrepancies between their desired and actual self-images under conditions where pessimists would accept them (Carver & Scheier, 1992).

A variant of the comparative approach has been to distinguish between classes of situations rather than classes of people. For example, people have been characterized as using rational processes when not under time demands, but as taking shortcuts when under them (Payne, Bettman, & Johnson, 1993; Reder, 1987), as using spatial strategies when given instruction in visualization and algorithmic strategies when taught an algorithmic solution (Kyllonen, Lohman, & Snow, 1984; Sternberg & Ketron, 1982; Sternberg & Weil, 1980), and as employing systematic strategies under conditions of high involvement and heuristic ones under conditions of lower involvement (Chaiken, 1980).

Why Have Universalist and Comparative Approaches Been So Popular?

All of these models, both the universalist and the comparative ones, depict each individual as consistently behaving in a particular way within a particular situation. Their basic claim is: "This is what this class of people does when faced with this situation." One explanation for the pervasiveness of such depictions is that they reflect reality; perhaps individuals really do approach higher level cognitive tasks in very consistent ways. Another possibility, though, is that the models overstate the degree of consistency, and that there is considerable within-subject as well as between-subject variability, even under essentially identical conditions (i.e., same child, same problem, same task instructions, same experimental context, measures obtained close in time).

Why might psychological models depict people as thinking in very consistent ways if their thinking is actually quite variable? Three types of reasons seem likely: pragmatic, perceptual, and technological.

Pragmatic Reasons for Underestimating Cognitive Variability

Portraying cognition as simpler and less variable than it really is has a number of practical advantages. Models that say that a given individual will always proceed in a particular way are simpler and easier to test than models that recognize that people think in different ways on different occasions, even regarding identical problems. Another practical reason for understating cognitive variability is that widely used methods, such as chronometric analyses, tend to yield more orderly results when data are averaged over many trials. Recognizing that performance on different trials was generated via different processes raises complex data analysis issues. Related to these reasons, straightforward, easily tested models and use of standard data-analysis methods help in achieving personal and professional goals of investigators, such as publishing the research in prestigious journals, getting it described in textbooks, and enticing other researchers to extend the work.

Perceptual Reasons for Underestimating Cognitive Variability

Research on social perception suggests another reason why models, in particular comparative models, might depict members of an age, ability, personality, or cultural group as being more consistent than they really are: People are biased toward exaggerating between-group behavioral variability and minimizing within-group variability (Fiske & Taylor, 1991). Information that enhances between-group differences is especially likely to be encoded and remembered; information that indicates variability within individuals is especially likely to be forgotten or not learned in the first place (Krueger, Rothbart, & Siriam, 1989; Park & Hastie, 1987). Psychologists who attempt to describe groups defined by age, ability, personality, or culture are unlikely to be immune to these influences on how people perceive other people. Thus, selective perception and memory, as well as pragmatic factors related to personal advancement and to communication and testing of models, may predispose us to underestimate within-subject variability.

Technological Reasons for Underestimating Cognitive Variability

Research is limited by available technologies, as well as by the conceptual understanding of the researcher. Appreciation of the full degree of variability that is present in cognition depends on being able to accurately assess each subject's thinking on each trial. Until recently, this was almost impossible. Researchers needed either to settle for simple measures, such as percent correct or mean solution times, or for less formal, often unreliable, on-line observations of behavior.

In recent years, however, ability to obtain precise and reliable trial-by-trial assessments has been greatly enhanced by videocassette technology. This technology allows detailed observation of the audible and visible concomitants of higher level cognition. In so doing, it also allows more valid inferences about processes underlying the observable behavior than could be achieved without it. Thus, as often happens, technological innovations have led to scientific progress.

Prior to the advent of high quality, low cost videorecording systems, it was at best difficult to obtain reliable observations of the behavioral concomitants of higher level cognition. Often, it was impossible. This can be illustrated with regard to assessments of strategy use. Dedicated observers, notebooks in hand, could watch children and scribble impressions while trying not to miss anything. The limits of this method were obvious, though. In all but the simplest cases, part of the challenge is to classify the strategies. Ideally, strategy classification is an iterative process, in which hypothesized classification systems are revised as often as necessary to meet the twin goals of minimizing the number of categories and maximizing their fit to observed behavior. Without a permanent record of the behavior, however, such iterative revision is impossible; the experiment often will be over, and children's behavior gone, before a good classification system can be reached.

Videorecording provides a solution to this problem. We can try out alternative coding systems until we settle on one that seems best; then we can apply that system to all of the behavior that has been recorded. Videorecordings also allow repeated scrutiny of behavior on particular trials, thus enhancing the accuracy of classification on each trial. Moreover, the technology can lead to breakthroughs in understanding, by allowing repeated analysis of especially revealing episodes.

Videorecording technology has proven especially useful in studying young children's thinking. Response methods that are widely used with adults, such as button boxes, keyboards, and voice-activated relays, cannot generally be used with infants, toddlers, or preschoolers. The children's lack of typing skills, tendency to forget which button goes with which response, and high frequency of unsolicited vocalizations generally rule out these methods. In contrast, by bringing together for each trial the overt behaviors that accompanied processing, the answer that was stated, the time it took to produce that answer, and the verbal description of strategy use, videorecording makes possible reliable and valid trial-by-trial strategy assessments for young children as well as older individuals.

To summarize, pragmatic, perceptual, and technological considerations have militated toward investigators portraying cognition as less variable than it really is. They have exercised this effect both directly, as described above, and indirectly, through their impact on the theories that became accepted as the major ones in the field and the tasks that became viewed as critical. Below I describe some of the experiences that have led to my own increasing conviction that cognitive variability is a pervasive and important phenomenon.

The Variability of Higher Level Cognition

I was not always so impressed with the variability of individual children's thinking. When first studying children's thinking, I thought that cognitive development was best described as a sequence of increasingly sophisticated rules for solving problems. I applied this approach to describing development of understanding of balance scales, projection of shadows, and fullness (Siegler, 1976; 1978; Siegler & Vago, 1978), conservation of liquid quantity, solid quantity, and number (Siegler, 1981), and time, speed, and distance (Siegler, 1983; Siegler & Richards, 1979).

These rule-based models painted a very orderly picture of development; in fact, they were as clear an example of the one-child:one-way-of-thinking approach as any that could be cited. The Figure 3.2 model of development of competence in solving balance scale problems illustrates this orderliness. In Rule I, children judge solely on the basis of the relative amounts of weight on the two sides of the fulcrum. In Rule II, they also consider relative distances from the fulcrum, but only when the weights on the two sides are equal. In Rule III, they generalize their consideration of distance to include all situations. Finally, in Rule IV, they proceed as in Rule III, unless one side has more weight and the other side more distance. In this case, they compute torques and choose the side with greater torque as the one that will go down. Thus, moving from Rule I to Rule II involves consideration of a new dimension, moving to Rule III involves generalizing consideration of this new dimension to all cases, and moving to Rule IV involves identifying a quantitative formula that solves all problems.

These rule-based descriptions fit the data well. The primary evidence came

Model of Rule I

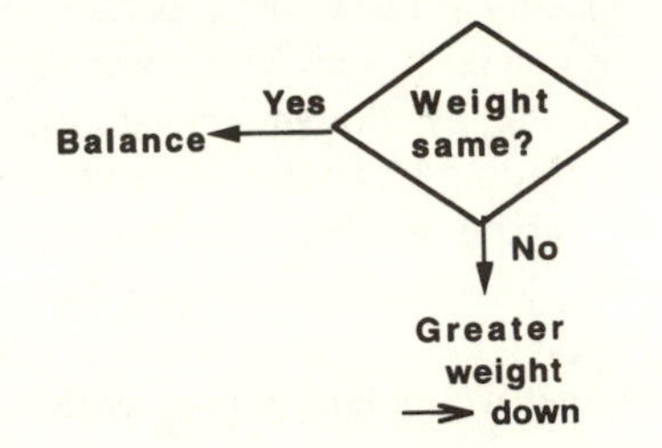

Model of Rule II

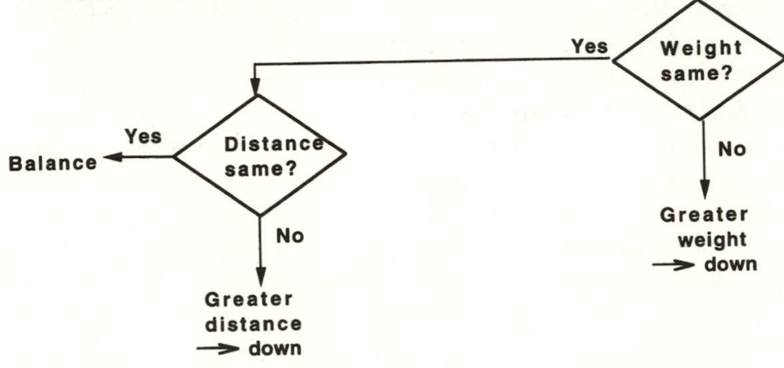

Model of Rule III

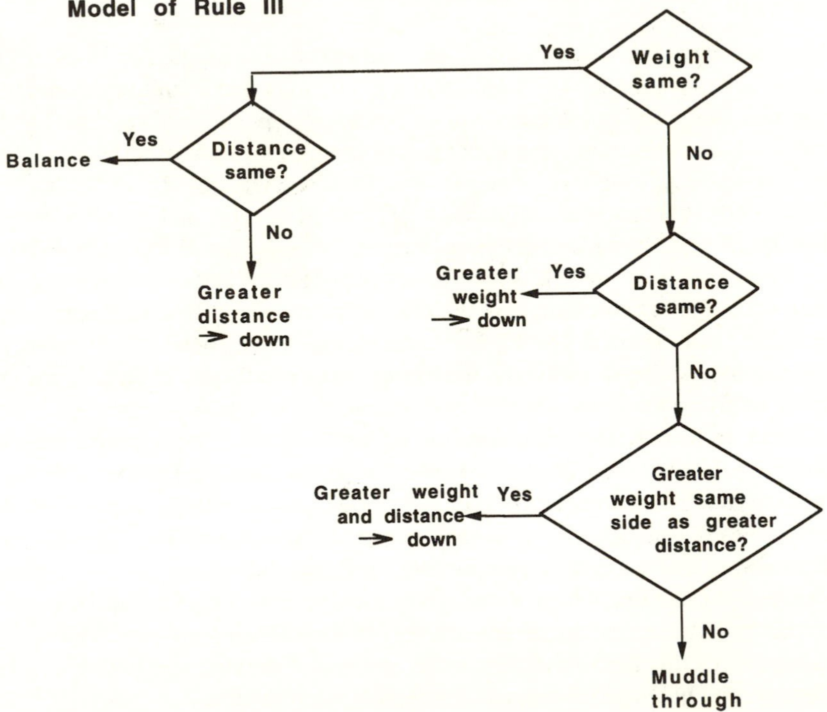

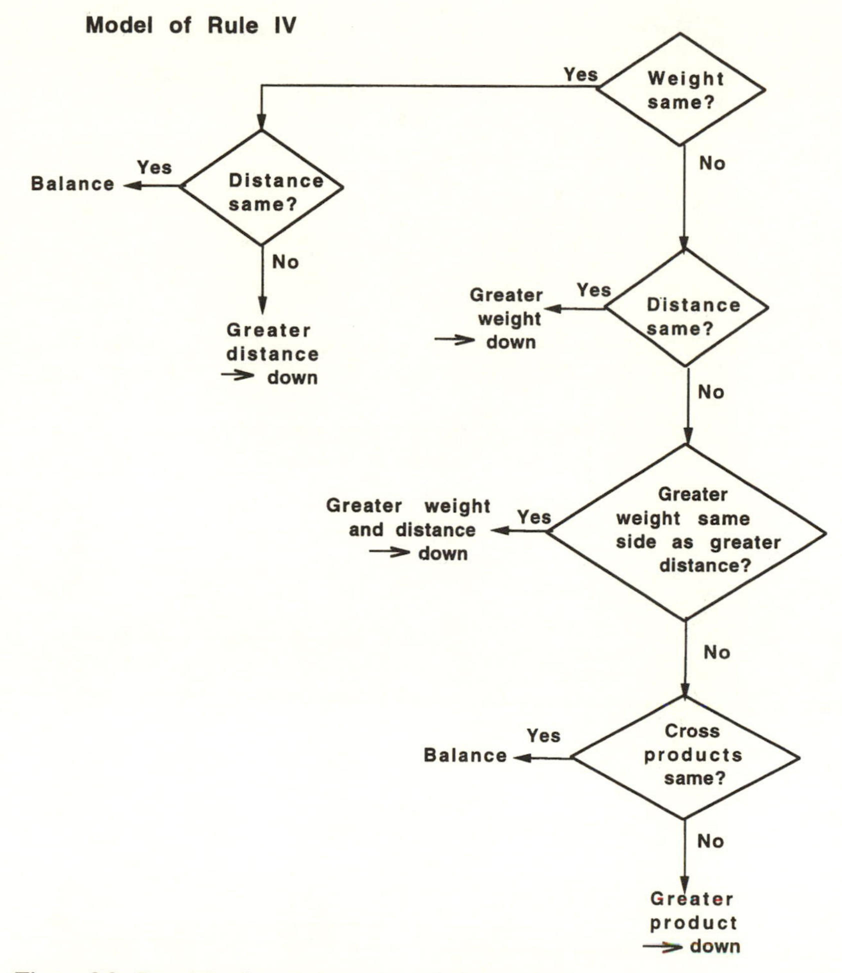

Figure 3.2. Four rules for solving balance scale problems.

from patterns of correct answers and errors. On all of the above-cited tasks, the responses of at least 80% of children fit the pattern predicted by one of the hypothesized rules on at least 80% of trials. Figure 3.3 illustrates the closeness of the fit on six types of balance scale problems.

Other evidence also supported the view that cognitive development could be described in terms of sequences of rules. The rules accurately predicted the specific errors that a given child would make, as well as how often they would err. Explanations and judgment data yielded similar assessments of most children's rules (e.g., Siegler, 1976). Classifications were stable over time. For example, when children in Siegler (1981) were presented balance scale, shadow projection, and probability problems on two occasions, one month apart, most children used the same rules on the two occasions. In addition, the rules provided a common language for describing development over very long periods, in several cases from age 3 to adulthood (Siegler, 1981). Beyond this, the rule classifications allowed

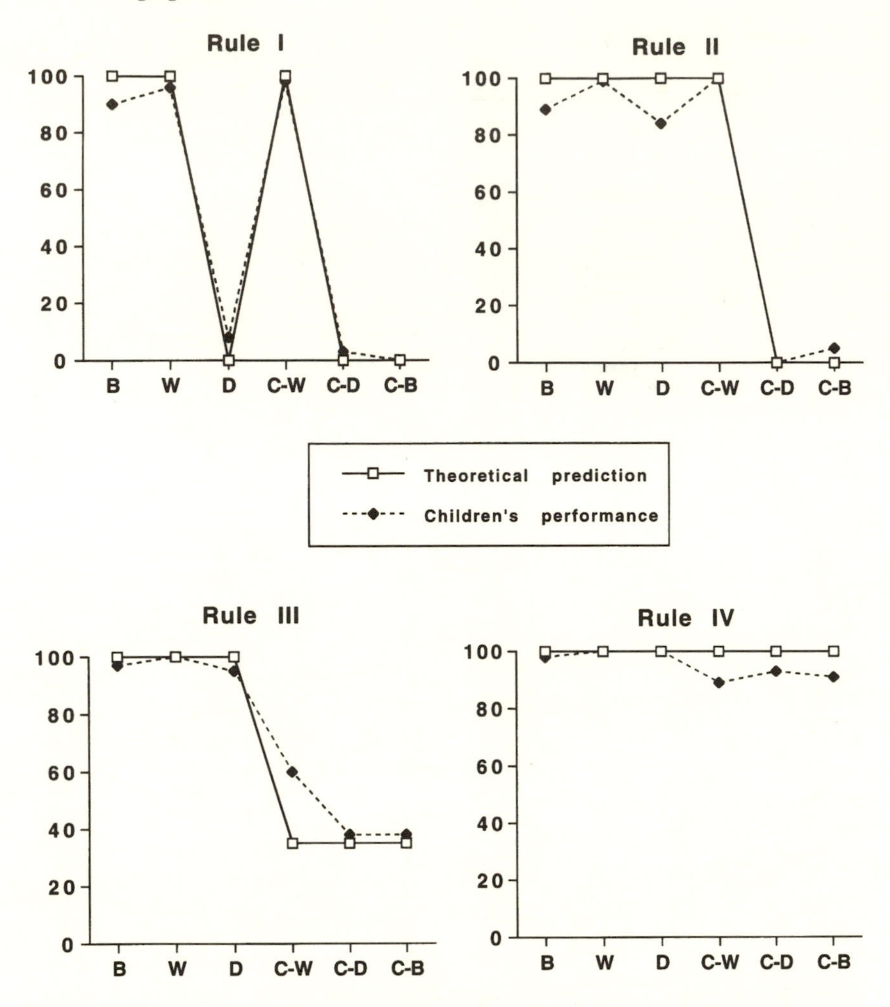

Figure 3.3. Fit of percent correct answers of children classified as using each balance scale rule to predicted percentage of correct answers for children using that rule.

accurate predictions of learning of new rules from specific types of experience (Siegler, 1976; 1983). These are among the properties that have motivated a number of researchers to construct computer simulations of the development sequences. Development of balance scale capabilities, as described in the rule sequences, has been simulated in OPS5, SOAR, PRISM, and PDP architectures (Klahr & Siegler, 1978; Langley, 1987; McClelland, 1995; Newell, 1990; Shultz et al., 1995).

Along with this positive evidence for the usefulness of viewing development in terms of rule sequences, a nagging question arose. It did not involve the fit of the models to the data; the fit was very good. Instead, the doubt involved how broadly such rule sequences applied. The tasks on which clear sequences of rules had been identified by myself and others (e.g., Case, 1974; 1985; Inhelder & Piaget, 1958; Levin, Wilkening, & Dembo, 1984; Ravn & Gelman, 1984; Strauss,

1982) had two characteristics in common. First, all were unfamiliar tasks that children generally would never have encountered before participating in the experiment. Second, all could be simply described as having two or more discrete dimensions, one of which tended to dominate young children's judgments (e.g., weight on the balance scale, height of the liquid column in quantity conservation, stopping point in time, speed, and distance estimates). I began to wonder whether these were coincidental characteristics of the tasks that had been studied or whether they defined the types of situations in which such rule sequences were likely to be observed.

Adding to the concern was the plausibility of a particular argument for why the two characteristics might yield especially frequent use of a single, consistent strategy. The unfamiliarity of the tasks would mean that children would have had little opportunity to discover or invent diverse strategies that might be applicable to the task. Presence of a single, dominant dimension might suppress behavioral evidence of other strategies that children knew or could devise. Alternative strategies might compete with the dominant one, but if they consistently lost the competitions, they would not be evident in the child's pattern of correct answers and errors. This was exactly the depiction yielded by the McClelland (1995) connectionist model of development on the balance scale task.

These concerns have led me since the early 1980s to examine thinking and reasoning on a different class of tasks: tasks that children have encountered before coming into the laboratory. By definition, these tasks play a greater role in children's everyday lives than the novel ones. The tasks I have examined include counting, arithmetic, reading, spelling, time telling, serial recall, and physics problems. Ages of subjects in the experiments have ranged from 3 years to adulthood. The choice of age groups within each task has been guided by a hunch I labeled the *Moderate Experience Hypothesis: Use of multiple strategies is most likely when people have moderate amounts of experience with the problems being studied.* Presented an unfamiliar problem, people sometimes will adopt a particular approach and use it consistently (as with the balance scale and other problems studied earlier). After massive amounts of experience with a set of problems, people sometimes will settle on a single approach to that class of problems. However, in the broad middle range, where people have some experience, but not massive amounts, with a particular set of problems, use of diverse approaches seems especially likely.

One source of evidence for this hypothesis came from an experiment with the balance scale (Siegler & Taraban, 1986). If children ordinarily have essentially no experience with balance scales, and if multiple strategy use is most likely when people have moderate experience with a task, then providing experience with balance scale problems should give rise to more variable strategy use. This proved to be the case. As children were given repeated experience with particular balance scale problems, they began to use a mix of retrieval and rule-based strategies on them. Eventually, when they had a great deal of experience on those items, they came to retrieve answers to them quite consistently, while continuing to use the rule-based approaches on other, structurally similar problems that they had not been presented. The pattern was exactly that predicted from the

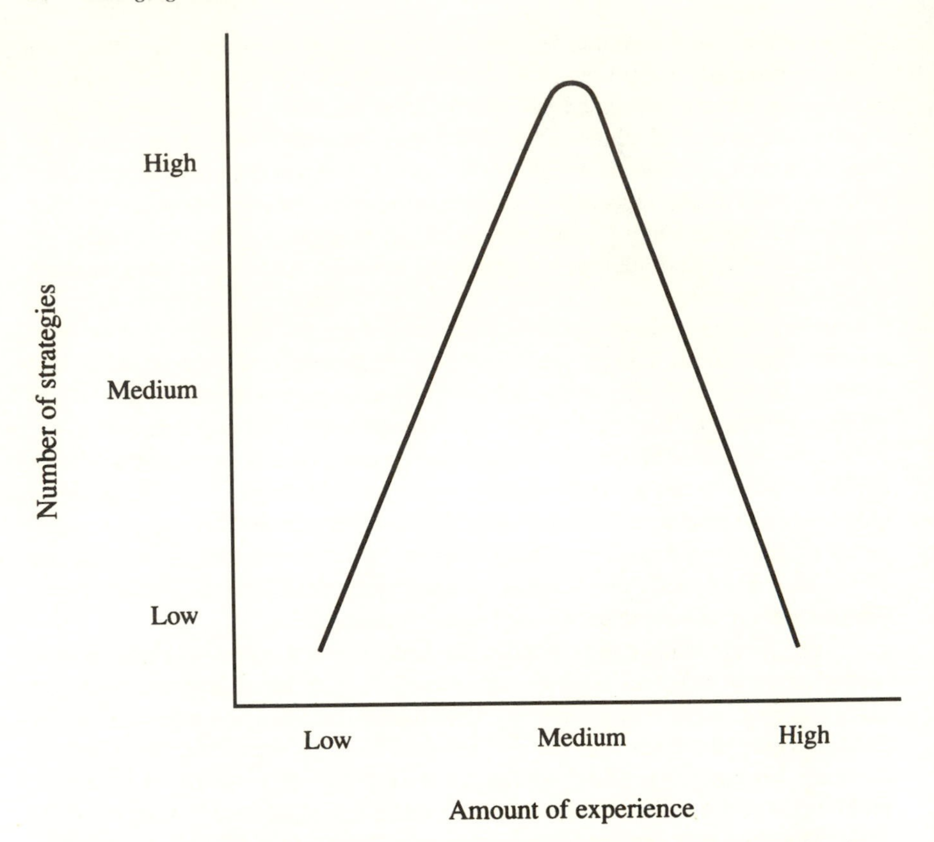

Figure 3.4. The moderate experience hypothesis: An inverted U pattern of change in variability of thinking with experience.

moderate experience hypothesis: Variability of strategies was greatest following moderate experience with the task.

This hypothesis does not imply that people generally think in only a single way in situations where they have very little or very much experience with particular problems. Within-subject variability in thinking is also often substantial in these situations. However, the diversity is hypothesized to be greatest when people have moderate amounts of experience with the problems. The expected relation is illustrated in Figure 3.4.

What mechanisms would generate variable thinking? Among the sources that likely are influential are spontaneous neural activity, impasse-driven learning, and instruction. Even before birth, there is considerable spontaneous neural activity. The way in which this spontaneous neural activity could give rise to variability in thinking is described in Changeux and Dehaene's (1989) account of prerepresentations (see chapter 2, pp. 41–42). In contrast to such spontaneous cognitive variability, which by definition occurs in all types of situations, impasse-driven learning occurs when existing means of thinking fail to reach a goal, and people generate new, more effective approaches in response to the failure. Mechanisms through which such impasse-driven learning can occur are described by Newell (1990) and by Jones and Van Lehn (1991). The third source of cognitive variability, instruction, involves the way in which the cognitive system learns what it is taught by other people directly or through the mediation of tools such as books and other media. Anderson's (1993) ACT-R simulation demonstrates how this form of learning could lead to new ways of thinking, and thus increase cognitive variability, through the mechanisms of knowledge representation, knowledge compilation, and production tuning.

The main purpose of this chapter is to describe some of the extensive evidence for the variability of higher level cognition. The chapter will consider the central areas of higher level cognition—problem solving, reasoning, memory, language, and conceptual understanding—and describe some of the evidence for variability of children's thinking in each. The evidence documents variability in the strategies that children use, in their theories, in their forms of reasoning, in their grammar and phonology, and in their beliefs. Demonstrations of the reliability and validity of the assessments of children's thinking will also be discussed in some depth, because accurate assessment is critical to claims that children are thinking in varied ways. The first area to be considered, and the one described most extensively, is young children's single-digit arithmetic.

Arithmetic

From an adult's perspective, simple arithmetic might seem a doubly unpromising area in which to study the variability of higher level cognition. First, the cognition does not seem very high level; only the ability to retrieve an answer from memory seems necessary. Second, the cognition does not seem highly variable; most adults retrieve answers to most problems.

At younger ages, however, the situation is different. Children in the process of learning arithmetic use a wide variety of strategies to solve what for them are real problems. The strategies are crisp and easily described, children can accurately report which strategy they used on each trial, and the distribution of strategies that they use changes substantially over a period of several years. Thus, although simple arithmetic would not be anyone's first choice for studying the variability of higher level cognition in adults, it has many advantages for studying it in children.

Preschoolers' Addition

I first became aware of the diversity of children's arithmetic strategies while pursuing a project with a quite different goal. The goal of this project (Siegler & Robinson, 1982) was to identify what children know about numbers when they enter school and how that knowledge develops during the preschool years. In pursuit of this goal, Mitch Robinson and I examined and modeled 3-, 4-, and 5-year-olds' competence in counting, magnitude comparison, number conservation, and addition. Although the addition experiment was planned as only one part of the larger whole, the results that it yielded were sufficiently interesting that they became the center of my research for several years to follow. For this reason, and because the procedure is representative of those used in many experiments on cognitive variability, I will describe the procedure and results of the Siegler and Robinson (1982) addition experiment in some detail.

Siegler and Robinson examined 4- and 5-year-olds' strategy use on the 25 problems with both addends 1 to 5. At the beginning of the session, children were told:

> I want you to imagine that you have a pile of oranges. I'll give you more oranges to add to your pile; then you need to tell me how many oranges you have altogether. Okay? You have *m* oranges and I give you *n* to add to your pile. How many do you have altogether?

After four or five problems, many children indicated that they preferred to hear the problem in the form "How much is $m + n$?" We complied with their requests.

Children performed the problems while sitting at a desk with a bare top; no external objects were present for them to manipulate as they solved the problems. Correct answers were rewarded with praise and a star that children could affix to their record book. Sessions lasted approximately 5 to 10 minutes. Each child participated in six sessions, with each problem being presented once in the first three sessions and a second time in the final three sessions. All sessions were videotaped, with the goal of being able to identify from overt behavior what strategies children used.

Analysis of the videotapes suggested that children employed four strategies. Three were overt (visible or audible) approaches. Sometimes the preschoolers raised fingers corresponding to each addend and counted them (the *counting fingers strategy*). Other times, they lifted fingers corresponding to each addend but answered without any apparent counting (the *fingers strategy*). Yet other times, they counted aloud (or moved their lips in a visible silent counting sequence), but without any obvious external referent (the *counting strategy*). The fourth approach involved no visible or audible behavior; this was classified as *retrieval.*[1]

As shown in Table 3.1, the four strategies differed in their frequency of use, in the time they required, and in their accuracy. Of particular importance, the times on trials classified as retrieval were much faster than the times when the 4- and 5-year-olds used any of the other three strategies. This, together with the lack of overt behavior on these trials, was what led us to conclude, at least tentatively, that most of these trials involved retrieval of answers from memory.

The multiple strategy use did not reflect one child consistently using one

Table 3.1. Preschoolers' Addition Strategies

Strategy	Trials on which strategy used (%)	Mean solution time (sec.)	Correct answers (%)
Counting fingers	15	14.0	87
Fingers	13	6.6	89
Counting	8	9.0	54
No visible strategy	64	4.0	66

Note. Data from Siegler and Robinson (1982).

strategy and other children consistently using other strategies. Most individuals, 80%, used multiple strategies. Of the 30 preschoolers in the study, 23% used two strategies, 30% used three strategies, and 27% four strategies. Thus, variable strategy use was evident within individual children as well as between them.

Especially striking, the variability was evident even within a single child solving the same problem on two occasions. Children were presented the same 25 arithmetic problems in two successive weeks. On 34% of pairs of trials for a given problem, they used different strategies on the two occasions. This did not reflect progress from the earlier to the later session. For each pair of strategies, children were only slightly more likely to move from the less to the more sophisticated strategy than to move in the opposite direction (with retrieval defined as the most sophisticated strategy, counting fingers the least, and the other two in-between).[2]

Jeff Shrager and I followed up this initial study with a further examination of preschoolers' addition (Siegler & Shrager, 1984). One goal was to see whether similar variability of strategy use would be apparent with children from a different preschool solving different problems. A second goal was to see what strategies children would use on problems that presented obstacles to use of their usual strategies.

Children were presented one of three sets of problems. The preschoolers in Group 1 received the same set of problems as in the earlier study, problems on which neither addend exceeded 5, and on which the sum therefore did not exceed 10. Those in Group 2 also received problems with sums of 10 or less, but half of the problems included an addend between 6 and 9. Children in Group 3 received half of their problems from the same set as in Group 1; the other half of their problems had one addend between 6 and 11 and a sum of 11 or 12. Thus, the problems given to children in the three groups varied in whether the sum could be consistently represented on both hands and in whether each addend could consistently be represented on one hand.

The results for the two groups of children who encountered problems with sums no greater than 10 closely paralleled those in the earlier study. The strategies that they used, the frequency with which they used them, and the relative speeds and accuracies of the strategies were all similar. Performance on about 90% of trials in which sums could range as high as 12 was also similar. However, in response to the problems with sums of 11 and 12, where the usual strategies were unlikely to work, children adopted (or invented) some previously unseen strategies as well. One approach was for the child to count up to the value of one addend without putting up any fingers, then to put up fingers to represent the other addend, and then to count the raised fingers starting with the number that was one greater than the result of their initial counting procedure. Another approach involved putting up and counting 10 fingers and then arbitrarily naming a number larger than 10 if both addends were not totally represented. A third approach, used by one child, was to count as she put up her 10 fingers, and then to whistle the number of times needed to represent the remaining numbers. This idiosyncratic method produced 96% correct answers on these difficult problems, the highest percentage of any child in the experiment (of course, the whistler was my daughter).

Subsequent investigators have obtained similar findings. For example, Geary and Burlingham-Dubree (1989) presented preschoolers the same set of problems used by Siegler and Robinson, that is, problems with addends no greater than 5 and sums no greater than 10. They observed the identical strategies and also found similar absolute and relative accuracies and solution times for the four strategies. The same type of diverse strategy use has been observed in Chinese as in U.S. preschoolers (Geary, Fan, Bow-Thomas, & Siegler, 1993).

Results from other studies indicate that the precise strategies that preschoolers use vary with children's backgrounds. Illustratively, Chinese preschoolers use the same strategies as those in the United States, but they use them in different proportions. U.S. children count on their fingers more often; Chinese children count internally more often. U.S. children also rely on retrieval more often, but they are much less accurate when they do so (Geary, Fan, et al., 1993).

Elementary School Children's Addition

These findings about preschoolers' addition differed substantially from the comparative models of young elementary school children's addition that were most prominent from the early 1970s through the mid 1980s. Within these models, first and second graders were depicted as always using a single strategy. One possibility was that both conclusions were correct, that preschoolers use diverse strategies but that by early elementary school, children settle on a single consistent approach. Another possibility, however, was that young elementary school students, like preschoolers, use diverse strategies, but that the methods that had been used in the earlier studies were inadequate for detecting them.

The most prominent of the comparative models was Groen and Parkman's (1972) *min model*. Groen and Parkman postulated that young elementary school children use the *min strategy* to solve single-digit addition problems, and that older children and adults retrieve answers to the same problems. The min strategy involves counting up from the larger addend the number of times indicated by the smaller addend. For example, a child using the min strategy to solve 3 + 6 would solve the problem by starting at 6 and counting "7, 8, 9." Within this min model, the only source of variation in solution times on different problems was the number of counts needed to solve the problem. Thus, 3 + 4, 4 + 3, and 6 + 3 would all require the same amount of time, because all required three upward counts. A problem such as 2 + 9 would require less time, even though its sum was larger, because it would require only 2 upward counts. A further assumption of the min model was that each count requires the same amount of time. Thus, the min model predicted that young children's solution times would be a linear function of the smaller addend, because children always solve problems by counting on from the larger addend, and the larger the size of the smaller addend, the more counts (and the more time) required to reach the sum.

Groen and Parkman (1972) tested the min model by presenting first graders a set of simple addition problems. Consistent with the model's predictions, they found that size of the smaller addend accurately predicted children's mean solution times on different problems (Figure 3.5). The prediction was accurate in both relative and absolute terms. The predictor associated with the model, size of the

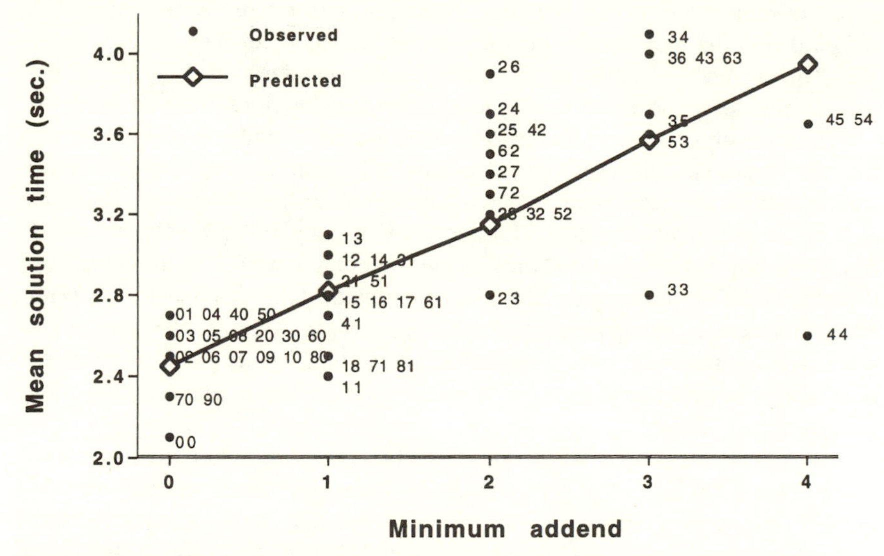

Figure 3.5. Solution times predicted by the min model and observed in first graders' performance on addition problems with sums below 10. For each pair of numbers in the figure, the first number indicates the first addend, and the second number indicates the second addend. Thus "01" corresponds to 0 + 1. Note that as the smaller addend in the problem increases, children take longer to solve the problem. Data from "A Chronometric Analysis of Simple Addition," by G. J. Groen and J. M. Parkman, 1972, *Psychological Review, 79*, p. 335. Copyright 1972 by American Psychological Association. Reprinted with permission.

smaller addend, accounted for roughly 70% of the variance in solution times, much higher than the amount accounted for by any other model that they considered.

A variety of subsequent findings were consistent with the min model as a description of how young elementary school children add. Other investigators replicated Groen and Parkman's finding that smaller addend size was the best predictor of such children's solution times (Ashcraft, 1982; 1987; Kaye, Post, Hall, & Dineen, 1986; Svenson, 1975). Like Groen and Parkman, they found that it was a good predictor in absolute as well as relative terms, accounting for between 60% and 75% of the variance in mean times on different problems. The model accurately predicted performance of children in Europe as well as North America, and children in special education classes as well as typical ones (Svenson & Broquist, 1975). It also fit the pattern of solution times produced by individual children, as well as group averages (Groen & Resnick, 1977; Kaye, et al., 1986; Svenson, 1975).

The model also was extended in an important way by Ashcraft (1982). Ashcraft found that the best predictor of first graders' solution times was the size of the smaller addend, that the best predictor of fourth graders' times was the sum squared (a predictor thought to reflect retrieval, due to its often being the best predictor of adults' solution times), and that the two were equally good predictors of third graders' times. From this, Ashcraft inferred that the first graders consistently used the min strategy, that the fourth graders (like adults) consistently used retrieval, and that third grade was the time of transition between the two strategies. This seemed a plausible account, given the demand of most U.S. school systems that children memorize the basic addition facts by third or fourth grade.

Thus, the chronometric data provided considerable evidence consistent with the min model. The one discordant note came from a different type of data, mathematics educators' descriptions of young children's arithmetic (Fuson, Richards, & Briars, 1982; Hebbeler, 1976; Houlihan & Ginsburg, 1981; Yoshimura, 1974). They reported that children said they added by counting from 1; by counting from the larger addend; by using 5s, 10s, and tie problems (e.g., 5 + 5, 6 + 6) as reference points; and by using a variety of other approaches. Although the descriptions were largely anecdotal, they were sufficently similar to raise doubts about the accuracy of models that depicted first and second graders as always using a single strategy.

How could the good fit of the min model to the solution time data be reconciled with the self-reports of diverse addition strategies? One possibility was that the self-reports were epiphenomenal. Even adults often cannot accurately report on their cognitive processes (Nisbett & Wilson, 1977; Wilson & Stone, 1985); the problem may be worse with children (Brainerd, 1973). The mathematics educators' reports that described the diverse strategies did not include converging evidence from solution time or error patterns. Thus, children's self-reports might have been inaccurate.

Another possibility, however, was that children's self-reports did accurately reflect their addition strategies, and that the apparent fit of the chronometric models was artifactual. This possibility was especially interesting to me, because it opened the possibility of more valid assessments of strategy use than the ones I had used in the studies of preschoolers. Equating absence of an observable strategy with retrieval had always made me uneasy. On the one hand, children's fast solution times and their answers to informal questions suggested that they often used retrieval on these trials. On the other hand, the answers to the informal questions also suggested that on some such trials, children had used strategies without visible accompaniments, such as counting in their heads. Systematically obtaining verbal reports provided a potential means for determining more precisely what children were doing on these "no visible strategy" trials (the name used to describe them in Siegler & Robinson, 1982).

Thus, both to test whether young elementary school children, like preschoolers, used diverse strategies, and to determine whether obtaining immediately retrospective self-reports could aid in strategy assessment, Siegler (1987a) presented kindergarteners, first graders, and second graders with 45 problems, 9 in each of 5 sessions. The smallest problem was 4 + 1, the largest was 17 + 6. Children were told that they could solve the problems in any way that they wanted, and that the experimenter was interested in how children their age solved math problems. Consistent with this expressed interest, the experimenter asked immediately after each problem, "How did you solve that problem?"

Strategy classifications were based on both the children's self-reports and the videotaped record of overt behavior. When overt behavior indicated what the

Table 3.2. Addition Strategies of 5-to-7 Year Olds

	Strategy					
	Retrieval	Min	Decomposition	Count All	Guessing	Total
% Use	35	36	7	8	14	100
% Correct	94	83	94	46	29	77
Mdn RT (sec.)	2.1	5.6	3.8	15.2	5.0	4.0

Note. Data from Siegler (1987a).

child had done, it was the basis of strategy assessment. When overt behavior was absent or ambiguous, the child's verbal report provided the basis for classification. This procedure allowed highly reliable strategy assessments. Two research assistants who independently assessed the strategies agreed on 94% of their initial classifications; they discussed the other 6% until they reached agreement.

Results of the study replicated both the chronometric findings that gave rise to the min model and the verbal reports described by the mathematics educators. In accord with the standard chronometric finding, mean solution time on each problem was a linear function of the size of the smaller addend. Smaller addend size accounted for 76% of the variance in the mean solution times. In keeping with the prediction of the min model, this was far more variance than could be accounted for by any other predictor.

On the other hand, as shown in Table 3.2, the classifications of children's strategy use on each trial (derived from their overt behavior and self-reports) suggested that children of each age used a variety of strategies. Of the 68 children, 99% were classified as using at least two strategies, and 62% as using at least three. Although the min strategy was the single most common method, it was used on only 36% of trials. At no age did children use it on more than 40% of trials. This was a far different picture than suggested by the min model, which predicted that children would use the min strategy on 100% of these problems.

Obtaining both types of data on each trial allowed analysis of whether it was the children's verbal reports or the chronometric techniques that were misleading. The critical data analysis involved dividing the solution times according to the strategy the child was classified as using on that trial, and then performing separate chronometric analyses for the mean times classified as having been generated by each strategy. If the strategy classifications were valid, this would be expected to yield predictors that were intuitively related to the characteristics of the strategy hypothesized to have produced the data on that subset of trials. The separate chronometric analyses would also be expected to yield more precise prediction of the solution times than analyses based on data averaged over all trials (and all strategies).

The results yielded exactly those results. On trials where children were classified as using the min strategy, the min model was a better predictor of solution times than in any past study or in the data set as a whole. It accounted for 86% of the variance in mean solution time on the 45 problems. In contrast, on trials where children were classified as using one of the other strategies, the min model was never a good predictor of performance either in absolute terms or relative to other predictors. It never accounted for as much as 40% of the variance in the mean solution time on each problem, and was never either the best or the second best predictor of the times.

The best predictors of performance when children were assessed as using other strategies provided further evidence for the validity of the strategy assessments. For example, on trials where children were assessed as counting from one, the sum, which corresponded to the number of counts they would need to make if they used this strategy, was the best predictor of solution times. Results of analyses of percent errors on each problem paralleled results of the solution time analyses. This and subsequent experience with the methodology has led to my using immediately retrospective verbal reports as well as overt behavior to assess strategy use in almost all studies conducted after this one (studies published after 1988).

These results raised the question of why, if children used the min strategy on only a minority of trials, the min model would account so well for the averaged data. At least three factors conspired to produce this effect: the relative frequency of use of each strategy, the variance on the dependent measure generated by each strategy, and covariance among predictor variables. Specifically, two strategies were used most often: the min strategy and retrieval. Together, they were used on 70% of trials. Although they were used on essentially the same percentage of trials (36% and 35%), the min strategy generated far more systematic variance in solution times on different problems. As a result, when data from the two sets of trials were combined, the smaller addend size was a very good predictor of the mean solution times, despite the min strategy being used no more often than retrieval (Figure 3.6). Further, the fact that all strategies generated shorter solution times on problems with small addends increased the absolute magnitudes of all of the correlations between predictor and dependent variables. The three factors together allowed the min model to do an excellent job of predicting solution times and error rates, despite children using the hypothesized strategy only about one third of the time. (See Pellegrino & Goldman, 1989, and Appendix A of Siegler, 1987a, for in-depth discussions of how these factors can distort conclusions from data averaged over strategies.)

In conclusion, there seems little doubt that rather than invariably using a single strategy, young elementary school children use multiple strategies to solve addition problems. In subsequent investigations, this was found to be true for third and fourth graders (Goldman, Mertz, & Pellegrino, 1989; Ladd, 1987), for children with learning disabilities (Geary, 1990; Geary & Brown, 1991; Geary, Brown, & Samaranayake, 1991), for gifted children (Geary & Brown, 1991), for children from both middle and lower income backgrounds (Kerkman & Siegler, 1993), and for children from Brazil and China as well as the United States (Geary, Fan, & Bow-Thomas, 1992; Schliemann, 1992).

Subtraction

The recent history of research on young children's subtraction has closely paralled that of research on their addition. In the early 1970s, chronometric models were proposed that depicted children of a given age as consistently using a particular strategy. Like the models of addition, these subtraction models accounted

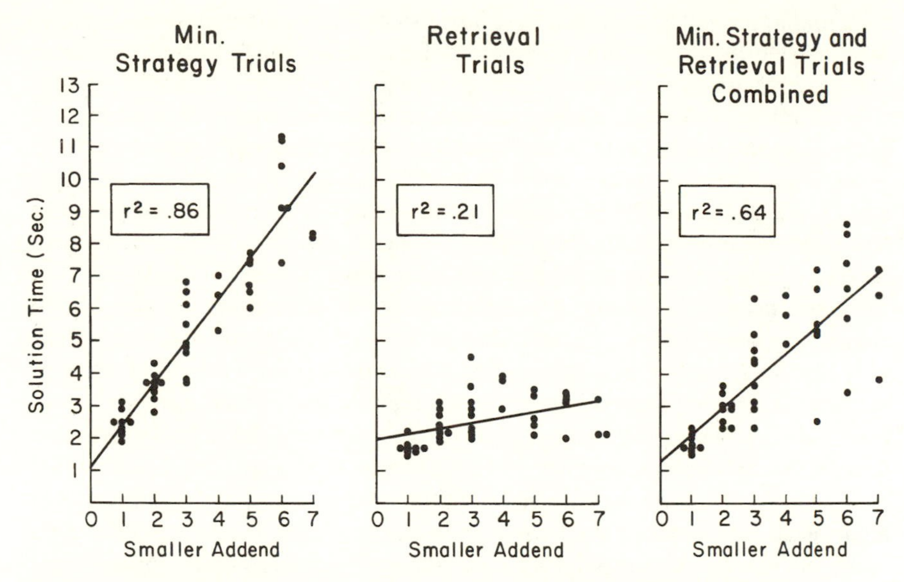

Figure 3.6. Relation between size of the smaller addend and median solution time on each problem on trials on which children reported using the min strategy (left panel), on trials on which they reported retrieving the answer (middle panel), and on trials on which they reported using either of the two approaches.

quite well for data on mean solution times on each problem. Also, as in addition, the one serious inconsistency was mathematics educators' reports suggesting that young elementary school children in fact used diverse strategies. As described in this section, the resolution also has been the same: Young children use multiple subtraction strategies, not just one.

In the 1970s and much of the 1980s, the most prominent model of children's subtraction was Woods, Resnick, and Groen's (1975) *smaller-count model.* This model reflected the hypothesis that children always execute whichever of two counting procedures, counting-down or counting-up, can be executed with fewer counts on the particular problem. The counting-down procedure involves counting down from the minuend (first number) the number of counts indicated by the subtrahend (second number) and stating as the answer the number at which counting stops. Thus, on 12 – 3, children would count "12, 11, 10, 9" and advance 9, the stopping point, as the answer. The counting-up procedure involves counting up from the second number to the first one and stating as the answer the number of counts required to reach that point. For example, on 12 – 9, children would start at 9, count "10, 11, 12," and advance 3, the number of counts, as the answer. A child behaving in accord with the smaller-count model would always count down on 12 – 3 and would always count up on 12 – 9, because this would minimize the number of counts needed to solve the problems.

The smaller-count model was consistent with a substantial body of data. It accounted for roughly 50% of variance in U. S. second and fourth graders' solution times on single-digit subtraction problems (Woods, et al., 1975). It accounted for a similar percentage of variance in Swedish children's solution times on somewhat more difficult problems (Svenson & Hedenborg, 1979). In both studies, it was superior to alternative models in accounting for the performance of individual children as well as for data averaged over the entire sample of children. For example, in the Woods, et al. study, it was the best predictor of solution times for 30 of 40 second graders and for all 20 fourth graders. The smaller-count model also explained almost 70% of variance in first graders' solution times on open sentence addition problems, such as 4 + ? = 7, which, like subtraction problems, can be solved either by counting up or by counting down (Groen & Poll, 1973).

In contrast, my own observations of preschoolers' subtraction (Siegler, 1987b) suggested quite a different picture. They indicated that individual 4- and 5-year-olds use diverse strategies, just as they do in addition, and that the particular strategies they use also resemble those in addition. The observations of mathematics educators suggested that early elementary school children also use diverse subtraction strategies (Carpenter, 1986; Carpenter & Moser, 1984; Fuson, 1984; 1988; Steinberg, 1983). As with addition, though, these strategy assessments of elementary school students did not include any validation from alternative measures. They also did not explain why the smaller-count model fit the solution time data as well as it did.

To determine whether early elementary school children in fact use multiple subtraction strategies, Siegler (1989a) presented to second and fourth graders problems on which subtrahends ranged from 5 to 17, minuends from 1 to 14, and differences from 1 to 8. Strategies were assessed on each trial using both videotapes of overt behavior and self-reports.

As in the parallel study of addition, the results replicated both the previous chronometric findings and the previous observations of strategy use. The smaller-count model was the best predictor of the data averaged across all trials, accounting for 52% of the variance in different problems' mean solution times. In contrast, the trial-by-trial strategy assessments, based on the videotapes of overt behavior and the immediately retrospective self-reports, suggested that children used at least six distinct approaches. Beyond the previously noted approaches of retrieving answers, counting down, and counting up, children also converted problems to simpler forms by subtracting 10 from each number, drew analogies to related addition problems, and guessed. Fully 99% of children used at least two strategies, 91% at least three, 72% at least 4, and 41% at least five.

The smaller-count model proved to be a poor predictor of when each strategy was used. On problems where children were predicted to always count down (because counting down required fewer counts), they counted down on only 32% of trials. On problems where children were expected never to count down (because counting down required more counts), they counted down on 31% of trials. Worse yet, on problems where children were predicted always to count up (because the smaller count involved counting up), they only counted up on 4% of trials. Overall, children were classified as using the hypothesized strategy on only 19% of trials. Only 2 of 74 children used the expected strategy on 50% or more of problems.

Dividing the solution times by the strategy believed to generate them again supported the validity of the strategy assessments. On trials where children were classified as counting down, the predictor that should have been the most accurate, the required number of downward counts, was by far the best predictor of solution times. It accounted for 81% of variance in the mean solution time on each problem. Also as expected, on the few trials where children were classified as counting up, the best predictor of the solution times was the number of upward counts required. The same types of factors that led to the min model accurately predicting the addition data led to the smaller count model accurately predicting the subtraction data (Siegler, 1989a). Thus, contrary to the depiction of the smaller-count model, preschoolers through fourth graders use diverse strategies to subtract, as they do to add.

This variability is far from unique to arithmetic. As illustrated in the remainder of this chapter, it is omnipresent in all four of the core areas of higher level cognition: problem solving and reasoning, memory, language, and conceptual understanding.

Problem Solving and Reasoning

When young children are first learning arithmetic, the task requires considerable problem-solving skills. Thus, their use of multiple arithmetic strategies demonstrates that they at least sometimes use multiple strategies to solve problems. Like any domain, however, arithmetic has idiosyncratic aspects that could limit the generality of observations. This raises the issue of whether comparable variability of thinking is observed in other situations that demand problem solving and reasoning.

Scientific Reasoning

In both children and adults, varied scientific concepts and types of reasoning coexist and compete for substantial periods of time. In one of the first studies to demonstrate this phenomenon, Kuhn and Phelps (1982) observed 10- and 11-year-olds' strategies for identifying the individual and joint effects of several potentially important variables on an outcome. Even after children discovered a systematic experimentation strategy, they continued to use a variety of unsystematic strategies as well. This was true of literally every subject in the study. The variability was present in strategies for generating hypotheses, strategies for generating new experiments, and strategies for drawing conclusions.

Schauble (1990) reported similar results with the same age group on a different scientific reasoning problem. In her task, the 10- and 11-year-olds needed to identify the effects of several factors that they were told might influence a race car's speed within a computerized microworld. Children had strong prior beliefs and theories about which factors mattered; the microworld was designed so that the prior beliefs proved correct in some cases and incorrect in others. For example, children's expectation that engine size mattered was true in the microworld, but their expectation that large wheels would increase the car's speed was not. When the 10- and 11-year-olds encountered evidence that disconfirmed their prior beliefs, they did not respond by dropping the beliefs and substituting new ones. Instead, they cited both old and new beliefs for a number of sessions, often through the end of the study. Variability of reasoning based on these beliefs was at times evident even within a child's statements on a single trial. Over the eight sessions of the experiment, children's beliefs became increasingly accurate, but alternative beliefs continued to compete for a prolonged period. As Schauble wrote, "Even after a belief was disconfirmed by the evidence, children did not necessarily abandon it altogether. Rather, the belief often resurfaced repeatedly, appearing finally to fade rather than conclusively being rejected" (p. 52).

College students' physics problem solving shows similar diversity. Learning in this area is often characterized as movement from an intuitive or Aristotelian theory to an understanding consistent with the principles of modern physics (e.g., Halloun & Hestenes, 1985; McCloskey, Washburn, & Felch, 1983). However, trial-by-trial assessment of reasoning on momentum and kinetic energy problems reveals that college students, both those taking their first physics course and those who have taken as many as seven courses, apply varied reasoning, legitimate and illegitimate, to essentially identical problems (Maloney & Siegler, 1993). For example, the college students sometimes analyzed kinetic energy problems in terms of the kinetic energy construct, sometimes in terms of momentum, sometimes in terms of force, sometimes in terms of weight, and sometimes in terms of other physical and intuitive concepts. As in children's reasoning, this variability was present within as well as between subjects; two thirds of students used three or more separate conceptualizations in trying to solve a given type of problem. The diversity was present even when two versions of a problem differed only in the particular objects involved. Half of the college students, both science and nonscience majors, used at least two different strategies on such trivially different versions of the same problem. Thus, in adults' physics reasoning as in preschoolers' single-digit addition, diversity of strategy use is a prominent characteristic of problem solving.

Block Stacking and Counting

Wilkinson (1982) created a problem-solving task in which 3- to 6-year-olds were given blocks of varying heights, with a hole drilled through the middle of each block, and asked to stack the most blocks possible on a vertically oriented rod. The optimal means of solving this problem was to select and maintain a goal of always choosing the shortest block not yet chosen. Problems varied in how many blocks of each height were available and in the number of dimensions along which the blocks varied.

To examine the stability of problem solving, Wilkinson presented identical problems twice within a single session. Children who had been correct on the first trial fairly often erred on the second, despite the problems being identical. Similarly, children who had been incorrect on the first trial were quite often correct on the second. Overall, children switched on 30% of the pairs of trials.

There appeared to be two sources of this variability. One involved initial interpretation of the goal; this was evident in children at times choosing as their first block one that was not the shortest available, but better understanding the task by the second time they encountered the problem. The other source of variability involved switching goals. Many children followed the optimal strategy of choosing the shortest block available for several trials before deviating from it. Irrelevant variation in other dimensions (width and depth) increased the likelihood of such deviations, especially among the youngest children in the study, the 3-year-olds.

Wilkinson (1984) described similar variability on a set of tasks involving counting of objects. The more demands placed on children as they counted, the more variable their counting became. Wilkinson suggested that this was due to the relatively difficult tasks burdening the executive processes responsible for coordination of components, and this greater burden on executive components resulting in more variability in choices among components.

Time Telling

Even when presented the identical problem on two successive days, older children, like the younger ones studied by Wilkinson (1984), fairly often use different strategies on the two occasions. This was evident in a study (Siegler & McGilly, 1989) in which second and third graders, just learning to tell time on an analog clock, were presented with a series of clockfaces and asked to tell the time on each one. The identical clockfaces were presented on two successive school days.

Children used five strategies. The most common strategy was retrieval, followed by counting forward by 1's from an earlier 5-mark, counting forward by 5's or by 5's and 1's from the hour, counting backward by 1's from a later 5's mark, and counting forward by 1's from the hour. As in arithmetic, variable strategy use was not just a group-level phenomenon. All 33 children used at least three strategies.

Most striking, this variability was evident on the two presentations of the identical time. Individual children used different strategies on 34% of the pairs of presentations of the identical setting. Learning of the times in the period between the two presentations was not a plausible explanation, because the direction of change in strategy use was inconsistent. For example, if we divide the trials into the 50% on which children retrieved the answer and the 50% on which they used one of the other strategies (collectively labeled *back-up strategies*), children moved from a back-up strategy to retrieval on 39% of trials, from retrieval to a back-up strategy on 29% of trials, and from one back-up strategy to another on 32% of trials. These data, along with the similar data from preschoolers' addition (Siegler & Shrager, 1984), are strong evidence for the variability of strategy use being present even under essentially identical circumstances: same child, same problem, same tester, same test situation, minimal opportunity for learning between testing occasions.

Memory Strategies

Memory strategies are as varied as strategies for reasoning and problem solving. This can be illustrated with regard to serial recall and search strategies.

Serial Recall

Serial recall involves presenting lists of arbitrary items, usually numbers, letters, or unrelated words, and asking subjects to recall them verbatim. It is perhaps *the* prototypic task for studying development of memory strategies, and a great many experiments have been performed regarding it (Brown & DeLoache, 1978; Dempster, 1981).

In most such experiments, a waiting period is imposed between presentation of the list and the time when children can respond. Children often use strategies to maintain their memories during this waiting period. The standard depiction of developmental changes in use of these strategies is that 5-year-olds rarely rehearse, but that children aged 7 and older generally do. For example, Flavell, Beach, and Chinsky (1966) classified 10% of kindergartners, 60% of second graders, and 85% of fifth graders as rehearsing. Subsequent studies replicated these findings, showed similar changes at later ages in special populations such as children with mental retardation or learning disabilities, and showed that teaching children to transfer training to new situations is difficult but possible (see Schneider & Pressley, 1989, for a comprehensive review of these findings).

There was reason to suspect, however, that the conceptual framework that motivated these studies, and the strategy-assessment methods used in them, led to underestimation of the variability of strategy use at all ages. The main question being asked concerned the age at which children made the transition from not rehearsing to rehearsing. In some studies, strategy use was inferred from the presence of primacy effects in serial position curves, despite this pattern being only weakly correlated with rehearsal activity (Crowder, 1976; Huttenlocher & Burke, 1976). Other studies used the more direct method of observing lip movements on each trial. The direct observations allowed detection of overt activity, but not of any covert activities that were occuring, the same problem that arose in my own early studies of arithmetic strategies. A third method was to ask children at the end of the session how they tried to remember. The problem with this method is the low validity of such delayed verbal reports, which occurs because the time interval between the processing and the verbal report is so long that the relevant information is no longer in working memory (Ericsson & Simon, 1991). Thus, all three methods seemed likely to underestimate both the frequency of young children's rehearsal and the variability of their ways of rehearsing.

To provide more valid assessments of serial recall strategies, McGilly and Siegler (1989) used the same type of trial-by-trial assessment procedure as proved effective in arithmetic and time telling: immediately retrospective self-reports following each trial and videotapes of ongoing behavior on the trial. Other than this, it was a standard study of the development of serial recall strategies. Kindergartners, first graders, and third graders were presented lists of three or five numbers and asked to recall them verbatim. A waiting period of either 5 or 15 seconds elapsed between the end of the experimenter's recital of each list and a signal for the child to repeat the numbers.

At all ages, children used three approaches (Table 3.3). Sometimes, they recited the list over and over until the waiting period ended (*repeated rehearsal*).

Table 3.3. Percentage Use of Each Serial Recall Strategy

Grade	Strategy		
	Repeated rehearsal	Single rehearsal	No rehearsal
Kindergarten	24	56	20
First	63	29	8
Third	78	16	5

Note. Data from "How Children Choose Among Serial Recall Strategies," by K. McGilly and R. S. Siegler, 1989, *Child Development, 60,* pp. 172–182. Copyright © 1989 by Society for Research in Child Development. Reprinted with permission.

Other times, they recited the list once and then stopped and waited for the signal (*single rehearsal*). Yet other times, they simply waited (*no rehearsal*). Even the youngest children in the experiment, 5-year-olds, rehearsed on the majority of trials. The majority of 5-year-olds also used the most sophisticated strategy on at least some trials.

These strategy assessments yielded considerably higher estimates of kindergartners' use of repeated rehearsal than did simple observation of the children's overt activities in previous experiments (e.g., in Flavell et al., 1966). This could be interpreted in two ways. One interpretation was that the requests for verbal reports artificially inflated the amount of strategy use by creating an implicit demand that children use strategies. The other possibility was that the verbal reports allowed detection of covert strategies that children were using, and would have used even without any questions being asked.

To distinguish between these interpretations, we conducted a second study in which we randomly assigned kindergartners, second graders, and fourth graders to self-report or no self-report conditions (McGilly & Siegler, 1990). Children in the self-report condition were asked immediately after each trial what, if anything, they had done in the waiting period. Those in the no self-report condition were given identical problems, but not asked to describe their strategy. Strategy use on each trial was assessed in two ways: solely on the basis of overt behavior, and on the basis of the verbal self-reports as well as the overt behavior (as in the earlier study).

When the strategy use of children in both groups was scored solely on the basis of overt behavior, children in the self-report condition were classified as rehearsing no more often (in fact, slightly *less* often, 39% vs. 47%). Mean number of distinct strategies used by each child also did not differ between the groups. These findings argued directly against the possibility that the questions about strategy use were leading children to rehearse more than they otherwise would have. If the questions had increased children's frequency of rehearsing, the results should have been evident in their overt behavior.

Including the children's verbal reports as evidence indicated that they were rehearsing on almost twice as many trials, 74% versus 39%, as was evident from their overt behavior. Together with the data on elementary school children's arithmetic that were reviewed earlier, these findings indicate that examining both ongoing overt behavior and immediately retrospective verbal reports provides a sensitive index of strategy use on each trial, without itself influencing the strategies that children use.

Search Strategies

In some situations, even 1-year-olds use multiple strategies. DeLoache (1984) noted that after seeing an object hidden and being told they later would need to retrieve it, 1-year-olds engaged in several mnemonically relevant activities during the delay period. They talked about where the object was hidden (e.g., saying "Big Bird chair" when a Big Bird doll was hidden under a chair), loitered in the vicinity of the hiding place, and stared at and pointed to the hidden object's location. DeLoache's interpretation that these were strategies for remembering was supported by her finding that the toddlers engaged in the same activities less often when the "hidden" object was visible (for example, when the Big Bird doll was under a transparent chair).

Oral and Written Language

Like theories of memory and problem solving, theories of the development of oral and written language often have postulated a developmental sequence in which children progress through a series of approaches, using a single approach at each age. Again, however, closer examination has revealed much greater variability.

Phonology

Much research on phonological development has emphasized identification of *the* basic unit guiding children's pronunciation and how that unit changes with age. At a given point in development, a child would operate with a particular basic unit, progressively mastering the distinctions at that level of analysis. For example, Jakobson (1968) hypothesized that children discover different phonemic distinctions at different ages, with the discoveries proceeding in a fixed sequence. As Ferguson (1986) commented, "for linguists viewing phonological development as the acquisition of phonemic oppositions (Jakobson, 1968) or the refinement of realization rules (Smith, 1973), variability was an inconvenience, to be acknowledged but not attended to" (p. 44).

More recent findings, however, have led to a revision in emphasis sufficiently great that it led Leonard, Rowan, Morris, and Fey (1982) to conclude, "one of the hallmarks of early language development is phonetic variability" (p. 55). This variability is especially striking in initial speech. It is present within individual words as well as in pronunciation of the same phoneme in the context of different words. For example, after a 1-year-old was introduced to the new word "pen," the child produced 10 different pronunciations of the word within a single session (e.g., "peh," "pin," "ben") (Ferguson, 1986). The variability is not limited to new words introduced by an experimenter; Scollon (1976) observed that in a naturalistic context, a child just short of her second birthday pronounced "I want" in seven different ways within a half hour period.

This variability in an individual's pronunciation is not unique to toddlers just beginning to use language; it continues throughout childhood and adulthood (e.g.,

Hindle, 1978; Labov, Yaeger, & Steiner, 1972). Variations in the linguistic environment and the speaker's goals cannot account for the variability; it is evident even when speakers are asked to pronounce twice a given word in a constant environment (Peterson & Barney, 1952). The variability is smaller in later childhood than when children first start speaking, and smaller in adulthood than in childhood; nonetheless, it is clearly present throughout life (Labov, 1969).

Syntax

How children produce past tense forms has been a central issue in language development at least since the 1950s. The most influential model in this area, and one of the most influential in all of developmental psychology, was proposed by Berko, R. A. Brown, and their colleagues (Berko, 1958; Brown, Cazden, & Bellugi, 1969; Brown, 1973; Ervin, 1964). The model postulates three stages. In Stage 1, children produce correct terms for the small number of regular and irregular verbs on which they attempt to use the past tense. In Stage 2, they use the "infinitive + ed" rule both for regular verbs, where it produces correct forms, and for irregular verbs, where it does not. Thus, they produce such overgeneralized forms as "comed," "goed," and "hitted." Finally, in Stage 3, they limit the "ed" rule to regular verbs and produce correct irregular forms. Brown and his colleagues suggested that children make this progression quite rapidly, moving from Stage I to Stage III between 18 months and 3 years.

Subsequent data have revealed much more variability, however. Kuczaj (1977) examined past tense verb use of 14 children ranging in age from 2.6 to 5.6 years. All children—2-year-olds, 3-year-olds, 4-year-olds, and 5-year-olds—produced more than 50% correct irregular past tense forms. Most, however, also produced substantial numbers of overgeneralizations. Overgeneralized forms were produced on 25% to 40% of uses. The same pattern was evident in Kuczaj's longitudinal study of an individual child whose progress he followed from age 2.6 to 5.0. On five of the six testing occasions, the child produced substantial numbers of both overgeneralized and correct irregular forms. Other investigators have found that overgeneralized past tense forms are fairly common as late as first grade (Marcus, Pinker, Ullman, Hollander, Rosen, & Xu, 1992; Menyuk, 1969) and that they still occur occasionally at age 11 (Kuczaj, 1977).

Adding to the variability, the children in Kuczaj's study produced two distinct types of overregularized forms, in addition to the correct irregular one. One overgeneralized form followed the familar "verb + ed" rule. The other took the form "past tense + ed". With the verb "eat," the first overgeneralization would generate "eated," the second "ated." Kuczaj observed a clear trend away from the first and toward the second type of error, but both types of errors were evident for several years. Kuczaj indicated that the varying forms were present even within a single verb; thus, the same child produced "goed," "wented," and "went" on different occasions close in time. Clearly, there is far more variability in use of these morphological forms than usually recognized.

Reading

When we read, we encounter material that makes varying processing demands. We respond to these varying demands, and to our own varying goals, by adopting different reading strategies. Goldman and Saul (1991) identified three commonly used strategies for reading text: *once through*, *review*, and *regress*. As the name suggests, the once-through strategy involves sequential reading of text from beginning to end. The review strategy involves reading the passage from beginning to end and then rereading some or all of it. The regress strategy involves rereading before reaching the end of the passage.

Goldman and Saul asked college students to read eight passages from introductory textbooks in the social and biological sciences. The students controlled the presentation of sentences on the computer screen in a way that allowed recording of the sequence in which they read them.

In reading the eight passages, 97% of students used at least two of the strategies. Roughly a third of students used all three. This was not attributable to differences in the difficulty of the passages; all elicited roughly equal percentages of use of each strategy. Students who used a greater number of strategies recalled more of the material than did those who used fewer of them. Thus, using diverse strategies may have aided the students' recall.

Spelling

Use of diverse strategies has also been documented in both children's and adults' spelling (Baron, Treiman, Wilf, & Kellman, 1980; Lewis, 1980; Marsh, Friedman, Welch, & Desberg, 1980). To learn more about these strategies, I asked 28 second graders to spell a set of words. Words were chosen from the second grade spelling book the children were using and the third grade book they were scheduled to use the next year. Their lengths varied from three to seven letters and they were chosen so as to represent a broad sampling of sound-letter correspondences. Children were provided paper and pencil so that they could generate and try to recognize alternative spellings. They also were asked to bring their dictionary from the classroom, so that they could look up words if they wished.

As shown in Table 3.4, children used at least four spelling strategies: retrieval, sounding out, writing alternative spellings, and looking up words in the dictionary. These approaches had different advantages and disadvantages. For example, sounding out took much less time than writing alternative spellings or looking up words in the dictionary. However, it also was less accurate.

An interesting feature of the spelling data was that looking up words in the

Table 3.4. Second Graders' Spelling Strategies

Strategy	Trials on which strategy used (%)	Mean solution time (sec.)	Correct answers (%)
Retrieval	74	9.2	88
Sounding out	15	13.5	51
Dictionary	11	1:20.8	67
Writing out alternatives	1	53.5	67

dictionary did not produce perfect spelling. Children erred on one third of trials on which they looked up the word. There were two reasons for this. On about half of the trials on which such errors occurred, children miscopied the word. On the other half, they did not even know the spelling well enough to find the word, and eventually gave up without locating it. Even seemingly error-free strategies do not guarantee error-free results.

Conceptual Understanding

Forms of Conceptual Representation

Conceptual representation has been a stronghold of theories that posit 1:1 relations between age and type of thought. The theories of Piaget, Vygotsky, Werner, and Bruner differ in many ways, but all agree that older children can represent concepts in ways that are impossible for younger children. Older children are said to be able to form taxonomic concepts, but younger children only thematic ones; older children to form separable concepts, but younger ones only integral ones; older children true concepts, but younger ones only chain ones; and so on.

More recent data, however, have challenged this assumption. They have shown that even young children can form complex as well as simple conceptual representations of a single type of content. Minor variations in experimental procedures often elicit different modes of thought.

This can be illustrated in the context of thematic and taxonomic concepts. When preschoolers are asked to indicate which objects belong together, they frequently produce thematic sortings; they may put together dogs and frisbees, rather than dogs and mice, because dogs like to play with frisbees. However, when the same children are asked to explain what dogs and mice have in common, they have no difficulty doing so (Smiley & Brown, 1979), thus illustrating that they sometimes think of the same content taxonomically.

This is not a new development late in the preschool period; even 1-year-olds at times use taxonomic concepts. For example, Bauer and Mandler (1989) presented 1-year-olds with sets of three objects. They pointed to the target object and asked, "See this one? Can you find another just like it?" One of the choices was related to the target thematically, the other taxonomically. For example, in one problem, the target object was a monkey, the thematically related choice was a banana, and the taxonomically related choice was a bear. More than 85% of the 1-year-olds chose the taxonomically related objects (the monkey and the bear) as being alike, rather than the thematically related ones (the monkey and the banana). Thus, rather than being limited to thematically based concepts, the 1-year-olds could form taxonomic concepts as well.

Biological Theories

Children's concepts of the nature and properties of living things have been the subject of a great deal of recent investigation. Carey (1985) proposed that up to age 7, children have a naive theory of psychology that they apply to judgments regarding biological as well as psychological characteristics. In particular, they rely on similarity to human beings, rather than biological categories (e.g., "mammal") to infer whether various creatures breathe, reproduce, and eat. In Carey's terms, the children rely on similarity-based, rather than categorical, inference. Carey also hypothesized that sometime between ages 7 and 10, children develop true biological theories, and therefore switch to relying on biological categories.

More recently, Keil (1992) demonstrated that children much younger than 7 also can think about living things in truly biological, as well as psychological, ways. Keil followed Carey's procedure of telling children that people possess a property and then observing the children's judgments of whether other animals, plants, and inanimate objects also possess it. Some children, however, were provided a biological context along with the information about people. For example, they were shown a picture of a person and told "This person eats because he needs food to live and grow. If he doesn't eat, he will get skinnier and skinnier and he will die." Given this context, 4-year-olds concluded that other mammals and fish also ate food and possessed other properties whose biological functions had been described. The children did not blindly generalize to all biological entities; for example, they did not infer that plants had bones. However, their pattern of responses left little doubt that that their inferences were based on biological categories rather than on similarity to human beings. The data indicated that young children possess biological concepts, but that they apply them in a narrower range of contexts, and at times to a narrower range of entities, than do older individuals. Manipulating the context influences which mode of construal (Keil, 1992) is chosen for thinking about the phenomenon, but not the fact that both younger and older children possess both biological and psychological concepts.

Conservation

Conservation concepts also have been viewed as progressing through a consistent, age-related sequence. The hypothesis is that children initially base their thinking on a single relation and later consider multiple influences. For example, Piaget (1952a) claimed that preoperational children base number conservation judgments on a single dimension, usually the relative lengths of the rows of objects, whereas concrete operational children consider length and density, as well as the type of transformation that was performed.

Subsequent research indicated greater variability than implied in this account. Even 3- and 4-year-olds often solve number conservation problems involving small sets of objects, while failing to solve problems with larger sets (Gelman, 1972; Winer, 1974). Children also understand the effects of addition and subtraction transformations at a time when they do not understand that simply spreading out or pushing together a row of objects does not change the number of objects (Siegler, 1981).

Trial-by-trial analysis of number conservation strategies indicates yet greater variability. Siegler (1995) presented 5-year-olds with a set of large number conservation problems in which the children both judged on each trial which, if either, row had more objects and explained their judgments. Children used a variety of strategies, sometimes relying on the type of transformation, sometimes on the length of the row, sometimes counting the objects in each row, and sometimes indicating that they simply did not know. All children used at least two of these approaches, and more than 85% used three or more. Thus, the same child would rely on length on one trial, on the type of transformation on a second, and on counting on a third. Rather than having a single concept of number conservation, children had several notions that competed for use.

Other evidence suggests that even a single number conservation response can reflect competing ways of thinking. Church and Goldin-Meadow (1986) observed both that children often gestured as they explained their number conservation responses and that, surprisingly frequently, their gestures and explanations did not go together. Thus, children sometimes explained their liquid quantity conservation answer by saying that the water in one glass was taller, while at the same time gesturing with their hands in a way that emphasized the cross-sectional areas of the liquid columns. The children who most often showed such variability within a single response also were the most likely to benefit from a conservation training procedure. The authors' explanation was that the differing gestures and verbal explanations indicate competition between different ways of conceptualizing the problem, which in turn aids learning through producing cognitive conflict. Siegler (1995) also found that variability in thinking, in this case as measured by frequency of producing two different types of thinking on a single pretest trial, was positively related to subsequent conservation learning.

Use of a quite different method yielded similar conclusions regarding children's understanding of conservation. Acredolo and O'Connor (1991) asked each of a group of kindergarten through sixth grade children to estimate the probability that each of several answers to number and area conservation questions were correct. On the number conservation task, 33% of children assigned non-zero probabilities to at least two solutions. On the area conservation task, 74% of children did so. There seems little question that on conservation, as elsewhere, children often think about a single concept in several ways.

Conclusions

The data presented in this chapter argue for a move away from universalist and comparative approaches and toward approaches that recognize as a central phenomenon the pervasive variability in children's thinking. This variability seems to be present in every area of higher level cognition, just as at all lower levels. The findings examined in this chapter alone documented cognitive variability in such diverse areas as addition, subtraction, scientific reasoning, problem solving, memory for hidden objects, serial recall, reading, spelling, phonology, syntax, biological concepts, and conservation. The variability was pervasive at all ages. Examples involved people ranging from one year to adulthood (the next chapter includes an example of such variability in infants less than a year old).

This variability also was shown to be present at a wide variety of levels of analysis. It is not limited to between-subject variability. When ways of thinking have been assessed on a trial-by-trial basis, individual children typically have been found to use three or more approaches on a given task. Nor is it limited to children using one approach on one type of problem but a different approach on another type of problem. In three experiments in which a single problem was presented on two occasions close in time, individual children used different strategies on roughly one third of the pairs of trials. The variability can at times even be seen within a single trial. Children's verbal explanation on a given trial may indicate one way of thinking, their gestures another.

Substantial variability in higher level cognition also has been found at all levels of competence. In the context of phonology, it appears to decrease with linguistic experience. In the context of physics problem solving, substantial variability remains present even among undergraduate science majors who have taken a number of physics courses. However, the moderate experience hypothesis seems to capture the most common developmental pattern. The relation between cognitive variability and age-experience seems usually to be curvilinear, with the greatest variability being present when children have had moderate amounts of experience in the domain. The progression was demonstrated most directly in the Siegler and Taraban (1986) balance scale study, in which children showed such a progression within a single experiment, but similar patterns are evident when we compare performance across age groups in such domains as arithmetic, spelling, memory strategies, and scientific reasoning.

A key factor in making possible analyses of variability in higher level cognition is reliable and valid methods for assessing thinking on a trial-by-trial basis. Otherwise, what looks like cognitive variability may just be unreliability of measurement. Several types of evidence indicate that the combination of videotaped observations of overt behavior and immediately retrospective self-reports produce reliable and valid assessment. In both addition and subtraction, separating solution times on each problem according to the strategy believed to have generated those solution times allowed more accurate prediction of the data than did analyzing the entire set of solution times. In one case, the method resulted in a strategy that had been believed to generate all of the data being shown to generate only a little over one third of it. In the other case, the method showed that no children used the strategy that all children had been hypothesized to use. Analyses of performance on serial recall tasks indicated that the assessment method was non-reactive. Asking children to provide immediately retrospective self-reports of strategy use did not lead them to use more strategies, or different strategies, than children who were presented the same serial recall task but not asked to provide self-reports. However, obtaining the self-reports allowed detection of strategy use that was not evident in overt behavior. These data indicate that at least for ways of thinking that are generated in a moderate amount of time (perhaps 2–30 seconds), this assessment method allows reliable, valid, and nonreactive measurement of what subjects are doing on each trial.

One reaction to these findings might be: "OK, there is a lot of variability in higher level, as well as lower level, cognition, but how important is it? Can't we achieve a good understanding of cognitive development without wallowing in this messy variability?" I believe not, for two reasons. First, not focusing on the variability of cognitive development leads us away from recognizing central phenomena, such as how children choose among the varying ways of thinking and how their choices change with age and experience. Second, not focusing on the variability makes cognitive change extremely difficult, and maybe impossible, to understand. The next chapter illustrates the benefits of recognizing cognitive variability for understanding changes in children's thinking.

Notes

1. It may seem counterintuitive to think of retrieval as a strategy—it is definitely not as prototypic as counting on one's fingers, for example. However, its use responds to the same types of variables as do more prototypic strategies. Thus, it is used most often on problems where it is fast and accurate relative to other strategies and when it has been successful on past trials within the session (Reder & Ritter, 1992; Siegler, 1987a). Similarly, early in the learning process, use of retrieval to solve a given problem, like use of other strategies, varies from trial to trial. Successful retrieval of an answer one day in no way implies that the same answer will be retrieved the next day nor that retrieval will be used at all (Siegler & Shrager, 1984). Finally, contemporary analyses, which emphasize spreading activation and parallel distributed processing, indicate that retrieval, like other strategies, is not a simple unitary act. Thus, it seems useful to think of retrieval as a strategy, albeit a nonprototypic one.

2. This lack of clear progress from one session to the next might seem surprising; how would children ever learn to add if they do not move toward more sophisticated strategies? The key consideration to keep in mind is the time scale. Learning to consistently retrieve the correct answer to single-digit addition problems takes most children several years and hundreds, if not thousands, of trials. Thus, progress from one session to the next would be expected to be minimal.

4

Strategic Development: Trudging up the Staircase or Swimming with the Tide?

As described in the previous chapter, children's thinking is highly variable. The present chapter focuses on implications of this variability for understanding development.

Thinking about a pair of visual metaphors may help facilitate recognition of these implications. The first, which I believe underlies most depictions of development, is the *staircase metaphor*. The second, which I believe offers a superior alternative, is the *overlapping waves metaphor.*

Two Metaphors for Cognitive Development

The Staircase Metaphor

Cognitive developmentalists have often phrased their models in terms that suggest that children of a given age think about a given task in a single way. *N*-year-olds are said to have a particular mental structure, a particular processing limit, a particular theory, strategy, or rule that gives rise to a single type of behavior. Change involves a substitution of one mental entity (and accompanying behavior) for another.

The basic conceptualization that seems to underlie these models is aptly captured in the title of Robbie Case's (1992) recent book *The Mind's Staircase*. The visual metaphor that this title evokes is, I believe, central to most cognitive-developmental treatments of change: Children are depicted as thinking in a given way for an extended period of time (a tread on the staircase); then their thinking undergoes a sudden, vertical shift (a riser on the staircase); then they think in a different, higher way for another extended period of time (the next tread); and so on.

This view of development is most closely identified with Piagetian and neo-Piagetian approaches, such as those of Piaget and Case. Thus, as shown in Figure 4.1, we see development depicted within Piaget's theory as involving sensorimotor activities from birth to about 2 years; preoperational thinking from 2 to 7 years; concrete operational thinking from 7 to 12 years; and formal operational think-

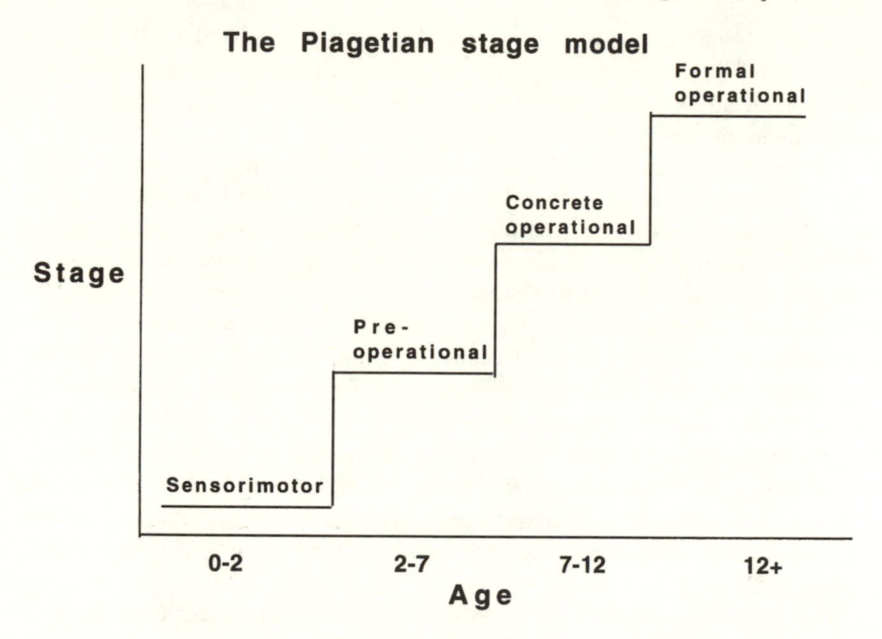

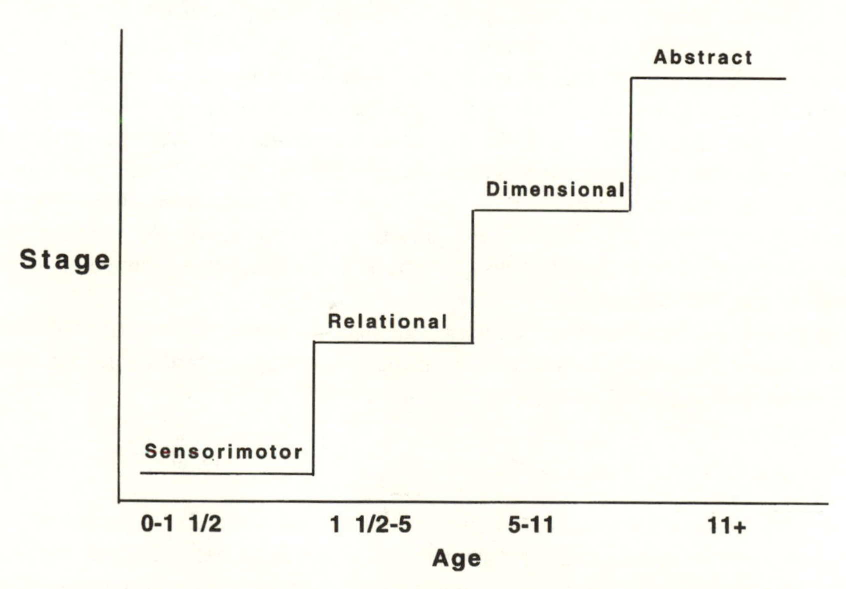

Figure 4.1. Piaget's and Case's (1985) staircase depictions of cognitive development.

ing from 12 years onward. Within Case's theory, we see thinking depicted as advancing from the sensorimotor level between birth and 18 months, to the relational level from 18 months to 5 years, to the dimensional level between 5 and 11 years, and to the formal level at age 11 and beyond.

Although this view of development is associated with the Piagetian and neo-Piagetian traditions, it is far from unique to them. Indeed, it is omnipresent. For example, researchers who try to identify children's implicit theories describe children's thinking in very different terms than Piagetians and neo-Piagetians; they also often look for and find much greater early competence. However, the form of their depiction of development is similar. Two-year-olds are said to have a desire theory of mind, whereas 3-year-olds are said to have a belief-desire theory (Wellman, 1990). Three-year-olds are said to have nonrepresentational theories of mind, whereas 5-year-olds are said to have representational theories (Perner, 1991). Four-year-olds are said to have a psychological theory of biology, whereas 10-year-olds are said to have a truly biological theory (Carey, 1985). As with the Piagetian and neo-Piagetian approaches, the staircase metaphor captures the basic idea about the course of development theorized in these approaches (Figure 4.2).

The depictions of information processing researchers differ from those of Piagetian, neo-Piagetian, and theory-theory researchers not only in vocabulary but in their emphasis on very precise descriptions of the cognitive processes that produce the behavior. Again, however, they usually portray development as a series of 1:1 equations between ages and ways of thinking. For example, Ashcraft (1987) depicted acquisition of expertise on simple addition problems (e.g., 3 + 7) as involving the following developmental sequence: 4- and 5-year-olds rely on counting from one; 5- to 8-year-olds rely on counting from the larger addend; older children and adults rely on retrieving the answer from memory. My own depiction of development of number conservation (Siegler, 1981) indicated that most 3- and 4-year-olds base judgments on the relative lengths of the two rows, some older 4-year-olds and most 5-year-olds base judgments on the results of counting the objects in the two rows, and 6-year-olds and older children base judgments on the type of transformation that was performed (Figure 4.3).

As discussed earlier, these staircase-like depictions are radically at odds with current understanding of children's thinking. This suggests that a different way of thinking about development may be more useful.

The Overlapping Waves Metaphor

Suppose we adopt alternative orienting assumptions about development that, I believe, are both more consistent with the data and more helpful in understanding change. Within this set of assumptions, children typically use multiple approaches over prolonged periods of time. Rather than development being seen as a stepping up from Level 1 to Level 2 to Level 3, it is envisioned as a gradual ebbing and flowing of the frequencies of alternative ways of thinking, with new approaches being added and old ones being eliminated as well. To capture this perspective in a visual metaphor, think of a series of overlapping waves, like that

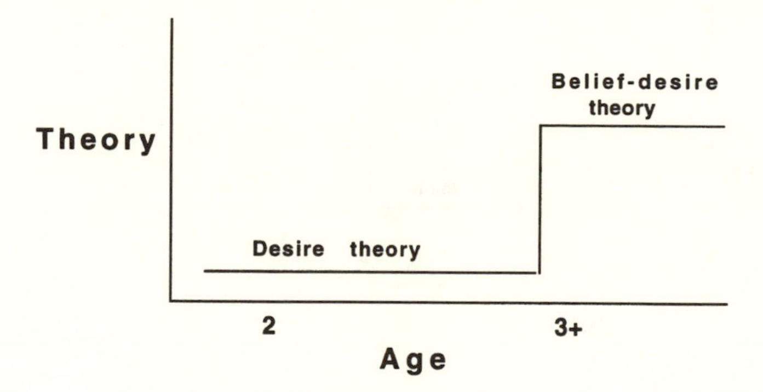

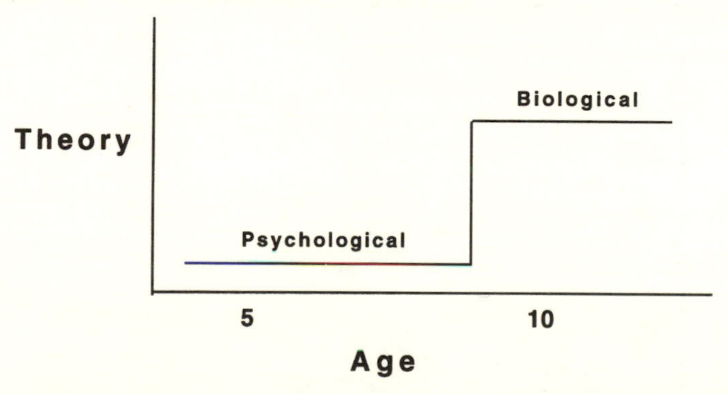

Figure 4.2. Wellman's (1990) and Carey's (1985) staircase depictions of development of theories of mind and biology.

shown in Figure 4.4, with each wave corresponding to a different rule, strategy, theory, or way of thinking. Contrasting the overlapping waves metaphor with the staircase progressions shown in Figures 4.1, 4.2, and 4.3 conveys some of the differences between the two approaches.

One immediately apparent difference is that rather than claiming that children use only a single way of thinking at each point in development, the overlapping waves depict the relative frequencies of multiple ways of thinking at each point in time (the vertical dimension of the figure). A second clear difference is that cognitive change is depicted as continuously changing frequencies of alternative ways of thinking, rather than substitution of one way for another.

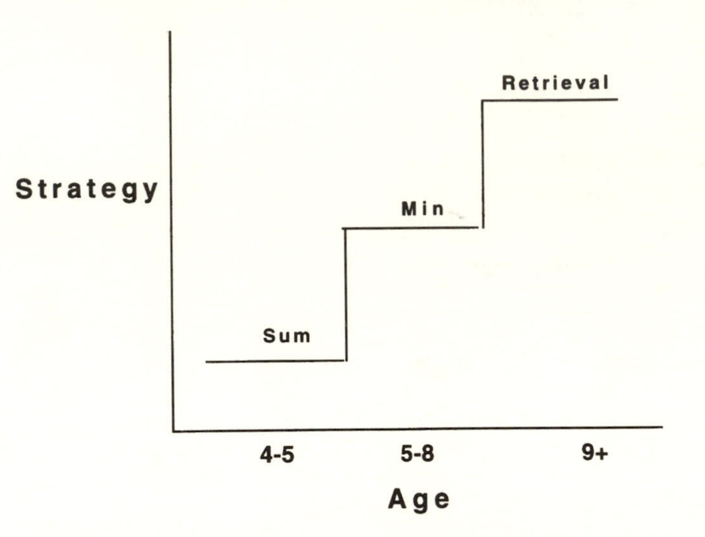

Siegler's (1981) number conservation model

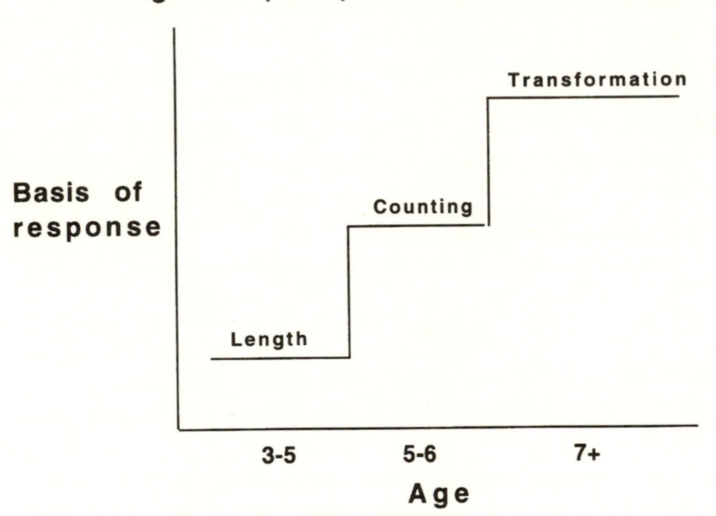

Figure 4.3. Ashcraft's (1987) and Siegler's (1981) staircase depictions of development of single-digit addition and number conservation.

If, on a given task, children think in only a single way at a given time, and occasionally suddenly shift to more advanced ways of thinking, the Figure 4.4 depictions collapse into staircase progressions like those in Figures 4.1 to 4.3. Thus, the overlapping waves depiction encompasses the staircase depiction as a limiting case involving the minimum number of ways of thinking and the maximum suddenness of change that are possible. However, the overlapping waves approach also allows

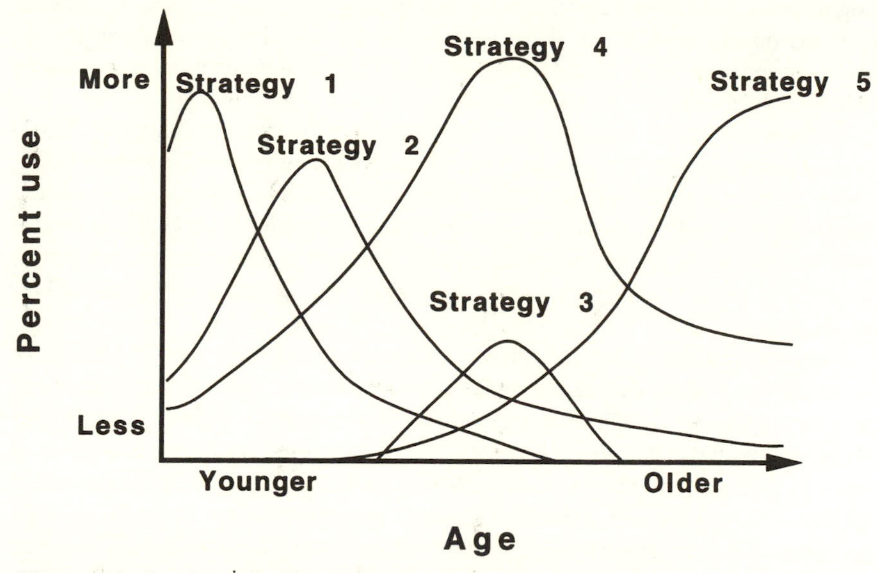

Figure 4.4. Overlapping waves depiction of cognitive development.

depiction of the situation that I believe is more typical, in which multiple ways of thinking coexist for prolonged periods, with development involving changes in their relative frequencies as well as introduction of new approaches.

The overlapping waves approach also opens up for investigation both descriptive and explanatory issues that would not otherwise be examined. Regarding description, knowing that children use varied approaches for substantial periods of time makes clear the need to examine separately developmental changes in the frequency, speed, accuracy, automaticity, and breadth of applicability of each approach. This can lead to a much more differentiated description of development than would be obtained by averaging over different approaches. For example, it can tell us whether age-related increases in speed of performance are due to older children acquiring new strategies that are faster than any previous approach, to their relying more often on the faster strategies from among those they already used, to their executing the same strategies more quickly, or to more than one of these potential sources of change.

Regarding explanations of development, the overlapping waves perspective moves to center stage a number of questions that have been backstage or offstage altogether in traditional approaches. What leads older children to choose different ways of thinking than younger ones? Is it that younger children don't have available the same ways of thinking as older ones? Or is it that they have the same ways available but use different algorithms for choosing among them? Or do they have available the same ways of thinking and use the same algorithms for choosing among them, but possess a smaller database that leads to the same algorithm generating different choices? This approach also raises the question of how new ways of thinking are discovered, and how, once discovered, they are integrated into the existing repertoire.

The overlapping waves metaphor also raises the more general question of why cognitive activity would be structured to give rise to multiple ways of thinking over periods of many years. Why, for example, when children discover a new, more advanced strategy, would they continue to rely heavily on old, less advanced strategies for prolonged periods of time?

This issue will be analyzed in greater depth in the next few chapters, but to anticipate the answer in a general way, consider the main task of the developing child: to learn. Childhood, especially early childhood, is a period in which the importance of high quality current performance is minimized relative to what it will be later in life. In contrast, learning new skills and competencies, and how to acquire yet greater knowledge, is absolutely essential. Learning is *the* central task of childhood.

The implication is that properties that facilitate learning may in general be especially prominent during childhood. Cognitive variability seems to represent one such property. Consider an example of how cognitive variability facilitates learning. Siegler and Jenkins (1989) examined 4- and 5-year-olds' discoveries of the min strategy for adding numbers. When the discoveries first occurred, use of the new strategy did not improve children's performance on the small number problems that were presented in this phase of the study. The min strategy was neither faster nor more accurate than counting from one. Thus, if new strategies were only generated when they benefited immediate performance, the children would not have discovered the min approach. For a substantial number of sessions after the initial discovery, the children used the new approach only occasionally on the small number problems that were being presented. Counting from one continued to be the children's predominant counting strategy even after they discovered the min approach.

However, when the preschoolers later were presented more challenging problems, such as 2 + 21, a disjuncture arose. Children who had previously discovered the min strategy used it often to solve the challenging problems, and thereafter used it considerably more often on all kinds of problems. In contrast, children who had not discovered the min strategy on the small number problems were simply overwhelmed by the new, more difficult problems. They neither solved them via the approaches they knew nor generated the min strategy in response to them. Thus, having available a variety of strategies can prove useful for adapting to new situations, even when one or more of the strategies is not used much and does not convey immediate benefits. The benefits parallel those of the immune system having available white blood cells that respond to a wide variety of antibodies, even though the cells may never have proved useful in the past (chapter 2, pp. 35–36).

Figures 4.5 and 4.6 illustrate how the overlapping waves model can be used to describe real-world empirical data. Figure 4.5 displays findings from Feldman's (1980) study of one child's map drawing on five occasions over a three-year period. During this time, Level II and III map drawings decreased in frequency; Level IV drawings first increased and then decreased; and Level V drawings gradually increased. At each time of measurement, the child produced four different levels of drawings, but the relative frequencies of the levels changed dramatically over time.

Figure 4.6 displays similar data for children's addition. It depicts results of a

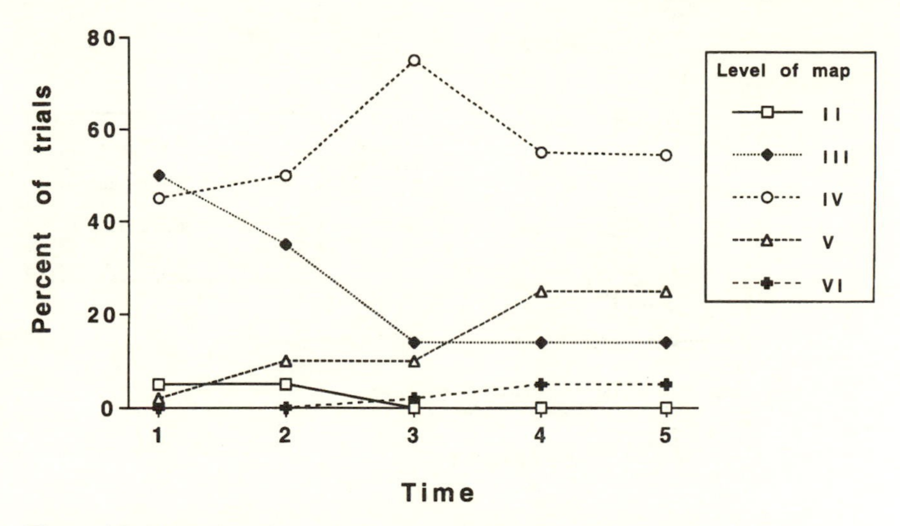

Figure 4.5. Variability of one child's map drawing over a 3-year period. Data from *Beyond Universals in Cognitive Development*, by D. H. Feldman, 1980, Norwood, NJ: Albex. Copyright 1980 by Ablex. Reprinted with permission.

short-term longitudinal study, in which 4- and 5-year-olds were presented roughly 30 sessions of experience solving single-digit addition problems over an 11-week period. For each child, some strategies increased in frequency, others decreased, yet others increased and then decreased, and yet others stayed at relatively constant levels of use.

The remainder of this chapter reports data on cognitive change that have arisen from detailed analyses of a variety of types of development: arithmetic, language, motor skills, moral reasoning, and interpersonal interactions among them. The examples include data from infants, preschoolers, elementary schoolchildren, young adults, and old adults. These data, and the overlapping waves conception, allow us to describe development in a way that, I believe, is both more accurate and more interesting than the portrayal that emerges from the staircase depictions.[1]

Much of this chapter is devoted to a detailed portrayal of the development of addition skills. The area seemed worth examining in depth because addition is a basic human competence, present in all societies; because its development covers a prolonged period from infancy through adulthood; because there is an extensive and high-quality database regarding it; and because that database allows us to distinguish six types of changes that contribute to strategic development:

1. Acquisition of new strategies
2. Changes in frequency of existing strategies
3. Changes in the speed of execution of the strategies
4. Changes in the accuracy of execution of the strategies
5. Changes in the automaticity of execution of the strategies
6. Changes in the range of problems to which each strategy can be applied.

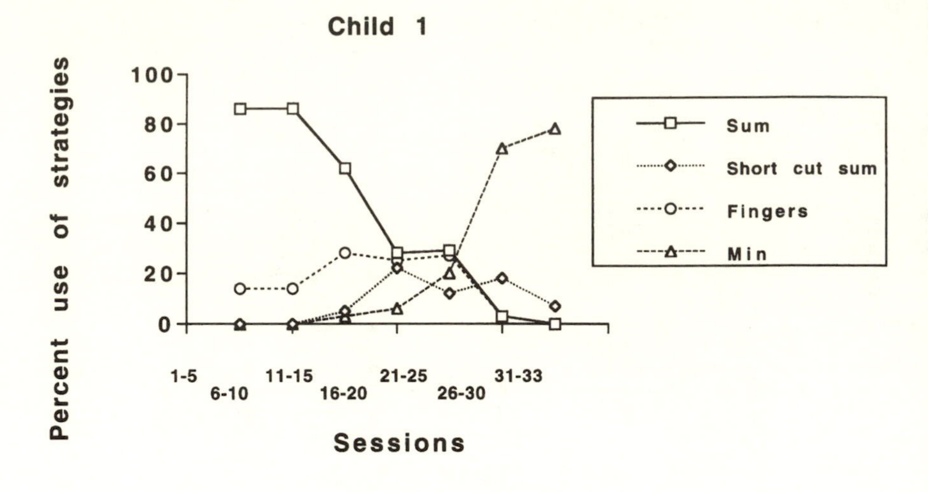

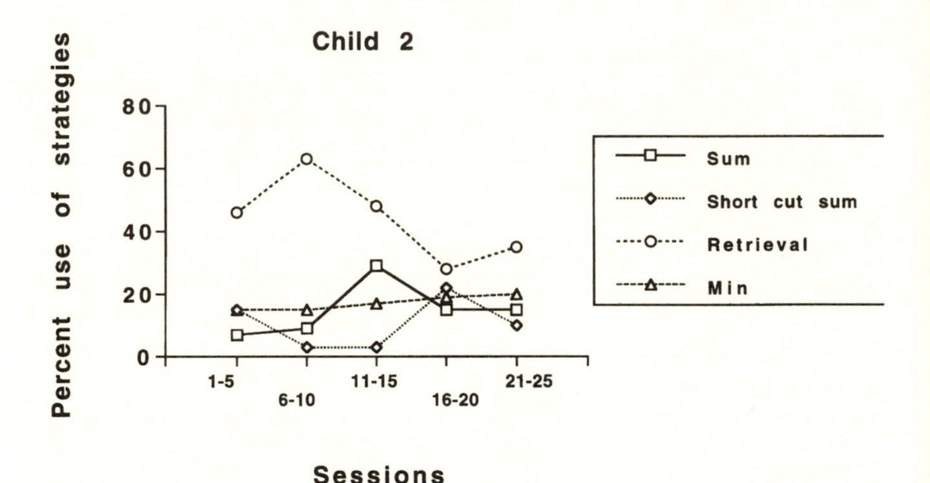

Figure 4.6. Variability in two children's simple addition strategies over an 11-week period (data from Siegler and Jenkins, 1989).

Thus the example illustrates two ways in which traditional portrayals of development can be enriched by the present approach: by depicting the strategic diversity that is present over prolonged periods of development and by differentiating among the multiple dimensions and providing data on each of them. As illustrated later in this chapter, most of the dimensions in this list also can be used to describe development in contexts where the unit of interest is not strategies, but rather beliefs, theories, rules, structures, or other units of cognition.

Development of Addition

Development in the Preschool Period

Strategy Use

From ages 2 to 4 years, children's knowledge of the sequence of number words and their ability to count objects to establish the cardinality of a set grows greatly (Fuson, 1988; Gelman & Gallistel, 1978). These acquisitions provide an essential base for the acquisition at ages 4 and 5 years of initial addition strategies such as counting fingers, putting up fingers but answering without counting them, counting imagined objects, and retrieval.[2]

During the preschool period, children increasingly use counting strategies and decreasingly rely on guessing. When young preschoolers are presented addition problems without physical objects present (as when asked "how much is 2 + 2"), they appear usually to guess. For example, the 4- to 4 1/2-year-olds observed by Levine, Jordan, and Huttenlocher (1992) did not use any overt strategy on 97% of trials, and answered only 9% of these problems correctly. The combination of absence of overt strategies and very low accuracy suggests that the children were guessing on these trials. Counting from one represented the leading edge of their competence; they always answered correctly on the 3% of trials on which they counted. Almost identical results were obtained when the problems were presented in story form ("Mike had two balls, he got two more, how many did he have then?").

With experience solving simple arithmetic problems, older preschoolers come to rely more heavily on overt strategies, particularly ones involving counting. The 4 1/2- to 6-year-olds studied by Siegler and Robinson (1982), who like the children observed by Huttenlocher, Jordan, and Levine were presented problems with addends of 5 or less, used overt strategies on 36% of trials versus 3% in Huttenlocher et al. In both studies, the counting that was observed consistently started with the number "1."

Speed and Accuracy of Strategies

Preschoolers' several approaches differ in speed and accuracy. Answering without generating overt behavior is by far the fastest strategy, putting up fingers but answering without counting them the next fastest, and the two counting strategies the slowest (Table 3.1, p. 62). Counting fingers and putting up fingers but answering without counting are generally more accurate than counting imagined objects or answering without any overt behavior.

Development in the Early Elementary School Period

Strategy Use

Children's proficiency changes dramatically when they begin to solve large numbers of addition problems in first grade. Virtually all children begin to use the *min strategy* (counting from the larger addend). Some children (usually the more mathematically advanced ones) also begin to use *decomposition* (dividing a prob-

Table 4.1. Percentage of Use of Each Strategy by Children of Early Elementary School Age

	Strategy				
Grade level	Retrieval	Min	Decomposition	Count from one	Guess or no response
Kindergarten	16	30	2	22	30
Grade 1	44	38	9	1	8
Grade 2	45	40	11	0	5

Note. Data from Siegler (1987a).

lem into two simpler ones, as in adding 9 + 4 by thinking "10 + 4 = 14, 9 is one less than 10, 14 – 1 = 13, so 9 + 4 = 13). Other strategies that had been quite frequent, such as counting from one, decrease and then disappear. Yet other strategies, such as retrieval, increase steadily in frequency and are extended to a greater range of problems. These developments are not unique to the present time or place. The progression from counting strategies to decomposition and retrieval was described by Brownell and Chazal (1935) and has been observed in China and Europe as well as in North America (Geary et al., 1993; Svenson & Sjoberg, 1983).

The developmental trend in strategy use is illustrated in Table 4.1.[2] Use of retrieval and decomposition increases greatly from kindergarten to second grade, whereas use of counting from one and guessing decrease substantially. Use of the min strategy increases some during this age range, and at all points seems much greater than that among preschoolers (recall that in Siegler and Robinson, 1982, and Geary and Burlingham-Dubree, 1989, all counting that was observed started from one). A longitudinal study in which the performance of the same children was assessed in both first grade and a year later in second grade showed similar trends (Geary, Brown, & Samaranyake, 1991).

Comparable trends were evident in a longitudinal sample of Swedish children (Figure 4.7). In this study, 13 children were asked to solve all problems with addends of at least 1 and sums less than or equal to 13. Their strategy use was assessed on a trial-by-trial basis early and late in first grade, second grade, and third grade. The data provide another nice illustration of the overlapping waves pattern, with some strategies steadily increasing, others decreasing, and yet others first increasing and then decreasing.

These data are aggregated over a number of types of problems; they show the general trends, but not the patterns of development, within each type of problem. Figure 4.8 illustrates the pattern of development for one type of problem, problems where both addends are between 5 and 10. Use of retrieval to solve such problems increases a little from kindergarten to first grade and much more from first to second grade. Counting from one and guessing are quite frequent in kindergarten, but decline sharply in use thereafter. The min strategy is used a little by kindergartners to solve such problems, becomes the most frequent single strategy by first grade, and then declines in frequency by second grade. Use of decomposition steadily increases, though it never becomes very common. Again, the pattern clearly fits the overlapping waves depiction better than it does the staircase.

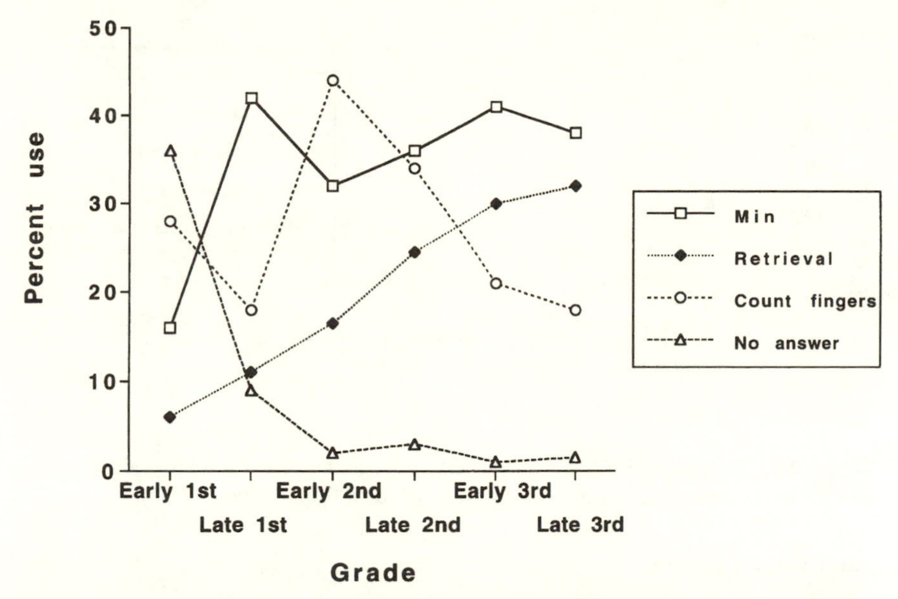

Figure 4.7. Variability of Swedish first, second, and third graders' addition strategies. Data from "Evolution of Cognitive Processes for Solving Simple Additions During the First Three School Years," by O. Svenson and K. Sjoberg, 1983, *Scandinavian Journal of Psychology, 24*, p. 121. Copyright 1983 by Scandinavian University Press. Reprinted with permission.

Speed and Accuracy

During the early elementary school period, children change not only which strategies they use, but how quickly and accurately they use them. Overall, second graders took less than half as long as kindergartners to solve the problems presented in Siegler (1987a) (Table 4.2, top). The speedup reflects a mixture of improvements in the speed with which each strategy is executed and movement toward more frequent choice of the faster strategies. Retrieving the answer to a problem, using the min strategy, and solving problems via decomposition all take second graders much less time than they take kindergartners. Beyond this, the fastest strategies, retrieval and decomposition, are the ones whose use increases the most; the slowest strategy, counting from one, is the one whose use decreases the most (Table 4.1).

Changes in the accuracy with which children execute each strategy are even more dramatic. Overall, the second graders in Siegler (1987a) made less than one tenth as many errors as the kindergartners (Table 4.2, bottom). Again this reflected both increasing use of the more accurate strategies and more accurate execution of each strategy. Retrieval and decomposition, the two most accurate strategies at all ages, were used increasingly; counting from one and guessing, the least accurate strategies, were used decreasingly. Similarly, each individual strategy was executed more accurately by older children. Thus, both increasing use of faster and more accurate strategies and increasing speed and accuracy of execution contribute to the developmental improvements along these dimensions.

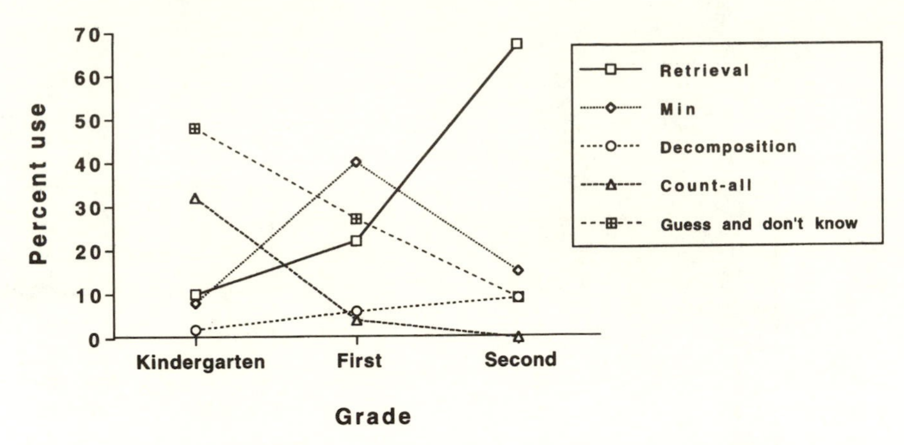

Figure 4.8. Variability in U.S. kindergartners', first graders', and second graders' addition strategies on problems with addends of 5–10 (data from Siegler, 1987a).

Later Development

Strategies

Children's addition strategies continue to change after second grade, but the change process is surprisingly slow and often fails to reach the usually envisioned endpoint of consistent use of retrieval. By third grade, children retrieve answers on about 70% of trials on single-digit addition problems (Ladd, 1987). The min strategy is used on most of the rest of trials. Thereafter, use of the min strategy decreases, and use of decomposition and reference to related problems becomes increasingly prevalent. By college, decomposition and reference to related problems are used more often than the min approach (Ladd, 1987, LeFevre, Sadesky, & Bisanz, 1996).

The really surprising finding that has arisen from studies of performance in

Table 4.2. Errors and Solution Times Generated by Early Elementary School Children's Strategies.

	Strategy					
Grade level	Retrieval	Min	Decomposition	Count from one	Guess or no response	All trials
Median solution times						
Kindergarten	3.9	6.0	6.9	15.2	4.2	6.0
Grade 1	2.1	6.9	4.1	16.3	7.4	3.8
Grade 2	1.8	3.9	3.2	——	3.7	2.7
Percentage of errors						
Kindergarten	19	29	9	55	89	51
Grade 1	4	17	8	50	38	13
Grade 2	3	7	3	——	7	5

Note. The final column in each section of the table is not an unweighted average of the numbers in the column, because the strategies were used on different numbers of trials. Instead, they are the overall mean for each age based on all responses. Data from Siegler (1987a).

later childhood, adolescence, and adulthood is that at no age do most people consistently retrieve answers to single-digit addition problems. For example, Ladd (1987) studied strategic development between second grade and adulthood, using the same type of immediately retrospective self-reports as used by Siegler (1987a). He found that on the 100 single-digit addition problems, second graders retrieved on 53% of trials, third graders on 76%, fourth graders on 69%, sixth graders on 69%, and college students (at Northern Colorado University) on 72%. Others have obtained similar findings. Geary and Wiley (1991) found that University of Missouri undergraduates used retrieval on 88% of trials, and LeFevre et al. (1996) found that undergraduates at Carleton University (in Ottawa, Canada) used retrieval on 71% of trials. The phenomenon cannot be attributed to a few math-phobic students. Fully 81% of subjects in LeFevre et al. used at least two strategies for solving these simple problems. Nor can the inconsistent retrieval be attributed to North American educational systems being worse than those elsewhere in the world; Svenson (1985) found that Swedish undergraduates used strategies other than retrieval on 22% of problems. Thus, although retrieval becomes the main strategy for solving single-digit addition problems, even college students, who if anything would be expected to retrieve more often than the general population, continue to use other strategies as well.

Despite the variety of studies in which college students have been found to use strategies other than retrieval, the finding seemed so counterintuitive that substantial converging evidence seemed necessary before accepting it. LeFevre et al. (1996) provided such converging evidence. Their method involved collecting solution time as well as strategy use data on each trial and contrasting the solution time patterns generated by the strategies that undergraduates reported using to those that would have been expected if the students were doing what they said they were.

As would have been expected if the self-reports were accurate, solution times were faster and less variable on trials where the undergraduates reported retrieving the answer than on trials on which they reported using back-up strategies. Similarly, on trials where the undergraduates reported using the min strategy, their solution times were very well predicted by the size of the smaller addend, as it should be, given that the smaller addend corresponds to the amount of counting needed to solve problems via this strategy. Further, the strategies that were used varied systematically with the problem, again in ways that would have been expected. For example, on the most difficult problems, such as 7 + 9 and 9 + 8, students reported retrieving on less than half of trials, whereas on the easiest, such as 1 + 1 and 2 + 2, they reported retrieving on nearly 100%. Adding yet more evidence, the undergraduates' self-reports of strategy use were systematically related to their standardized test performance. Undergraduates who attained high scores on standardized tests of arithmetic competence reported using retrieval considerably more often than did those who attained lower scores. This converging evidence left little doubt that the undergraduates' self-reports were valid indexes of their strategy use and that they use back-up strategies on a surprising percentage of single-digit addition problems.

There is one group of subjects who apparently do use retrieval consistently—

elderly adults. The elderly adults (mean age of 71 years) studied by Geary and Wiley (1991) reported retrieving answers on 98% of trials. One explanation for the difference between their performance and that of current undergraduates is that more emphasis was placed on memorizing the arithmetic facts when the older adults attended school. Another explanation is that the older adults had more reason to memorize the facts, because calculators were unavailable when they attended school. Whatever the reason for the difference, the result insures that there was nothing in the self-report method that pre-ordained the result that college students often do not retrieve answers to simple addition problems.

Speed and Accuracy

By the end of second grade, children add very accurately (95% or more correct in most experiments), leaving little room for further improvement on this dimension. However, speed continues to increase throughout childhood and adolescence. For example, Ladd (1987) reported mean solution times on the 100 single-digit problems of a little over two seconds for second graders, between one and two seconds for third, fourth, and sixth graders, and less than one second for college students. The differences among the strategies also decrease, due to large increases in the speeds of strategies other than retrieval. For example, the undergraduates in LeFevre et al. executed all strategies in less than 1.1 seconds. Retrieval was faster and less variable than the other strategies, but the range of mean times from the fastest to the slowest strategy was only 750 to 1100 milliseconds.

These changes in speed and accuracy suggest a possible explanation for why use of strategies other than retrieval continues into adulthood. The alternative strategies may be sufficiently fast that there is little reason to retrieve consistently. Habits that might be worth changing if they entailed large disadvantages sometimes are not worth changing when the disadvantages are small. This satisficing explanation (Simon, 1955) cannot be the whole story; it leaves unanswered the question of why some people, such as the high ability subjects in LeFevre et al. and the older adults in Geary and Wiley, do consistently use retrieval. However, habit and the small cost incurred seem likely to be part of the explanation for why many adults continue to use back-up strategies to solve such simple problems.

Automaticity

As children become increasingly expert in addition, their performance becomes not only faster and more accurate, but also increasingly automatic. It requires decreasing amounts of cognitive resources and becomes increasingly difficult to inhibit. LeFevre, Bisanz, and Mrkonjic (1988) developed a particularly clever way of assessing automaticity. Their task involved presentation of a problem such as 4 + 5 and then, a fraction of a second later, presentation of a single digit such as 9 slightly to the right of the first two numbers. What subjects needed to do was to say whether the number on the right had been one of the addends in the problem. Thus, the answer for the above problem would be "no," because 9 was not one of the addends in 4 + 5. Automaticity was assessed by contrasting the time to say no when the number on the right was the sum of the digits with the time required to say no when the number was wrong but not the sum. If activation of the sum was automatic, subjects would be slower to say no when the rightside number was the sum than when it was not (due to interference from activation of the sum slowing performance). Thus, when presented 4 + 5, subjects would be slower to say no when the number on the right was 9 than when it was 8.

Some degree of automaticity appears to be present from quite early in the learning of the easiest addition problems, but it only gradually spreads to the full range of problems (LeFevre, Kulak, & Bisanz, 1991; LeFevre & Kulak, 1994; Lemaire, Barret, Fayol, & Abdi, 1994). The youngest children thus far studied, second graders, show the interference effects associated with automatic processing, but only on small number problems (both addends of five or less). Third graders show the effects on both small and medium problems (one addend of six or more), but not on large number problems (both addends of six or more). Fourth and fifth graders and adults show evidence of automatic processing on all single-digit addition problems: small, medium, and large.

External Validation

As with preschoolers, older children's arithmetic strategy use is related both to their standardized test scores and to their ability to execute specific cognitive processes. With regard to the psychometric data, mathematics achievement test scores are quite strongly related to elementary school children's strategy use. For example, third and fourth graders' frequency of correct retrieval was found to correlate strongly ($r = .73$) with performance on the SRA test of mathematics achievement (Geary & Brown, 1991). At the level of specific cognitive processes, frequency and accuracy of use of advanced strategies is related to both working memory span and speed of processing in young elementary school children. This has proven true with both U.S. and Chinese samples (Geary et al., 1992), and with children who are gifted, typical, or learning disabled (Geary & Brown, 1991; Geary et al., 1991).

Range of Problems

Another major dimension of development involves extending competence to a widening range of problems. After learning single-digit addition problems to a high degree of proficiency, children are taught algorithms for adding multi-digit numbers that make use of these facts. They successively learn to apply the algorithm to one-digit plus two-digit, two-digit plus two-digit, two-digit plus three-digit, and eventually to arbitrarily large numbers. Once they learn to apply this algorithm, which is a main focus of instruction during second grade in the United States, children can in principle solve all addition problems when they have paper and pencil available.

Many multi-digit problems also can be solved through mental computation. It is not surprising that given the varied strategies children and adults use on single-digit problems, they also use a variety of strategies on multi-digit problems. One dimension on which the strategies vary is whether they involve adding from left to right or right to left. Another is whether they involve complete or partial decomposition of the problem. On 52 + 27, complete decomposition would involve the procedure: 50 + 20 = 70, 2 + 7 = 9, 70 + 9 = 79. Partial decomposition would involve the slightly compressed procedure 52 + 20 = 72, 72 + 7 = 79.

Both adults and third graders, in both the United States and the Netherlands, have been found to use these procedures (Hamann & Ashcraft, 1985; Widaman, Geary, Cormier, & Little, 1989; Wolters, Beishizen, Broers, & Knoppert, 1990).

At present, relatively little is known about the acquisition of these algorithms. For example, no one knows how people come to add from left to right, despite the written algorithm taught in school proceeding from right to left. The key point, though, is that once children learn multi-digit algorithms, they are in a position to solve all problems in the domain if pencil and paper are available and a great many problems even if they are not.

Conclusions Regarding the Development of Addition

Development of addition skills illustrates the kind of depiction of development yielded by the overlapping waves approach. It includes not just the ebb and flow of multiple ways of thinking, but also the multiple dimensions along which development occurs.

What the addition example clearly illustrates is that development occurs simultaneously along multiple dimensions, and that just focusing on qualitative aspects, or just on quantitative aspects, yields an incomplete and biased depiction. Children's strategies change; so do the speed, accuracy, and automaticity with which they can execute those strategies; so does the range of problems to which children can apply the strategies and the particular types of problems to which each strategy is most often applied.

The type of multidimensional description of development that this approach yields is illustrated in Table 4.3. The particular ages are approximations that depend on the individual, the types of formal and informal instruction that the individual encounters, and a host of other factors. More important is the illustration of the multiple dimensions along which addition development occurs, and of how the overlapping waves approach can provide a rich and encompassing characterization of development.

Considerations of space preclude presentation of comparably detailed depictions of development in other domains. However, both common sense and available data suggest that acquisition of addition is not an atypically complex phenomenon, and that adequately describing other areas of development in which children use diverse approaches will demand comparably multifaceted descriptions. The remainder of this chapter focuses on illustrating more briefly the changing patterns of thinking that occur in other domains and the applicability of the overlapping waves model to characterizing cognitive development in them.

Development in Other Domains

Multiplication

Most children in technologically advanced societies receive initial instruction in multiplication in second or third grade. From very early in the learning process,

Table 4.3. Dimensions of Addition Development

	Age/(Grade)			
Dimension of Development	3–4.5 (Preschool)	4.5–6 (Preschool + K)	6–8 (1st & 2nd Grade)	(Third grade and beyond)
Available processes & strategies for adding	Guessing, subitizing, sometimes counting from 1.	Subitizing, counting from 1, fingers, guessing, retrieving	Subitizing, counting from 1, fingers, guessing, retrieving, min, decomposition	Same
Relative frequency	Mainly subitizing on small number problems, guessing on larger ones	Increasing counting from 1, fingers, & retrieval; decreasing guessing	Increasing min, decomposition, retrieval; decreasing counting from 1, guessing	Increasing decomposition, decreasing min
Range of solvable problems	Sums < 5	Sums < 10	First sums < 18; then 2-digit addends, then 3-digit addends	All sums
Accuracy	High on sums < 5, low elsewhere	Increasing	Increasing	Asymptotic
Speed	High on sums < 5, low elsewhere	Increasing	Increasing	Increasing
Automaticity			Small single-digit problems	Small and medium, then large 1-digit problems

they use diverse strategies. Despite substantial changes in teaching methods and educational philosophy over the past half century, children's multiplication strategies have remained the same (Brownell & Carper, 1943; Cooney & Ladd, 1992; Siegler, 1988a). In both the 1940s and the 1980s, and in France as well as the United States (Lemaire & Siegler, 1995), the most common strategies are *retrieval* from memory, *repeated addition* of one of the multiplicands the number of times indicated by the other, and *representing and counting* objects that correspond to the problem (for example, solving 3 X 4 by writing 3 sets of 4 hatchmarks on a piece of paper and counting or adding the hatchmarks).

These studies also tell basically the same story regarding the development of multiplication strategies. With experience in multiplication, the frequency of retrieval and of relying on related facts (e.g., solving 3 X 8 by recalling 8 X 3) increases. Conversely, with experience, the frequency of using repeated addition and being unable to advance any answer decreases.

Consider results of a study in which French children were asked to solve in their heads single-digit multiplication problems on three occasions: early, in the middle, and late in second grade, the year in which they were being taught single-digit multiplication (Lemaire & Siegler, 1995). As shown in Figure 4.9, changes in strategy use came at different times on different classes of problems. Even very early in the year, children usually retrieved answers to the easiest problems. By the middle of the year, they extended retrieval to more difficult problems and became able to solve via repeated addition many problems on which they previously could only say "I don't know." By the end of the year, they quite consistently used retrieval on all but the most difficult problems, and rarely said "I don't know." A study 50 years ago of U.S. third, fourth, and fifth graders (Brownell and Carper, 1943) showed a very similar progression.

As in addition, frequency of retrieval of answers to multiplication problems seems to more or less stabilize beyond the first few years of learning. For example, LeFevre, Bisanz, Hubbard, Buffone, Greenham & Sadesky (in press) found

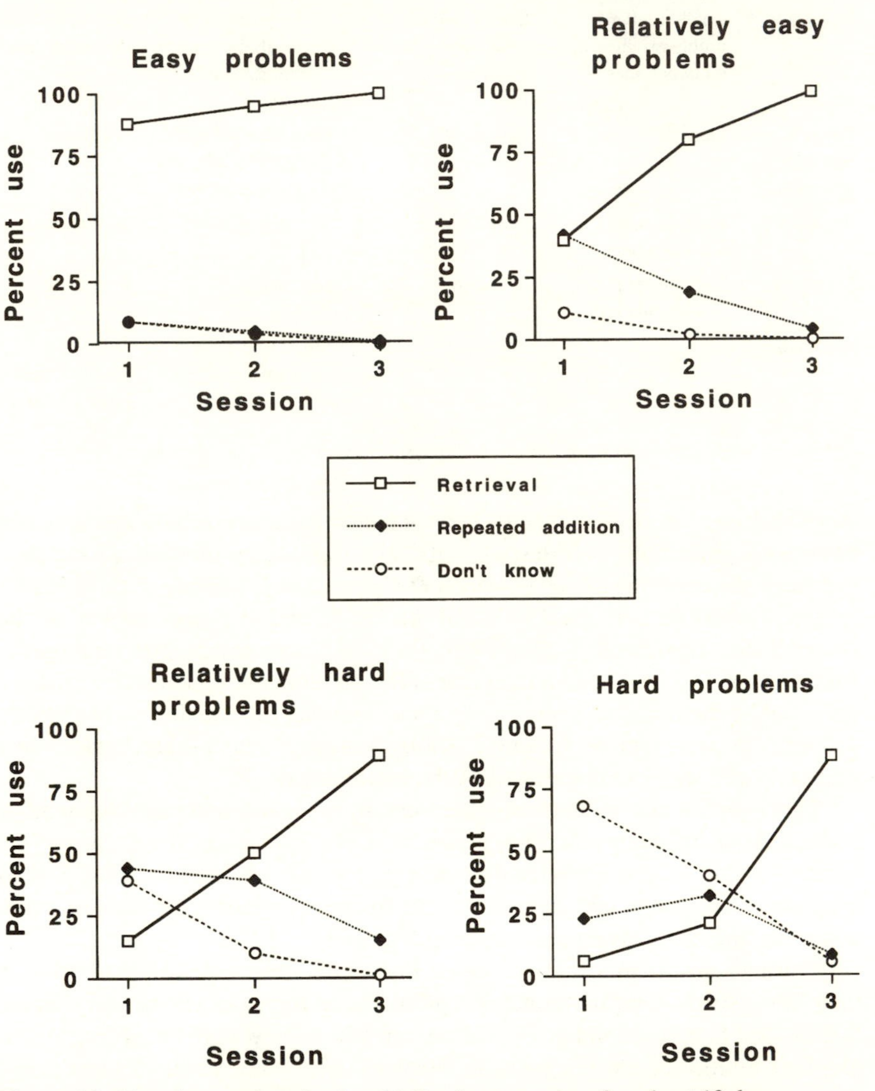

Figure 4.9. French second graders' multiplication strategies after about 10 days (Session 1), 2 months (Session 2), and 4 months (Session 3) of formal instruction in multiplication (data from Lemaire & Siegler, 1995).

that both ninth graders and adults retrieved answers to 83% of trials on the 100 single-digit multiplication problems. On the other trials, they sometimes based answers on rules (especially on problems involving zeros and ones), sometimes used repeated addition, and sometimes decomposed a single difficult problem into two easier ones (e.g., 6 X 7 = (6 X 6) + 6). As in the previous studies, patterns of solution times lent converging validation to the verbal reports. For example, solutions generated by rules or by retrieval took less than half as long as those generated via decomposition, which in turn took less than half as long as those generated via repeated addition.

As children gain experience with arithmetic, their diversity of strategies decreases to an extent on single-digit multiplication problems. However, the diversity continues to be very large on multi-digit problems. On these problems, older children and adults have some experience, but not the overwhelming amount they have with single-digit problems. To illustrate this point, Siegler and Ashcraft (in preparation) presented to college students a set of problems with multiplicands between 11 and 30. The same type of variability, both within and between subjects, was present among the college students solving these 2-digit X 2-digit problems as among third graders solving 1-digit X 1-digit problems. For example, on 22 X 18, some adults rounded the 22 down to 20 and proceeded by multiplying and adding, some rounded the 18 up to 20 and proceeded by multiplying and subtracting, some used the standard right to left multiplication algorithm, and some used the insightful shortcut $(a + b)(a - b) = a^2 - b^2$ (so 22 X 18 = (20 + 2) X (20 – 2) = $20^2 - 2^2$ = 396). The finding supported the moderate experience hypothesis: When adults have moderate amounts of experience with a particular class of problems, they, like children, tend to use diverse strategies. Even with truly massive experience, however, the variability of strategy use does not disappear entirely.

These descriptions have all involved arithmetic. However, as shown in the following sections, when investigators have assessed children's approaches on each trial in other, very different, domains, they have observed similar age-related changes.

Infants' and Toddlers' Locomotion

Observations of the development of crawling and walking shows that the overlapping waves pattern is present even in the first year of life (Adolph, 1993; 1995; Adolph, Eppler, & Gibson, 1993; McGraw, 1935). When faced with a need to go down moderately steep ramps (with a consequence of tumbling down into the arms of an experimenter if the slope is too difficult for their capabilities), 5- to 15-month-olds adopt a variety of approaches. Sometimes they try the approaches that they usually use on flat surfaces (crawling or walking), sometimes they slide headfirst like Superman flying, sometimes they slide in a sitting position, sometimes they slide feet first, and sometimes they refuse to descend altogether. For example, Adolph (1993; Experiment 2) observed that when infants who usually crawled on their hands and knees decided not to crawl down the ramps (usually when the ramps were too steep for them to crawl successfully), they slid headfirst on 41%

of trials, feet first on 29%, in a sitting position on 10%, and refused to go down altogether on 19%. The variability was evident within individual infants as well as between them. Often, a single child used several approaches within a single session. These alternatives to the children's usual approaches for navigating along flat surfaces were accompanied by a variety of exploratory behaviors, such as hesitating before deciding what to do, stooping to touch the ramp, and assuming several postures before going down the ramp.

There also are large individual differences among infants along a dimension of cautiousness to recklessness. Adoph (1995) distinguished among four groups of 14-month-old walking infants. Some walked down only those ramps that they could consistently traverse successfully; some tried to walk down those ramps and also others slightly beyond their capabilities; others tried to walk down those and also ramps that were fairly far beyond ones they could handle; and yet others were utterly fearless, and attempted to walk down any ramp they encountered.

In a longitudinal study, Adolph (1993; Experiment 2) observed infants on a weekly basis from the week in which they started crawling (on average 7 months) through at least 10 weeks after they started walking (on average 15 months). As the infants gained experience in crawling, they learned to crawl down considerably steeper slopes without losing their balance. However, when they started walking, babies could succeed only on much shallower slopes, and had to learn to walk down the steeper slopes. More surprising were the corresponding changes in the infants' judgments of when they could walk. With practice crawling, they learned to crawl down only those ramps on which they could succeed quite consistently—attempts to crawl down ramps that were 2 to 8 degrees beyond their assessed crawling capabilities declined from 89% to 23% of trials from the beginning to the end of the period in which crawling was their standard means of locomotion on flat surfaces. When they started to walk, however, most children had to start the perceptual learning process anew. In the first session after they started to walk, the toddlers attempted to walk down 78% of ramps that were 2 to 8 degrees beyond their assessed walking abilities. With walking experience, they learned which slopes they could and could not traverse by walking, as they earlier had with crawling. By the last session, they attempted to walk down the slopes 2 to 8 degrees beyond their capabilities on only 38% of trials.

Examination of the learning of individual toddlers demonstrates that the variability was present within as well as between individuals, and that it conformed to the basic overlapping waves model. Figure 4.10 illustrates the strategies used by "Baby Jack" to descend down risky slopes (defined as slopes beyond his capabilities) from the first week of his crawling through his fifth week of walking. The pattern closely matches that which would be expected from the overlapping waves characterization. For the first five sessions, crawling was his most common approach, then backing down had a brief ascendency, then sliding down prone became his most common approach, then walking down did, and finally sliding down in a sitting position became the most common. He did not abandon the approaches that he relied on earlier; he just used them less often.

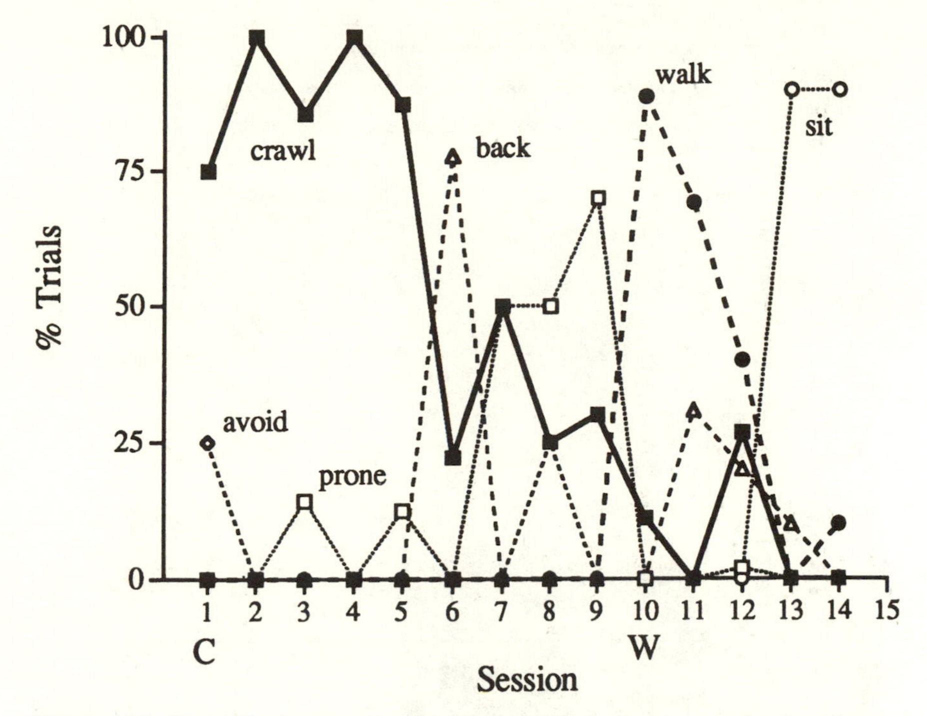

Figure 4.10. Variability between 7 and 16 months in Baby Jack's strategies for going down a ramp. For the first 9 sessions, crawling was his main mode of locomotion on flat surfaces; after that, walking was. Data from "Learning New Ways of Moving: Variability in Infants' Discovery and Selection of Motor Strategies," by M. A. Wechsler and K. E. Adolph, April, 1995. Poster presented at the meeting of the Society for Research in Child Development, Indianapolis, IN. Reprinted with permission.

Language Development

As noted in chapter 3, children generate at least three types of past tense verb forms: correct (e.g., "ate"), overregularized base (e.g., "eated"), and overregularized past (e.g., "ated"). Some individual children generate the overregularized forms quite often; others do so only rarely (Marcus, et al., 1992). Among those children who use them reasonably often, their use can persist for a surprisingly long time. For example, in a very intensive sampling of one child's spontaneous use of past tense forms between ages 2 years 5 months and 5 years (more than 2,000 observations of past tense verbs), Kuczaj (1976) observed the following systematic but gradual pattern of change: Use of correct past tense forms slowly increased (68%, 76%, and 82% at ages 2, 3, and 4 years), use of the overregularized base decreased (27%, 20%, and 14% at the three ages), and use of the overregularized past stayed at a low but constant level (4%, 5%, and 4%).

Reliance on spontaneous language production often results in underestimates of the degree of competition among alternative forms. The reason is that children (and adults) avoid using forms when they are unsure which is right. Thus, someone unsure of whether to say "He hanged it on the wall" or "He hung

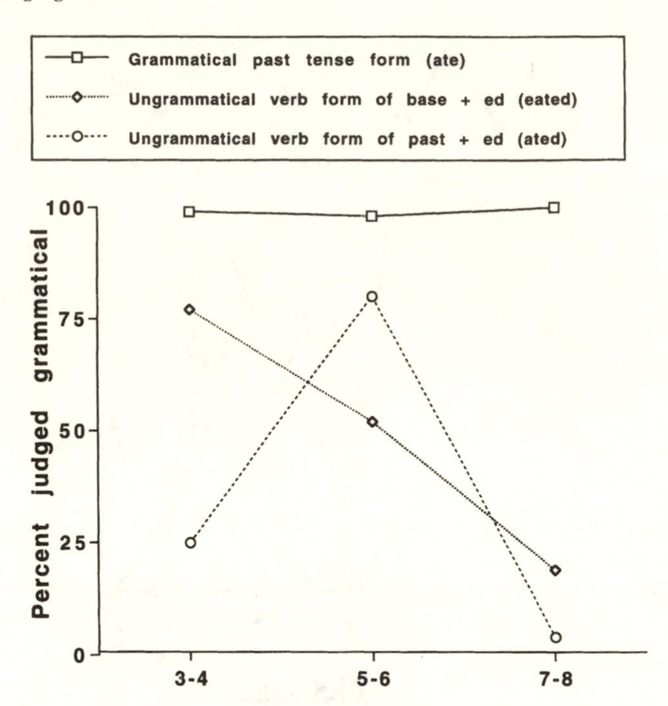

Figure 4.11. 3- to 8-year-olds' judgments of acceptability of past tense verbs. Data from "The Acquisition of Regular and Irregular Past Tense Forms," by S. A. Kuczaj, 1977, *Journal of Verbal Learning and Verbal Behavior*, 16, pp. 589–600. Copyright 1977 by Academic Press. Reprinted with permission.

it on the wall" will often opt out of the problem by saying "He put it on the wall."

Having children judge the acceptability of alternative phrasings is one way to circumvent this methodological problem. Applying this logic, Kuczaj (1977) presented 3- to 8-year-olds with past tense verb forms of the three kinds described above, and asked them to judge whether each was "OK" or "silly." As shown in Figure 4.11 (top), the results revealed more competition than was apparent in spontaneous use of the verbs. The 3- and 4-year-olds consistently judged the correct form to be acceptable, but usually also thought that the overregularized base (e.g., "eated") was OK. The 5- and 6-year-olds consistently judged the correct form to be acceptable, but also usually judged the overregularized past tense form (e.g., "ated") to be OK. Not until age 7 did children think that only the correct form was correct. The pattern was paralleled by the same children's performance on an elicited production task (Figure 4.11, next page), in which the experimenter said a sentence in the future tense (e.g., "I will drive the car") and the child needed to transform it to the past tense (e.g., by saying "I already drove the car").

Thus, in learning syntax, as in many other areas, there is a prolonged compe-

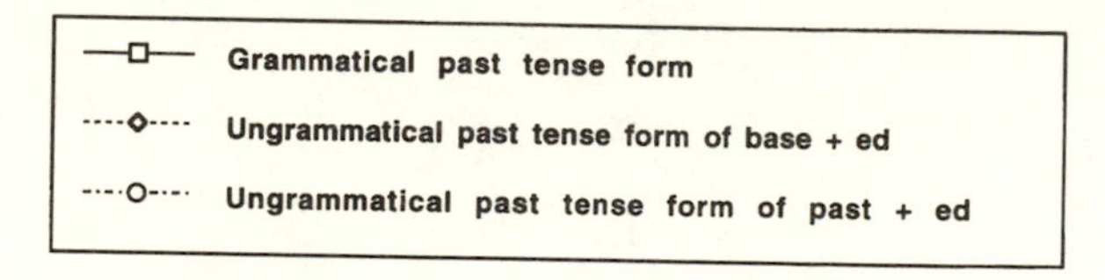

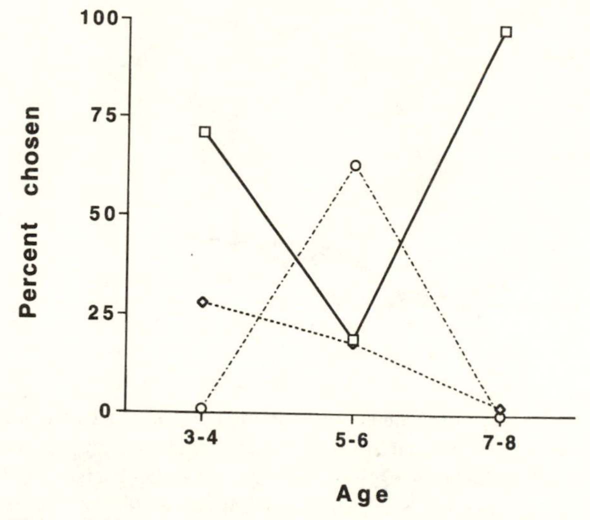

Figure 4.11 (*continued*). 3- to 8-year-olds' choices of past tense forms that they would use. Data from Kuczaj (1977).

tition among alternative forms. Eventually, it is resolved in favor of consistent use of, and preference for, the correct forms, but along the way, multiple incorrect forms also compete.

Moral Development

Some of the most striking illustrations of the overlapping waves pattern come from research on moral reasoning. Data reported by Kohlberg (1969) and his colleagues provide particularly compelling examples of the applicability of this approach over a very broad period, ranging from age 7 to age 36. The data come from people's reactions to moral dilemmas in which protagonists' needs conflict with societal rules. The basic developmental model is well known, but it may be worthwhile to briefly review the proposed sequence of types of moral reasoning.

Stage 1: Heteronomous morality: Morality of actions evaluated in terms of whether they elicit punishment.

Stage 2: Instrumental orientation: Morality evaluated in terms of gaining rewards as well as avoiding punishment.

Stage 3: Mutual-interpersonal expectations: Evaluations based on other people's approval. Intent to adhere to rules considered.

Stage 4: Social systems and conscience: Emphasis on accepting society's rules to maintain order.

Stage 5: Social-contract approach: Morality evaluated in terms of the consis-

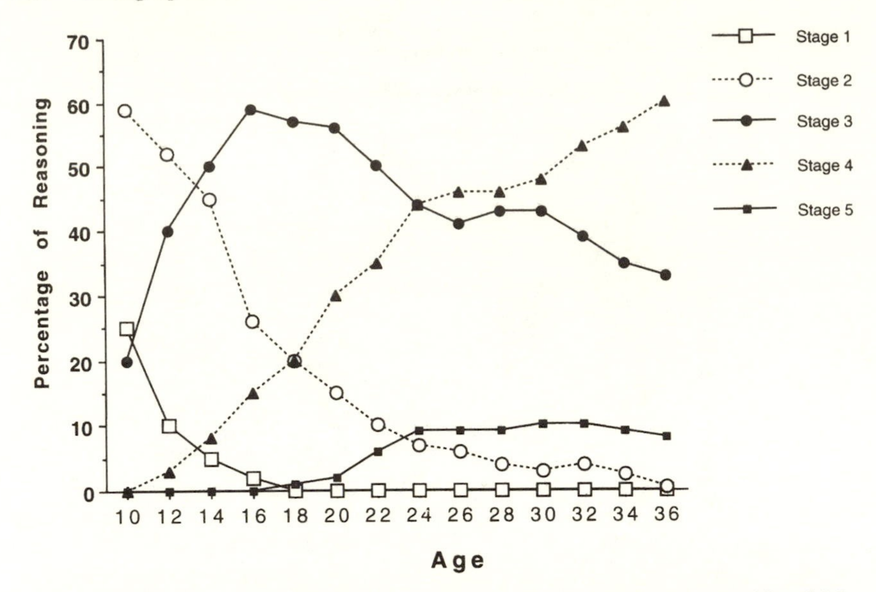

Figure 4.12. Frequency of several stages of moral reasoning between ages 10 and 36 years. Data from "A Longitudinal Study of Moral Judgement," by A. Colby, L. Kohlberg, J. Gibbs, and M. Lieberman, 1983, *Monographs of the Society for Research in Child Development, 48* (Serial No. 200), p. 46. Copyright 1983 by Society for Research in Child Development. Reprinted with permission.

tency of the actions with laws, with emphasis on working to change laws considered unjust.

Stage 6: Universal ethical principles: The individual's principles are the ultimate arbiter of an action's morality.

Although these types of reasoning have often been referred to as stages (by Kohlberg himself, as well as others), the data on them that he and his collaborators collected look nothing like the staircase progression implied by the stage model. Instead, as shown in Figure 4.12, they resembled the overlapping waves pattern. At most ages during this prolonged period, three or four "stages" of reasoning were common. The particular ones that were most common changed considerably. Between ages 10 and 20, Stage 2 reasoning went from being the most common to being quite rare, whereas Stage 3 reasoning went from being relatively uncommon to being the most common approach. During adulthood, Stage 3 reasoning declined from its peak, whereas Stage 4 reasoning became the most frequent form. Stage 5 reasoning was present for many years, though it never became very common.

Moral reasoning varies within individuals as well as between them. Colby, Kohlberg, Gibbs, & Lieberman (1983) presented Kohlberg's moral development interview to the same people 6 times over a 20 year period; subjects were 10-16 years at the outset of the experiment and 30-36 at the end. Even within a single interview form, involving responses to three moral dilemmas, 62% of children and adults showed reasoning at two or more stages. This was true at all ages and for almost all individual subjects on at least one of the three inteview forms (Colby et al., 1983, Table 13). Most often, the reasoning included two adjacent types (e.g., Stages 3 and 4 reasoning), though at times three different levels of reasoning were apparent within a single session. Only 1% of subjects reasoned at the same level on all nine problems.

The classic Kohlbergian moral dilemma problems are not the only context in which the diversity of moral reasoning has been documented. When children have been asked to reason about other types of moral issues, similar diversity has been apparent. Consider reasoning regarding the type of situation in which one's own needs and desires conflict with those of others, but in which no universal moral principle, societal rule, or authority dictates a resolution. The general developmental trend of reasoning about such situations moves from an early emphasis on satisfying one's own goals (hedonistic reasoning) to a later emphasis on meeting the needs of others, to still later reasoning based on more abstract and self-reflective considerations (e.g., stereotypes of a good or bad person; considerations of how you or the other person would feel if certain actions were taken).

This general description does not begin to address the complexity and variability of the reasoning, however. Consider the data reported by Eisenberg, Miller, Shell, McNally, and Shea (1991) on the development of prosocial moral reasoning between ages 4 and 16. This was a longitudinal study in which the same individuals' reasoning was observed seven times during the preschool, elementary school, and adolescent periods.

As is evident in Figure 4.13, multiple types of prosocial moral reasoning were observed at each age. In the preschool period, *hedonistic reasoning* was the most common, with substantial amounts of *needs-oriented reasoning* (reasoning based on the physical or psychological needs of the other person) also present. During

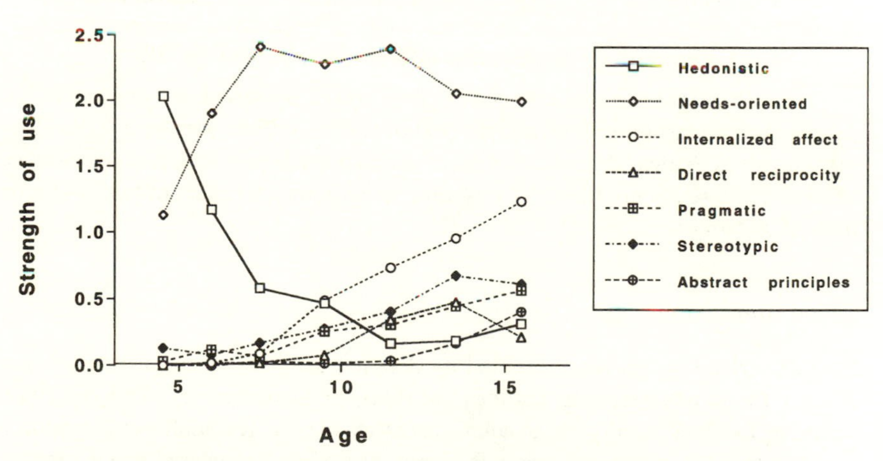

Figure 4.13. Prosocial moral reasoning categories used by 4- to 16-year-olds. Score of 0 = no use, 1 = some use, 2 = clear use, 3 = strong use. Data from "Prosocial Development in Adolescence: A Longitudinal Study," N. Eisenberg, P. A. Miller, R. Shell, S. McNally, and C. Shea, 1991, *Developmental Psychology, 27*, p. 853. Copyright 1991 by American Psychological Association. Reprinted with permission.

the elementary school period, these remained the most common approaches, though hedonistic reasoning decreased in frequency and needs-oriented reasoning increased. They were joined by several other approaches, such as reasoning based on *direct reciprocity*, *stereotypes* of good and bad people, and *pragmatic factors*.

All of these types of reasoning remained present in adolescence, and were joined by yet others. The many particular kinds of reasoning that became more common in adolescence can be grouped into two general classes: *self-reflective empathic considerations*, such as when children explicitly have the protagonist take the role of the other person or anticipate how they would feel if they had taken certain actions; and reasoning based on *internalized abstract values*, such as self-respect or broader societal norms. After becoming less frequent from preschool to early adolesence, hedonistic reasoning made a bit of a comeback in middle adolescence. This comeback was almost entirely the product of teenage boys increasing their use of hedonistic reasoning.

Children's reasoning about yet other moral issues shows similar heterogeneity. For example, consider the distinction between social practices that are due to cultural conventions (e.g., insisting that all children in a classroom participate in show and tell) and practices believed to reflect universal morality (e.g., insisting that children not hit each other). Children differentiate between the two types of domains from at least age 3 (Smetana, 1981), though the differentiations grow sharper and are more comprehensively and consistently applied with age (Turiel, 1989). Most important for the present purposes, however, is the diversity of ideas that underlie children's reasoning about these moral issues over a wide age span—ideas of collectivism, individualism, cooperation, freedom from coercion, and so on. As Turiel and Davidson (1986) noted:

> These research findings do not allow classification of individuals within broad social categories, such as individualistic or collectivistic, egalitarian or hierarchically oriented, autonomous or conformist. All these orientations have been found to *coexist* in that each is reflected in the individual's judgments. (p. 106)

Thus, as in other domains that have given rise to prototypic stage models, the data on moral reasoning show a great deal of within-subject variability. Development involves gradual shifts toward more sophisticated reasoning and coexistence of less and more mature forms of reasoning at all points in time, not just at special transition periods.

Social Interaction

Similar variability has been revealed by detailed analyses of social interactions. Among the most interesting findings are those of Eckerman and Didow (1989) regarding toddlers' reactions to an adult's invitation to play. The adult would approach the play material, pause and look at the child, play with the material in a distinctive way, step back, and again look at the child. Illustratively, on one task the adult approached a chute, rolled a ball down it, said "Down it goes," and looked at the child.

At all ages studied (16–32 months), children reacted in three main ways. The most frequent class of children's behavior was "coordinated responses," which

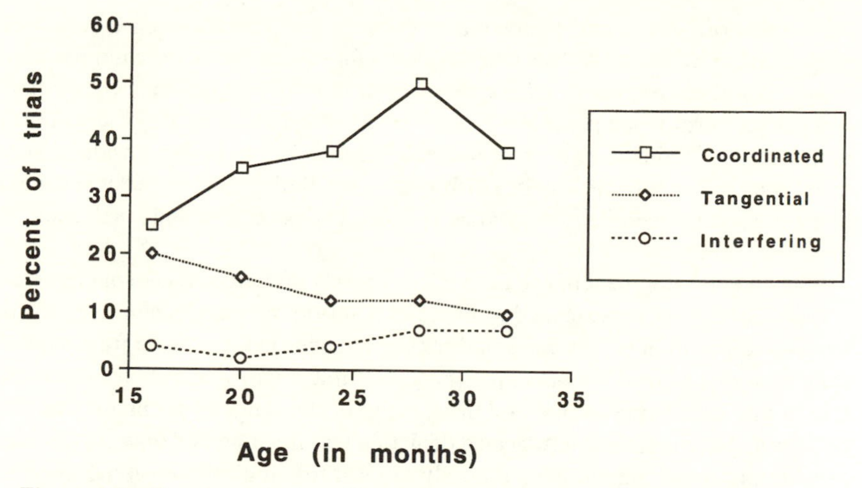

Figure 4.14. Reactions of 16- to 32-month olds when adults invite them to play. From "Toddlers' Social Coordinations: Changing Responses to Another's Invitation to Play," by C. O. Eckerman and S. M. Didow, 1989, *Developmental Psychology, 25*, p. 798. Copyright by American Psychological Association. Reprinted with permission.

involved acting in a way that was related to the adult's action and that enabled the adult to continue her own activity. The next most frequent class was "tangential responses"; here the toddler interacted with the same material as the adult, but without any relation to the adult's activity. The least frequent class was "interfering responses," in which the child prevented the adult from continuing her action, for example by taking the ball away.

Among the youngest children, coordinated and tangential responses were similarly frequent, with interfering responses less frequent (Figure 4.14). With age, the frequency of coordinated responses increased. Coding of alternative responses to the experimenter's activities (attempts to involve the adult in activities unrelated to the adult's original actions) revealed further variability. Vocalizations started out as highly frequent parts of this category and progressively decreased with age. Verbal repetition of what the adult had said, followed by verbalization describing the child's own activity, progressively increased. Verbal statements intended to influence the adult's activity and introduction of new verbal topics were not evident early in the period. However, they were introduced and became increasingly prevalent during the later portions. As in all of the diverse areas we have examined, variability was a hallmark of children's activity, with development involving changes in the relative frequency of existing approaches along with introduction of new approaches.

Conclusions

The evidence presented in this chapter suggests two main conclusions. First, in a wide range of domains, the overlapping waves metaphor provides a more useful way of thinking about development than does the traditional staircase metaphor. Regardless of whether we consider development of arithmetic, locomotion, language, moral reasoning, or social interaction, multiple approaches coexist and compete for prolonged periods. Changes in all of these domains occur as much in the relative frequencies of the competing approaches as in the introduction of novel approaches and elimination of obsolete ones. Rather than important changes being limited to delimited transitional periods, changes large and small seem to occur constantly.

Second, development of even a single, narrowly demarcated area of cognition is multifaceted. As the extended example of addition indicated, cognitive growth involves acquisition of new ways of thinking; changes in the relative frequency of existing ways; improvements in the speed, accuracy, and automaticity of execution of the varied approaches; and broadening of the range of problems that can be solved. Although this multifaceted depiction was documented only for the case of addition, development is doubtlessly at least this multidimensional in other domains.

At a very general level, these conclusions may seem unsurprising. Few would argue against the proposition that development occurs along multiple dimensions or that during transitional periods (of whatever length), a variety of ways of thinking compete. Part of the message of this chapter is that we should act on this knowledge, that our descriptions of development should be as multifaceted as the phenomena we are trying to explain.

Another part of the message calls for a more fundamental revision in the way we think about development. Rather than viewing transition periods as apart and special, we need to recognize that all of development is a transitional period, with new approaches being introduced frequently, competing with existing approaches, and continuously changing in relative frequency. In some domains, such as acquisition of syntax, substantial variability exists for years before people settle on a particular approach. In other domains, such as moral reasoning, the competition never is resolved; more and more approaches join the competition, and few if any are eliminated. In yet other domains, such as single-digit arithmetic, some people eventually rely on a single approach, but others never do. Accounting for change demands accounting for the overlapping waves of change that actually occur, rather than the idealized staircase patterns that provide convenient shorthands.

This approach may seem to make accounting for change more difficult, because there is more to explain. I suspect, though, that it actually will make it easier. What is genuinely difficult, maybe impossible, to explain is why, after children have thought about a class of phenomena in a single way for several years, they would suddenly switch to a different way of thinking. When introduction of new approaches and gradual changes in frequency of existing approaches are accepted as continuously operating processes, however, explaining them becomes considerably easier. Examples of such explanations of change are provided in chapters 6 and 7. Before considering them, however, we need to consider another critical aspect of development—how children choose among alternative approaches in ways that promote both effective current performance and adaptive changes over time.

Notes

1. Another metaphor that seems useful for thinking about age-related changes in children's thinking is that of a cognitive ecology. Just as the distribution of plants and animals within an ecosystem changes over time, so does the distribution of children's ways of thinking. An advantage of this metaphor is that it captures the cooperative and competitive relations among the different entities—plants and animals, like strategies, cooperate and compete with each other for survival, which waves do not. On the other hand, the overlapping waves model captures in an easy-to-visualize way the typical course of development and contrasts directly with staircase conceptions. The cognitive ecology and overlapping waves metaphors seem complementary, in that each points to a different central aspect of the relation among changing ways of thinking: their comptitive and cooperative relations in one case, their changing distribution in the other. Multiple metaphors, like multiple strategies, can be useful.

2. Wynn (1992) observed that infants look longer when an object is added to another object and (through trickery) only one object appears than when two do. She argued that this is an early form of addition. However, it seems at least as likely that it is a form of object permanence, since it is limited for years after to sets of 1–3 objects (Starkey, 1992). In light of the uncertain relation between this competence and arithmetic, it seemed best to start the developmental story with acquisitions in the preschool period that are definitely central to the development of addition.

3. The lower percentage of retrieval among the older children whose performance is summarized in Table 4.1, relative to that among the younger children whose performance is described in Table 3.1, may seem anomalous. It is attributable to differences in problem sets and strategy assessment techniques. The older children were presented problems with sums as great as 23, whereas the younger ones were presented problems with sums no greater than 10. Further, the verbal reports obtained from the older children led to detection of strategies on trials that would have been classified as retrieval in the earlier study of the younger children.

5

The Adaptivity of Multiplicity

By itself, cognitive variability would be an interesting curio, but no more. What makes it important is the potential it offers for adapting to task and situational demands. Realizing this potential, however, requires wise choices among the available alternatives. If children know two strategies—one faster, the other more accurate—they will benefit only if they choose the faster strategy when speed is most important and choose the more accurate when accuracy is. Choosing randomly will yield worse performance than always using the approach that on average yields the best outcome. Thus, the higher the quality of choices among alternative approaches, the greater the benefits of cognitive variability.

How well do children choose? The conclusions of developmental psychologists have tended to emphasize the negative. Those interested in metacognition have focused on findings that children who have been taught new strategies often do not use them when they later are free to choose (e.g, Ghatala, Levin, Pressley, & Goodwin, 1986; Keeney, Cannizo, & Flavell, 1967; Paris & Lindauer, 1982; Williams & Goulet, 1975). Those interested in decision making have focused on situations in which children choose alternatives with lower expected values over ones with higher values (Byrnes & McClenny, 1994; Klayman, 1985). Those interested in planning have focused on situations in which children who have heard the virtues of planning extolled nonetheless fail to plan (Friedman, Scholnick, & Cocking, 1987). Those interested in scientific reasoning have emphasized cases in which children who have discovered advanced experimentation strategies nonetheless continue to choose less advanced ones (Kuhn, Amsel, & O'Laughlin 1988).

These and related findings have led to generally negative conclusions about children's ability to choose wisely among alternative ways of thinking. To cite two examples:

> Children do not monitor well and often fail to make appropriate executive decisions. For instance, children often do not monitor comprehension problems when reading text . . . and they fail to recognize when they do not have enough information to complete a task. (Schneider & Pressley, 1989, p. 91)

> Certainly one of the lessons from research across many areas of cognition is that children often do not use their available knowledge. . . . A child might know

that rehearsal is a good strategy for remembering a list of chores that need to be done, but not rehearse because he or she lacks time, energy, capacity, or motivation to exert the effort. (Flavell, Miller, & Miller, 1993, p. 261)

It is easy to generate reasons why children often choose strategies that, at least from an adult's perspective, seem less than optimal. Consider one strategy choice—to plan or not to plan—and some reasons why children might choose not to plan even in situations in which planning would help them succeed on a task (Ellis & Siegler, in press):

1. Planning often requires inhibition of more activated procedures.
2. Planning takes time, and children often value speed over accuracy.
3. Generating plans is no guarantee of successful outcomes.
4. Planning is often subjectively unpleasant because it is difficult, tedious, or anxiety-producing.
5. Unplanned action can be enjoyable in its own right, since it can place children in novel, interesting situations.

Thus, it is easy to find reasons for why children's strategy choices are not always successful, at least from an adult perspective. What is remarkable, however, is how rarely such excuses are needed. As we shall see in this chapter, in a wide range of situations, children finely calibrate strategy choices to the demands of tasks and situations and to their own changing capacities. Even infants and toddlers do so. The capacity is evident in children's problem solving, reasoning, memory, locomotor activity, academic skills, and even, under some circumstances, in their planning.

The present chapter includes four main sections. The first is a discussion of what it means for a choice to be adaptive. The second and third examine two important types of adaptation: adjustments to inherent problem characteristics and adjustments to fluctuating situational demands. The fourth focuses on how, with age and experience, adaptation to problem characteristics and situational demands increases beyond its initial high level.

What Makes a Choice Adaptive?

Judgments of quality are always relative to the criteria on which they are based. Past pessimistic impressions of the adaptiveness of children's strategy choices may be more indicative of inadequacies in the criteria than anything else. In this section, three commonly used criteria for evaluating the quality of children's choices are analyzed, and then a fourth, which seems more appropriate, is introduced.

Criteria Emphasizing the Choices That Are Made

Probably the main source of the impression that children's strategy choice processes are flawed is that much of what they do seems unwise. For example, in basic arithmetic, they count from one rather than counting from the larger addend and use buggy algorithms rather than the correct one.

Concluding from such evidence that their choice *processes* are flawed, however, confuses process with product. In particular, it fails to distinguish the quality of the cognitive processes used to choose actions with the success of the actions that are taken. Children frequently face situations in which successful action is impossible. Sometimes, they lack the factual knowledge necessary for accurate retrieval; other times, they lack the procedural knowledge needed to effectively execute a backup strategy; yet other times, they lack the processing capacity needed to keep all relevant data in memory. Suboptimal choices by themselves are not evidence that the process that generated the choices is suboptimal. Rather, they may arise from the children having only suboptimal alternatives to choose among.

An example may help make the point concrete. Low-achieving elementary school students often are said to choose strategies poorly, on the evidence that they frequently use strategies that are neither fast nor accurate, such as counting their fingers to solve addition problems (e.g., Borkowski & Krause, 1983; Pressley, Borkowski, & O'Sullivan, 1984). Teachers frequently push such students to alter their strategies. When I once interviewed a teacher and asked how many days she had told a particular student not to use his fingers, she responded, "How many days have there been in the school year so far?"

Yet, at least at times, the choice processes of low achieving students are of high quality. They closely calibrate their choices to problem characteristics and to the advantages and disadvantages of each strategy on the particular task. For example, Kerkman and Siegler (1993) examined the addition, subtraction, and word identification performance of a sample of low-income, predominantly African-American, inner-city first graders. The sample included many children who did poorly on standardized achievement tests. Yet they were as systematic as middle-income, predominantly Caucasian, suburban first graders in relying on retrieval when they could do so accurately, and using alternative strategies increasingly often as accurate retrieval becomes increasingly difficult. Certainly it would be better if the low-income children could have consistently retrieved the correct answer on all problems. The difficulty, however, was that they lacked the knowledge of particular problems that would make accurate retrieval possible, rather than that they chose badly among available strategies. Thus, use of immature strategies is not evidence of maladaptive choice processes; it can instead reflect limits of the knowledge base.

Mathematical Optimization Criteria

A second, related, approach is to evaluate the quality of choice processes by comparing the choices they yield to a criterion of mathematical or logical optimality. This approach differs from the first one primarily in the explicitness of the criteria against which the choices are measured. It has received its greatest development within the field of economics, under the heading of rational choice theory. This theory is used normatively to assess whether behavior is proceeding optimally to gain specified ends, and if not, what changes are needed to have it do so.

Within psychology, rational choice models have been especially common in studies of decision making. In some such studies, choices are evaluated with regard to how well they maximize expected value. In other cases, they are evaluated with regard to whether they violate logical criteria, such as transitivity (if you prefer A to B and B to C, you should not prefer C to A), and dominance (if A is better than B on all relevant criteria, you shouldn't choose B over A).

Evaluating choices in relation to mathematical and/or logical criteria has led to a number of elegant analyses of the rewards of using alternative decision rules under varying conditions (e.g., Keeney & Raiffa, 1976). It also has led to discovery of many interesting paradoxes, in which people seem to act irrationally by making nontransitive choices and selecting dominated alternatives (Shafir & Tversky, 1992). Framing effects, in which the choice made depends on how the situation is presented, also have been documented repeatedly.

As several researchers who study decision making have noted, however, such normative approaches, like the absolute quality criteria described in the last section, focus on products rather than processes. They also tend to exclude from consideration important costs to decision makers of choosing in ways other than they do (Payne, Bettman, & Johnson, 1993; Simon, 1981). In particular, the normative approaches often ignore the information processing cost involved in executing the mathematically optimal approaches. They also typically do not examine whether superior strategies are known to the participants in the experiment. If people do not know a strategy, they cannot choose it; again, the problem is their knowledge base rather than the choice process. At the heart of each of these problems is the focus on the quality of the choices that are made rather than the quality of the choice processes that generated them.[1]

Metacognitive Process Criteria

The quality of choices can also be evaluated by the degree to which they are reached through rational, conscious, verbalizable consideration of the strengths and weaknesses of alternative approaches. For example, Kuhn (1989) argued that the quality of children's strategy choice processes should be evaluated by how well they understand such issues as why the chosen strategy is appropriate, how each component contributes to its usefulness, when the strategy is applicable, and why other strategies are less desirable.

This metacognitive approach has the advantage of focusing attention on the choice process. It also is useful for studying the subset of choices that are made through such metacognitive processes. However, when used as a standard against which to evaluate strategy choices in general, it represents too narrow a view of adaptive choice processes. Suppose that a child always chooses the most effective approach available on each problem, but does not know why the approach works or why other approaches would not work. The choices are still adaptive, even if they were not reached through conscious metastrategic analysis.

This is not just a logical possibility. Many of the most adaptive decisions do not derive from explicit, rational, metacognitive analysis. Again an example from basic arithmetic illustrates the point. The 4- and 5-year-olds studied by

Siegler and Shrager (1984) generated very adaptive choices among alternative strategies. The harder the problem, the more often they relied on strategies other than retrieval, such as counting fingers. This allowed them to solve easy problems both quickly and accurately, and to solve difficult problems more slowly but still accurately. However, when asked whether each problem was very hard, kind of hard, or easy, the children's metacognitive judgments were only moderately correlated with either the objective difficulty of the problems or with their own strategy choices. The choices were no less adaptive for having been made with limited explicit knowledge of problem difficulty. Rather, the example illustrates that such explicit knowledge is not necessary for strategy choices to be adaptive.

The Present Approach

Like the metacognitive approach, the present perspective on adaptive choice emphasizes the processes by which the choices are reached. However, it does not presume that this process will consistently, or even usually, follow an explicit, rational, metacognitive model or fit a mathematical optimizing formula. Rather, it is based on the view that choice processes are adaptive to the extent that they most often select from among the choices available to the individual those that best meet the individual's short-term and long-term goals.

Several features of this approach should be noted. First, the adaptiveness of the choice process is defined relative to the choices available to the individual. If a person does not know a potentially optimal strategy, or can only execute it badly, not choosing that strategy does not indicate that the choice process is flawed. Second, adaptiveness is defined relative to the activity meeting both short- and long-term goals. These sometimes conflict, as when using a newly discovered strategy leads to sub-optimal performance on the given occasion but produces learning that enhances future performance. Under such conditions, an adaptive approach might be to use better-learned strategies when successful performance is essential but to more often use the novel strategy when successful performance is not imperative. Third, the approach allows for adaptive choices being produced through application of either implicit or explicit knowledge. Adaptive choices can be generated in a variety of ways, and it seems misleading to say that choices based on implicit, non-verbalizable processes are by definition less than optimal.

What specific types of behavior would be indicative of adaptive choices? Three characteristics seem particularly important:

1. Choices vary in ways responsive to problem characteristics.
2. Choices vary in ways responsive to fluctuating situational demands.
3. With age and experience, choices meet the first two goals increasingly effectively.

The main point of this chapter is that children's choices are adaptive in all three senses.

Adapting to Problem Characteristics

In school and out, children must constantly choose what to do. The choices can be divided into two main types: whether to state a retrieved answer or to use a *back-up strategy* (any strategy other than retrieval), and which back-up strategy to use. From early in development, children adapt both types of choices to the characteristics of particular problems.

Choosing Between Retrieval and Use of a Backup Strategy

Perhaps the most frequent strategy choice that people make is whether to state an answer they've retrieved from memory or to use a back-up strategy. The need for this choice arises in any domain in which people have enough experience that retrieval of an answer is an option, and not so much that retrieval is automatic. In a typical school day, a third grader might make such choices in arithmetic (whether to retrieve the answer to 9 X 6 or add six 9s), reading (whether to retrieve the pronunciation of the word "Chicago" or "sound it out"), spelling (whether to retrieve the spelling of the word "business" or look it up in a dictionary), geography (retrieving whether Norway or Sweden is larger versus examining a globe), and history (retrieving the dates of the Civil War versus asking your mother). This section focuses on how children make such strategy choices in a variety of domains.

Addition

As noted in chapter 3, preschoolers' addition was the context in which I first became aware of the variety of strategies that children used to solve a single problem. It also was the context in which I first realized that it could be useful to group together strategies other than retrieval into a single category of "back-up strategies."

This decision did not come about as a result of any a priori logical analysis. Instead, it came through a protracted effort to make sense of a data pattern. Once I noticed the variety of strategies preschoolers were using to add, I wanted to determine which factors led them to use one or another approach. Previous chronometric analyses of arithmetic (e.g., Groen & Parkman, 1972; Svenson & Broquist, 1975) indicated that problems with larger addends and sums took longer to solve. I reasoned that such factors might also influence which strategies children used to solve each problem. To test this hypothesis, I computed correlations between frequency of use of each strategy on each problem and structural variables associated with that problem, such as the problem's sum, its larger addend, its smaller addend, and so on. The results indicated a number of fairly high correlations (*r*'s = .50 to .70) between frequency of use of individual strategies on each problem and the structural features of the problem. The number of such correlations and their failure to fall into any discernible pattern led me to suspect that a stronger relation was present that underlay all of these particular relations. This led me to graph the data in different ways to see if any such underlying relation could be found.

One graph I drew, without any particular expectation of it being uniquely revealing, related percentage of errors on each problem to percentage of use of retrieval on that problem. The very strong relation I had been looking for jumped out—when I computed the correlation, it was $r = -.91$. The strong negative correlation reflected the fact that on the problems that elicited the fewest errors, such as 1 + 1, 2 + 1, and 2 + 2, children almost always retrieved the answer, but on the problems that elicited the most errors, such as 4 + 3 and 3 + 4, they rarely used retrieval.

As suggested by this analysis, when I computed the correlations between percentage of errors on each problem and frequency of use of the three other strategies that the preschoolers used to add—counting fingers, putting up fingers but not counting them, and counting aloud without any obvious external referent—they were all quite positive (r's = .50 to .75). This led me to think about what these strategies had in common.

One clear commonality was that all of the alternative strategies took much longer to execute than did retrieval. A year earlier, in a different context, I had proposed that reliance on unidimensional reasoning on problems such as balance scales and conservation was a fallback strategy—a strategy that children would use if they did not have enough knowledge of the task to use a more advanced approach (Siegler, 1981). Drawing an analogy to this idea, I wondered whether all addition strategies other than retrieval served as fallback, or back-up, strategies for retrieval. That is, they would be used when a more advanced strategy (retrieval) was unavailable.

This line of reasoning brought me back to my original question of what determined frequency of use of each strategy on each problem. Percentage of errors on each problem could be thought of as a measure of problem difficulty—the harder the problem, the more errors it would elicit. It would make sense for children to use retrieval on easy problems and back-up strategies on more difficult ones. Retrieval is fast, but cannot always yield accurate answers. Back-up strategies, such as counting one's fingers, are slower, but often can generate correct answers on problems where retrieval cannot. Using retrieval on easy problems and back-up strategies on more difficult ones would allow children to be fast and accurate when that was possible and to be slower but accurate when answering quickly and accurately was impossible.

This interpretation implied that a very high correlation should also be present between percentage of use of back-up strategies on each problem and another measure of problem difficulty, mean solution time on the problem. When I tested this prediction, the expected relation was clearly present; the correlation was $r = .92$. The fineness of the calibration of strategy choices to problem difficulty was especially striking. Four- and five-year-olds are not notoriously systematic, yet the extremely high correlations indicated that their strategy choices responded systematically to even small differences in problem difficulty.

The more I thought about the relation between problem difficulty and strategy choices, the more sense it made. Children could use the fast, effortless retrieval strategy when they could execute it accurately, and could fall back on the back-up strategies when they could not. A much less interesting alternative interpretation was also plausible, however. Perhaps relative frequency of use of back-up strategies was causing the relative problem difficulties rather than reflecting them. To illustrate, if retrieval consistently produced 90% correct performance on a problem and back-up strategies 60% correct performance on it, the more often that back-up strategies were used on the problem, the less accurate performance on it would be. Within this view, use of back-up strategies was actually harmful, in that it caused the inaccurate performance on problems where back-up strategies were often used. If children had consistently used retrieval, they would have been more accurate.

I tested this alternative interpretation by conducting a new experiment that included two conditions: one in which preschoolers were allowed to use back-up strategies, the other in which they were not (Siegler & Shrager, 1984). In the condition in which children were not allowed to use back-up strategies, they were told to state the first answer that came to mind and were required to answer within 4 seconds, too short a time for such young children to execute a back-up strategy. The children in the condition in which back-up strategy use was allowed were considerably more accurate than those in the condition where it was not, 74% versus 47%. This provided evidence that use of back-up strategies decreased errors, rather than increasing them.

These data led me to conclude that the construct of back-up strategies was useful, that it made sense to group together strategies other than retrieval. One advantage was that doing so revealed a commonality among the back-up strategies—percentage of use of each one was positively related to problem difficulty. A second advantage was that the construct was applicable to a broad range of domains, any area in which both retrieval and other approaches were used. A third advantage was that the correlations between measures of problem difficulty and frequency of back-up strategy use provided a quantitative index of the adaptive quality of children's strategy choices that could be compared across domains and age groups. These considerations led me to examine in greater depth children's choices between back-up strategies and retrieval.

The first follow-up study also concerned preschoolers' addition. Because I had not predicted the relation between problem difficulty and use of back-up strategies, it seemed critical to replicate it and determine whether it extended beyond the original set of addition problems. The original problems were ones on which each addend could be represented on one hand (making execution of the fingers and counting fingers strategies especially easy). Regardless of how systematic the strategy choices were, they would be of limited interest if they only occurred on such simple problems.

To find out, Siegler and Shrager (1984) presented 4- and 5-year-olds a mix of problems. Half were from the same set as those in Siegler and Robinson (1982). The other half had sums of 11 or 12, and one addend greater than 5, so that the sum could not be represented entirely on the child's fingers.

The strong relation between problem difficulty (as measured by percentage of errors on each problem) and percent use of back-up strategies was again present; the correlation was $r = .81$. Preschoolers used back-up strategies most often on the most difficult problems, such as 5 + 7; next most often on problems of intermediate difficulty, such as 10 + 2; and least often on easy problems, such as 2 + 2. They used the same back-up strategies on problems with sums above 10 as they had on problems with smaller sums.

The strong relation has also proved to be general across demographic groups. Kerkman and Siegler (1993) sampled a population of low income first graders, 80% of whom came from homes sufficiently impoverished that they qualified for the federally subsidized lunch program; 71% were African-American. Most had standardized math achivement test scores that were well below average for their grade. However, the adaptiveness of their addition strategy choices was as high as that of the previously studied middle income samples.

In subsequent studies of addition, similarly strong relations between the difficulty of each problem and frequency of back-up strategy use on it have been found for third and fourth graders with learning disabilities presented problems with addends ranging from 2 to 9 (Geary, 1990; Geary & Brown, 1991), for college students presented problems with addends ranging from 0 to 9 (LeFevre et al., 1996), and for both college students and elderly adults presented problems with addends ranging from 2 to 9 (Geary & Wiley, 1991). Clearly, people of a variety of ages, ability levels, and backgrounds choose adaptively whether to state a retrieved answer or use a backup strategy to add numbers.

Subtraction

The above-described analysis of the relation between problem difficulty and use of back-up strategies led me to suspect that the relation was far from unique to addition. Simple subtraction seemed a logical starting point for examining the generality of the relation across tasks. The same types of back-up strategies, relying on use of fingers and counting, can be applied to subtraction as to addition. Moreover, skill in the two areas develops at roughly the same age. These considerations led Siegler and Shrager (1984) to present the exact inverse subtraction problems to 5- and 6-year-olds as had been presented by Siegler and Robinson (1982) to 4- and 5-year-olds. That is, there were 25 subtraction problems, ranging in size from 2 – 1 to 10 – 5.

As shown in Figure 5.1A and 5.1B, the relation of problem difficulty to back-up strategy use was just about as strong in subtraction as in addition. Percentage back-up strategy use on each problem correlated $r = .83$ with percentage errors on the problem and $r = .90$ with mean solution time on the problem. These relations were stronger than the relation of percentage back-up strategy use on each problem to any of the structural variables associated with the problems: sizes of the minuend, subtrahend, difference, or sum.

The relations were similarly strong in the low income first grade sample studied by Kerkman & Siegler (1993). Percentage use of back-up strategies on each subtraction problem correlated $r = .92$ with percentage errors on all trials on that problem and $r = .79$ with mean solution time on all trials on the problem.

Multiplication

The relation between problem difficulty and choices among multiplication strategies was first reported 50 years ago by Brownell and Carper (1943). These inves-

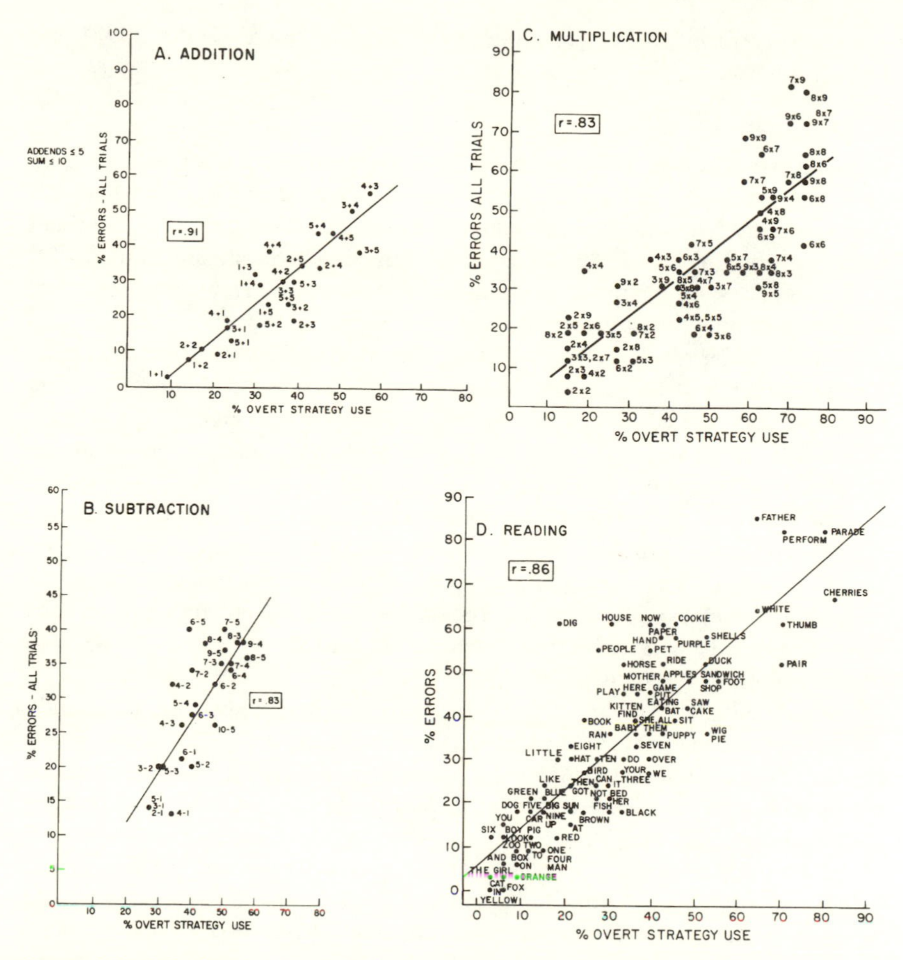

Figure 5.1. Relations on four tasks between percent use of overt strategies on each problem and the difficulty of the problem, as measured by its percent errors (data from Siegler, 1986). Note that the more difficult the problem, the more often children resort to overt strategies on all four tasks.

tigators contrasted strategy use on easy and difficult single-digit problems, and found that children in the first year of multiplication instruction (end of third grade and beginning of fourth grade) used strategies other than retrieval roughly three times as often (60% vs. 20%) on the hard problems as on the easy ones. By fifth grade, retrieval predominated on both easy and difficult problems, but back-up strategies remained more common on the difficult problems.

The same relation remained present 45 years later (Siegler, 1988a). Presented the 81 multiplication facts with multiplicands 1 to 9, third graders' percentage of use of back-up strategies on each problem correlated highly with their percentage of errors on that problem (Figure 5.1C). A similarly strong correlation was present between percent back-up stategy use and median solution time on that problem ($r = .86$). Comparable findings have been reported by Cooney, Swanson, and Ladd (1988) with American children and by Lemaire and Siegler (1995) with French children.

Reading and Spelling

The next step was to test whether the generality of the relation between problem difficulty and use of back-up strategies extended beyond arithmetic and beyond the types of back-up strategies used on arithmetic tasks. Young elementary school students' word identification and spelling seemed to be promising domains for such tests. They are important in children's daily lives and elicit strategies quite different than those used in arithmetic.

First consider results regarding first graders' word identification strategies. The words in this study (Siegler, 1988b) were taken from the children's reading textbook; they ranged in length from two letters ("in") to eight ("sandwich"). About 70% of the words had appeared in the portion of the children's textbook they had read before the experiment.

The findings closely paralleled those from the studies of addition, subtraction, and multiplication (Figure 5.1D). Again, frequency of back-up strategy use on each word was closely related to the word's difficulty, measured either in terms of speed or accuracy. Specifically, percentage use of back-up strategies on each word correlated $r = .83$ with percentage errors for that word and $r = .83$ with median solution time for it.

A later, parallel experiment, conducted with the low income, predominantly African-American sample studied by Kerkman and Siegler (1993) yielded closely similar results. Their percentage back-up strategy use on each word correlated highly with both percentage errors for the word and solution times on it ($r = .86$ in both cases).

In the study of spelling, second and third graders were asked to spell a set of words, half from their spelling book and half from the spelling book they would be using the next year. The words varied in length from three to seven letters. Children were presented paper, pencil, and a dictionary, and allowed to use any strategy they wanted. As noted in chapter 3, they chose such back-up strategies as sounding out the word, writing alternative spellings and trying to recognize the correct one, and looking up the word in the dictionary.

The relation between percentage errors on each word and percentage use of back-up strategies on the word was of comparable magnitude to that in the studies of arithmetic—$r = .87$ among second graders and $\underline{r} = .76$ among third graders. Also as in the arithmetic findings, this measure of problem difficulty was a stronger predictor of percentage use of back-up strategies on the item than any of the structural variables that were examined: word length, number of syllables, number of consonant clusters, or number of vowel clusters. Thus, across a considerable range of tasks, ages, and income groups, choices between reliance on retrieval and use of back-up strategies vary closely with the difficulty of the problems.

Individual Differences

Stable individual differences in strategy choices across tasks and over time have also been found. In one study (Siegler, 1988b), first graders performed three tasks:

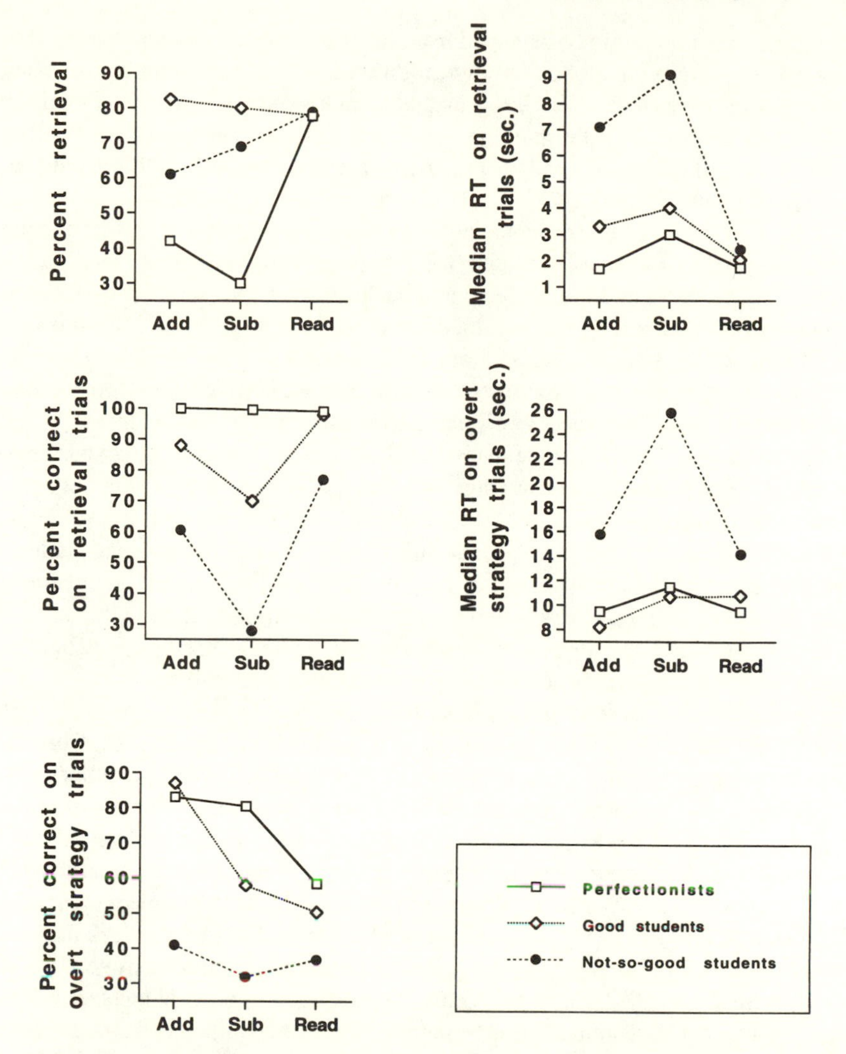

Figure 5.2. Speed and accuracy of good students, not-so-good students, and perfectionists in addition, subtraction, and reading (word identification) (data from Siegler, 1988b).

addition, subtraction, and word identification. The addition and subtraction problems had sums and minuends of 18 or less; the word identification items were the 2- to 8-letter words described in the previous section.

A cluster analysis of the children's percentage use of retrieval, percentage correct on retrieval trials, and percentage correct on back-up strategy trials on the three tasks indicated that there was considerable consistency across tasks in the children's choices of strategies.[2] The clustering program divided the children into three groups, which were labeled the "good students," the "not-so-good students," and the "perfectionists."

The contrast between good and not-so-good students was evident along all of the dimensions that might be expected from the names. Good students more often succeeded in retrieving answers to both addition and subtraction problems. They were correct more often on both retrieval and back-up strategy trials on all three tasks. They also were faster than the not-so-good students in executing back-up strategies on all three tasks and faster in using retrieval on both addition and subtraction problems (Figure 5.2).

The relation of the performance of the perfectionists to that of children in the other two groups was more complex. Despite their being as fast and as accurate as the good students on both retrieval and back-up strategy trials, the perfectionists chose retrieval less often even than the not-so-good students. This was true on all three tasks: addition, subtraction, and reading.

Four months after the experiment, all children were given the Metropolitan Achievement Test. Differences between perfectionists and good students on the one hand and not-so-good students on the other echoed those in the experimental setting. The perfectionists' average mathematics scores were at the 86th percentile, the good students' at the 81st percentile, and the not-so-good students' at the 37th percentile (Table 5.1). Thus, differences between not-so-good students and the other two groups would have been evident on standardized achievement tests. However, differences between good students and perfectionists would not have been. Instead, these seem to be alternative strategic preferences, both of which lead to high achievement in early mathematics and reading.

One factor that united children in all three groups was the adaptiveness with which they varied their strategy choices to fit problem characteristics. Correlations between percentage use of back-up strategies on each problem and percentage errors on the problem exceeded $r = .75$ in all of them. Even the not-so-good students closely fit the strategies they used to problem characteristics, though they answered less accurately and less quickly than would have been optimal.

The same three individual difference groups are evident in low income samples (Kerkman & Siegler, 1993). Proportions of children in the three groups also are similar in lower and middle income samples. In the low income sample, 30% of children were classified as good students, 24% as not-so-good students, and 46% as perfectionists. In the middle income sample, the corresponding percentages were 34%, 24%, and 42%. Differences in standardized test performance of the three groups are also similar for children from low and middle income backgrounds.

To study how these initial individual differences were related to change over

Table 5.1. Achievement Test Percentile Scores of Perfectionists, Good Students, and Not-So-Good Students: Experiment 1

Measure	Perfectionists	Good Students	Not-So-Good Students
Total math	86	81	37
Math computation	84	68	22
Total reading	81	83	52
Word recognition	79	84	54

Note. Data from Siegler (1988b).

time, the same low income sample was presented the same problems during second grade (35 of the original 41 children still attended the school). Exactly two thirds of children remained in the same individual difference group as in first grade. Of the one third who changed, the large majority substantially increased their percentage use of retrieval on the problems and therefore were classified as good students. The changes seem due to the children's increasing knowledge of these simple arithmetic and word identification problems leading to more advanced performance on them. By this argument, even greater stability of the classifications over time might have been evident if we had presented items as difficult for second graders as the items in this study were for first graders.

Almost every time I have described these results, people have asked whether there were sex differences. Their hypothesis has been that the perfectionists sound like stereotypic little girls and the not-so-good students like stereotypic little boys. In fact, none of the five experiments on individual differences that my colleagues and I have conducted have shown such sex differences. The percentages of boys and girls in each group have almost perfectly mirrored the percentages for the sample as a whole. Thus, contrary to the stereotype, boys and girls are equally likely to fit the perfectionist profile, at least in first and second grade. The stereotypic differences may arise later in development, they may have been present at an earlier historical time but no longer, or they may just be myths.

A different type of individual difference analysis has shown that young children's choices of strategies are related to the types of abilities measured on psychometric instruments. The sophistication of kindergartners' and first graders' choices among strategies for solving arithmetic problems is positively related to the child's performance on both the arithmetic subtest of the WRAT (Wide Range Achievement Test) and the arithmetic, block design, and maze subtests of the WPPSI (Wechsler Preschool Intelligence Instrument) (Geary & Burlingham-Dubree, 1989). In contrast, the sophistication of the strategies is uncorrelated with performance on nonmathematical subtests of these standardized instruments, such as information, vocabulary, similarities, and comprehension. These findings contributed both convergent and discriminant validation to the strategy assessments as indices of early mathematical competence.

Are these individual difference patterns present at older ages, or are they limited to young children? A recent study of ninth graders' strategies for solving mental multiplication problems (Hubbard et al., 1994) suggests that comparable individual differences are present at least as late as early adolescence. In that study, about 60% of the ninth graders fit the good student pattern, retrieving consistently and doing so quickly and accurately. A smaller group, 25% of the sample, showed the perfectionist pattern of less consistent use of retrieval but quick and accurate performance when they did retrieve. Finally, the remaining 15% showed the not-so-good student pattern of inconsistent use of retrieval and slower and less accurate performance even on those trials. Longitudinal data are needed to determine whether the same children who early-on show a given pattern continue to manifest it years later, but existence of parallel patterns of individual differences across years of schooling suggests that they might.

Choosing Among Backup Strategies

Children choose not only whether to use retrieval or a back-up strategy, but also which back-up strategy to use. Although the particular back-up strategies from which they choose vary a great deal across tasks, the processes through which the choices are made seem to have much in common. Below, a general theoretical analysis of how people choose among back-up strategies is provided, followed by data from several areas testing the validity of the analysis.

Theoretical Analysis

Determining the factors that influence choices among back-up strategies is surprisingly difficult. The difficulty comes because the frequency with which a strategy is used reflects not only how effective that strategy is, but also the effectiveness of alternative approaches.

Consider use of the min strategy on two problems, 2 + 1 and 7 + 8. In absolute terms, first graders use the min strategy on similarly low percentages of trials on the two problems (Siegler, 1987a). However, the reasons are quite different. On 2 + 1, the min strategy can be executed quickly and easily, but retrieval provides an even quicker and easier way of solving the problem. The min strategy isn't used because it isn't needed. On 7 + 8, first graders cannot usually retrieve the correct answer, but they cannot use the min strategy effectively either. The min strategy isn't used because it isn't effective.

If similar frequency of choices of strategies occur for different reasons, how can we identify the determinants of how often each strategy is chosen? Thinking about the choice between retrieval and use of a back-up strategy provides a good place to start. The influence of retrieval and back-up strategies on each other's frequency of use on a given problem seems to be asymmetric. Ability to accurately retrieve the answer to a problem influences frequency of use of back-up strategies on that problem. When accurate retrieval of the answer to a problem is possible, most people would rather use that fast and easy-to-execute approach. In contrast, ability to accurately execute back-up strategies on a problem exerts minimal influence on frequency of use of retrieval. If accurate retrieval is possible, that approach will usually be used, even if back-up strategies also would yield correct answers. We all can solve 2 + 2 by putting up two fingers on each hand and counting them, but how often do we bother to do so?

This analysis can be generalized into the principle that the influence of faster and slower strategies on each others' frequency of use will in general be asymmetric. If faster strategies can be executed accurately on a problem, they will usually be chosen regardless of the accuracy of slower strategies on it. In contrast, slower strategies will be frequent only if faster ones cannot be executed accurately. Thus, children's choices among strategies might be approximated by the following algorithm: Choose the fastest strategy that you can apply accurately.[3]

The analysis also points to a dependent measure that may be useful for identifying factors that influence strategy choices: the probability that a given strategy is used on a problem, given that a faster strategy is not used on it. This conditional probability can be stated as:

$$CP(Strategy_a) = P(Strategy_a) / (1 - P(Faster\ Strategy))$$

The utility of this approach for revealing the factors that influence strategy choices can be illustrated by returning to the problems used in the previous example, 2 + 1 and 7 + 8. Suppose that on 2 + 1, first graders use retrieval on 70% of trials, the min strategy on 20%, and counting from 1 on 10%—and that retrieval is fastest, the min strategy is next fastest, and counting from 1 is the slowest. The children's conditional probability of using the min strategy on that problem would be their 20% absolute probability of using it divided by the 30% probability of not using the faster retrieval strategy on it—that is, .67. Now suppose that on 7 + 8, they used retrieval on 10% of trials, the min strategy on 20%, and counting from one on 70%, and the order of speeds of the three strategies was the same. The conditional probability of using the min strategy on that problem would be the 20% absolute probability of using it divided by the 90% probability of not using the faster retrieval strategy—that is, .22.

The two conditional probabilities—.67 on 2 + 1 and .22 on 7 + 8—would indicate that when first graders cannot accurately retrieve an answer, they are more likely to use the min strategy on problems where it is easy to execute, such as 2 + 1, than on problems where it is difficult to execute, such as 7 + 8. In contrast, the absolute probabilities would have indicated only that the min strategy was used on 20% of trials on both problems. Thus, relying on the conditional probabilities of not using a faster strategy seems likely to prove useful for understanding children's choices among backup strategies. Consider two applications of the approach:

Addition

My first application of the conditional probability approach was to kindergartners', first graders', and second graders' addition (Siegler, 1987a). Presented 45 problems ranging in size from 4 + 1 to 17 + 6, the children used five main strategies. In order of speed, they were retrieval, decomposition, the min strategy, counting from one, and guessing.[4]

As shown in Table 5.2, the conditional probability approach (center columns) led to identification of predictors of use of each strategy that both accounted for a high percentage of variance in how often each strategy was used on each problem and that were intuitively reasonable. Retrieval was used predominantly on problems where the sum of the addends was small (i.e., on problems like 4 + 1 rather than 17 + 6). Decomposition was used predominantly when one of the addends was larger than 10 (e.g., on 13 + 4, a child might think "3 + 4 = 7; 10 + 7 = 17"). The min strategy was used predominantly when either the smaller addend was very small (resulting in easy execution of the strategy) or when the difference between the addends was large (resulting in the min strategy being much quicker and more accurate than counting from 1). Thus, it would be used particularly often on problems such as 2 + 14, where it could be executed easily and counting from 1 was difficult. Finally, when the choice came down to counting from 1 or guessing, children chose counting from 1 when the square of the sum (and other indicators of overall problem size) were relatively small. That is,

Table 5.2. Best Predictor of Conditional and Unconditional Probabilities of Use of Each Strategy on Each Addition Problem

	Conditional Probabilities		Unconditional Probabilities	
Strategy	Best Predictor	R^2	Best Predictor	R^2
Retrieval	– Sum	70	– Sum	70
Decomposition	+ Bigger 10	58	+ Bigger 10	54
Min	– Min / + Difference	79	+ Sum^2	57
Count all	– Sum^2	74	– Difference	59
Guessing	Inapplicable	—	+ Sum^2	65

Note. A minus sign in front of a predictor means the smaller the size of the predictor variable on a problem, the more often the strategy was used on it. Thus, the first line means that the smaller the size of a problem's sum, the more often retrieval was used on it. Data from Siegler (1987a).

children counted from 1 on relatively difficult problems and guessed on the most difficult ones.

Analyses of the seemingly more straightforward unconditional probability of use of each strategy on each problem (rightmost columns) yielded less-interpretable results. This can be illustrated in the context of the min strategy. The best predictor of absolute probability of use of the min strategy was the sum squared: The *greater* the sum squared, the more often the min strategy was used. The only straightforward explanation of this result that I can generate is that retrieval was used very often on problems with small squared sums, thus limiting use of the min strategy to problems with large squared sums. Note that this logic, emphasizing the impact of frequency of the faster retrieval strategy on the slower min strategy, is essentially identical to the argument for conditionalizing probability of use of each strategy on not using faster strategies on the problem.

Subtraction

The same approach yielded similarly sensible results regarding second and fourth graders' choices among subtraction back-up strategies (Siegler, 1989b). The children were presented 36 problems ranging in size from 5 – 1 to 17 – 12. Half of the problems were among the 100 basic subtraction facts; half were not.

The children's six main subtraction strategies, listed in order of speed, were retrieval, referring to a related addition problem, deleting a 10, counting down from the larger number, counting up from the smaller number, and guessing.

As shown in Table 5.3, the majority of variance in the conditional probability of use of each strategy could again be accounted for through a single, intuitively reasonable, predictor. Retrieval was used primarily on problems where the sum of the minuend and subtrahend was small. Thus, children were more likely to retrieve answers to problems like 5 – 1 than to problems like 16 – 12. Conditional probability of referring to a related addition problem was predicted by whether the problem was a basic subtraction fact (and therefore by whether the inverse problem was a basic addition fact). Thus, more children would solve 14 – 8 by saying that 8 + 6 = 14 than would solve 17 – 11 by saying that 11 + 6 = 17. Conditional probability of deleting a 10 was highest when the problem was not a basic fact, which in this problem set meant that there was a 10 that could be deleted

Table 5.3. Best Predictor of Conditional Probability and Unconditional Probability of Use of Each Strategy on Each Subtraction Problem

	Conditional Probabilities		Unconditional Probabilities	
Strategy	Best Predictor	R^2	Best Predictor	R^2
Retrieval	– Sum	55	– Sum	55
Addition Reference	+ Basic Fact	55	+ Smcnt[a]	74
Delete 10s	– Basic Fact	78	– Basic Fact	64
Count Down	– Subtrahend	91	+ Smcnt[a]	36
Count Up	+ Subtrahend	61	+ Subtrahend	48
Guessing	———	—	+ Subtrahend	86

Note. A minus sign in front of a predictor means the smaller the size of the predictor variable on the problem, the more often the strategy was used on it. Data from Siegler (1989a).

[a]Smcnt indicates counting up or down, whichever solves the particular problem with fewer counts.

from the minuend (e.g., 17 – 6) or from both minuend and subtrahend (e.g., 17 – 12). Conditional probability of counting down from the minuend was highest when the subtrahend was small; thus, children counted down more often on problems like 14 – 2 than on ones like 14 – 12. Conversely, conditional probability of counting up was highest when the subtrahend was large—more frequent on 14 – 12 than on 14 – 2. These results, along with those on addition, indicated that the conditional probability approach was useful for identifying determinants of when different strategies are used.

Causal Reasoning

Adaptive choices among alternative ways of thinking are also evident in children's approaches to inferring causal connections between events. Among the bases on which people infer causes of physical events are generative mechanisms, temporal contiguity, spatial contiguity, and covariation. That is, we might choose A rather than B as the cause of C because we understood the mechanism through which A generated C, because A occurred in close temporal or spatial proximity to C, or because A consistently preceded C.

Shultz, Fisher, Pratt, and Rulf (1986) presented 3-, 5-, and 7-year-olds with situations in which these potential bases of causal inference conflicted. For example, one potential cause might produce the effect through a comprehensible mechanism, but covariation and contiguity information might point to an alternative cause.

The choices of children of all three ages reflected a hierarchical pattern of preferences. If information about generative mechanisms was present, children usually relied on it, regardless of what other information was available. If such information was not present, and the situation was relatively simple, they generally relied on the consistency of the covariation of cause and effect. If neither condition was met, they most often relied on perceptually salient information, such as temporal contiguity. Again, this seemed a reasonable way to choose among competing lines of causal reasoning, in that the most predictive sources of information were given preferred status. The pattern paralleled the choices children made among the addition and subtraction strategies, with the most preferred approach being understanding of generative mechanisms rather than retrieval, and other types of information relevant to causation (e.g., contiguity and covariation) assuming the roles of back-up strategies.

Adapting to Situational Variations

All of the above examples involve adaptation to inherent differences among problems. Another large class of adaptations involves responses to more transitory situational constraints. Sometimes the situation calls for speed, other times for accuracy; sometimes it calls for winning, other times for not losing; sometimes it calls for finding the solution with the highest expected value, other times for the solution that is highest on the most important attribute. This section focuses on how children adjust to three of the most common types of situational demands: demands on cognitive resources, demands to balance goals of speed and accuracy, and demands to balance long- and short-term goals.

Adapting to Demands on Cognitive Resources

Limited cognitive resources force people to select approaches that meet key goals without imposing excessive processing demands. This type of adaptation has received particular attention in decision-making research. A standard method used in this area involves presenting response alternatives that vary in their values along several dimensions, and asking subjects to choose the best one. Such factors as time pressure, number of competing alternatives, and number of relevant dimensions are varied to determine how people adapt to processing demands.

Basic to much of this work is the assumption that people use simplifying heuristics to make complex decisions. They might choose the first alternative they find acceptable on all attributes (Simon's, 1957, satisficing heuristic); might identify the most important dimension and choose the alternative with the highest value on it (Tversky's 1969, lexicographic heuristic), or might do a first pass to eliminate alternatives that fail on one or more important dimensions and then do a more complete analysis of the remaining possibilities (Russo & Dosher's, 1983, majority-of-confirming-dimensions heuristic). The greater the amount of information to be processed, and the less time provided to do so, the more adults use strategies that minimize the processing load (Payne, Bettman, & Johnson, 1993).

Far less research using such paradigms has been done with children than adults. The few studies that have been done, however, suggest that the choice process is similar. In one study, Klayman (1985) asked 12-year-olds to decide which of several used bicycles they would buy. The bicycles varied in cost, number of speeds, body condition, tires condition, appropriateness of size, and so on. Children were presented information boards containing cards; each card indicated the value of a given bicycle on a given dimension. When they wanted to obtain a piece of information, they had to ask the experimenter to turn over the relevant card (e.g., "Please turn over the card with the cost of Bicycle A"). The simplest problems included three alternatives (three bicycles), each varying along three dimensions (e.g., cost, number of speeds, size); the most complex problems included six alternatives varying along six dimensions. The methodology allowed Klayman to identify the information each child considered before deciding which bicycle to buy.

Like adults in prior studies, the children responded to increasing amounts of information by searching the information more selectively. The more alternatives on the board, and the more dimensions along which the alternatives varied, the lower the percentage of cards that children examined. Increasing the information load also led to increased use of the satisficing strategy (defined as choosing a bicycle without considering any information regarding at least one of the other bicycles). With increasing information, children also focused more on the alternatives that initially appeared most promising. These particulars fit the generalization that as the amount of information increases, children increasingly focus on informative subsets of it. This allows them to make reasonable choices without execessive processing demands.

Balancing Goals of Speed and Accuracy

Children also frequently need to balance considerations of speed and accuracy. Two contexts in which their balancing act has been examined are route planning and reading.

Planning

Contrary to children's reputation as poor planners, 4- to 9-year-olds plan in ways that effectively adapt to competing demands of speed and accuracy (Gardner & Rogoff, 1990). In this study, children were presented mazes of varying complexity, and received instructions that either emphasized both speed and accuracy or accuracy alone.

Faced with relatively simple mazes, or provided instructions that emphasized speed as well as accuracy, both younger and older children generated partial plans, executed them, and used the situation that emerged to help them decide what to do next. Presented demanding mazes and instructions that emphasized accuracy alone, both younger and older children usually planned complete routes in advance of any drawing on the mazes. Making complete plans reduced the number of errors on both simple and complex mazes, but the gains were larger on the more complex ones. This showed the value of the children's choices. When they could succeed reasonably well without making complete plans, they did so, thus avoiding the time consuming and effortful process of formulating a complete plan. When complete plans were necessary for success, however, the children usually generated them.

Reading

Children whose reading achievement is seriously below grade level often seem to place too great an emphasis on speed, not enough on accuracy. For example, their performance on the MFFT (Matching Familiar Figures Test) frequently fits the impulsive profile of above average speed and below average accuracy on a test that requires careful consideration of multiple alternatives (Kagan, Rosman, Day, Albert, & Phillips, 1964). Despite this tendency, such children do adjust their strategy choices appropriately to situational emphases on speed or on accuracy (Brent & Routh, 1978).

The children studied were fourth graders whose reading achievement was at least 1.5 grades below average and who fit the impulsive profile on the MFFT. When given a reading pretest, their solution times averaged around 2 seconds, a time sufficiently fast to suggest that they used retrieval on the large majority of trials (in Siegler, 1988b, median time on retrieval trials on a similar reading task was 1.9 s). The children also erred on 20% of the words they were asked to read on the pretest.

However, when they were given 40 nickels and told they would lose a nickel for each word read incorrectly, their approach changed dramatically. Their solution times increased to a mean of 5 seconds, considerably longer than retrieval would take. This suggested that they shifted to more time consuming back-up strategies, such as sounding out words. The threat of losing their nickels also led to a decrease in the impulsive children's percentage of errors from 20% to 10%. In contrast, children in a control condition showed no decrement in errors or increase in solution times in their second session.

Thus, although children who are labeled impulsive may emphasize speed over accuracy in their typical reading, they do react appropriately to situational contingencies that place a premium on accuracy. Their goals may be different than we would prefer, but their choices respond appropriately to circumstances.

Balancing Long-Term and Immediate Goals

In domains with multiple competing goals, people face a basic challenge: how to make their strategy use flexible enough to deal with shifting situations without losing track of more enduring objectives. Such domains are often ones in which an individual's actions must be responsive to those of other people: driving in traffic, speculating on the stock exchange, or playing chess, for example. People operating in these domains have enduring goals, such as getting home as quickly as possible, maximizing the expected value of investments, or not losing the game. But achieving these goals is not entirely under the individual's control. The shortest route may be clogged with other drivers, prices of the most promising stocks may have been bid up so high as to make investment in them unacceptably risky, and even a strong chess opponent may blunder, thus creating unexpected opportunities to win rather than just not to lose. These impasses create short-term goals that may supersede the longer term ones.

Choosing adaptively in the face of changing circumstances requires that individuals change goals and strategies flexibly but without losing track of the enduring objectives. In chess, for example, pursuit of an unanticipated chance to win must not be so single-minded that it opens the way for counterattack and defeat. Similarly, a hot tip may lead an investor to plunge into the market, but the longer term goal of maximizing return subject to acceptable levels of risk must not be forgotten. Two domains in which children encounter such conflicting demands are tick-tack-toe and arithmetic.

Tick-tack-toe

The simple game of tick-tack-toe exposes quite young children to direct conflict among competing goals. In this game, as in many others, the competing goals are winning and not losing. Because focusing on one can lead to neglect of the other, children must strike a balance between long-term considerations (the best way to play the game in general) and circumstantial ones (whether they are going first or second; whether they have a realistic chance to beat the particular opponent).

Children adjust their strategies in sensible ways toward winning or not losing (Crowley & Siegler, 1993). This was evident in games that kindergartners and first graders played against a computer program. Going first increased the children's emphasis on the goal of winning. They detected a higher percentage of potential winning moves when they went first than when they went second. Conversely, going second increased their emphasis on the goal of not losing. They blocked a higher percentage of potential wins by the computer when they went second than when they went first. The emphases made sense, given that the player going first is much more likely to win if the opponents are at all equally matched.

The children also adjusted their tick-tack-toe strategies to varying instructions. When told that the most important goal was to win, they more consistently detected their own potential winning moves. When told that the most important goal was to prevent the computer from winning, they more consistently blocked its potential victories.

How did children achieve this balance between long-term and situational goals? One important piece of evidence was that the absolute time spent on winning moves was always shorter than the time spent on blocking moves. This suggested that children maintained the long-term goals by always first trying to win and then trying not to lose. They appeared to adjust to the situation by varying the amount of time spent pursuing the two goals. When the situation emphasized winning, they would search for a winning move for a longer time; when the situation emphasized not losing, they would turn to that goal more quickly. This was evident in winning always being faster than blocking, but the mean time to identify winning moves being longer when winning was emphasized (reflecting more time spent searching for a win before giving up on that goal). A computer simulation was built based on these ideas (Crowley & Siegler, 1993). It demonstrated that the combination of pursuing the goals in the hypothesized invariant order, and adapting to the situation by varying the time spent pursuing each goal, led to the patterns of solution times and errors observed in the study

Arithmetic

Children seem to adopt a similar approach to maintaining both long-term and immediate goals in arithmetic. Consider a study of second graders' subtraction that I conducted in which situational demands were varied. Before one set of problems, children were told that the only important goal for these problems was to answer correctly. For another set of problems, they were told that the only important goal was to answer quickly. For a third set of problems, they were told that the two goals were equally important. All children received all three types of instructions, with the order counterbalanced across children, and each instruction paired with each set of problems equally often.

The children responded sensibly. They were most accurate when the instructions emphasized only accuracy, and least accurate when the instructions emphasized only speed. Conversely, they answered fastest when the instructions emphasized speed alone and slowest when the sole emphasis was on accuracy. Instructions that emphasized both speed and accuracy resulted in intermediate performance on both dimensions.

This adaptation did not come about through children changing their strategy use in response to the different contingencies. Percentage use of retrieval and percentage use of each back-up strategy did not differ significantly with the instructions. Similarly, the order of solution times of the strategies was the same in all conditions: retrieval was the fastest approach, deleting 10s of intermediate length, and counting down from the minuend the slowest approach. Instead, as in tick-tack-toe, children responded to changing circumstances by varying how quickly and accurately they executed the strategy they chose rather than changing the basic strategy choice process.

This approach to balancing short-term and long-term goals does not appear to be limited to children. Payne, Bettman, and Johnson (1988) reported a similar finding in a study of adults' decision making. When under moderate time pressure, the adults chose their usual strategies, but executed each of them faster. Only when under severe time pressure did they abandon their preferred strategies in favor of inherently faster ones. The general point is that in a variety of domains and under a variety of circumstances, children and adults adapt to situational demands by maintaining the usual choice process, but varying the way in which they execute the approach they choose.

Changes in Adaptiveness with Age and Experience

As illustrated by the above examples, children choose adaptively among strategies from early in life. This does not imply, however, that the early choices are as adaptive as they ever will be. Instead, choices seem to become increasingly adaptive with age and experience. This ability to benefit from experience can be seen as another dimension of adaptiveness. The growing adaptiveness characterizes both changes within an experimental session and changes over longer periods.

Changes Within an Experimental Session

Children's strategy choices often change adaptively from the beginning to the end of a single experimental session and even from one trial to the next. Both types of within-session changes were apparent in a study of development of serial recall strategies (McGilly & Siegler, 1989). The kindergartners, first graders, and third graders in this study were presented a series of lists of digits and asked to recall each one.

One change within the experimental session involved increasing frequency of use over trials of the most advanced strategy, repeated rehearsal. The increases were present among children of all three ages.

A more intriguing type of change within the session involved strategy switches from one trial to the next. Two characteristics of performance on trial N influenced which strategy children chose on trial $N + 1$: whether children rehearsed the earlier list and whether they successfully recalled it. When children had not rehearsed and then failed to recall correctly, they were much more likely to switch strategies than under any other circumstance (Figure 5.3). Again, the pattern was present at all three ages.

These trial-to-trial changes make a great deal of sense. If one answers correctly, there is no strong impetus to switch, regardless of how the correct answer was generated. Complementarily, if a person is wrong, but used the most accurate approach they know, there is no reason to think that switching strategies will improve the situation. It is only when the approach used fails to yield a correct answer, and a more accurate approach is known, that there is compelling reason to switch.

Changes Over Longer Periods

School-Age Children's Arithmetic

Studies of the adaptiveness of strategy choices have not generally focused on changes with age in that adaptiveness. The fact that such choices are so adaptive so early has discouraged this kind of investigation, because it suggested that there was little development to investigate. However, a recent study (Lemaire & Siegler, 1995) suggests that this conclusion was premature.

In the study, French children were presented single-digit multiplication problems at three times (January, April, and June) in the year in which they learned

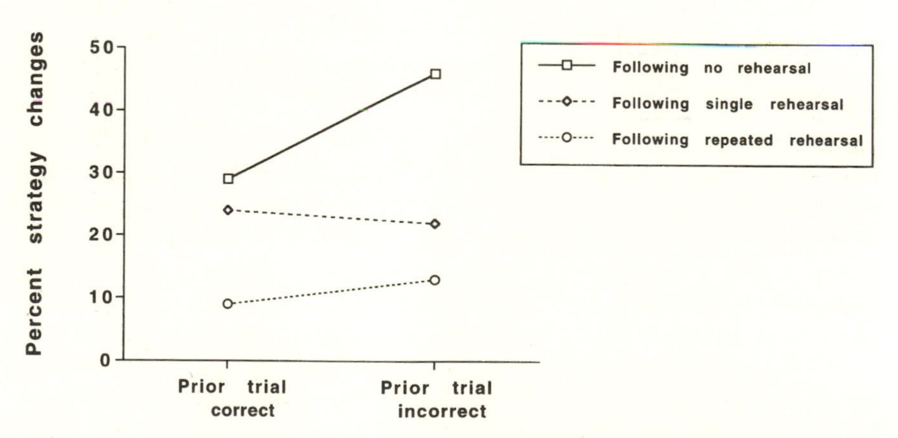

Figure 5.3. Probability of switching serial recall strategies from one trial to the next. The probability is greatest when the child had not rehearsed on the preceding trial and had then been unable to recall the list correctly on that trial (data from McGilly & Siegler, 1989).

multiplication (second grade). On each occasion, they needed to solve the 81 items with multiplicands 1 to 9 inclusive. At the time of the first testing session, children had had roughly a week of instruction in the multiplication facts.

The results demonstrated two important phenomena regarding development of adaptiveness of strategy choices. First, the choices were quite adaptive from early in learning. Even on the first testing occasion, frequency of use of back-up strategies on each problem correlated $r = .80$ with percentage errors on the problem and $r = .50$ with mean solution time on it. Second, despite this strong early relation, the correlations increased considerably with learning. The correlation of back-up strategy use on each problem with mean solution time on it increased from $r = .50$ in the first session to $r = .75$ in the second and $r = .80$ in the third. The correlation of percentage back-up strategy use with percentage errors on the problem increased from $r = .80$ in the first session to $r = .90$ in the second session, before ceiling effects (0% errors on the majority of problems) led to it declining to $r = .69$ in the third session. It thus appears that the choice between retrieval and back-up strategies is quite adaptive from early in learning about the domain, but that it becomes more adaptive with experience in it.

Infants' Locomotion

Developmental trends in the strategy choices of infants who are learning to crawl and walk parallel those in elementary schoolchildren's arithmetic. This was apparent in Adolph's (1993; 1995) study of 14-month-olds walking up and down ramps of varying steepness.

Adolph characterized the toddlers' locomotor decision making in several ways. Of their overall approach she wrote,

> (1) If children did not perceive risk from a quick glance at the slope, then they plunged ahead. . . . (2) If children perceived something amiss, then they stopped, looked, and touched. These cautious probes served to turn up information about whether the slopes were safe for walking. (3) If children did perceive danger from falling, then they generated alternatives and tried them out before going. This means/ends exploration is a form of problem solving, and it occurred after children recognized that the hill was too steep to walk down. (Adolph, 1993, p. 90)

The toddlers used several approaches to go down the ramps: walking, crawling down on hands and knees, sliding down headfirst, sliding down feetfirst, sliding down while sitting, or refusing to go altogether. One interesting strategy choice they needed to make was whether to locomote down the ramp using their standard method of locomotion, walking, or some other approach. A reasonable solution would be to walk down all ramps that could be traversed without falling, and to walk down fewer and fewer ramps as falling became increasingly likely.

All children tried to walk down the large majority of ramps within their capabilities. Beyond this point, the further the slope beyond the toddlers' capabilities, the less likely they were to try to walk down.

Adolph (1993) also reported a longitudinal study, in which infants' and toddlers' locomotion down ramps was studied from the time they learned to crawl to a number of weeks after they learned to walk. The results illustrated how learning to choose adaptively among strategies can be specific to the particular strategies available at the time of learning. To quantify the relation between the toddlers' strategy choices and the steepness of the ramps, Adolph computed a "go ratio," the percentage of trials on which the child attempted to locomote down the ramp in their usual way (crawling or walking). The go ratio was computed relative to the child's capability, defined as the steepest angle at which the child descended without falling on at least two thirds of attempts.

At the beginning of the experiment, infants crawled down many ramps that were beyond the boundary at which they could descend without falling (Figure 5.4). However, even in the first session of the study, they were less likely to crawl down ramps that were far beyond their capabilities than other ramps. With experience, they increasingly often refused to crawl down ramps that were too steep. This can be seen as a process of the infants learning the limits of their crawling abilities, and adjusting their strategy choices accordingly.

The learning process was repeated when walking became the standard means

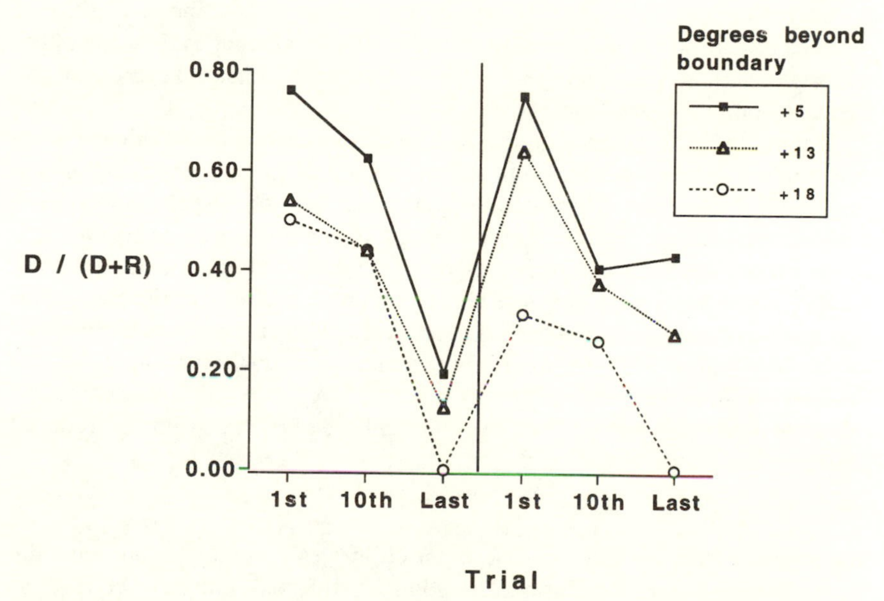

Figure 5.4. Probability of babies' attempting to descend down ramps from the first to the last session in which their predominant mode of locomotion was crawling (left of vertical line) and from the first to the last session in which their predominant mode of locomotion was walking (right of vertical line). D is the infants' total number of attempts to descend down the ramps using the usual mode of locomotion. D+R is the total number of trials, including refusals to descend in the usual way. The dark circles indicate the D/D+R ratio on ramps within 5 degrees of those on which the babies could descend without falling at the time of the session. Data from *Perceptual-Motor Development in Infants' Locomotion Over Slopes*, by K. E. Adolph, 1993, unpublished doctoral dissertation, Emory University, Atlanta, Georgia. Reprinted with permission.

of locomotion (average age = 13 months). At first, the toddlers tried to walk down most ramps, including ones that were 18° beyond the steepest ramps that they could descend down without falling. With experience walking, their calibration of their own capabilities became increasingly precise, so that they again discriminated more sharply between ramps where they could succeed and ramps where they were likely to fall. They walked down the former but not the latter. Despite the many cognitive, perceptual, and motor developments between when infants started crawling and when they started walking, they still needed experience with the new strategy of walking to learn which slopes were safe using that new approach.

Memory Strategies

With changing ability to use strategies, the particular choices that will be most adaptive also change. This was apparent in McGilly and Siegler's (1990) study of serial recall. In it, kindergartners, second graders, and fourth graders were asked to recall ascending contiguous lists (4, 5, 6, 7, 8), descending contiguous lists (8, 7, 6, 5, 4), and random lists (6, 4, 7, 5, 8).

On the random lists, the usual developmental pattern of increasing use of repeated rehearsal was observed. In contrast, on the contiguous lists, the opposite pattern was present: With age, frequency of repeated rehearsal decreased, and frequency of no rehearsal increased.

Despite the differences among age groups in frequency of use of each strategy, children of each age seemed to choose adaptively, given their ability to execute the strategies. When presented the contiguous lists, fourth graders were very accurate regardless of whether they rehearsed; they answered correctly on 100% of the contiguous lists on which they did not rehearse. In contrast, unlike the fourth graders, kindergartners were correct on only about half of the contiguous lists and were considerably more successful when they used repeated rehearsal on the contiguous lists than when they used no rehearsal on them. Thus, the younger children benefited (through increased accuracy) by using repeated rehearsal on contiguous lists, and the older children benefited (through reduced effort) by fairly often not using them.

Selective Attention

Sometimes strategies that increase older children's accuracy do not have the same effect on younger children. The younger children's failure to benefit has been said to indicate a *mediation deficiency* (Reese, 1962) or a *utilization deficiency* (Miller & Seier, 1994). The pattern is best documented in selective attention tasks. On such tasks, children are shown a matrix of locations (e.g., two rows of six locations each), with each location containing one of two categories of stimuli (e.g., animals and furniture). Each location within the matrix has its own door, which is marked with a picture representing the category of the item inside (e.g., 6 of the 12 doors have a picture of an animal; the other 6 have a picture of a house). Before each trial, children are told which category they will need to remember on that trial. Then, during a study period, children can open whichever doors they want. After the study period, children are asked the locations of the particular entities within the relevant category (e.g., Where is the dog, where is the cat?).

The most selective strategy is for children only to open doors whose contents are in the relevant category (as indicated by the picture on the doors). However, at young ages, children often search either exhaustively or haphazardly. More surprising, the selectivity of their searches is uncorrelated, or minimally correlated, with their recall.

Why might selective strategies not increase young children's recall? One explanation emphasizes the demands of executing new strategies. When children first use a strategy, they tend to execute it less effectively, and at greater cognitive cost, than when they are more experienced in its use (Guttentag, 1984). Consistent with this interpretation, having the experimenter execute the selective attention strategy (opening only the relevant doors) leads to young children's recall benefiting from the strategy. This presumably occurs because having the experimenter execute the strategy frees processing capacity that the child would otherwise need to expend on the strategy's execution (Miller & Seier, 1994).

What is more challenging to explain is why the young children use the selective attention strategy at all, given that their recall does not benefit from it. One possibility that would have quite broad implications for thinking about how adaptive strategy choices develop is that the cognitive system may operate as if it knew the law of practice. With practice, any new procedure is likely to become faster, easier, and more accurate. If a new approach is even approximately as useful as an established one, it makes sense from a long-term perspective to use the new procedure, because substantial improvement in its effectiveness is more likely. This seems an extremely adaptive approach for a cognitive system to take. The model of strategy choice described in the next chapter incorporates a mechanism that produces such effects.

Conclusions

From infancy to adolescence, children choose adaptively among strategies in such diverse contexts as solving arithmetic problems, reading and spelling words, recalling lists of numbers, inferring the causes of events, selectively attending to relevant information, deciding among alternative purchases, playing tick-tack-toe, planning how to traverse mazes, and crawling and walking down ramps. Children adjust their choices in entirely reasonable ways both to inherent characteristics of problems and to transitory situational demands. The sensible choices extend both to choosing between stating a retrieved answer and using a back-up strategy and to choosing which back-up strategy to use. They are evident in changes over trials and changes with age, as well as in performance at any one time. They are present among children labeled gifted, typical, and learning disabled; among children from low income as well as middle income backgrounds; and early in learning of a skill as well as later. In short, adaptive choices among available alternatives seems to be a general characteristic of children's thinking. The frequent conclusion that children's choice processes are flawed appears to reflect inadequate criteria for evaluating them, rather than any inadequacy in the choice processes themselves.

But through what mechanisms are these adaptive choices generated? This is the focus of the next chapter.

Notes

1. Simon's (e.g., 1955) theory of bounded rationality represents a response to these difficulties and resembles in many ways the present view of adaptive strategy choice. The main difference is that his theory emphasizes how information processing constraints lead to the single choice that subjects most often make, whereas the present approach emphasizes how they choose among alternative approaches, all of which they sometimes use.

2. This analysis was suggested and performed by Jamie Campbell, who contributed substantially to the individual differences research; see Siegler and Campbell (1989) for another description of the work.

3. Speed and accuracy are not the only factors that influence strategy choices, but they seem usually to be the most powerful ones.

4. Guessing was treated somewhat differently than the other strategies, because it was viewed as a default strategy, to be used only when no other strategy could be executed accurately. Therefore, even though it was not the slowest strategy, it was assumed to be considered last in the sequence, and to be used only when no other strategy seemed likely to yield a correct answer. The fact that it was faster than some other strategies does not imply that it was considered before them, since solution times for each strategy include time to execute the strategy as well as the order in which they were considered and guessing takes less time to execute than other backup strategies.

6

Formal Models of Strategy Choice

Pittsburgh has many beautiful old houses, most of which have thick plaster walls. The walls are good in the sense that they effectively reduce noise coming from other rooms, but bad in the sense that they sometimes force me to interact with plasterers. My experience with plasterers has not been fun. The ones who have come to do repairs on my house haven't put drop cloths below where they worked, have resisted or ignored requests not to smoke in the house, and have flicked cigarette ashes wherever they went. Several of them smelled bad and had alcohol on their breath, even at 8:00 A.M.

On the other hand, they were really good at plastering. They fixed cracks and holes quickly and without apparent difficulty. The finished product, once painted, matched the surrounding wall or ceiling remarkably well.

My own attempts at plastering have been much less successful. These attempts have taught me quite a bit, but unfortunately not how to do the job. I have learned that plastering requires many good strategy choices. Home plastering kits indicate how much plaster powder and water to mix together, and roughly when to apply the mixture, but that is only the beginning of the problem. When exactly has the plaster jelled sufficiently to apply it? If it's too watery, it will run; if it's too thick, it will be wavy, and soon will crack. The instructions also do not illustrate the wrist movements for applying the plaster. The package directs the reader to apply the plaster with "flexible," "supple," and "smooth" movements, but what does that mean? Despite considerable time spent thinking about how to plaster, and some time spent watching plasterers, my decisions invariably lead to wavy, cracked surfaces resembling those of an artistically challenged kindergartner.

I occasionally have asked the plasterers who came to my house how they know when the plaster is ready and how it should be applied. Their replies: "You just look at it." "You can see when it's ready." "You put it on smoothly." True enough, I'm sure, but not helpful.

There may be a general lesson about strategy choice in this tale of competence and incompetence. I would like to think that my general intelligence, decision-making skills, and metacognitive knowledge at least match those of the plasterers. Yet in terms of deciding when and how to apply plaster, I'm not in their league. Making highly skilled strategy choices, then, may depend less on general metacognitive knowledge, decision-making skills, and reasoning abilities than on implicit, unconscious knowledge derived from experience in the specific domain. Relying on more general reasoning and decision-making abilities may be what we do when we lack the directly relevant experience that would make possible truly skillful choices. There was a good reason why Newell (1990) labeled reliance on general knowledge and reasoning as a "weak method."

My adventures in plastering raise the two central questions of this chapter: How are people able to choose strategies so adaptively in domains in which they are experienced, and how does ability to make such adaptive choices develop (or not develop, in some cases)? To address these questions, I first identify five basic findings regarding strategy choice, and then consider the ability of several types of models to account for the findings.

Five Fundamental Phenomena of Strategy Choice

Variability

As discussed throughout this book, children and adults often use multiple strategies on a given task. The domains in which they have been found to do so range from arithmetic to spelling to reading to time telling to serial recall to crawling down ramps to searching for hidden objects to block stacking to causal and moral reasoning. The variability is present not just from one child to another, but also within a single child. It also is not just present from one item to another, but within a single item. Even a single child solving a single problem on two consecutive days fairly often uses different strategies on the two occasions. Not infrequently, a child gives evidence of multiple ways of thinking on a single trial.

Generating similar variability seems an essential quality for models of strategy choice. If children of a given age use five different approaches to solve a problem, models of the form "Children of age *N* use strategy *X* on this type of problem" cannot accurately depict their behavior. Only models that recognize the variability present within individual children solving individual problems can accurately describe their strategy choices.

Adaptiveness

As discussed in chapter 5, children's strategy choices are adaptive in at least four ways. One involves their choice of whether to state a retrieved answer or to use a back-up strategy on a given problem. The more difficult the item, defined either in terms of the percentage of errors or the length of solution times it elicits, the more often children use back-up strategies on it. This pattern of strategy choice is adaptive, because it enables children to use the faster retrieval approach on problems where it yields correct answers and to use slower back-up strategies on problems where they are necessary to produce accurate performance. Second, children choose adaptively among back-up strategies. They tend to choose the fastest back-up strategy that yields accurate answers on the particular problem. Third, they react appropriately to changing circumstances, such as situational emphases on speed or on accuracy. Fourth, they show adaptive patterns of change; the adaptiveness of choices increases over trials within a session, over repeated sessions, and with age.

Change

As described in chapters 4 and 5, four main changes in strategy use occur with age and experience: acquisition of new strategies, increases and decreases in frequency of use of existing strategies, more efficient execution of strategies, and better choices among strategies. In traditional depictions of cognitive development, overwhelming emphasis has been put on the first type of change: acquisition of new strategies. However, changes also occur along the other three dimensions, and these changes have large effects on the efficiency and effectiveness of performance. All four types of changes are important phenomena for models of strategy choice to generate.

Individual Differences

Recognizing the variability of strategy use within individuals raises the issue of whether strategy use also varies in interesting ways across individuals. Although research on broad cognitive styles has not identified many strong consistencies in strategy use (Kogan, 1983; Sternberg, 1985), results from studies of more narrowly defined strategy choices have been more encouraging. The consistent patterns of differences among good students, not-so-good students, and perfectionists, described in chapter 5, provide one such case. Similar differences have been found among both White, suburban children from middle income backgrounds and Black, urban children from lower income backgrounds. Models of strategy choices should account not just for overall patterns of performance, but also for individual differences in those patterns.

Generalization

Effective strategy choices also require generalization of the lessons of past experience to new problems and situations. Some degree of generalization is a basic human tendency; even 3-month-olds who learn that kicking can make a mobile emit interesting sounds generalize the lessons to new mobiles (Rovee-Collier, 1989). However, observation of children in the weeks after they first discover a strategy indicates that the generalization process often takes a long time, at least when children possess alternative strategies that work fairly well (Kuhn, 1995; Schauble, 1990; Siegler, 1995; Siegler & Jenkins, 1989). Models that generalize, but that do so only gradually (at least when other relatively effective strategies are known), appear necessary to fit the data.

These five phenomena—variability, adaptiveness, change, individual differences, and generalization—provide benchmarks against which to evaluate the adequacy of alternative models of choice. The next section examines models intended to account for adults' choices (and in some cases, the choices of nonhuman animals); the section after that examines models of children's choices.

Models of Adults' Choices

In this section, I briefly describe three prominent models of choice, and examine the degree to which they account for the five phenomena described previously. None of the approaches has been used much to model cognitive development, but all are serious attempts to understand decision making, and all incorporate interesting ideas about how people decide what to do. The models also have the advantage of illustrating the way that choice is thought of by scholars in neighboring disciplines concerned with behavior—economics, political science, sociology, anthropology, and so on.

Rational Choice Theory

The economic theory of rational choice, or optimal choice as it is sometimes called, is among the most influential theories in all of the social sciences. Herrnstein (1990, p. 356) claimed "No other well articulated theory of behavior commands so large a following in so wide a range of disciplines," and I suspect that he was right. Rational choice theory is widely used not just in economics but in political science, sociology, social psychology, comparative psychology, ethology, and other fields that attempt to explain behavior. It has been applied to governmental decision making, functioning of the criminal justice system, voting behavior, animals' foraging for resources, altruistic behavior, and many other tasks in which there are choices to explain.

The basic tenet of rational choice theory is that choices maximize total utility, where utility is defined in a way similar to the way in which reinforcement is defined within psychology. The theory has been formalized by a variety of axioms, such as the axiom of transitivity. (For any three choices, if A is preferred to B and B to C, then A should be preferred to C.)

Rational choice theory is used in two distinct ways: as a normative theory of what people should do and as a descriptive theory of what they actually do. Fishbein and Ajzen's (1975) theory of voting behavior provides a straightforward example. They postulated that a rational person would vote in accord with the following formula: Multiply the probability with which you believe that a candidate favors a certain policy by how positively or negatively you view that policy and by how important the issue is to you; sum the products over all issues for each candidate; vote for the candidate with the highest sum of products. Normatively, this does seem a rational way to vote. Descriptively, it predicts the choices of most voters.

A number of problems have arisen regarding the descriptive accuracy of rational choice theory, however. Numerous paradoxes have been identified in which people violate the most basic axioms of the theory, such as transitivity (e.g., Lichtenstein & Slovic, 1971; 1973). Theoretically irrelevant variables, such as the wordings of questions, the order of choices, and the context in which they are framed (e.g., whether they are posed as potential gains or as avoidance of potential losses), profoundly influence people's choices (Shafir & Tversky, 1992). As Herrnstein (1990) concluded, although rational choice theory provides a useful normative theory against which to compare behavior, its predictions do not in general predict people's choices particularly accurately.

One approach that in some ways fits into the rational choice category, and that does appear useful for analyzing strategy choices, is Anderson's (1990) ACT-R model. This model derives its predictions both from analyses of the statistical structure of the environment and from psychological data on learning. Results of an initial attempt to apply ACT-R to modeling strategy choices (Lovett & Anderson, in press) were quite promising. It proved possible to model within ACT-R the influence on strategy choices of both problem characteristics and each strategy's history of success or failure. Consistent with predictions from ACT-R, but inconsistent with the predictions that followed from several alternative models, the two variables combined additively to predict how often each strategy was used on each problem. The ACT-R model has not to date been used to model children's strategy choices, but may well prove useful in that context as well.

Matching Law Models

Recognizing the inaccurate predictions yielded by rational choice theory in its pure form, other investigators have formulated formal models with different idealized choice formulas. One of the most prominent of these is the matching law (Herrnstein, 1970; Davison & McCarthy, 1988):

$$\frac{\text{\% Choice of A}}{\text{\% Choice of A or B}} = \frac{\text{Reward for Choosing A}}{\text{Reward for Choosing A or B}}$$

The matching law has been applied most frequently to the behavior of rats and pigeons in two-choice situations. It often very accurately predicts their behavior in those contexts. Results of studies with human adults also have frequently shown that the matching law's predictions are accurate, even when nonintuitive. This has been especially the case in situations in which choosing one alternative alters the payoff associated either with it or with both alternatives, so that the relative value of choices changes with the time period being considered. An example of such a situation in the environment outside the lab is drug use. When people use addictive drugs such as crack, the reward both of that activity and of alternative activities changes with the amount of drugs consumed (Herrnstein, 1990). The more drugs used, the higher the reward of further drug use relative to the reward of other activities. Overeating provides a parallel example; the heavier people get, the more the reward of eating relative to other activities, such as exercising. Under such conditions, both people and other animals often choose on the basis of the immediate reward relations, even when this yields distinctly non-optimal long-term consequences.

The matching law, and its accompanying proposed mechanism of *melioration* (always moving toward aligning percentage of choices of a given alternative with percentage of rewards for that alternative) have also been criticized on several grounds. Under some circumstances, the matching law yields inaccurate predictions (Staddon, 1991). Certain aspects of the theory also are less well specified than they first appear. For example, the time horizon over which melioration is applied is left undefined, even though length of the time period is the critical variable in yielding the effects that best discriminates its predictions from those of rational choice theory (Staddon, 1991). Another problem involves the range of applicability of the approach. In typical human contexts outside the laboratory, in which speed, accuracy, effort, and other variables associated with each activity vary, how can reward be defined except circularly in terms of the choices that are made (Premack, 1965)? Thus, the matching law seems very useful for predicting some choices, particularly those in which long- and short-term contingencies differ, but also has important shortcomings as a general model of choice.

Models of Decision Making

Researchers interested in decision making have proposed a number of formulas hypothesized to describe people's choices among alternatives. One is *weighted averaging*, a close cousin of rational choice theory (Keeney & Raiffa, 1976). Another is the *equal weight heuristic*, which differs from weighted averaging only in assigning equal weight to information from all relevant dimensions (Dawes, 1979). Another is *satisficing*, in which the choice made is the first alternative considered that has adequate values on all relevant dimensions (Simon, 1955). Two others are *lexicographic approaches*, in which the alternative with the highest value on the most important dimension is chosen (Tversky, 1969; Tversky et al., 1988), and the *majority of confirming dimensions approach*, in which pairs of alternatives are compared, the one with the higher value on most dimensions is chosen, and then the winner is compared to the next alternative (Russo & Dosher, 1983).

Each of these approaches has been found to be the best predictor of the overall pattern of choices under some circumstances (Payne et al., 1993). The particular approach that best fits the data is influenced by the relative importance of accuracy and speed/effort in the particular situation. When motivation to perform accurately is high, and time limits are generous or nonexistent, people's choices are best predicted by weighted averaging. As speed demands and required amount of processing increase, simplifying strategies such as lexicographic approaches emerge as better predictors.

Payne et al. (1993) developed the interesting perspective that these algorithms could themselves be viewed as distinct strategies among which people choose. They formulated a production system model that chose among the algorithms depending on the importance within that situation of accuracy and speed. The problems presented to the model varied in number of choices, number of attributes per alternative, payoff for accurate answers, and time constraints on problem solutions, among other variables.

Payne et al. explicitly stated (p. 142) that their model was not intended to simulate how humans reach their decisions. Instead it was a point of comparison indicating the costs and benefits of each algorithm under a variety of circumstances. The model was highly successful in this way. For example, it helped to explain why people quite often rely on lexicographic rules, by showing that under certain circumstances they achieved 90% of the accuracy of the weighted averaging rule with only 40% as many elementary information processes. More generally, the model showed that people respond quite rationally to increasing amounts of information. The higher the processing demands, the more they shift toward choices that yield most of the benefits of the more difficult-to-execute algorithms with less of the processing cost.

Another prominent approach to decision making, the heuristics and biases approach, can be analyzed similarly. This family of approaches, like the matching law, was generated in large part as an attempt to improve on rational choice theory. The heuristics and biases that have been studied tend to be widely applicable back-up strategies that can be used when specific knowledge is lacking. For example, Tversky and Kahneman (1973) suggested that people use the availability heuristic to estimate a wide range of features of particular objects, events, and phenomena. Within this heuristic, the more easily the object, event, or phenomenon comes to mind, the more of the quality of interest it must have. Consistent with the idea, people judge well-known countries to have greater populations and land areas than less well-known countries of the same populations and areas, judge well-publicized causes of death to be more frequent than less well-publicized causes of the same objective frequency, and so on.

On the other hand, the heuristics and biases accounts, like the more formal decision-making models, are at best partial stories. They do not account for variability of choices either within or between subjects, do not indicate when a given heuristic will be used (or how much weight to assign to a given heuristic on a particular estimate), and do not address how changes in choices occur.

Evaluation

These approaches to choice have a number of appealing aspects. They illuminate a variety of decision rules that people could use, describe them in a clean and simple way, and, in the Payne et al. model, describe how adaptive choices among them could be made.

However, the models do not get us very far in understanding several of the central phenomena regarding strategy choice that were described earlier. None of the models generates variability like that in people's choices. If you specify the problem and task characteristics, each model will make the same choice every time. Even more important from the present perspective, they do not address the issue of how change occurs. The models are static; they make the same choices at all times, regardless of their prior experience. These facts do not mean that the models are faulty, because they are intended to pursue different goals. However, they do mean that the models are limited, and that they exclude from consideration some of the most interesting and best documented phenomena regarding choice.

It is probably not coincidental that these models were generated to describe adults' decision making. Variability and change seem especially prominent characteristics of children's thinking. I am convinced that they are also vital for understanding adult's cognition, but they seem even more basic to understanding the thought processes of children.

Consistent with this view, models of how children choose among alternative strategies have paid greater attention to the variability of choices and how they change with experience. In the rest of this chapter, I describe three generations of efforts specifically directed at understanding how children choose among alternative strategies.

Metacognitive Models of Strategy Choice

Children's use of strategies first became a major topic of research in the mid 1960s (e.g., Flavell et al., 1966; Keeney et al., 1967). Much of the early research focused on memory strategies, such as rehearsal and organization. The research soon revealed an intriguing set of phenomena. Most 5- and 6-year-olds did not seem to use such strategies spontaneously. Given appropriate instruction, they could learn the strategies, and using them led to greater recall. However, despite these benefits, the children soon stopped using the strategies and reverted to earlier approaches.

This puzzle was an important impetus for the first generation of models of the development of strategy choices. These models were labeled "metacognitive," because they focused on how knowledge about cognition could be used to control cognitive activities. Their fundamental assumption was that young children's failure to use new strategies reflected their limited understanding of their own thinking and of why the new strategies were needed.

It is important to note that these metacognitive models focused on explicit, rationally derived, conscious, metacognitive knowledge. At times, the term *metacognitive* also has been used to refer to processes that are implicit, not derived from rational consideration, and unconscious. For purposes of clarity, however, the term is used here only in its original sense of explicit, rationally derived, conscious knowledge about cognition.

Two Metacognitive Models

Metacognitive approaches assume that strategy choices are made through the cognitive system's explicit knowledge of its own workings. This knowledge is often said to be used by an "executive processor," which decides what the cognitive system should do (Case, 1978; Kluwe, 1982; Sternberg, 1985). Schneider and Pressley (1989) described the executive processor's role as follows: "This executive is aware of the system's capacity limits and strategies. The executive can analyze new problems and select appropriate strategies and attempt solutions" (p. 91).

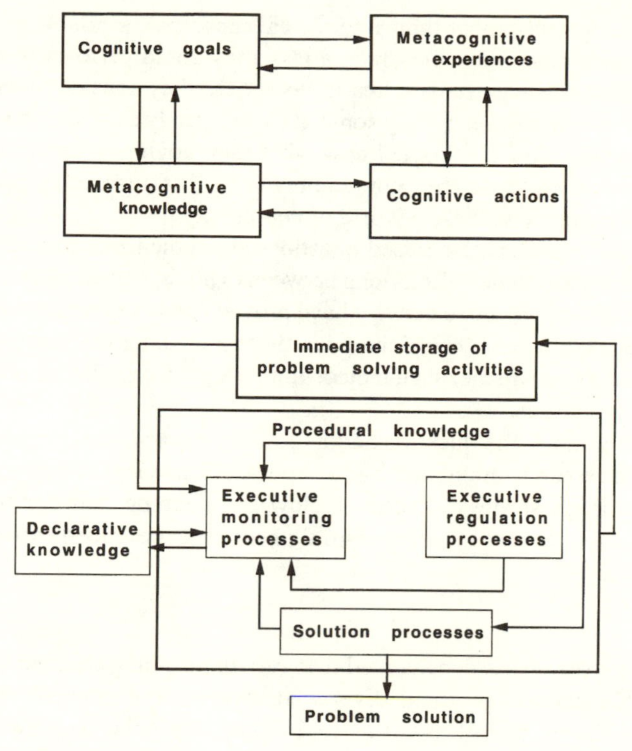

Figure 6.1. Two metacognitive models of the executive processor: Flavell's model (top) and Kluwe's model (bottom). Top model from "Cognitive Monitoring," by J. H. Flavell, 1981, in *Children's Oral Communication Skills* (p. 40), P. Dickson (Ed.), New York: Academic Press. Copyright 1981 by Academic Press. Reprinted with permission. Bottom model from "Cognitive Knowledge and Executive Control: Metacognition," by R. H. Kluwe, 1982, in *Animal Mind–Human Mind* (pp. 201–224), by D. Griffin (Ed.), New York: Springer. Copyright 1982 by Springer. Reprinted with permission.

Kuhn (1984) described the way in which metacognitive knowledge influences strategy selection similarly: "In order to select a strategy as appropriate for solving a particular problem, the individual must understand the strategy, understand the problem, and understand how the problem and strategy intersect or map onto one another" (p. 165).

Models of the executive processor that are based on such conceptions of how metacognitive knowledge exercises its effects generally have been high level, rather abstract, characterizations of types of relevant knowledge used to govern cognition. A less and a more elaborate model of this type are shown in Figure 6.1.

Such metacognitive models are useful for conveying hypotheses about relations among different types of knowledge and for pointing to one way in which adaptive strategy choices can be generated. However, they also have a number of weaknesses, both theoretical and empirical (Brown & Reeve, 1986; Cavanaugh & Perlmutter, 1982; Siegler, 1988a). As statements of theory, they have been vague about the mechanisms that produce the phenomena of interest. Do people make explicit judgments about their intellectual capacities, available strategies, and task demands every time they face a task they could perform in multiple ways? If not, how do they decide when to do so? Do they consider every strategy they could use on the task or only some of them? If only a subset, how do they decide which ones? How do people know what their cognitive capacity is on a novel task or what strategies they could apply to it? The apparent simplicity of the metacognitive models masks a world of complexity.

Empirical evidence has also raised questions about the fundamental assumption that underlies the models. Relations between explicit, verbalizable metacognitive knowledge and cognitive activity have proven much weaker than expected (Cavanaugh & Perlmutter, 1982; Schneider 1985; Schneider & Pressley, 1989). This has cast doubt on whether such metacognitive knowledge plays a central role in most strategy choices.

On the other hand, the questions addressed by metacognitive research are important, and research stimulated by the approach has yielded intriguing data regarding children's strategy choices. Below we examine findings from this research that are relevant to the five central phenomena described earlier.

Variability

Metacognitive research has documented that even quite young children have conscious, statable knowledge about diverse strategies. For example, Kreutzer, Leonard, and Flavell (1975) asked 5- to 10-year-olds what they could do to remember to bring their skates to school the next day. At all ages, children generated a variety of strategies for solving the problem. Studies of other tasks (e.g., ways of remembering a forgotten idea) have obtained similar results and have demonstrated that the number of strategies generated increases with age at least into early adolescence (Yussen & Levy, 1977).

Adaptive Choice

The metacognitive perspective suggests a way of thinking about how children choose among alternative strategies. The models generally are not explicit, but the implicit causal pathway seems to be:

Metacognitive knowledge → *Strategy choice* → *Performance*

For example, knowledge that a given list of words was too long to be remembered without using a memory strategy could lead the executive processor to choose to repeatedly rehearse the words, which, in turn, could increase recall.

The type of research suggested by this approach is exemplified in an experiment by Justice (1985). Children were presented videotapes of a 10-year-old executing several strategies that might benefit recall and then were asked to judge the likely effectiveness of the strategies. Older children's judgments of the strategies' relative value were generally more accurate. The conclusion was that older children's typically superior choice of strategies stemmed in large part from their superior knowledge about the strategies.

However, even when children know abstractly that one strategy is superior to another, they often do not choose that strategy. Such choices may reflect lack of motivation, lack of time, overreliance on sheer effort, or belief that the strategy is unnecessary (Flavell & Wellman, 1977; Wellman, 1983). For example, Fabricius and Hagen (1984) found that among a sample of children taught a new strategy that consistently improved their performance, only a minority continued to use it when no longer instructed to do so. The children who continued to use it were predominantly those who attributed their improved success to adopting the strategy. Other children, who attributed their improvement to trying harder, to being lucky, or to other factors usually stopped using the new approach.

Even when significant relations between metacognitive knowledge and strategy choices are present, they often are insufficient to account for the very strong relations between problem difficulty and strategy choices that have been observed. This can be seen in children's arithmetic. Recall that the frequency with which children use back-up strategies on a given arithmetic problem is highly correlated with the problem's difficulty. This relation could be mediated by metacognitive judgments of problem difficulty as follows:

True problem difficulty → *Judged problem difficult* → *Strategy choice*

A difficult problem could lead a child to think, "This is a difficult problem; I'd better use a strategy such as *X* that can solve problems like that."

However, Siegler and Robinson (1982) found only moderate links between each of these steps. True problem difficulty (as measured by the percentage of errors the problem elicited) correlated $r = .47$ with the children's judgments of its difficulty. Judged difficulty of each problem correlated $r = .51$ with percentage use of back-up strategies on the problem. These correlations were significant, but not nearly high enough to account for the very strong correlation ($r = .91$) between problem difficulty and percentage use of back-up strategies on the problem. As illustrated by this case, young children's conscious, explicit metacognitive knowledge may contribute to their extremely adaptive strategy choices, but often falls well short of explaining them.

Change

Metacognitive knowledge increases greatly during childhood and adolescence. Older children know more strategies, often choose more adaptively among them, and are better at learning new strategies as well (Schneider & Pressley, 1989). They are more realistic in assessing their own memory capacities, more accurate in assessing the relative importance of different parts of a task, and more knowledgable about interactions among factors that influence performance. This growing knowledge could lead children to base strategy choices increasingly on metacognitive understanding. Alternatively, however, with age, children may rely decreasingly on metacognitive knowledge. As suggested by the plasterers, implicit knowledge, derived from experience with tasks, provides an increasingly effective alternative basis for choosing. As children gain experience with more and more tasks, they may rely increasingly on such implicit knowledge. A third possibility is that both types of changes occur and that the effects cancel out. Available evidence is inadequate to address the issue, because it rarely indicates what kinds of knowledge children use to make particular choices.

Generalization

When children learn a strategy, they often do not generalize it to new situations. One reason may be that they often realize fewer benefits in increased accuracy, and incur greater costs in cognitive effort, from using new strategies than they will once the strategies become better practiced (Guttentag, 1984; Miller & Seier, 1994). Thus, they have less reason to generalize, at least in the short run.

Even with well-practiced strategies, however, it is surprisingly difficult to override usual strategy selection procedures through metacognitive means. Recall the previously described results of a study I conducted on second graders' subtraction. The children were given problems under conditions in which they were told either that only accuracy was important, that only speed was important, or that both speed and accuracy were. They heeded the instructions; they were fastest and least accurate when told that only speed was important and were slowest and most accurate when told that only accuracy was important.

Despite the instructions influencing speed and accuracy, they had no effect on strategy choices. Instead, the children just executed the same strategies more carefully or more quickly, depending on the instructions. Thus, at least in domains such as arithmetic, in which children have substantial experience, strategy choice seems to be a relatively automatic, hard-to-change process. This may underlie the slow generalization of newly taught strategies, so frequently observed and lamented (e.g., Brown, Bransford, Ferrara, & Campione, 1983). As noted by Kuhn, Schauble, and Garcia-Mila (1992), learning not to use old strategies may often be as large a challenge as learning to use new ones.

Individual Differences

Do children who have greater metamnemonic knowledge also remember more? There appears to be some relation between the two, but not a very strong one. For example, two meta-analyses of the literature, one weighted by sample size and the other unweighted, yielded identical average correlations of $r = .41$ between individual children's metacognitive knowledge about memory and their recall (Schneider, 1985; Schneider & Pressley, 1989). Thus, a child's factual knowledge about memory is only moderately helpful in predicting how much the child will remember.

Even these moderate correlations may overstate the relation between enduring metacognitive knowledge and performance. The studies in the meta-analyses include ones in which the assessments of metacognitive knowledge were done after the relevant performance, as well as ones in which the assessments were done before it. The timing makes a big difference: When metamnemonic knowledge was measured after the task had been performed, the correlations averaged $r = .54$. When such knowledge was measured before the task was performed, the correlations averaged only $r = .25$ (Schneider & Pressley, 1989, p. 117). The higher correlation when metamnemonic knowledge was measured after the child performed the task may reflect children using short-term episodic memory to guide their metacognitive judgments, rather than the usual assumption of enduring metacognitive knowledge governing strategy use.

Evaluation

These first generation models, which emphasized explicit, verbalizable metacognitive knowledge, were clearly insufficient to explain how children choose among alternative strategies. As the evidence became increasingly clear, investigators drew different conclusions about how to proceed. Some emphasized the need for better assessments of metacognitive knowledge (e.g., Cavanaugh & Perlmutter, 1982). Others highlighted the need to determine the conditions under which metacognitive knowledge is most strongly related to strategy use (e.g., Schneider & Pressley, 1989; Wellman, 1983). Yet others focused on potential educational gains of teaching metacognitive knowledge and skills to children. Although such knowledge is not strongly correlated with strategy choices in typical populations, teaching it to low-achieving children has often proved useful (Baker & Brown, 1984; Palincsar & Brown, 1984; Paris, 1988; Pressley & Levin, 1987). Perhaps the most common reaction was to conclude that what was really interesting about this research was what it indicated about children's developing understanding of themselves and other people. Researchers who drew this conclusion formed much of the core of the movement to study development of theories of mind (e.g., Astington, Harris & Olson, 1988; Flavell, Green, & Flavell, 1986; Leslie, 1987; Perner, 1991; Wellman, 1990).

Perhaps because I was not involved in studying metacognition earlier, the findings had a different effect on me. I found it fascinating that such an intuitively likely relation failed to emerge. It made me ask: How can children choose as adaptively as they do if not by reasoning from explicit metacognitive knowledge? Thus, when I observed preschoolers' highly adaptive choices among addition strategies (Siegler & Robinson, 1982), and found that their explicit ratings of the difficulty of the problems were not nearly accurate enough to account for the adaptiveness of their choices, it struck me that implicit knowledge must be giving rise to the adaptive choices. The goal of finding out how this could occur is what motivated Jeff Shrager and me to develop a model of strategy choice quite different than the previous metacognitive ones. For purposes of this discussion, I have labeled it a second generation account of strategy choice, because it used as a point of departure what had been learned from research on explicit, verbalizable, metacognitive knowledge.

The Distributions of Associations Model

The distributions of associations model was developed by Siegler and Shrager (1984) to show how adaptive strategy choices could emerge without explicit

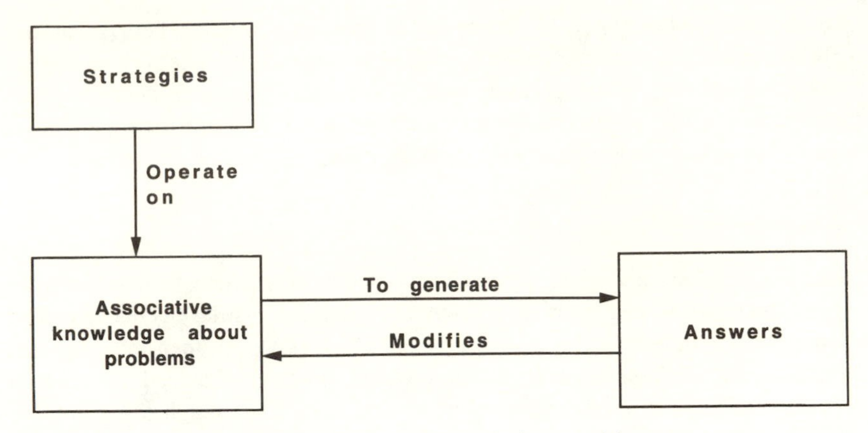

Figure 6.2. Overview of distributions of associations model.

metacognitive knowledge. It was specifically aimed at accounting for preschoolers' strategy choices in solving simple addition problems.

The Model's Basic Structure

The two main parts of the distributions of associations model are (a) a representation of knowledge about particular problems and (b) strategies that operate on the representation to produce answers. The answers, in turn, reshape the representation; the model learns by doing. Figure 6.2 illustrates the hypothesized relations among strategies, associative knowledge of problems, and the answers that are generated.

Within this model, the representation of knowledge is hypothesized to include associations between problems and potential answers, both correct and incorrect. For example, 3 + 5 would be associated not only with 8, but also with 6, 7, and 9 (Figure 6.3). Each problem's associations with various answers can be classified along a dimension of *peakedness*. In a problem with a *peaked distribution*, such as that on the top of Figure 6.3, most of the associative strength is concentrated in a single answer, ordinarily the correct answer. At the other extreme, in a *flat distribution*, such as that on the bottom of Figure 6.3, associative strength is dispersed among several answers, with none of them forming a strong peak.[1]

The process that operates on the representation involves three sequential phases, any one of which can produce an answer: retrieval, elaboration of the representation, and application of an algorithm. In the specific case of preschoolers' addition, children would first try to retrieve an answer. If not sufficiently confident of any answer, they would elaborate the representation of the problem, perhaps by putting up fingers to represent the two addends. If they still did not know the answer, they would use the algorithm of counting the objects in the elaborated representation, in this case the fingers that were up. The three sequential phases are present in all distributions of associations models (the Siegler, 1987b, simulation of 5- and 6-year-olds' subtraction learning and the Siegler, 1988a, simulation of 8- and 9-year-olds' multiplication learning, as well as this model of addi-

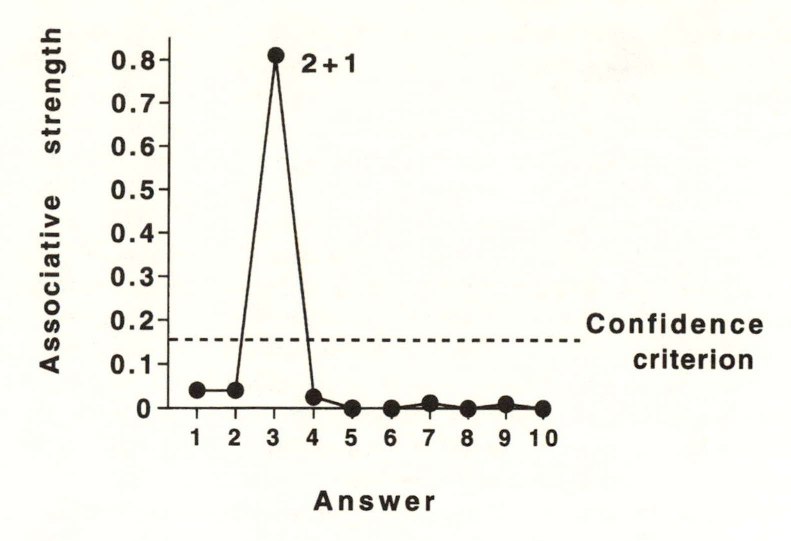

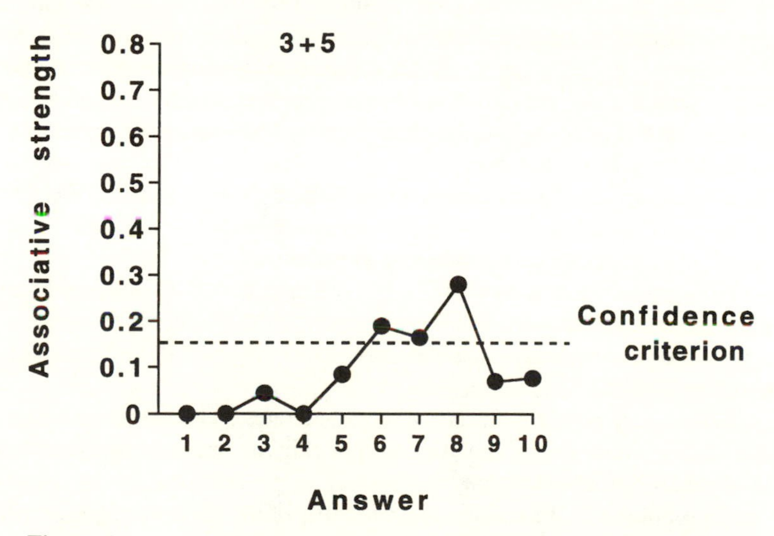

Figure 6.3. A peaked (top) and a flat (bottom) distributions of associations.

tion). The way in which retrieval occurs is also constant across the models, though the particulars of the other two phases are specific to each task.

The retrieval mechanism is central within the model. When presented a problem, children are hypothesized to set two parameters: a *confidence criterion*, which determines how sure they must be to state a retrieved answer, and a *search length*, which determines how many attempts they will make to retrieve an answer before resorting to a different approach to solving the problem. After setting these parameters, the child retrieves an answer. Probability of retrieving any given answer to a problem is proportional to that answer's associative strength relative to the total associative strength of all answers to the problem. For example, if a given answer had an associative strength of .4, and the total associative strength of all answers was .8, then that answer would be retrieved on 50% of retrieval efforts. This retrieval procedure closely paralleled that hypothesized by Gillilund and Shiffrin (1984) and like it, is a specific instantiation of the Bradley-Terry-Luce mathematical model of choice (Bradley & Terry, 1953; Luce, 1959).

The retrieved answer is stated if its associative strength exceeds the confidence criterion. For example, if a girl had a distributions of associations and a confidence criterion like that shown for 3 + 5 in Figure 6.3, she would state the answer if she retrieved 6, 7, or 8, but not if she retrieved any other answer.

If the answer's associative strength does not exceed the confidence criterion, and the number of retrieval attempts has not exceeded the search length, the child again retrieves an answer from the problem's distribution of associations. She states it if its associative strength exceeds the confidence criterion.

If the retrieval process fails to yield such an answer within the allotted number of searches, the child elaborates the representation. In the case of simple addition, this occurs through putting up fingers corresponding to the number of objects in each addend or forming a mental image of objects corresponding to that number of objects. A single further retrieval attempt is made to see if the kinesthetic and/or visual cues associated with the elaboration allows retrieval of an answer whose strength exceeds the confidence criterion. If this criterion is met, the answer is stated; if not, the child uses an algorithmic procedure to solve the problem. In the case of addition, the algorithm involves counting the number of objects in the elaborated representation.

The distributions of associations model initially was formalized within a running computer simulation of 4- and 5-year-olds' addition (Siegler & Shrager, 1984). Its operation can be summarized as follows:

1. The simulation is presented the 25 problems with both addends between 1 and 5. Frequency of presentation corresponds to the frequency with which parents present that problem to preschoolers (as established in an empirical study reported in Siegler and Shrager, 1984).

2. Before each problem, the simulation generates a confidence criterion and a search length, whose values vary randomly within the limits set by the simulation.

3. Probability of retrieving an answer is proportional to its associative strength compared to the associative strengths of all answers to the problem. A retrieved answer is stated if its associative strength exceeds the current confidence criterion. Retrieval attempts continue until either the associative strength of a retrieved answer exceeds the confidence criterion or the number of searches matches the search length.

4. If no answer has been stated and the search length has been reached, the program generates an elaborated representation. The particular elaboration varies with the operation being modeled; in all cases, though, it may lead directly to a statable answer. In the case of addition, the elaboration involves either forming a mental image of objects corresponding to the addends or putting up fingers to represent each addend. The visual and/or kinesthetic cues associated with these

elaborations add associative strength to the answer corresponding to the number of objects represented, which is usually the correct answer.

5. If no answer has been stated, the model uses an algorithmic back-up strategy, which again is specific to the operation being modeled. This algorithmic strategy always yields a statable answer. In the case of preschoolers' addition, the algorithm involves counting the objects in the mental image or the fingers that were put up.

6. Crucial to the overall working of the model is the learning mechanism. Every time the system advances an answer, the association between that answer and the problem increases. The increment is twice as great for correct answers, that presumably are reinforced, as for incorrect answers, that presumably are not. The change in the association between problem and answer is identical regardless of whether the answer is produced through retrieval or through use of a back-up strategy.

The Model's Performance

Data on the model's performance were obtained by running the simulation in two phases: a *learning phase* and a *test phase*. During the learning phase, performance on each trial altered the associations between the problem and the answer that was stated. The analogy was to experience that children would have had prior to entering the experimental situation. During the test phase, in contrast, the associations remained constant. The analogy was to children's performance in the experimental situation, after having had a given amount of pre-experimental experience. The results yielded by the simulation can be organized around the five key strategy choice phenomena described earlier in the chapter.

Variability

Variability of strategy use is built into the distributions of associations model. Each strategy can be, and is, applied to any problem. Thus, Siegler and Shrager (1984) found that in the course of the simulation's run, all four strategies were applied to each of the 25 problems. The assignment of strategies to problems is far from random. Problems with peaked distributions of associations elicit greater reliance on retrieval, and problems with flatter distributions elicit greater reliance on the three back-up strategies. Nonetheless, strategy use is variable within problems as well as between them.

Adaptive choice

At the heart of the distributions of associations model is its procedure for adaptively choosing whether to use retrieval or a back-up strategy on a problem. The procedure illustrates how adaptive strategy choices can be generated without any homuncular executive processor.

Adaptive strategy choices between retrieval and back-up strategies are seen as arising because the peakedness of a given problem's distributions of associations determines both problem difficulty and the likelihood of using a back-up strategy. To understand this view, it is useful to compare the model's workings on problems with peaked and flat distributions of associations.

Relative to a peaked distribution, a flat distribution elicits a higher percentage of use of back-up strategies. The reason is that flat distributions, by definition, lack a single answer with high associative strength. This lack means that no answer will be stated when confidence criteria are moderate or high. The absence of such a strongly associated answer leads to children often being unable to state any retrieved answer and instead using a back-up strategy.

The flat distribution also elicits a higher percentage of errors. The reason is that the difference between the strength of association of the correct answer and incorrect ones will be smaller in the flatter distribution, leading to more frequent retrieval of wrong answers and to their being stated on a higher percentage of trials when they are retrieved.

Finally, the flat distribution leads to longer solution times. The flatter the distribution, the less likely that an answer whose associative strength exceeds the confidence criterion will be retrieved and stated on an early retrieval attempt.

Thus, within this model, the strong correlations between percentage use of back-up strategies on a problem and percentage of errors and mean solution times on it arise because all three variables are governed by the same underlying factor: the peakedness of the problem's distribution of associations.

The data on children's performance demonstrated the sufficiency of the hypothesized mechanism to generate adaptive choices between retrieval and back-up strategies. Within the simulation, correlations between strategy choices (percentage of use of back-up strategies on each problem) and the measures of problem difficulty (percentage of errors and length of solution times on that problem) exceeded $r = .90$. The simulation's strategy choices also paralleled those of children. Percentage back-up strategies on each problem generated by the simulation and by the children in Siegler and Shrager (1984) correlated more than $r = .80$. Thus, the adaptive strategy choices of the simulation paralleled the adaptive strategy choices of the children.

The simulation also made a specific, nonintuitive prediction regarding the source of these correlations: The high correlations among percentage of back-up strategies, percentage of errors, and length of solution times on each problem should derive primarily from correlations among percentage of back-up strategies, percentage of errors *on retrieval trials*, and length of solution times *on retrieval trials* on each problem. The reason is that only on retrieval trials do percentage of errors and length of solution times stem from the peakedness of the distributions of associations—the same variable that governs strategy choices. In contrast, speed and accuracy on back-up strategy trials derive from a different variable, the difficulty of executing the back-up strategies.

Analyses of 4- and 5-year-olds' performance supported this prediction (Siegler & Shrager, 1984). Correlations between percentage of back-up strategy use and percentage of errors on retrieval trials on each problem were significantly higher than correlations between percentage of back-up strategy use and percentage of errors on back-up strategy trials on the problem. The same was true for the corresponding correlations involving solution times rather than errors. These nonintuitive predictions arose specifically from the distributions of associations model; it is very unlikely that they would have been made without it.

Change

The distributions of associations model focused on two closely related issues regarding change: how problems come to have increasingly peaked distributions of associations and why this process occurs faster on some problems than others.

First consider how learning occurs in general. The basic assumption of the model regarding creation of distributions of associations for each problem is that people associate whatever answer they state, correct or incorrect, with the problem on which they state it. Thus, the more often correct answers are stated on a problem, and the less often incorrect ones are, the faster that learning occurs. Early in learning, children almost always generate answers via back-up strategies, because associative strengths are too weak to make retrieval possible. Back-up strategies, such as counting from one, generate the correct answer more often than any other answer, leading its associative strength to grow more rapidly than that of other answers. As the associative strength of the correct answer grows, it becomes both more likely to be retrieved and more likely to exceed any given confidence criterion. This leads to increasingly frequent retrieval of the correct answer, which increases that answer's associative strength yet further. The same increase in associative strength leads to performance becoming increasingly fast and accurate (because retrieval, the fastest strategy, can be used increasingly often, and because the associative strength of the correct answer is increasing more rapidly than that of any other answer).

Why, then, do some problems develop peaked distributions of associations faster than others? Three factors hypothesized to be influential are (a) differences in difficulty of executing back-up strategies on the problems, (b) differing influences of related problems, and (c) different frequencies of encountering problems.

First consider differences among problems in difficulty of executing back-up strategies. In preschoolers' addition, the most common back-up approach is the sum strategy. Children are more likely to correctly execute this back-up strategy on problems with small addends, because such problems can be solved via the sum strategy with fewer counting operations, and therefore less chance of error, than other problems. Generating the correct answer via back-up strategies on a greater percentage of attempts on these problems results in their coming to have more peaked distributions of associations.

Intrusions from related operations also influence the rate of acquiring peaked distributions. Knowledge from one numerical operation often intrudes into performance on another. For example, among fourth graders, 4 + 3 fairly often elicits the answer "12" and 4 x 3 the answer "7" (e.g., Miller & Paredes, 1990). Among preschoolers, knowledge of the counting string often intrudes into addition, leading them to state wrong answers (e.g., 3 + 4 = 5, 3 + 5 = 6) but also right ones (e.g., 1 + 2 = 3, 1 + 3 = 4). This cross-operation influence would slow acquisition of peaked distributions on the first set of problems, but hasten it on the second.

Frequency of presentation also differs among problems and seems likely to influence the rate of learning. For example, parents present to their children tie problems, such as 2 + 2 and 3 + 3, more often than other problems (Siegler &

Shrager, 1984). More frequent presentation of these problems should contribute to their more quickly coming to have peaked distributions.

These three factors—ease of execution of back-up strategies, intrusions from related operations, and frequency of problem presentation—all influence the rate at which different problems are learned. For example, regression analyses were conducted in which each of the three factors was used to predict preschoolers' percentage of errors on each the 25 addition problems with addends 1 to 5. All three factors added significant independent variance to that which could be accounted for by the other two factors. Together, they accounted for more than 80% of the variance among problems in percentage of errors (Siegler & Shrager, 1984).

The simulation incorporated all three influences on problem difficulty. Probability of errors on each problem when children used back-up strategies was a function of the number of the counts that were needed to solve it. Intrusions from knowledge of the counting string was modeled by temporarily increasing the associative strength of the answer one greater than the second addend on ascending series problems (e.g., 1 + 3 = 4; 3 + 4 = 5), where such counting associations were most likely. Presentation of each problem was proportional to parental presentation rates.

These features of the simulation led to its rate of learning of different problems paralleling that of children. Correlations between the simulation's behavior and that of children increased substantially during its run. When a test phase was run before the learning phase, thus reflecting the model's initial competence but not its learning from experience, correlations between its performance and that of children were minimal. The correlation between the model's and the children's frequency of back-up strategy use on each problem was $r = -.03$; the correlation between their solution times was $r = .00$. When the test phase was run after the 80 trials/problem of the learning phase, the corresponding correlations were substantial, $r = .87$ and $r = .80$ respectively. Thus, not only did the model's absolute level of performance change in the way that children's does, the relative performance it generated on different problems also increasingly closely resembled that of children.

Generalization and Individual Differences

The simulations embodying the distributions of associations model were silent about both generalization and individual differences, but for different reasons. Their silence about generalization was due to their inherently not being able to generalize. All learning was specific to the particular problems that were encountered.

The silence regarding individual differences was not due to any such conceptual difficulty. Rather, it reflected a lack of implementation within the simulations of ideas regarding individual differences. Such implementations could have been undertaken, but they weren't.

Evaluation

The distributions of associations model had a number of strengths. It was far more explicit than the previous metacognitive models regarding how strategy choices are made, why they change over time, and why the changes take the form they do. It accounted straightforwardly for a number of key phenomena regarding strategy choices and made specific, testable, sometimes nonintuitive predictions that proved to be correct. It illustrated the viability of an alternative to the metacognitive perspective: Rather than adaptive strategy choices implying a knowledgable and insightful executive processor, the choices could arise through the operation of simple cognitive processes such as retrieval, execution of back-up strategies, and associative learning.

However, the model had certain weaknesses as well. It was too inflexible, too limited in its explicitness, and too dumb.

Inflexibility

The distributions of associations model was quite rigid. It always considered strategies in the same order, regardless of the circumstances. It also did not provide any obvious way in which new strategies could be integrated into the strategy choice process.

Both properties are at odds with what is known about strategy choices. People do not always attempt retrieval before other strategies. Instead, we at times first consider the strategy that seems the most likely to pay off, even when that strategy is not retrieval (Reder, 1982; 1987). Further, under time pressure, people often choose to use calculational strategies in less than the amount of time that retrieval requires (Reder & Ritter, 1992). Thus, strategy choice procedures clearly are more flexible than described within the distributions of associations model.

Another way in which the distributions of associations model was inflexible involved it always having the three phases: retrieval, elaboration of the representation, and use of a solution algorithm. This three-phase approach fit the particular strategies used in preschoolers' addition (and in somewhat older children's single-digit subtraction and multiplication as well), but was too restrictive to capture strategy choices in general.

Limited Explicitness

The distributions of associations model was far more explicit than previous metacognitive models of how strategy choices are made. However, the explicitness lay primarily in the depiction of the choice between stating a retrieved answer or using a back-up strategy. Procedures for choosing among alternative back-up strategies were left vague. For example, the choice between elaborating the representation by putting up fingers or by forming an internal representation was simply stated as a pair of probabilities. There was no account of how this decision was made.

Dumbness

The distributions of associations model was considerably less intelligent than children in at least two ways. First, it could not generalize from its experience. No matter how much problem-solving experience it had, it could not draw any implications regarding other problems, even the most closely related. Extensive experience solving 5 + 5 had no implications for learning of 6 + 5.

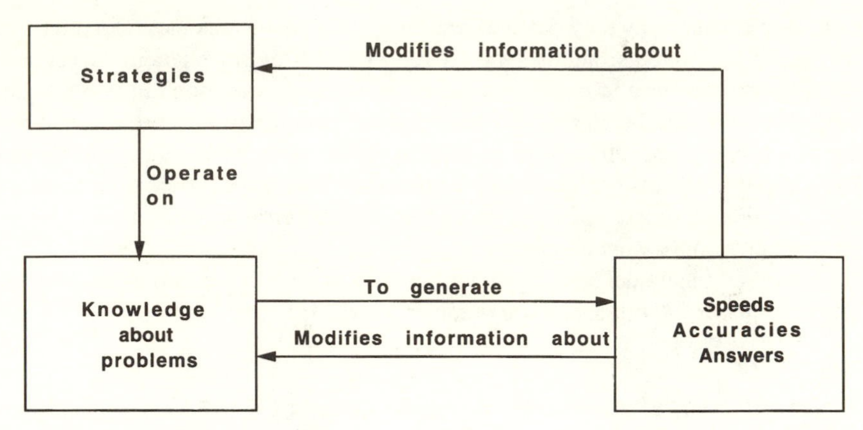

Figure 6.4. Overview of ASCM.

The model also had no abstract knowledge about the usefulness of strategies or the difficulty of problems. As described earlier, children's judgments of problem difficulty correlated about $r = .50$ with the actual difficulty of the problems (Siegler & Shrager, 1984). This is insufficient to account for their very adaptive strategy choices, but it also is not negligible. The model did not include any data that would provide a basis for such judgments.

In response to these limitations, Siegler and Shipley (1995) formulated a new strategy choice model, ASCM (*A*daptive *S*trategy *C*hoice *M*odel—pronounced "Ask-em"). The primary goal was to create a more flexible, precise, and intelligent model of strategy choice. A further goal was to simulate acquisition of knowledge not just of small addend problems in the preschool years, but of all single integer problems from the preschool period through adulthood.

ASCM

The Model's Structure

Figure 6.4 illustrates ASCM's organization. Strategies operate on problems to generate answers. The problem-solving process yields information not only about the answer to the particular problem, but also about the time required to solve the problem using that strategy and the accuracy of the strategy in answering the problem. This information modifies the database regarding the strategy, the problem, and their interaction.

The Database

The type of information in ASCM's database is illustrated in Figure 6.5. Through their experience solving problems, children are hypothesized to gain knowledge of both strategies and problems. Knowledge of each strategy can be divided into knowledge based on data and knowledge based on projections (inferences) from those data.

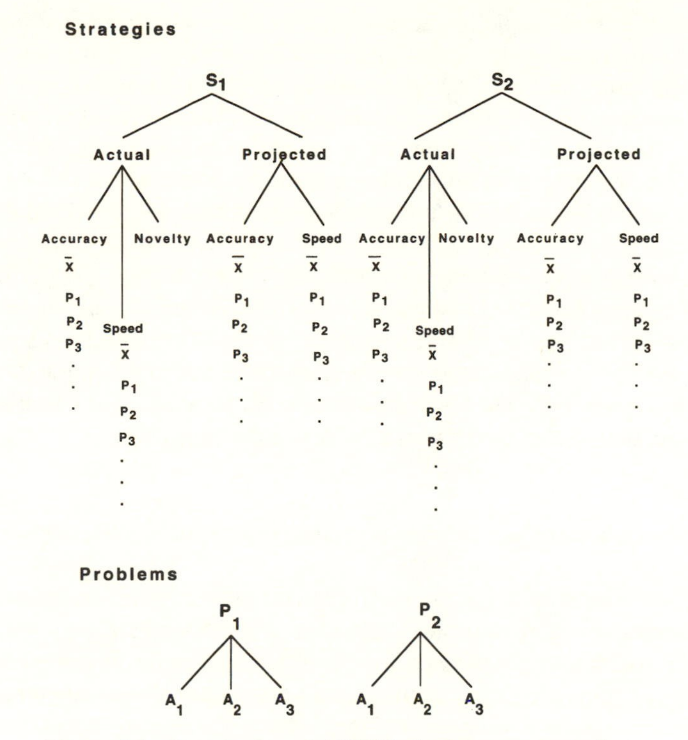

Figure 6.5. Organization of ASCM's databases on strategies and problems.

The data about each strategy include information on its past speed and accuracy aggregated over all problems *(global data)*, its speed and accuracy on problems with a particular feature *(featural data)*, its speed and accuracy on individual problems *(problem-specific data)*, and its newness *(novelty data)*. The roles of the first three types of data should be easy to comprehend, but that of the novelty data may require some explanation.

Inclusion of novelty data was motivated by an attempt to answer the question: What leads children to use new strategies in situations where existing strategies work reasonably well? For example, if a child can consistently solve a problem by using the sum strategy, why would the child ever try the min strategy on the problem? ASCM deals with this issue by assigning novelty points to newly discovered strategies. These novelty points temporarily add to the strength of new strategies, and thus allow them to be tried even when they have little or no track record. With each use of a new strategy, some of its novelty strength is lost, but information about its speed and accuracy is gained. This leads to the strategy's probability of use being determined increasingly by the expanding database on its effectiveness. If the new strategy proves useful, the strength contributed from the database more than offsets loss of the novelty points. If the new strategy does not work well, it gradually decreases in use.

The idea that novelty could be viewed as a kind of strength was suggested by the observation that people (especially children) are often interested in exercising newly acquired cognitive capabilities (Piaget, 1970). Its inclusion in the simulation was motivated by the realization that without a track record, a newly acquired strategy might never be chosen, especially if effective alternatives were available. The idea of novelty points also provides a potential account of utilization deficiencies, that is, of how children come to choose novel strategies even when the strategies do not at first enhance performance (Bjorklund & Coyle, 1995; Miller & Seier, 1994).

Whenever ASCM is presented a problem, it uses data on the performance each strategy has generated in the past to make projections concerning how well the strategy is likely to do now. If a strategy has never been used on a particular problem, ASCM's projections are based solely on global and featural data. If the strategy has never been used on the particular problem or on any problem with that feature, only global data are used to derive the projection.

The Model's Operation

ASCM is implemented as a running computer simulation; its operation proceeds as follows:

1. At the beginning of its run, ASCM knows only the two strategies that are most common among 4-year-olds—retrieval and the sum strategy—and basic procedures for choosing strategies, for collecting data on the outcomes they generate, and for projecting their future usefulness. These latter competencies are hypothesized to be basic properties of the human information-processing system and to be present from birth.

2. During the learning phase, the simulation is repeatedly presented the 81 basic addition facts formed by all combinations of addend values 1 to 9 inclusive. The problems are presented equally often. In the absence of data on presentation rates over the large age range being modeled, this seemed the most conservative assumption.

3. After a number of exposures to each problem (60 trials/problem in the simulation runs reported here), the min strategy is added to those initially available. This is done to correspond to the time, usually sometime during first grade, when children add the min strategy to their repertoire. The process of discovery of the min strategy is not yet modeled. Like its predecessor, the new simulation focuses on choices among existing strategies, rather than on how new strategies are constructed.

4. Strategy choices are based on the strength of each strategy (Table 6.1). This strength is a function of the strategy's past speed and accuracy on problems as a whole, on problems with features in common with the current one, and on the particular problem being solved. For new strategies, the strategy's novelty boosts its strength beyond what its past performance alone would justify.

5. A logistic equation weights data according to the amount of information they reflect. When a strategy has rarely been used on a particular problem, global and featural data are weighed most heavily. As more information becomes available about how well the strategy works on the particular problem, problem-specific information receives increasing weight, eventually exercising the largest

Table 6.1. General Equations Governing ASCM's Operation

$$\text{Strength (Strategy}_a) = f\text{ (speed, accuracy and novelty)}$$

$$P(\text{Retrieve Strategy}_a) = \frac{\text{Strength (Strategy}_a)}{\text{Strength of all Strategies}}$$

$$P(\text{Retrieve Answer}_a) = \frac{\text{Strength (Answer}_a)}{\text{Strength of all Answers}}$$

influence. The reasoning is that problem-specific information derived from a few uses of a strategy is inherently noisy, but when such information is derived from a substantial database, it is the best predictor of the strategy's future effectiveness on that problem. A similar logistic equation is used to weight data according to how recently they were generated. Again, recent performance is given greater weight because it is likely to better predict future performance.

6. Each time a problem is presented, these four types of data provide the input to a stepwise regression equation, which computes the projected strength of each strategy on the problem.

7. Probability of choosing a particular strategy is proportional to that strategy's projected strength relative to that of all strategies combined. The simulation attempts to execute whichever strategy is chosen. If a back-up strategy is chosen, it is executed to completion. If retrieval is chosen, a procedure identical to that within the distributions of associations model is followed. This means that when an answer is retrieved with associative strength that exceeds the confidence criterion, the answer is stated.

8. On trials where retrieval is tried but no statable answer is identified before the search length is reached, the model returns to the strategy choice phase and chooses among the back-up strategies. The process is the same as at the beginning of the trial, except for the exclusion of retrieval from the set of strategies under consideration (because it already was tried). Thus, the probability of a given back-up strategy being chosen at this point reflects its strength relative to that of all back-up strategies combined.

9. Probabilities of errors using the sum and min strategies are proportional to the number of counts required to execute the strategy on that problem. Errors arise through skipping or double-counting an object in the representation. Each count entails a probability of error; thus, the greater the number of counts, the more likely that an error will occur. On retrieval trials, errors arise through an incorrect answer being retrieved and having sufficient associative strength to be stated.

10. Solution times on back-up strategy trials are proportional to a constant times the number of counts that are executed. The constant is smaller for the sum than for the min strategy, because children take less time per count in counting from one than in counting from other numbers (Siegler, 1987a). Solution times on retrieval trials reflect a constant times the number of searches prior to locating a statable answer. This constant is much smaller than those used with the back-up strategies, reflecting the fact that retrieval is much faster than the sum or min strategies.

11. As in the distributions of associations model, each time an answer is

advanced, ASCM increases the association between that answer and the problem, and the increments are twice as great for correct answers as for incorrect ones. Unlike its predecessor, ASCM also adds information regarding the speed and accuracy with which the answer was generated to the database for the strategy.

12. Each execution of a back-up strategy also brings an increase in the strategy's speed and a decrease in its probability of generating an error. Thus, strategy execution improves with practice.

There are clear similarities between ASCM and the distributions of associations model; in part, ASCM is a generalized version of the principles inherent in its predecessor. Several differences between the two also should be noted, though. ASCM is smarter: It possesses mechanisms for generalizing its experience to unfamiliar problems. It also is explicit about how a broader range of strategy choices are made. Further, it is more flexible, in the sense of allowing strategies to be considered in any order.[2]

The Model's Performance

As in the tests of the distributions of associations model, the tests of ASCM's performance involved a learning phase and a test phase. During the learning phase, performance on each trial altered the database regarding strategies, problems, and answers. During the test phase, in contrast, the database remained constant, which allowed assessment of performance after the amount of experience in the learning phase.

The learning phases that were examined ranged from 60 to 1,250 trials per problem. This latter figure may at first sound high. However, to put it in perspective, 1,250 trials/problem works out to approximately 100 simple addition operations per school day over 6 years of elementary school (6 years, 180 school days/year, 81 problems). Given the torrent of addition problems that elementary school students receive from textbooks, workbooks, handouts, and fact quizzes, plus the embedding of simple addition within the multidigit addition and multiplication algorithms (a typical 3-digit by 3-digit multiplication problem entails 16 addition operations), this number does not seem unreasonable. Where not otherwise specified, the values reported for the simulation will be those attained after a learning phase of 750 exposures per problem, a point at which performance is very good but where ceiling effects are not a serious difficulty.

Parameters within the model were set on the basis of intuitive beliefs about what was reasonable; there was no attempt to optimize the parameter values. This approach reflected a general philosophy regarding the use of simulations to understand cognition. The effectiveness of many simulations is heavily dependent on particular combinations of parameter settings; in a word, they are brittle. This seems an unfortunate quality, because it leaves the model's validity dependent not only on the reasonableness of its general assumptions about structure and process, but also on the correctness of its parameter values. Meeting both criteria seems improbable, to say the least. The approach taken in ASCM, therefore, was to demonstrate that the main phenomena generated by the model would be stable over a broad range of parameter values.

The model demonstrated this type of stability, with one revealing exception: When statement of the correct answer led to increments in its associative strength no greater than the increments that occurred for statement of incorrect answers, ASCM's learning was severely slowed. The finding indicates that for reasonably paced learning to occur in the model, differential strengthening of correct answers is necessary. This seems a reasonable constraint, not just for ASCM but for a broad range of learning.

As with the distributions of associations model, ASCM can be understood in terms of how it generates variability, adaptive choice, change, generalization, and individual differences. Its performance on these dimensions highlights both similarities to, and differences from, its predecessor.

Variability

ASCM generates variability in the senses that the earlier model did. It uses diverse strategies both within and across problems. Although it tends to use strategies most often on the problems where they work best, strategy use varies within as well as between problems.

ASCM goes beyond its predecessor in generating some types of variability that the earlier model did not. In the distributions of associations model, strategies were always executed in a fixed order, with retrieval invariably being tried first. Within ASCM, in contrast, any strategy can be tried first. In practice, retrieval comes to be tried first in the large majority of cases (99% after a learning phase of 750 trials per problem). This is due to its always being the fastest strategy and usually being quite accurate when it is used. However, the same mechanism that allows the novelty points to add associative strength to a strategy also opens ASCM to situational influences that can temporarily boost the strength of competing strategies (for example, through instructions encouraging their use or through a child consciously thinking that it would be a good idea to try a particular strategy). The order in which back-up strategies are considered also varies in practice as well as in theory from trial to trial, unlike in the distributions of associations model, where their order was fixed.

Adaptive Choice

ASCM produced performance that was adaptive in the same ways as the performance generated by the distributions of associations model. Like the earlier model, it produced correlations exceeding $r = .90$ between percentage of use of back-up strategies on each problem and the difficulty of the problem.

As ASCM gained experience with problems, its strategy choices increasingly paralleled those of a group of 120 children whose arithmetic abilities were tested near the end of first grade (Siegler & Shipley, 1995). As shown in Table 6.2, at the outset of the simulation's run, its percentages of use of back-up strategies on each problem were almost uncorrelated with those of the children. However, as it gained experience, its performance increasingly resembled the children's. After 750 trials per problem, ASCM's percentage use of back-up strategies on each problem correlated $r = .93$ with that of the children. After this point, the correlations decreased, for a reason that is easy to understand. After a learning phase

Table 6.2. Correlations Between ASCM's and Children's Performance on Each Problem

	Learning Trials per Problem				
Measure	60	250	500	750	1,250
Percentage of Errors	.27	.78	.85	.85	.50
Mean Solution Times	.12	.55	.77	.90	.81
Percentage of Retrieval	.06	.21	.76	.93	.78

with 1,250 trials per problem, the percentage of strategies other than retrieval was quite low (5%). This led to there being too little variance among problems to produce the very high correlations seen after shorter learning phases. Nonetheless, even in this advanced state, the simulations still produced adaptive choices much like those of children.

ASCM also made a second type of adaptive choice, the choice of which back-up strategy to use, that the earlier model did not. The adaptiveness of ASCM's choices is evident in data on probability of min strategy use on each problem, given that retrieval was not used on it. After relatively brief learning phases (e.g., 120 trials per problem), the best predictor of this conditional probability was the size of the problem's smaller addend; the smaller this value, the higher the percentage of min strategy use on the problem. After greater numbers of trials, the best predictor of percentage of min strategy use on a problem was the difference between the problem's addends; the larger the difference, the greater the percentage of min strategy use on the problem. These are the same variables that best predict children's conditional probability of min strategy use on each problem (Siegler, 1987a).

Change

Perhaps the single most essential property of a simulation of acquisition of arithmetic knowledge is that it should progress from the relatively inaccurate performance characteristic of children just beginning to add to the consistently correct performance characteristic of older children and adults. ASCM met this test; after a learning phase of 60 trials per problem, it generated 31% correct answers, whereas after a learning phase of 1,250 trials per problem, it generated 99% correct answers. As shown in Figure 6.6, this improvement did not occur in sudden jumps; rather, it came steadily with increasing experience. Children show similar gradual improvement with experience in the accuracy of their addition (Kaye et al., 1986; Siegler, 1987a).

A second important type of change involved relative frequency of use of the three strategies. On this dimension also, changes in ASCM's behavior paralleled those of children. As shown in Figure 6.7, the simulation initially used only the sum strategy and retrieval (the only strategies it knew), with the sum strategy being employed on the large majority of trials. After the min strategy was added, it became the most frequently used strategy, with the sum strategy and retrieval also being used on substantial numbers of trials. This corresponds to children's performance toward the end of first grade. Beyond this point, use of both the sum and the min strategies decreased, and retrieval became increasingly dominant, again parallel to the typical pattern of learning.

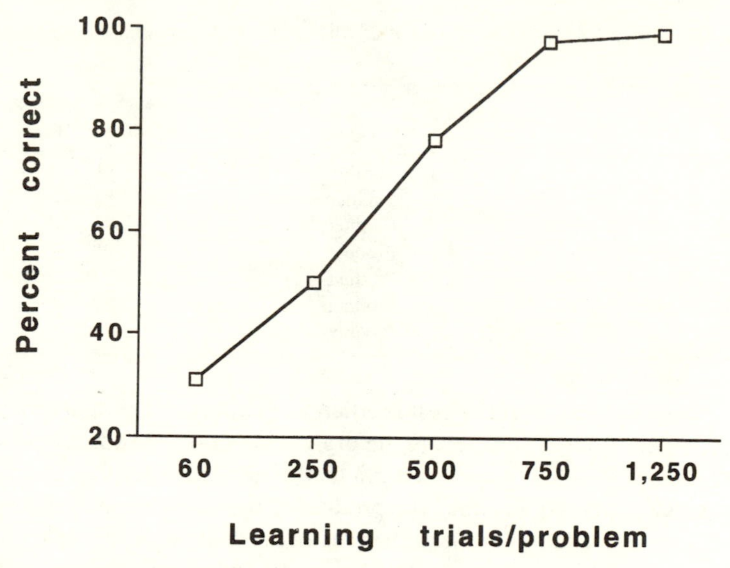

Figure 6.6. ASCM's percent correct after different length learning phases.

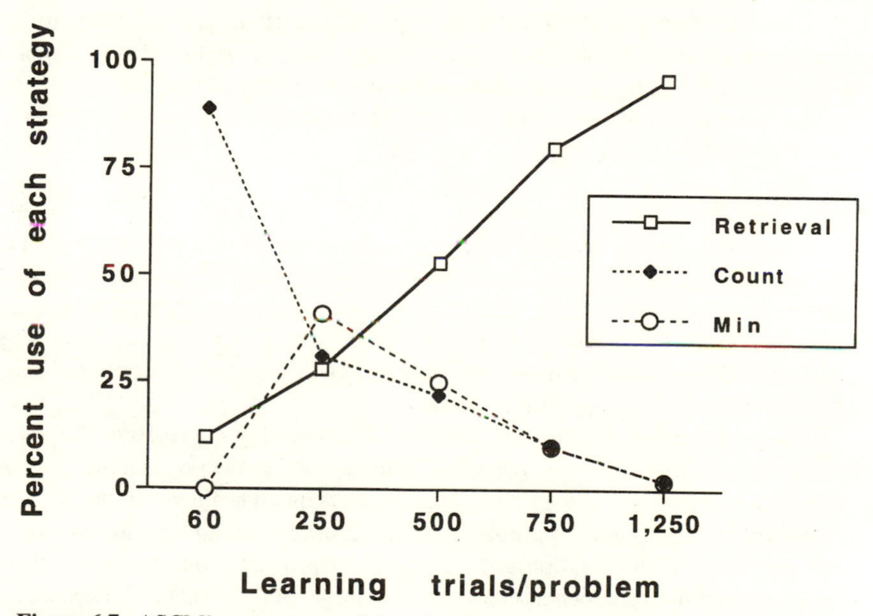

Figure 6.7. ASCM's percent use of the min strategy, sum strategy, and retrieval after learning phases of different lengths.

A third key type of progress shown by ASCM involved decrements in solution times. The overall decrement in times was produced by two factors: shifts from the slower back-up strategies to the faster retrieval approach, and faster execution of each strategy. More interesting, along with this general speedup, ASCM produced changes in the pattern of solution times on different problems, changes that paralleled those observed in children. Empirical studies of children's arith-

Table 6.3. Best Predictor of ASCM's Solution Times After Learning Phases of Different Lengths

Learning Trials Per Problem	Best Predictor	Percentage Variance Accounted for
60	Sum	91
120	Smaller addend	88
250	Product	93
500	Product	91
750	Product	79
1000	Product	93
1250	Product	92

metic have demonstrated that the best predictor of children's solution times on addition problems changes with age. In the preschool period, the size of the sum is the best predictor; in first and second grade, the size of the smaller addend is the best predictor; beyond this time, the product of the two addends tends to be most predictive. Accounting for these changes in the best predictors of solution times is a considerably more rigorous test of the simulation than simply producing faster solution times.

The simulation underwent the same type of changes in the best predictor of its solution times as did children (Table 6.3). At first, the best predictor of mean solution time on each problem was the sum of the addends. Later, the size of the smaller addend was the best predictor. Still later, product size was the most predictive variable.

Generalization

As noted earlier, a key requirement for a realistic model of arithmetic is that it be able to generalize its knowledge of strategies to new problems. A second grader who for the first time needed to mentally calculate 4 + 38 would be unlikely to know the answer, but almost certainly would choose to count from 38 rather than from 1. Inability to generalize in this way was one of the major limits of the distributions of associations model.

ASCM attempted to transcend this limit by projecting the relative effectiveness of each strategy on a novel problem. It made such projections on the basis of information about the strategy's past effectiveness on all problems in the domain (global information) and on problems with features in common with the novel problem (featural information). The features of problems that were coded by ASCM—sizes of first addend, second addend, larger addend, smaller addend, and difference between addends—provided a basis for predictions that a strategy that was the most promising on one problem might not be on another.

To test how well these projections allowed ASCM to generalize to novel problems, Siegler and Shipley conducted an experiment with it. We presented the simulation with a relatively brief learning-phase for each of 10 single-digit problems and then examined its strategy choices on the other 71 problems. We then repeated the procedure with a longer learning phase for each of the 10 problems, to see if generalization improved with experience. In this test of ASCM's ability to generalize, we were interested in whether it would choose the min strategy most often on problems where it was easiest to execute and/or where its advantage in reduced counting over the sum strategy was greatest. For example, would it choose the min strategy especially often on 9 + 1, a problem that has both of these properties.[3]

ASCM showed exactly this pattern of generalization. On the 71 problems that had not been presented during the learning phase, the best predictor of percentage of trials on which the min strategy was used was the difference between the addends. What this meant can be illustrated by considering use of the min and sum strategies on two specific problems: 9 + 8 and 9 + 1. On 9 + 8, where the difference between the addends was only one, the min strategy was used on 33% of trials during the generalization phase. In contrast, on 9 + 1, where the difference between the addends was 8, the min strategy was used on 76%.[4]

The differentiation between problems on which the min strategy was more and less helpful increased with learning; difference between the addends was a better predictor of percentage use of the min strategy on each novel problem after a longer learning phase than after a shorter one. This made sense, because with greater experience on familiar problems, the model could more accurately estimate the strategies' likely effectiveness on each novel problem. Even after the moderate length exposure, however, ASCM produced patterns of generalization quite similar to those shown by children.

Individual differences

Both the distributions of associations model and ASCM suggested that differences among good students, not-so-good students, and perfectionists could arise through child-to-child variation in peakedness of distributions of associations and in confidence criteria (Siegler & Campbell, 1989). The good-student pattern could arise from a combination of peaked distributions of associations and a wide range of confidence criteria. This would lead to frequent use of retrieval, because the highly peaked distributions would result in consistent retrieval of an answer that had sufficient strength to exceed most confidence criteria and therefore to be stated. This would ordinarily be the correct answer, which would lead to the highly accurate performance of the good students. The not-so-good student pattern would arise from flat distributions of associations and low confidence criteria. This would generate inaccurate performance, because incorrect answers would often be retrieved, and medium or low amounts of retrieval, depending on how low the confidence criteria were relative to the flat distributions of associations. The perfectionist pattern would arise from peaked distributions and very high confidence criteria. The peaked distributions of associations would lead to accurate performance, but the very high confidence criteria would lead to low frequencies of retrieval, because only the most peaked distributions would have an answer with enough associative strength to be stated.

To test this interpretation, Siegler and Shipley (1995) created three forms of ASCM. The forms differed only in their values on the two parameters hypothesized to underlie the individual differences: probability of correct execution of back-up strategies (which influenced the peakedness of distributions that were

Table 6.4. Performance Generated by ASCM Simulations of Individual Differences

Group	% Correct	% Retrieval
Good Students	96	84
Not-so-good Students	76	76
Perfectionists	96	69

formed) and range of confidence criteria. The simulation of the not-so-good students' performance executed back-up strategies less accurately than did the simulations of the perfectionists' and good students' performance, which were identical to each other in accuracy of execution of these strategies. The confidence criteria of the not-so-good students were consistently low, those of the perfectionists consistently high, and those of the good students included both low and high values. Other than these two parameter values, the simulations of the three groups were identical.

Variations in the two parameter values proved sufficient to account for the individual differences. As shown in Table 6.4, ASCM's simulation of the not-so-good students produced lower percentages correct than its simulations of the good students and perfectionists, which did not differ. Also as with children, ASCM's "good student" simulation produced the greatest amount of retrieval, its "not-so-good student" simulation the next most, and its "perfectionist" simulation the least. The simulations thus illustrated how the qualitatively different patterns of performance observed in children could arise through parametric variations within the same basic model of performance and learning.

Conclusions

Science progresses not only through increasingly precise description of an increasingly broad range of phenomena, but also through iterative efforts to explain the phenomena. Formal models are critical to this effort, because they indicate the range of phenomena that can be accounted for at any one time, and thus provide a benchmark against which the successes and failures of new explanations can be measured. Such models never have the solidity of facts and, somewhat unsatisfyingly, are never complete. Still, they are valuable, because they make clear where we are, both in relation to where we have been and in relation to where we'd like to be.

Many formal models of choice, particularly those aimed at explaining the choices of adult humans and nonhuman animals, have been aimed at identifying simple mathematical formulas for describing people's choices. Rational choice theory, the matching law, and the availability heuristic are prominent examples. The conciseness and precision of these models makes them useful points of comparison, and they do predict aggregated choices quite well. However, the models do not account for variability and change. To the extent that these phenomena are important, the usefulness of the models is limited.

Developmental models of choice have paid considerably more attention to variability and change. Metacognitive models depicted choices in terms of an executive processor that used explicit, conscious knowledge about cognitive capacities, strategies, and situational variables to decide which strategy to use. Change in this knowledge was hypothesized to lead to better choices among the strategies. The metacognitive approach was useful in identifying choices among strategies as a critical issue to be explained. However, the assumption underlying the approach that strategy choices are in general produced by explicit, rational understanding of situations, capacities, and strategies seems unlikely to be true.

The distributions of associations model recognized a broader range of variability: variability not just in strategies known to each child but also in answers associated with the problem and in individual children's application of their knowledge to the task of choosing strategies. Within this model, choosing whether to use a back-up strategy or retrieval reflected an interaction between the organization of the strategies and the peakedness of the distribution of associations for the particular problem. Changes in the peakedness of the distribution of associations altered the frequency with which each strategy was selected, as well as the speed and accuracy of performance. The key insight embodied within the distributions of associations model was that intelligent strategy choices did not require an intelligent executive processor. The model also was more explicit than the metacognitive models about how strategy choices are made and about the factors that contribute to changes in the choices. However, it also was too inflexible, too limited in the range of choices it explained, and incapable of generalizing its strategy choices to new problems.

ASCM expanded the range of phenomena that could be explained yet further. It not only attempted to account for variability in strategies, answers, and individual patterns of performance, but also for variability in the order in which strategies were considered. Its choices among the strategies made use of a considerably broader range of data—not just associations between problems and answers, but also global, featural, local, and novelty data about the strategies themselves. These data allowed ASCM to make adaptive choices on novel as well as familiar problems and to choose between alternative back-up strategies as well as between use of retrieval and use of some back-up strategy. Relative to its predecessors, ASCM also specified a larger set of contributors to change in strategy choices—not just changes in the peakedness of the distributions of associations, but also changing knowledge about all of the types of data regarding strategies that contribute to adaptive choices at any one time. The key insight was that the principles used by the distributions of associations model to choose between retrieval and a back-up strategy could be used to choose among any set of strategies and that the principles provided a basis for generalizing to novel problems as well.

ASCM provides a precise account of how children choose among existing strategies. However, it leaves unanswered a critical question: How are new strategies discovered? Evidence regarding children's discovery of new strategies is presented in the next chapter.

Notes

1. The values for each associative strength linking a problem and answer in Figure 6.3 were derived empirically from an overt-strategies-prohibited experiment reported in Siegler and Shrager (1984). In that experiment, children were presented addition problems and asked not to use any strategies but rather to just state the first answer that came to mind. They were also given a time limit too short for them to use backup strategies on the problems. The associative strength values in Figure 6.3 reflect the percentage of children who advanced each answer on that problem. Thus, for 2 + 1, 7% of children advanced the answer "1," 5% said "2," 79% said "3," and so on. Peaked distributions were ones where most children advanced a single answer (invariably the correct one); flat distributions were ones where no one answer predominated.

2. One further similarity between ASCM and the distributions of associations model is that both were written in symbolic programming languages. In each case, this was largely a pragmatic decision, reflecting the ease of simulating the type of sequential strategies used in arithmetic, rather than any principled conviction that symbolic modeling techniques are inherently more appropriate than neural networks for modeling strategy choices. Indeed, Anumolu, Reilly, and Bray (1992) demonstrated that neural network models also can effectively model strategy choices. Their simulation showed variability in strategy choices and changes in performance with experience that resembled the developmental data of Bray, Saarnio, Borges, & Hawk (1993) that were being modeled. It is interesting that the strategy choices of this neural network model were based on two of the three aspects of each strategy's database that are used to generate choices within ASCM: accuracy and novelty.

3. It might seem that using the min strategy would always be more advantageous than using the sum strategy, because it always involves less counting. However, at the time when children learn the min strategy, they are much more practiced at counting from one than from other starting points, and do so more accurately and efficiently. Thus, the advantage of the min over the sum strategy is not as great as the savings in number of counts would suggest. Some problems at first are solved more quickly via the sum strategy (Siegler & Jenkins, 1989).

4. Because these novel problems had no associative strengths connecting them to answers, retrieval could not be used on the generalization problems. Thus, in this particular run of the simulation, the min strategy was the fastest strategy available.

7

How Children Generate New Ways of Thinking

Cognitive variability ultimately depends on people's constructing novel ways of thinking even when we already possess reasonable alternatives. If we did not supplement existing approaches with new ones, there would be no variation in the approaches we use to solve a single problem, nor any need to choose adaptively among the alternatives. But how do we generate new approaches, and what leads us to do so when existing approaches already are adequate? This is the focus of the present chapter.

Despite the obvious importance of constructing new ways of thinking, we know little about how the process occurs. For every study focusing on how children generate new approaches, there must be a hundred that focus on how the thinking of different-age children differs.

Both conceptual and methodological considerations have contributed to this imbalance. Conceptually, the staircase approaches that have been dominant for the last 30 years have depicted generation of new ways of thinking as a rare event, too rare to be studied systematically. The outcomes of the generative process could be observed, as in the studies of age-related differences in reasoning, but not the generative process itself.

Methodologically, standard developmental approaches, whether cross-sectional or longitudinal, are not well suited to studying the process of change. Developmental psychologists' reliance on such approaches in part reflects the conceptual blinders imposed by the staircase conceptions of development. If generation of new approaches is a rare event, then these methods might be the best possible. Expedience also plays a role; cross-sectional methods in particular are cheaper and easier to use than methods more specifically designed to get at the process of change. Habit also plays a role; the standard methods are so prevalent, and have been for so long, that they almost inevitably are the first methods that come to mind when thinking about how to study a developmental issue.

However, they are not the only methods for studying development, nor the ones best suited to studying change processes. An alternative approach that seems especially promising for studying change is the *microgenetic method*. In the first part of this chapter, I describe this approach and its potential for advancing our understanding of cognitive development. Later, I present a set of microgenetic studies that illuminate how children discover new strategies when they are working individually, how they discover new strategies when they collaborate with other children, how conceptual understanding constrains the new procedures that children attempt, and how varying conditions of learning influence the change process.

Microgenetic Methods

A key characteristic for any method aimed at studying change is that it examine changes *while they are occurring*. Most methods used to study cognitive development do not meet this requirement. They are based on the strategy of trying to infer how a change occurred by comparing behavior before and after the change.

Unfortunately, this indirect strategy leaves open a very large number of possible pathways to change. Changes in children's thinking often do not proceed by the most direct route imaginable. For example, Karmiloff-Smith (1984) examined children as they repeatedly drew maps showing how ambulances should drive to hospitals. Examination of the set of maps drawn by each child showed that children often first drew efficient and informative maps, then regressed to drawing ones with considerable redundancy, then returned to the earlier efficient and informative depictions. Without examining performance as it was changing, the short-lived regressions would not have been detected. Thus, learning about the endpoints of change, though useful, is no substitute for detailed examination of changing competence.

This criticism often has been leveled at cross-sectional methods, but it applies equally to most longitudinal approaches. Examining the same child at one- or two-year intervals is informative regarding stability over time of the child's performance relative to that of other children. However, with regard to how change occurs, such longitudinal approaches are only slightly more informative than cross-sectional studies with equally infrequent sampling of performance. The same criticism holds for hybrid cross-sectional/longitudinal approaches, such as cohort sequential designs. They allow examination of differences among cohorts, as well as stability of individual differences, but again do not provide the density of information needed to understand the change process. The time between observations is simply too great.

A Definition of Microgenetic Methods

Microgenetic methods have three key characteristics: (a) observations span the period of rapid change in the competence of interest; (b) the density of observations is high relative to the rate of change in the competence; and (c) observations are subjected to intensive trial-by-trial analysis, with the goal of inferring the processes that gave rise to the change (Siegler & Crowley, 1991).

The second characteristic is especially important. Densely sampling changes while they are occurring allows the kind of fine-grain temporal resolution needed to inform our understanding of change processes. It provides the data needed to discriminate among alternative hypotheses about what actually goes on during periods of rapid change, rather than limiting understanding to what can be inferred from performance before and after them. The difference is analogous to that between two depictions of a hurricane: snapshots of a tidy, small town before and after a hurricane, and a movie depicting the town during the hurricane, as well as before and after it. What we would like is the movie; what we ordinarily get is the snapshots.[1] By densely sampling individual children's changing competence, microgenetic designs move us in the direction of movies of how change occurs.

Two variants of the microgenetic approach have been used. One is to choose a task from the everyday environment, hypothesize the types of experiences that typically lead to changes in performance on it, and provide a higher concentration of such experiences than would otherwise occur (e.g., Butterfield & Albertson, 1995; Butterfield, Siladi, & Belmont, 1980; Siegler & Jenkins, 1989). The other involves presenting a novel task and observing children's changing understanding as they interact with it (e.g., Karmiloff-Smith, 1992; Kuhn, Amsel, & O'Laughlin, 1988; Schauble, 1990). Both variants can yield data about the fine structure of change that could not be obtained via other methods. For example, studies using each approach have shown that previously hypothesized transition strategies in fact are not used, and have documented the existence of short-lived transition strategies that no one had hypothesized (Karmiloff-Smith, 1984; Siegler & Jenkins, 1989).

It might be objected that the changes examined in such microgenetic studies occur over minutes, days, weeks, or months, rather than years, and that they therefore address issues of learning rather than development (Liben, 1987). Several considerations militate against this argument, however. Important commonalities seem to underlie changes occurring on radically different time scales (Granott, 1991; 1993; Werner, 1948). The more precise our understanding of changes at any time grain, the better the chance of progress in identifying commonalities in changes at different time grains and thus of understanding long-term, as well as short- and medium-term, changes. It surely is better to have high quality information about some types of changes than about none. Finally, many of the most striking "developmental" phenomena involve differences in learning at different ages (as in the differences in learning of syntax at different ages documented by Johnson & Newport, 1989). Regardless of whether microgenetic methods are viewed as providing information about learning or about development, they allow us to compare the ways in which changes occur at different ages.

A Brief History of Microgenetic Methods

The concept of microgenetic methods and the rationale for using them go back at least as far as two of the forefathers of developmental psychology, Heinz Werner and Lev Vygotsky. As early as the mid-1920s, Werner was performing what he termed *genetic experiments*. These were experiments aimed at depicting the unfolding of successive representations that made up psychological events.

For example, Werner (1925) described how repeated presentation of highly similar tones led to increased perceptual differentiation of the tonal space. Although his own microgenetic studies focused on change within a single stimulus presentation or a single experimental session, he also noted that the approach could be applied to processes that continued over hours, days, or weeks (Werner, 1948).

Vygotsky (1978) agreed with Werner's arguments favoring this method, and argued more generally for studying concepts and skills "in the process of change" (p. 65). He condemned the usual practice of examining procedures whose development was essentially complete, commenting, "Previous investigators have studied reactions in psychological experiments only after they have become fossilized" (p. 68). As an alternative to such desiccated research strategies, Vygotsky advocated studying changes while they are happening.

In the ensuing years, a variety of investigators who agree on little else have advocated increased use of this approach. Consider the following testimonials from Piagetian, Vygotskyian, and information-processing oriented researchers:

> The most appropriate method for tracing the evolution of a process such as this is a method which permits the subject to have the opportunity for repeated learning experiences in order to activate his existing schemes and to increase the opportunity for interaction between these schemes and the emergent schemes which result from interaction with the problem environment. The unfolding of the subject's behavior during these repeated sessions constitutes what might be termed a microgenesis, or in other words, a telescoping of the much longer time span of macrogenetic development. (Inhelder et al., 1976, p. 58; translated from French)

> When it is possible to utilize microgenetic analysis, it has the great advantage of allowing the investigator to observe the genetic roots and the final form of a strategy within a single session. When one observes a subject during all phases of strategy development, one can better identify the transitional processes and limit alternate explanations. (Wertsch & Stone, 1978, p. 9)

> When questions about transition processes are central, the microgenetic approach seems to be the method of choice. (Siegler & Jenkins, 1989, p. 103)

It is not difficult to see why the method would appeal to those interested in understanding the process of change, regardless of their theoretical orientation. The microgenetic approach can reveal the steps and circumstances that precede a change, the change itself, and generalization of the change beyond its initial context.

Consider an example of the type of information the method can yield regarding the steps preceding a change. Karmiloff-Smith (1984) noted a consistent finding in microgenetic experiments she had conducted. Representational growth frequently followed success rather than failure. That is, children often stopped using approaches that had been producing success on the task and began using alternative approaches instead. Only direct observation of ongoing change could have yielded this type of information.

Next, consider an example of how the approach can yield information about the change itself. Lawler (1985) intensely observed his daughter's growing understanding of arithmetic, tick-tack-toe, and LOGO in the half year following her sixth birthday. He noted a number of insights and discoveries in the course of her learning and found that they tended to occur when two or more competing conceptualizations were suddenly realized to be sufficient to solve the same problem. As he put it, " The elevation of control was *not* necessity driven, but rather derived from the surprising confluence of results where no such agreement between disparate structures was expected" (p. 63). This view, quite different from the usual stereotype of discovery, illustrates the type of nonintuitive ideas that can emerge from intensive observation of changes.

Now, consider an example of the way in which the microgenetic approach can inform our understanding of how changes are generalized beyond their initial contexts. Kuhn and Phelps (1982) examined 10- and 11-year-olds' experimentation strategies over an 11-week period (one session per week). They found that even after children discovered a systematic experimentation strategy, they continued to use a variety of unsystematic strategies as well. This was true of literally every subject in their study. Schauble (1990) reported similar results with the same age group over eight weekly sessions on a different scientific reasoning problem, and found that the variability was present within as well as between subjects, and at times even within the same subject on a single trial. This variability in experimentation strategies was paralleled by variability in beliefs about the causal status of variables in the problems. Often, children performed a valid experiment to test the effect of a factor, recognized that the results indicated that the factor had no effect, yet later in the session indicated that the variable did matter. Schauble described such beliefs as "appearing finally to fade rather than conclusively being rejected" (p. 52). Adults are no different; they too continue to use less good approaches after they have discovered better ones (Kuhn, Garcia-Mila, Zohar, & Andersen, 1995). Again, it is difficult to see how such information could have been obtained without intense observation and analysis of changing competence.

Current Status

With all of these testimonials and positive examples, one might expect microgenetic experiments to be extremely prevalent. In fact, there are relatively few, perhaps 30 to 40 depending on the stringency of the definition of the term *microgenetic.*

The reason for the relative paucity of such experiments is not hard to grasp: They are time consuming and difficult to conduct. The children must be tested individually to obtain the type of detailed data that are essential for trial-by-trial analyses of performance. In studies involving repeated sessions, experimenters must exhibit considerable skill, ingenuity, and charm to keep children interested in the task. Determining when specific events (e.g., first use of a new strategy) occurred for each subject requires poring over the videotaped record of performance and, in cases where explanations are obtained on each trial, coding large numbers of verbal statements. In addition, the amount of time required for children to make a given change often is difficult to anticipate, variable across individuals, and heavily dependent on the fit between the capabilities of the children tested and the demands of the task. Given these difficulties, it is in some ways surprising that any such studies exist.

More than simply existing, however, the prevalence of such studies is growing. One reason is the increasingly widespread realization that there is something important to explain here, that children quite often generate new ways of thinking. Another is the availability of high-quality, relatively inexpensive videocassette recorders that have made such studies easier to conduct. Another reason is that expanding knowledge of the typical course of development has made possible better estimates of the most appropriate age groups for such studies. However, the most important reason is that it is increasingly evident that the value of the data yielded by microgenetic approaches more than compensates for the difficulties of running them. They can yield higher quality evidence about the process of change than can conventional developmental methods.

A Conceptual Framework for Thinking About Change

Using microgenetic methods forces us to think seriously about the dimensions along which changes occur. Five dimensions that seem particularly important are the *path, rate, breadth, variability,* and *sources* of change. Subsets of these dimensions have been examined within stage-based studies (e.g., Case, 1985; Piaget, 1952a), psychometrically based studies (e.g., Collins, 1991; McCall, Applebaum, & Hogarty, 1973), and training studies (e.g., Beilin, 1977; Field, 1987). The types of data on change yielded by microgenetic studies, however, require consideration of all of them. In this section, each dimension is briefly described. The examples in the rest of the chapter illustrate how the dimensional analysis can be used to study cognitive change.[2]

The Path of Change

One basic issue concerns whether children progress through a sequence of qualitatively distinct understandings on their way to mature competence, and if so, what the qualitatively distinct understandings are. This issue has been considered most often in the context of research on stages and sequences. For example, Flavell (1971) noted that one of the four main assumptions of stage theories is that children progress through an invariant sequence of qualitatively distinct knowledge states on their way to mature understanding of many concepts.

Describing the path of change becomes more complex when, as is often the case, individual children think about a given concept in multiple ways for a prolonged period of time. In such instances, cognitive growth is as much about shifting frequencies of existing ways of thinking as about discovery of new approaches. The combination of microgenetic methods and assessment of strategy use on each trial can be particularly helpful under such circumstances for studying the path of change. Together, they can yield information regarding when each child begins to use a new strategy of interest, whether short-lived transition strategies emerge shortly or not so shortly before the strategy of interest, and whether the new strategy is substituted for a particular previous approach or whether it to some degree reduces the percentage of use of all alternative approaches.

The combination of microgenetic methods and trial-by-trial assessments also facilitate efforts to address another issue regarding the path of change: that of U-shaped curves (Strauss, 1982). Development often follows paths that no one would imagine beforehand. Regressions in thinking about a given task are not uncommon (e.g., Bowerman, 1982; Grannott; unpublished; Karmiloff-Smith & Inhelder, 1977; Mehler, 1982), though their meaning remains quite controversial (Klahr, 1982; Stavy, Strauss, Orpaz, & Carmi, 1982). Densely sampling behavior while it is rapidly changing and assessing behavior on a trial-by-trial basis can help in documenting the prevalence of such (often brief) regressions, can indicate the conditions under which they occur, and thus can suggest why they occur.

The Rate of Change

A second basic issue regarding change is the rate at which it occurs. Flavell's (1971) analysis of stage theories referred to their stance on this issue as "the abruptness assumption." Relative to other approaches, stage theories depict important changes as occurring rapidly. Learning theories often reflect the opposite assumption—that changes occur only gradually.

Microgenetic studies are particularly well suited to examining this dimension of change, because they involve repeated presentation of the task to the same children and because the sessions are close enough in time to provide fine-grain information on the rate of change. In the context of strategy construction, such studies can tell us how quickly a new strategy comes to be used consistently after it is first employed on a given class of problems. For example, if children first use the min strategy on problems with one big and one small addend, how quickly do they come to use it consistently on such problems?

The Breadth of Change

Once children construct a new way of thinking, how widely do they generalize it? Flavell (1971) labeled the basic assumption of stage theories on this issue "the concurrence assumption." The idea was that many cognitive capabilities that share a common underlying logic are acquired close in time.

Subsequent research has shown that the concurrence assumption is not generally viable. A great many factors influence the timing of each acquisition, and broad unities in the timing of change have been difficult to identify (though see Case & Okamoto, 1996, and Halford, 1993, for some exceptions).

Thus, consideration has turned to whether understanding of a given task tends to be acquired in unified or piecemeal fashion. For example, when children acquire a new strategy, do they immediately apply it to all problems on which it is applicable, do they at first use it only on the types of problems on which it was discovered and later extend it to other types of problems, or do they at first overextend it and later restrict it to problems where it is especially advantageous? Again, microgenetic methods can provide crucial evidence, because of their dense sampling of the performance of individuals, both when they construct the new strategy and after.

The Variability of Individual Change Patterns

Issues regarding individual variation in change patterns have been investigated primarily within long-term longitudinal studies of individual differences (e.g., Applebaum & McCall, 1983; McCall et al., 1973; Nesselroade, 1990). Such studies have depicted cognitive changes at the relatively aggregated level of stability of overall test performance or factor structure, rather than in terms of specific cognitive processes. They also have examined performance at widely separated sessions. Thus, they have provided a useful overview of the stability of individual differences over time, but have been less helpful for understanding individual variation in the change process itself.

In contrast, most depictions of the development of understanding of specific concepts and problem-solving skills have ignored variability among individuals. They have characterized changes in unqualified terms that imply that the path, if not the rate, of change is universal. The monolithic character of these depictions seems unlikely to have sprung from any deep conviction that all children progress through the same path of change. Instead, it seems attributable to traditional methods not yielding sufficiently rich data to differentiate among individual children's change patterns, and to investigators therefore having little to say about variation in them. Microgenetic methods yield richer data regarding the path, rate, and breadth of change, which allows more precise depiction of individual differences along all three dimensions.

The Sources of Change

Issues regarding sources of change have been focused on most often within training studies. These studies have shown that many types of experiences can lead to change: exposure to rules, feedback, or both; observational learning; peer interaction; cognitive conflict; meaningful cover stories, stimuli, or both; and so on. Training studies have been less informative, however, regarding how the changes occur. The emphasis has been on outcomes: percentage of children who learn, stability of the learning over time, whether the learning transfers to untrained tasks, and whether it withstands counter-suggestions, rather than on the way that the transition is accomplished.

Many microgenetic studies resemble training studies in that they involve providing experiences that might promote cognitive growth and determining whether they do so. However, the trial-by-trial assessments of thinking that often are part of microgenetic studies allow them to yield useful data not only regarding what children learn, but also regarding how the learning occurred. For example, training studies might indicate that receiving feedback can lead to conservation learning. Microgenetic analyses also yield this type of information, but provide additional types as well. In particular, they can indicate whether exposure to the feedback leads children to progress through qualitatively distinct knowledge states; whether it gives rise to beneficial but short-lived transition strategies; whether different types of thinking coexist and continue to be expressed for substantial periods of time; and whether learning tends to be specific to individual problems or is general across classes of problems. Put another way, they indicate how sources of change exercise their effects.

The remainder of this chapter illustrates some of the ways in which microgenetic methods can advance understanding of each of these dimensions of change, and thus how they can contribute to a comprehensive and differentiated understanding of the change process.

Strategy Discovery in Addition

Even when children already know effective strategies for performing a given task, they often discover additional approaches. For example, when 6-year-olds discover the min strategy or decomposition as a strategy for adding small numbers, they usually can already add by counting from one, and often can retrieve answers to many problems as well. The key issues in such situations are how children discover the new strategy and how they come to choose it over previously learned approaches.

To address these issues, Siegler and Jenkins (1989) examined discovery of the min strategy. Neither teachers nor parents usually teach this strategy (Resnick & Neches, 1984). Instead, it appears that children discover it in the course of solving addition problems. Consistent with this hypothesis, most children discover it sometime during first grade, which is typically the first year in which they have substantial experience adding numbers. Thus, presenting slightly younger children, 4 1/2- and 5-year-olds, with concentrated experience solving addition problems seemed likely to elicit discovery of the new strategy and to parallel the circumstances under which it is discovered in the world outside the laboratory.

Siegler and Jenkins' microgenetic experiment involved two parts: pretest and practice. The purpose of the pretest was to identify children who could add via the sum strategy (the standard count-from-one approach) but who did not yet know the min strategy. Children were presented problems with addends from 1 to 5. They were asked after each trial how they solved that problem. In another part of the pretest, they were asked to recommend to a hypothetical younger child possible ways of adding numbers. After each suggestion, the experimenter asked, "Suppose they didn't want to do it that way; can you think of another way they could do it?" This continued until the subject indicated that the hypothetical other child could just do what he or she wanted.

The children who were selected to participate in the study were those who did not report counting from a number other than one on any of the pretest addition problems, did not give evidence of doing so on the videotapes, and did not recommend doing so to the hypothetical younger child. To guarantee reasonable prior knowledge of addition, the participants also needed to answer correctly at least 50% of the pretest addition problems.

This selection procedure led to 10 children being selected for participation in the training period. Of the 10, 8 finished the entire 11-week practice phase. One child did not finish because she took the experiment so seriously that she became upset when she could not generate the correct answer. The other child did not finish because of the opposite problem; he became bored and stopped trying. All of the data presented here are from the eight children who completed all phases of the experiment. As a group, they correctly answered 78% of the pretest addition problems. The sum strategy and retrieval were their most frequent approaches—they used them on 43% and 34% of pretest trials, respectively.

Children who met the pretest criteria then participated in an 11-week practice period. During this time, they were presented roughly three sessions a week, seven problems per session. The first seven weeks of the practice period were spent on *small-number problems*, problems with addends 1 to 5. A number of children discovered the min strategy during this period, but none generalized it very widely. Therefore, in Week 8, they were presented *challenge problems*, problems such as 22 + 3, on which counting from 1 and retrieval would work badly, but on which the min strategy would work well. The idea was to offer both a carrot for use of the min strategy and a stick to not use other approaches. In Weeks 9 to 11, the children were presented a mixed set of problems. Some were small number problems, some were challenge problems, and some were *medium-size problems* (larger addend ≥ 6, 8 ≤ sum ≤ 13).

Throughout the experiment, children's strategies were classified on a trial-by-trial basis, using both videotapes of overt behavior and immediately retrospective verbal reports. The advantages of this procedure for studying strategy discovery were that it allowed identification of the first trial on which each child used the new strategy, of the experiences that led up to the discovery, and of how the child generalized the new strategy beyond the context of its initial use.

To provide a general sense of performance at different points in the practice phase, sessions were grouped into trial blocks, with each block including five successive sessions. In the first trial block, children were correct on 80% of trials; by the last, they improved to 96% correct. Speed also improved, from a mean of 11 seconds per problem in the first trial block to a mean of 9 seconds per problem in the final block. (These numbers were computed on small number problems, which were the only ones presented throughout the experiment.)

As shown in Table 7.1, each child used at least five strategies. This variability was present within sessions as well as across them, and within a single problem presented in different sessions. The children who were quicker and more accurate at addition tended to use the more advanced strategies more often. The relation was far from perfect, though. For example, Whitney, the child who used retrieval the most often, was only average in her percentage of correct answers.[3] She often retrieved answers, but quite often they were wrong. Conversely, Jesse, the child who was the fastest and most accurate over all problems, was not very high in percentage use of retrieval.

The frequency of use of each strategy also changed over the sessions. As shown in Figure 7.1, the most marked changes were increasing use of the min strategy and decreasing use of the sum strategy.

Most important, seven of the eight children discovered the min strategy. This allowed us to examine what the discoveries were like, what led up to them, and how they were generalized beyond their initial context.

Table 7.1. Percentage Use of Each Addition Strategy by Each Child

Child	Sum	Retrieval	Shortcut Sum	Finger Recognition	Min	Guessing or Unknown	Counting from First Addend
Brittany	43	6	9	19	21	1	—
Christian	31	10	27	25	1	2	—
Danny	65	1	6	13	—	14	—
Jesse	—	23	68	1	2	4	—
Laine	69	5	1	6	1	17	—
Lauren	40	40	8	—	6	6	—
Ruth	13	42	9	8	17	3	6
Whitney	5	61	5	5	18	5	—
Total	34	22	17	11	9	6	1

Note. Data from Siegler & Jenkins (1989).

Discovery of the Min Strategy

Children differed greatly in how long they took to make the discovery. The first child to use the min strategy did so in her second session, and the second child in her fourth. At the other extreme, one of the eight children never discovered the strategy, and another first used it in the 29th of his 30 sessions.

The children's protocols convey a qualitative sense of what strategy discovery in this context was like. The following is the protocol from one girl's discovery trial:

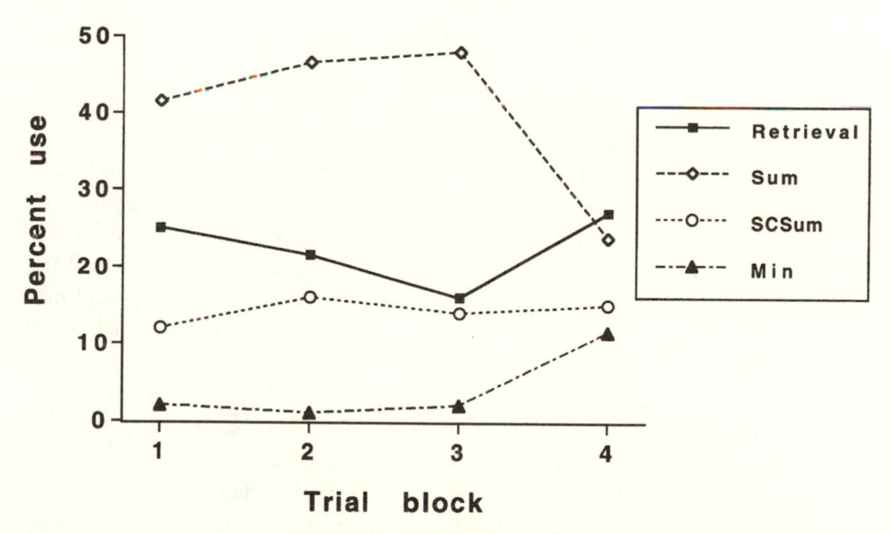

Figure 7.1. Change over trial blocks in 4- and 5-year-olds' use of addition strategies. Each trial block corresponds to 5 training sessions, the second the next 5, etc. Data from Siegler and Jenkins (1989).

Experimenter: *How much is 4 + 3?*
Ruth: *7.*
E: *OK, that's right, very good, how did you know that?*
R: *Counted—I started from 4.*
E: *Started from 4—can you tell me why you started from 4?*
R: *Because that's—that's—because I can um—can—I don't have to count a very long ways if I start from 4, I just have to do 3 more.*

As Ruth's example illustrates, some of the discoveries (slightly more than half) were accompanied by impressive insight into the new strategy's advantages. Others were not, however; several children either were unable to say what they had done or said they just remembered the answer, despite audible evidence to the contrary on the videotape of the trial.

The particular problems on which children first used the min strategy were quite diverse and seemed representative of the total set of problems: 2 + 5, 4 + 1, 3 + 9, 1 + 24, 5 + 2, and 4 + 3 (two children). The sums, larger addends, and smaller addends of these problems all were representative of the overall group of problems that the children encountered.

In contrast, the solution times that accompanied discovery of the min strategy did deviate markedly from performance on other trials. They were on average twice as long (medians of 18 vs. 9 seconds). The additional time on discovery trials reflected longer pauses before answering, more false starts in trying to use the new approach, and slower counting while executing the new strategy.

Changes Leading Up to the Discovery

Changes in Solution Times

The longer solution times that were present on the discovery trials were also evident on the trials just before the discovery. This could be seen in the performance of the five children who first used the min strategy on some trial other than the first trial of the session. On the trial just before the discovery, the median reaction time (RT) was just as long as on the discovery trial—18 seconds, versus an overall median of 9 seconds. A similar picture emerged for all trials before the discovery but within the same session. Here the median was 14 seconds.

What did these long times reflect? One possibility was that they were unusually difficult problems. This was not the case, however; 14 of the 16 problems preceding the discovery but within the same session were small-addend problems. Another possibility was that for some reason, children had unusual difficulty solving the problems in the session of discovery, and that this motivated them to generate an alternative approach. Again, however, this was not the case. The five children who discovered the strategy on a trial other than the first in the session had answered 12 of 16 problems correctly up to the point of discovery; 3 of the 5 children made no errors before the discovery. This, together with the fact that two other children used the min strategy for the first time on the first trial of a session indicated that incorrect answers are not necessary to motivate discovery of a new strategy. However, the long solution times just prior to the discoveries suggest a heightening of cognitive activity even without impasses to motivate it.[4]

Transition Strategies

Several earlier theories of the development of addition skills suggested that counting from the first addend mediates the transition from use of the sum to use of the min approach (Neches, 1987; Resnick & Neches, 1984; Secada, Fuson, & Hall, 1983). This view was based on a rational analysis of differences between the sum and min strategies. Within these theories, after a period in which children only counted from one, they would realize that counting from the first addend would yield the same answer. This would lead them to count from 4 on 4 + 2 and from 2 on 2 + 4. Later still, they would have the further insight that they could produce the same answer more efficiently by counting from the larger addend, regardless of whether it was first or second.

Microgenetic data are especially valuable in addressing such hypotheses regarding transition strategies. In the particular case, the data did not support the view that counting from the first addend mediated discovery of the min strategy. Only one of the eight children in the experiment ever counted from the first addend on trials where it was the smaller addend. Even this child already had used the min strategy before counting from the first addend. The other six children who discovered the min strategy never used the count-from-first-addend approach.

Another strategy that was not anticipated, but that was observed, seemed a better candidate as a mediator of discovery of the min strategy. This was the *shortcut sum* approach. Both conceptual and empirical considerations suggested that it was a likely transition strategy.

Conceptually, the shortcut sum strategy resembled the sum strategy in certain ways and the min strategy in others. On a problem such as 2 + 4, it involved counting "1,2,3,4,5,6," as opposed to the standard sum approach of counting "1, 2," "1,2,3,4," "1,2,3,4,5,6," or the min approach of counting "4,5,6." Thus, it was like the sum strategy in that it involved starting with one and counting up to the sum. It was like the min strategy in that it eliminated the need to quantitatively represent the addends twice.

There were also empirical grounds for viewing the shortcut sum approach as transitional to the min strategy. Of the seven children who ever discovered the min strategy, five started using the shortcut sum approach shortly before their first use of the min strategy. Two children first used it two sessions before using the min strategy, one first used it one session before, and two first used it earlier in the same session. Together, these conceptual and empirical considerations suggest that the shortcut sum strategy may mediate many children's discovery of the min strategy.

Generalization

Once children discover a strategy, they still need to extend it to the full range of problems on which it is useful. In the case of the min strategy, generalization was slow. Most children rarely used it in the sessions following their discovery. This was not due to their being able to retrieve answers to the problems and thus having no reason to use the new approach. In the first five sessions after each child's discovery, the child used it on an average of only 12% of the trials on which he or she used any counting strategy (min, sum, or shortcut sum). This slow generalization was why we decided to present the challenge problems.

Effects of Encountering Challenge Problems

The situation changed dramatically when the challenge problems were presented in Week 8 of the study. When children encountered problems such as 2 + 21, which were easy to solve via the min strategy but almost impossible (for them) to solve via retrieval or counting from one, they greatly increased their use of the min approach. Use of the min strategy, which had been below 20% of counting strategy trials jumped to 60% of such trials (Figure 7.2). Even more striking, the gains continued over the last three weeks of the experiment, when a mix of small-number problems, medium-number problems, and challenge problems was presented. Use of the min strategy reached 90% of counting trials by the end of the study.

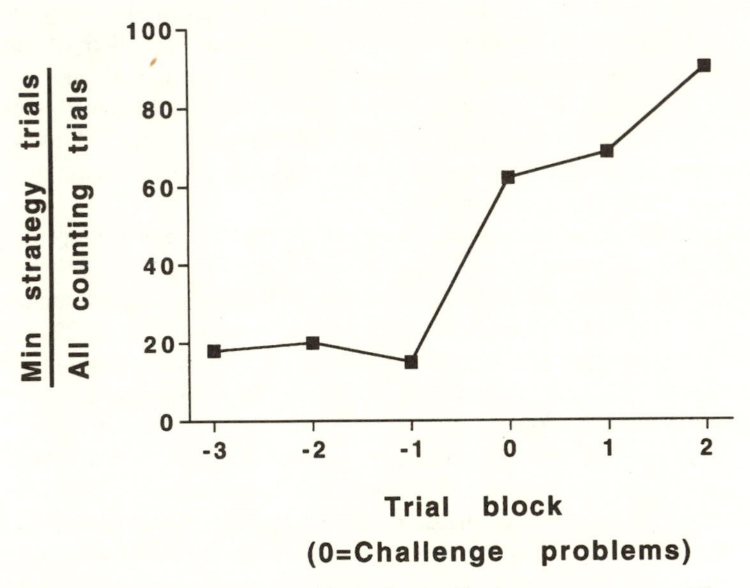

Figure 7.2. Change over trial blocks in use of min strategy among children who had discovered the min strategy by that time. Trial blocks are graphed relative to presentation of the challenge problems; thus, the -1 trial block involves the proportion of min strategy use for those children who used the min strategy at least once in the 5 sessions before the challenge problems were presented, the -2 trial block shows the proportion of min strategy use among children who used it at least once 6 to 10 sessions before the challenge problems, etc. Each child's data are included from the session of the child's first use of the min strategy. Data from Siegler and Jenkins (1989).

Effects of Consciousness of the Discovery

As previously noted, children varied greatly in the degree of insight that accompanied their discoveries. For purposes of analysis, we divided children into six who were aware that they had counted (they noted it in their verbal reports) and three who were not. (Two children first used the min strategy without explicit awareness and later with such awareness. Their performance after the initial use but prior to the conscious discovery was classified with that of the "low awareness" group. Their performance following the conscious discovery was classified with that of the "high awareness" group.)

Degree of awareness of the new strategy proved predictive of its frequency of use. Children who showed such awareness used the min strategy more, and their use increased with experience (Figure 7.3). Those who did not show such awareness never used the new strategy often.

One Child's Discovery

Microgenetic methods can yield enough data to allow analysis of the change processes of individual children. Describing a given child's discovery and generalization process may convey a sense of what these processes were like.

Brittany was 4 years, 9 months, at the beginning of the study. Her performance on the pretest suggested relatively poor knowledge of addition compared to that of other children in the study. She had the second lowest percentage correct of the eight children, 65%, and her median solution time was the second slowest, 13.6 seconds.

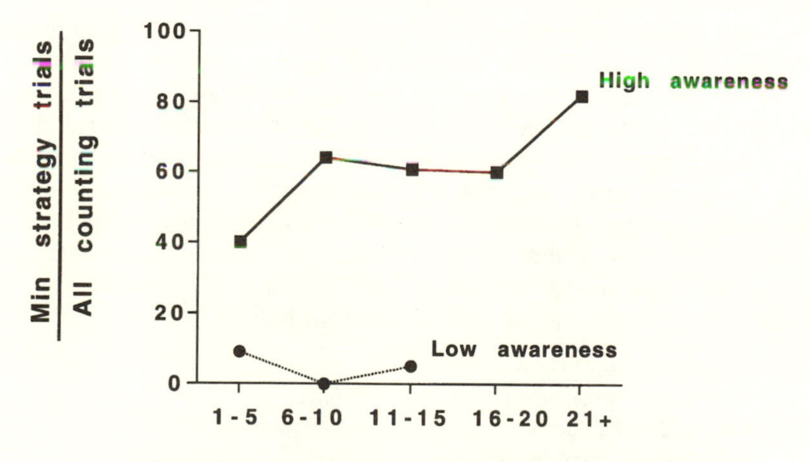

Figure 7.3. Change in proportion of use of min strategy among children who did or did not indicate awareness of having used that strategy. Each child's data are included from the point of the child's first use of the min strategy. The low awareness line stops at the 15th session, because no children continued to use the min strategy with low awareness for more sessions than that. Data from Siegler and Jenkins (1989).

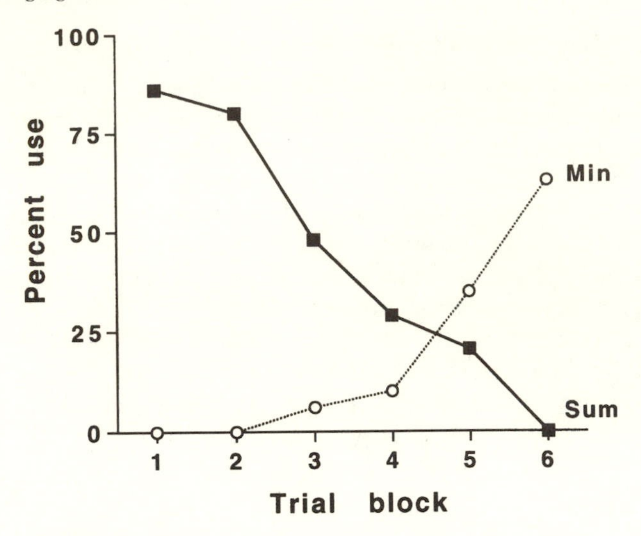

Figure 7.4. Changes in Brittany's use of the min and sum strategies. Data from Siegler and Jenkins (1989).

During the practice phase, her performance improved considerably. She answered correctly on 87% of the small number problems, much better than her 65% correct on such problems on the pretest. Her solution time on such problems decreased by 4 seconds to 9.6 seconds. She dealt especially effectively with the challenge and medium-size problems presented in the last four weeks of the experiment, answering 90% of them correctly.

A major source of her improvement came through increasing use of the min strategy and decreasing use of the sum approach (on trials where she counted) (Figure 7.4). At the outset of the experiment, Brittany usually used the sum strategy. In the 12th session she discovered the min strategy. At first, she relied on it only occasionally. However, when she encountered the challenge problems, she began to use it much more often and continued to do so thereafter. Eventually, she stopped using the sum strategy altogether, and used the min strategy on most trials.

Brittany first used the shortcut sum strategy in the same session in which she first used the min approach. Her initial use of the shortcut sum strategy was on the first trial of the session. The trial proceeded as follows:

E: *How much is 2 + 1?*
B: *One* (puts up finger), *two* (puts up a second finger on the same hand, then puts up a third finger on the other hand). *Oh that's easy, that's three.*
E: *How did you know that?*
B: *I never counted.*
E: *You just knew it?*
B: *I knew it . . . I just blobbed around.*

Brittany again used the shortcut-sum approach on the second problem of the session, 5 + 1. On the third problem, 4 + 1, she put up her fingers and recognized that there were five. On all three problems, her answers were fast as well as accurate, none requiring more than six seconds.

On the fourth trial of the session, Brittany discovered the min strategy:

Experimenter: *OK, Brittany, how much is 2 + 5?*
Brittany: *2 + 5*—(whispers) *6, 7—it's 7.*
E: *How did you know that?*
B: (excitedly) *Never counted.*
E: *You didn't count?*
B: *Just said it—I just said 6 after something—7—6, 7.*
E: *You did? Why did you say 6, 7?*
B: *Cause I wanted to see what it really was.*
E: *OK, well—so did you—what—you didn't have to count at 1, you didn't count 1,2,3, you just said 6,7?*
B: *Yeah—smart answer.*

Although Brittany seemed excited by her initial use of the min strategy, and complimented herself for giving a "smart answer," she did not immediately use the approach at all often. In the remainder of Session 12 and in Sessions 13, 14, and 15, she used the sum strategy 16 times, but never used either the shortcut sum or min approaches. Then, in Session 16, for no apparent reason, she used the two new strategies on all seven trials. She used the shortcut-sum approach six times and the min strategy once. This might have been expected to signal a permanent change in strategy use, but once again did not. In Sessions 17 to 24, Brittany used the min strategy on only 6 of the 49 trials and the shortcut-sum strategy on only 1 (as opposed to 15 uses of the sum strategy).

The situation changed dramatically with presentation of the challenge problems. On the seven challenge problems that Brittany received, she used the shortcut-sum approach three times and the min strategy three times. In the first session after the challenge problems, she used the shortcut-sum approach on three of seven trials. In the following session, she used the shortcut-sum strategy twice and the min strategy four times in seven trials. In the remaining seven sessions, she used the min strategy on 36 trials, the shortcut-sum strategy on 4, and the sum strategy on only 1.

The example illustrates the way in which microgenetic studies can contribute to theories of learning and discovery. The back and forth, now-you-see-it, now-you-don't quality of Brittany's use of the min and shortcut-sum strategies are not what anyone would posit on intuitive grounds. The role of the shortcut-sum strategy as a mediator of discovery of the min strategy also was surprising. It had not been proposed despite previous detailed task analyses and a number of cross-sectional and longitudinal studies of development of the min strategy. Only through following the change process on a trial-by-trial basis did the findings emerge.

Goal Sketches and Constraints on Strategy Discovery

To our surprise, none of the children ever attempted strategies inconsistent with the principles underlying addition. The situation was reminiscent of the classic conversation in *The Memoirs of Sherlock Holmes*:

Holmes: *But there was the curious incident of the dog in the nighttime.*
Colonel Ross: *The dog did nothing in the nighttime.*
Holmes: *That was the curious incident.*

In Siegler and Jenkins (1989), the curious incident was that not one child tried on even a single trial any strategy that violated the principles underlying addition. Several illegitimate strategies might have been tried, because they were procedurally similar to children's most frequent approach, the sum strategy. One example of such an illegitimate strategy is putting up fingers corresponding to the first addend twice and then counting all of the fingers. In superficial ways, this strategy is more like the sum strategy than is the min strategy. Counting the first addend twice, like the sum strategy but unlike the min strategy, involves counting from one, making three separate counts (for the two component numbers and the combined set), and always counting the first-mentioned addend first. Despite these superficial similarities, not one child used this or other illegitimate strategies on even one trial. This raised the question: "Why not?"

One possibility is that the strategy generation process was constrained by a *goal sketch.* Such a goal sketch specifies the hierarchy of objectives that a satisfactory strategy in the domain must meet. The hierarchical structure directs searches of existing knowledge toward subprocedures that can meet the goals, even if those subprocedures are parts of separate overall procedures. In so doing, it directs searches away from illegitimate procedures, that is, procedures that either fail to meet essential goals in the domain or that directly violate such goals. When legitimate procedures for meeting each goal have been identified, the goal sketch provides a schematic outline of how the components can be organized into a new strategy.

In the case of addition, such a goal sketch would include the information that each set being added must be represented, that a quantitative representation of the combined sets must be generated, and that a number corresponding to this quantitative representation must be advanced as the answer (Figure 7.5).

Such goal sketches, if they existed, would seem likely to be both widely useful and widely used. They could help direct search for new strategies in promising directions—that is, toward procedures that would meet essential and desirable goals of the domain. They might also keep children from trying flawed strategies that they thought of, on the basis that the strategies were not in accord with the key goals in the domain. Thus goal sketches would constitute a kind of metacognitive understanding, though one that often would be implicit. They would also provide the same type of conceptual guidance for learning as the constraints and principles that have been proposed for such domains as counting, language development, and acquisition of biological theories (Gelman & Gallistel, 1978, Keil, 1989; Markman, 1989; Newport, 1990).

But do children in fact possess such goal sketches and use them to evaluate potential new strategies? To find out, Siegler and Crowley (1994) conducted an experiment that directly assessed whether children of the age of the subjects in Siegler and Jenkins (1989) possess the type of information hypothesized to be

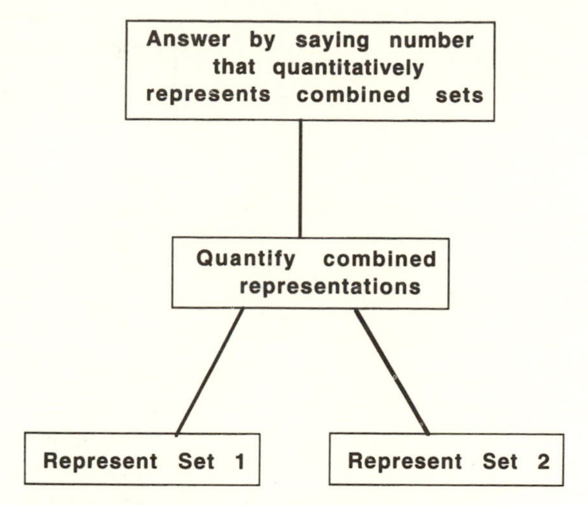

Figure 7.5. Goal sketch hypothesized to guide 5-year-olds' construction of new addition strategies.

included within goal sketches and if so, whether they can apply it to evaluating strategies that they do not yet use.

The experiment focused on 5-year-olds who either did or did not already use the min strategy. The experiment involved two sessions: a strategy use session and a strategy judgment session. In the strategy use session, children were asked to solve a number of addition problems, including ones such as 11 + 2, where children who knew the min strategy would be very likely to use it, because it was so much more effective than the available alternatives. In the strategy judgment session, children saw the experimenter demonstrate three strategies that she said had been used by students at another school. The task for the experimental subjects was to judge whether the demonstrated strategies were "very smart," "kind of smart," or "not smart." The three strategies were the sum strategy, which all children in the experiment knew; the min strategy, which some knew and some did not; and an illegitimate strategy (representing and counting the first addend twice), which was superficially similar to the sum strategy but that violated the principle that each addend must be represented once and only once. All children were presented the judgment session first and the performance session second, to ensure that no children would have had greater knowledge when they participated in the judgment session than when their own performance was examined.

As expected, the children who already used the min strategy judged it to be as smart as the sum strategy and judged both to be smarter than the illegal strategy. More interesting, the children who did not yet use the min strategy produced almost identical judgments (Figure 7.6). Clearly, children recognize the superiority of legal strategies that they do not yet use to illegal strategies that they also do not use. This finding indicated that in accord with the goal sketch hypothesis, the 5-year-olds had conceptual knowledge that allowed them to evaluate the relative merits of alternative strategies that they did not yet use.

This phenomenon is not limited to the domain of addition or to 5-year-olds. A

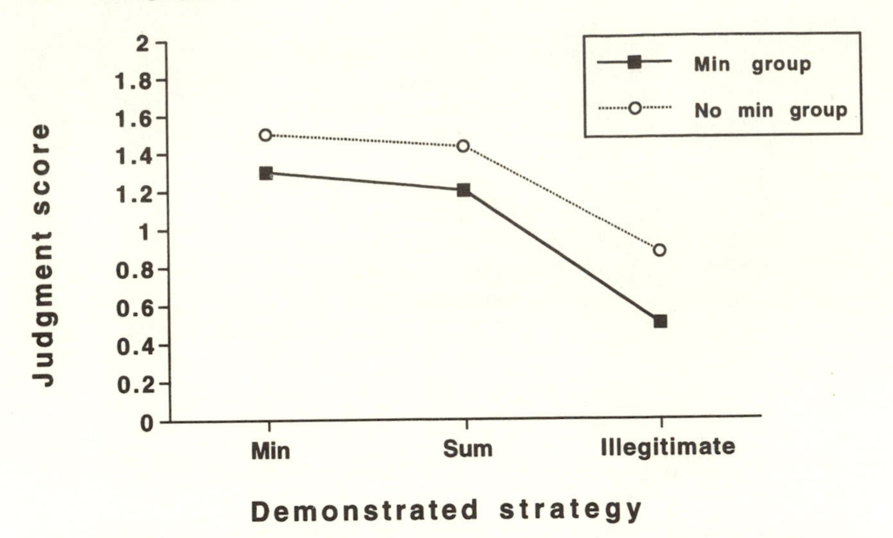

Figure 7.6. Judgments of smartness of three addition strategies that the experimenter demonstrated to 5-year-olds who did or did not use the min strategy in their own addition performance. Judgments of "very smart" were assigned a score of 2, judgments of "kind of smart" a score of 1, and judgments of "not smart" a score of 0. Data from Siegler and Crowley (1994).

second experiment in Siegler and Crowley (1994) indicated that 8- and 9-year-olds could perform similarly reasonable evaluations of tick-tack-toe strategies that they did not yet use. This relatively mundane game was chosen for study precisely because of its mundane nature. Numerical cognition may be a privileged domain; even infants have basic quantification and addition/subtraction abilities (Antell & Keating, 1983; Starkey, 1992; Wynn, 1992). This raised the possibility that goal sketches might be limited to domains in which evolutionary history has specially prepared children to learn (Carey & Gelman, 1991; Geary, 1995). Performing a parallel experiment regarding children's knowledge of strategies used to play tick-tack-toe, a game where special, evolutionarily based preparation seems extremely unlikely, allowed us to test the role of goal sketches in "ordinary" domains.

Almost all first and second graders, and about half of third graders, use the *win/block strategy* for playing tick-tack-toe, which incorporates in a transparent way the essential goals of winning and not losing (Crowley & Siegler, 1993). It involves first trying to identify a move that will produce an immediate win. If a win is not possible, children see if they can block a path by which their opponent could win on the opponent's next turn. If they can neither win nor block, they attempt to put two Xs in a row so that—if their opponent fails to block—they can win on their next turn.

By third grade, about half of children begin to use a more sophisticated approach, the *forking strategy*. This strategy includes a high level goal of trying to create a situation in which there are two separate winning paths. Even if the opponent blocks one, the player can win by completing the other. Creating the fork is not the player's only goal, however. On each turn, the player first looks for squares where a win is possible, then for squares where a block is needed, and then for possible forks (thus, the approach also could be called the win/block/fork strategy).

The experimental procedure used to test children's conceptual understanding of tick-tack-toe strategies paralleled that used to examine their understanding of addition strategies. It included two phases: a strategy-judgment phase, in which children judged the relative merits of strategies, and a strategy-use phase, in which children in the experiment played games themselves. First, during the strategy-judgment phase, third graders observed games where the moves conformed either to the win/block strategy or to the forking strategy. Children's task was to judge whether each strategy was very smart, kind of smart, or not smart. Then, during the strategy-use phase, children's own activities were examined to identify children who used the forking strategy (the *fork group*) and those who did not (the *no-fork group*). As in the addition experiment, the key data were the judgments of children who did not yet use the strategy of interest, in this case the forking strategy.

The results again demonstrated that children could accurately judge the value of strategies that they themselves did not yet use. Children who did not yet use the forking strategy, like those who did, judged the forking strategy to be very smart, much smarter than the win-block strategy that they themselves used (Figure 7.7).

These findings indicated that the type of knowledge envisioned within the goal sketch construct is not limited to "special" domains. On entirely mundane

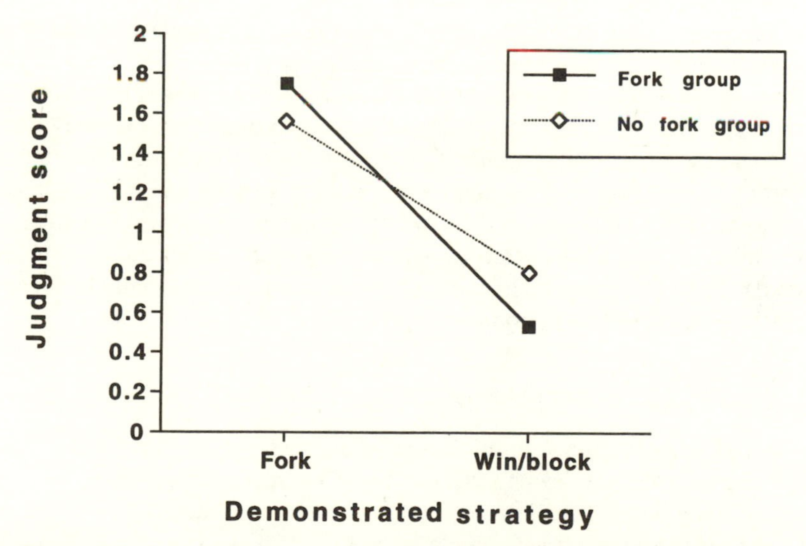

Figure 7.7. Judgments of smartness of two tick-tack-toe strategies by 8-year-olds who did or did not use the forking strategy in their own playing of the game. Data from Siegler and Crowley (1994).

tasks, such as tick-tack-toe, children also are able to anticipate the value of strategies even before they begin to use them. This is precisely the type of knowledge hypothesized to be especially useful for constraining strategy discoveries to promising avenues.

The findings raised the question: When are such goal sketches present? Present data are too limited to say with confidence, but my suspicion is that at minimum, goal sketches will be present consistently on tasks with which children have had substantial experience.

One reaction to this hypothesis might be to point out as a counter-example the buggy subtraction algorithms used by third and fourth graders (Brown & Burton, 1978; Van Lehn, 1986), or some similar case in which children use inherently flawed strategies. At first glance, use of such flawed approaches does seem like strong evidence that children lack the kind of conceptual understanding posited in goal sketches despite their having had substantial experience in the domain. Illustratively, how could a child who understood long subtraction use an approach such as the smaller-from-larger bug (subtracting the smaller number in each colum from the larger, leading to results such as 736 – 587 = 251)?

A recent application of the judgment paradigm used in Siegler and Crowley (1994), however, indicated that children who use buggy algorithms possess greater understanding than is evident in their subtraction performance (Siegler, in preparation). Virtually without exception, third and fourth graders whose subtraction performance manifested such bugs judged the correct subtraction algorithm to be superior to the buggy approach that they used, and to other buggy approaches as well. When asked to rate their confidence in their own procedure, most children who used buggy algorithms indicated that the approach they used was probably wrong. Difficulty in remembering what to do under the various situations that arise in multi-digit subtraction (borrowing from a zero, borrowing across a zero, borrowing from a number other than zero), rather than lack of understanding of the basic goals of subtraction, may underlie use of buggy algorithms.

The general point is that performance that violates principles in a domain does not necessarily reflect lack of principled understanding. Children may adopt flawed approaches as the best available alternative when they need to generate an answer and cannot access a procedure that will do so without violating one or more principles. Assessing understanding of the principles independent of requirements to execute a correct procedure may often reveal the type of conceptual understanding posited by the goal sketch construct, especially in domains in which children possess substantial experience.

How Was the Min Strategy Generated?

The data on strategy discovery and on goal sketches suggested a number of ideas concerning the processes leading to discovery of the min strategy. These ideas are currently being implemented as a computer simulation of the discovery process. Although the model is not yet complete, its central ideas can be described quite precisely.

The first step toward the simulation was a task analysis of the prerequisites for discovering the min strategy. The analysis indicated that five components were essential for executing the strategy:

1. Identifying the larger addend.
2. Reversing the addend order if the larger addend was second.
3. Quantitatively representing the larger addend by saying the number used to represent that addend in the original problem.
4. Counting on from the larger addend.
5. Keeping track simultaneously of the running total of counts and of the counts corresponding to the second addend, so that counting stops at the right point.

If children needed to master all of these skills at once, they might never discover the min strategy. However, this type of conceptual leap was unnecessary. Most 4- and 5-year-olds possess four of the five prerequisite skills: ability to identify the larger addend, reverse addend order, count on from the larger addend, and keep track of both the running total of counts and the counts corresponding to the second addend (Fuson, Richards, & Briars, 1982; Siegler & Jenkins, 1989).

The one remaining skill seems in some ways the simplest of the five. Quantitatively representing the larger addend by repeating the value of the number given in the problem (e.g., by saying "7" in 7 + 3), is superficially undemanding. However, many 6- and 7-year-olds who do not know the min strategy also lack this skill (Secada et al., 1983). None of the addition procedures used on the pretest by the 4- and 5-year-olds in Siegler and Jenkins (1989) showed such understanding. Thus, it seems likely to have posed the final barrier to discovery of the min strategy.

How might children acquire this final component? The goal-sketch construct suggested that one useful place to look was to components of existing strategies. Existing approaches need to meet the same general goals as new ones, and therefore provide procedures that can be recombined to meet the same goals in novel ways.

Consistent with this analysis, during the course of the Siegler and Jenkins study, children's execution of existing procedures changed in two ways that were likely to facilitate construction of the missing component. First, children increasingly often represented the value of each addend by just putting up that number of fingers, rather than by counting them out. If asked to solve 4 + 2, they simply put up 4 fingers rather than counting "1,2,3,4." Second, children became increasingly proficient at recognizing the number of fingers that were up. On problems such as 3 + 1, they increasingly just said "4" when they had put up 4 fingers. This suggests that in terms of the following productions, children already possessed P1 and P2 and through the mechanism of composition (Anderson, 1990), constructed P3:

P1: *IF your goal is to quantitatively represent N, THEN put up* N *fingers.*
P2: *IF your goal is to quantitatively represent* N, *AND you have put up* N *fingers, THEN say* "N" *to represent the quantity.*
P3: *IF your goal is to quantitatively represent* N, *THEN say* "N" *to represent the quantity.*

Once P3 is in place, the min strategy follows straightforwardly. The new strategy simply involves first executing P3, then executing the productions used in the short-cut sum strategy to keep track simultaneously of the running total of counts and of the counts corresponding to the second addend being counted, and finally saying whichever number is reached when that addend has been counted out.

Microgenetic methods have proved helpful in understanding how children construct strategies in many domains other than addition. The remainder of this chapter describes a few of these cases.

Self-Explanations as a Source of Strategy Construction

Training studies have always had the potential to allow detailed analysis of change. In practice, however, this potential has rarely been realized. Instead, such studies have focused on which treatments are most effective.

The way in which microgenetic analyses can enhance what we learn from training studies was illustrated in a study of number conservation (Siegler, 1995). Applying microgenetic methods to this task was of special interest because it allowed a rigorous test of the generality of one of the most consistent findings from microgenetic studies—that new strategies are acquired only gradually, even when children can provide clear and reasonable explanations of why the new strategy is superior to previously used ones. Recall the example of Ruth, the child who explained her initial use of the min strategy by noting that when she used it "I don't have to count a very long ways" and Brittany, the child who commented on her first use of the min strategy "Smart answer." They, like other children who seemed to understand the advantages of the min strategy, only gradually increased their use of it until they encountered the challenge problems. Other microgenetic studies also have consistently yielded the finding that uptake of a new strategy tends to be halting and gradual unless a very strong incentive for its use is present (e.g., Adolph, 1993; Alibali & Goldin-Meadow, 1993; Kuhn & Phelps, 1982; Kuhn et al., 1988; Schauble, 1990)

Number conservation provided a test of the generality of this finding because of the logical superiority of the new strategy to those previously available. This contrasts with other domains in which microgenetic methods have been used. Addition can be used as an example. The min strategy is more efficient than the sum strategy, in that it can be executed with fewer counts. Both are counting strategies, however, and both consistently generate the correct answer if correctly executed. It is hard to argue that one is logically superior to the other. In contrast, in number conservation, relying on the type of quantitatively relevant transformation (addition, subtraction, or doing neither) to determine whether the two rows have the same number of objects represents a different, and more advanced, logic than judging on the basis of the relative length of the rows or counting the number of objects in each and comparing the results. If sudden changes to reliance on more advanced approaches would be expected anywhere, they would be expected on tasks where the new approach was superior not only in its ability to generate correct answers, but in its whole logic.

In the experiment, 5-year-olds were first given pretest sessions to identify children who did not yet know how to solve number conservation problems. The problems presented on the pretest and in the subsequent training sessions involved three types of transformations: addition, subtraction, and null. On addition problems, one row was lengthened or shortened and an object was added, resulting in the transformed row having more objects. On subtraction problems, a row was lengthened or shortened and an object was subtracted, resulting in the transformed row having fewer objects. On null transformation problems (the traditional Piagetian problems), one row of objects was lengthened or shortened and nothing was added to or subtracted from it. On half of each type of problem, relying on the relative lengths of the rows led to the correct answer; on the other half, it led to incorrect answers.

Children whose pretest performance indicated that they did not yet know how to solve number conservation problems were then given four sessions of one of three training procedures. Children in one group received feedback alone; they were simply told on each problem whether their answer was correct. Children in a second group received feedback regarding their answers and were also asked to explain their reasoning. Children in a third group received feedback and were then asked by the experimenter "How do you think I knew that?"

This last condition, in which the child needed to explain the experimenter's reasoning, was of greatest interest. Studies of college students learning physics and computer programming have demonstrated that better learners tend to more actively explain to themselves textbook passages (e.g., Chi, Bassok, Lewis, Reimann, & Glaser, 1989). It remained unknown, however, whether the simple instruction to try to explain the reasoning of another, more knowledgeable, person would have similar effects on individuals who did not engage in the activity spontaneously. Trying such instructions with young children was of particular interest. Although young children can and do try to explain to themselves other people's reasoning, their frequent egocentrism and lack of reflection may lead them to do so less often than older individuals. If this is the case, then instructions to try to explain to oneself the reasoning of a more knowledgeable individual may be especially useful for such young children.

As hypothesized, asking children to explain the experimenter's reasoning resulted in their learning more than they did from the feedback alone or from the feedback in combination with being asked to explain their own reasoning (Figure 7.8). The differential gains were largely concentrated in the most difficult problems. Learning of children in the three groups was similar on the problems where the length cue led to the right answer; the differential effectiveness of the procedures was concentrated on the more difficult problems, where relying on the length cue led to the wrong answer.

This finding, though interesting, could have been obtained within conventional training studies. Other findings, however, could not have been obtained without the type of trial-by-trial analysis of change that characterizes microgenetic methods.

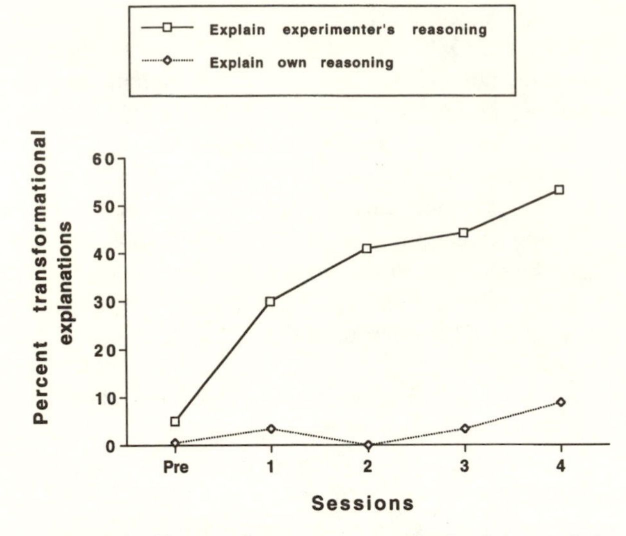

Figure 7.8. Changes from pretest to end of training period in percent transformational explanations by 5-year-olds asked to explain their own or the experimenter's number conservation judgments on length-inconsistent problems. Data from Siegler (1995).

Variability of Thinking

Even in a "logical domain" such as number conservation, a variety of ways of thinking coexisted both before and during training. Children's explanations indicated five different types of reasoning: relying on the type of transformation, relying on the relative lengths of the rows, counting the number of objects in each row, saying the objects were just moved back and forth, and saying "I don't know."

Such variability of reasoning was already evident on the pretest, before the experimental manipulations could have influenced it. Consider just the performance of children in the group that showed the most dramatic change, the group in which children were called on to explain the experimenter's reasoning (Figure 7.9). On the pretest, only 1 of 15 children in this group relied on a single strategy on all trials. In contrast, 11 of 15 used 3 or more strategies on it. The most frequent strategy was to rely on length, but a number of other strategies also were used.

Another surprising result from the pretest was that half of the children explicitly cited the type of transformation at least once. Overall percentage of citations of the type of transformation was low (9%). The low percentage was a necessary by-product of the criteria for participation in the study; children who cited the type of transformation on 25% or more of trials were excluded. Even within this sample, however, 23 of the 45 five-year-olds cited the type of quantitatively relevant transformation—addition, subtraction, or doing neither—to explain their judgments on at least one pretest trial. Thus, even before the training session

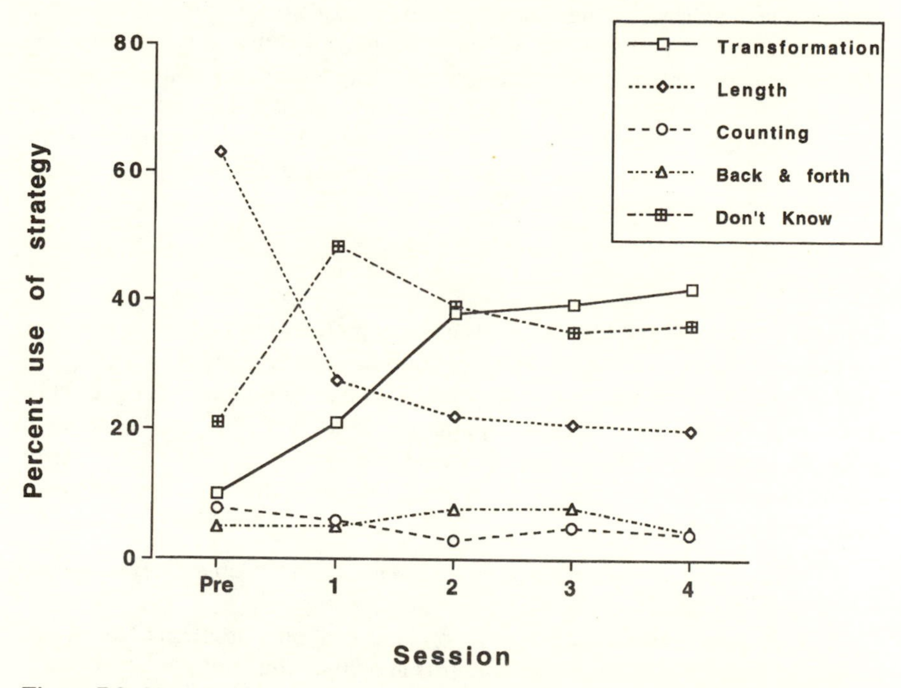

Figure 7.9. Changes over sessions in percent use of five number conservation explanations by children who were asked to explain the experimenter's reasoning. Data from Siegler (1995).

began, sophisticated transformational explanations coexisted with less sophisticated strategies, such as those based on length and counting.

This diversity of thinking continued during the four training sessions. In each of these sessions, very few children relied on a single strategy. The variability of strategy use was present throughout the training period—mean number of strategies used by each child was almost identical on the pretest, first two training sessions, and last two training sessions.

The microgenetic design also made possible detailed analysis of the process of change. The analyses described here focus on the changes of children who were asked to explain why the experimenter answered as she had, because this group showed the greatest change.

As shown in Figure 7.9, the pattern of change was much more akin to that envisioned in the overlapping-waves depiction than in the staircase one. On the pretest, children explained most of their answers by saying that the row they chose was longer (or by saying that the two rows had the same number of objects because they were equally long). When called on to explain the experimenter's reasoning in the training sessions, children cited the relative lengths of the rows much less often. In part, this was due to 50% of the experimenter's judgments not being predicted by the relative lengths of the rows. However, even when the length cue did predict the experimenter's answer, the children cited it on only 30% of trials. In the first training session, where children initially encountered the experimenter's judgments, they usually could not explain why she had answered as she had. They said "I don't know" why she generated that judgment twice as often as they cited the type of transformation to explain her reasoning. However, by the second training session, children cited the type of transformation just as often as they said "I don't know," and in the third and fourth training sessions, their most frequent explanation was to say that the experimenter based her judgment on the type of transformation.

Stability and Generalization of Learning

Children were presented identical conservation problems three times: once during the pretest, once during the first two training sessions, and once during the final two training sessions. This made it possible to determine whether once children advanced a transformational explanation on an item, they continued to do so on the same item when it was presented again—a direct index of the rate of change. In particular, the rate of change was measured through comparing two conditional probabilities:

1. P(Transformational explanation on later trial on a problem | Transformational explanation on earlier trial on that problem)
2. P(Transformational explanation on later trial on a problem | Non-transformational explanation on earlier trial on that problem)

Such comparisons were used both to examine stability of use of transformational explanations from the pretest to the training sessions, and to compare stability from earlier training sessions to later ones.

Some, but not great, stability of transformational explanations on identical items was evident from the pretest to the training sessions. On 43% of problems on which a child advanced a transformational explanation on the pretest, the child also advanced a transformational explanation when the problem was again presented during the training session. This was considerably greater than the 18% of problems on which children advanced transformational explanations in the training sessions after not having done so on the pretest. On the other hand, it indicated far from consistent reliance on transformational reasoning once it was employed, even on the identical problem.

More stability was evident across training sessions. When a child advanced a transformational explanation on a problem in one of the first two training sessions, that child did so again on 76% of trials when the problem reappeared in one of the last two training sessions. In contrast, when a child did not advance a transformational explanation on a problem presented in the first two training sessions, that child advanced such an explanation on only 13% of trials when the problem was again presented in the third or fourth training session. These data indicated that within the context of the training procedures, early use of a transformational explanation on a problem was quite predictive of later use of such reasoning on that problem. Even in this most favorable situation for demonstrating stability of reasoning, however, in which the child, the problem, and the questioning procedure were all constant, children reverted from using transformational explanations to not using them in 24% of cases.

The experimental design also allowed examination of the breadth of change—the spread of new forms of reasoning to different types of problems. There were two main types of problems: ones on which the length cue predicted the right answer (e.g., the longer row had more objects) and ones on which it did not. On the pretest, frequency of transformational reasoning was equal on the two types of problems. However, during the training sessions, children generated transformational explanations more often on problems where the longer row did not have more objects. Even the best learners in the experiment applied the logically more advanced reasoning twice as often on problems where it was necessary to account for the particular judgment of the experimenter as on problems where less advanced explanations were also consistent with the experimenter's judgment on that item. Thus, generalization of the new reasoning was quite narrow.

Individual Differences in Learning

At the level of the entire group of children who were asked to explain the experimenter's reasoning, the main changes in explanations were increasingly reliance on the type of quantitatively relevant transformation and decreasing reliance on length. The large amount of data on individual performance yielded by the microgenetic study also allowed analyses of what the changes looked like at the individual level. These analyses indicated that the main group-level change pattern did correspond to the single most common pattern of change at the individual level, but that two other patterns of change were also evident. In particular, identifying within each child's performance the type of explanation of the experimenter's reasoning that underwent the largest increase from the pretest to the last training session and the type of explanation that underwent the largest decrease over the same period indicated three distinct patterns of change: large increases in reliance on transformations and large decreases in reliance on length (8 children), large increases in saying "I don't know" and large decreases in reliance on length (4 children), and idiosyncratic patterns (3 children).

These changes in explanations proved highly predictive of changes in percentage of correct answers. The eight children in the decreased-length/increased-transformation group increased their percentage of correct answers from 49% on the pretest to 86% in the final session of the training period (Figure 7.10). The seven children in the other two groups did not show any increase; they answered correctly 52% of items on the pretest and 50% on the posttest (Figures 7.11 and 7.12). The effect was consistent over individuals within these groups. Of the eight children in the decreased-length/increased-transformation group, seven increased their percentage of correct answers by at least 30% in absolute terms from the pretest to the final training session. In contrast, zero of the seven children in the other two groups increased their percentage correct by as much as 20%.

This result left little question that the source of learning from explaining the experimenter's reasoning came from recognizing the role of quantitatively rele-

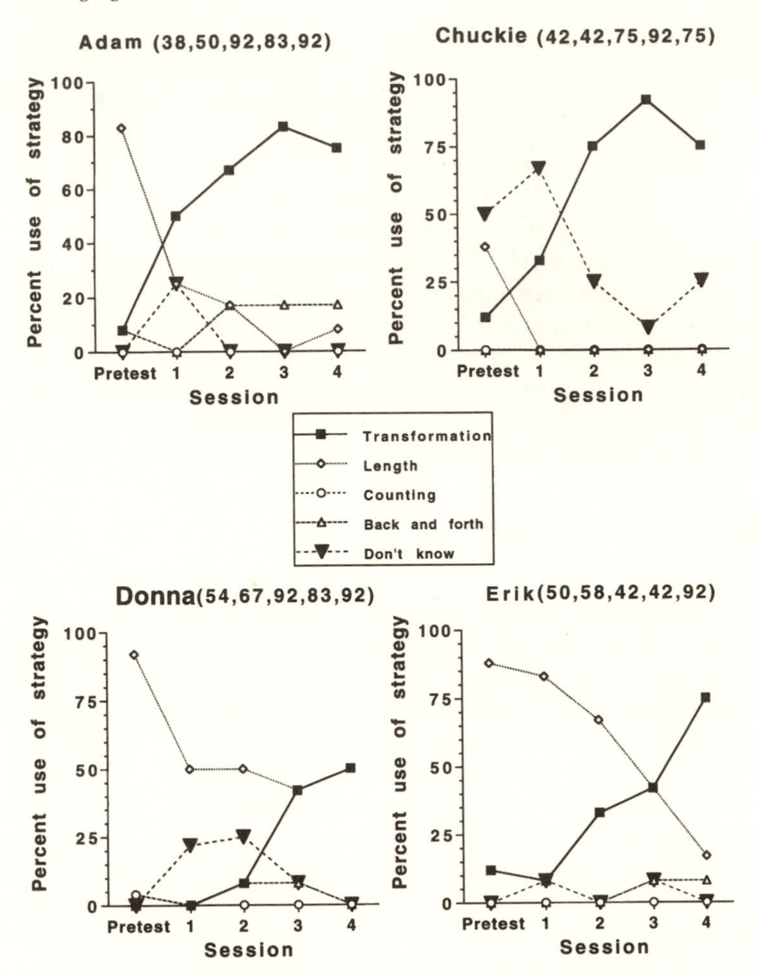

Figure 7.10. Changes over sessions in percentage use of number conservation explanations by individual children asked to explain the experimenter's reasoning. These children are in the "decreasing length/ increasing transformations" subgroup. The numbers in parentheses next to each child's name indicate that child's percentage of correct answers on the pretest and in each of the four training sessions. Data from Siegler (1995).

vant transformations in her reasoning. Those children who came to explain the experimenter's reasoning in terms of transformations substantially increased the percentage correct in their own judgments. Those children who did not change their explanations of the experimenter's reasoning in this way showed little or no improvement in the accuracy of their own judgments.

Why did some children learn and others not from the same procedure? A multiple regression analysis of pretest performance identified three significant predictors of the percentage of correct answers that each child obtained over the four training sessions. The first factor to enter the equation was number of distinct

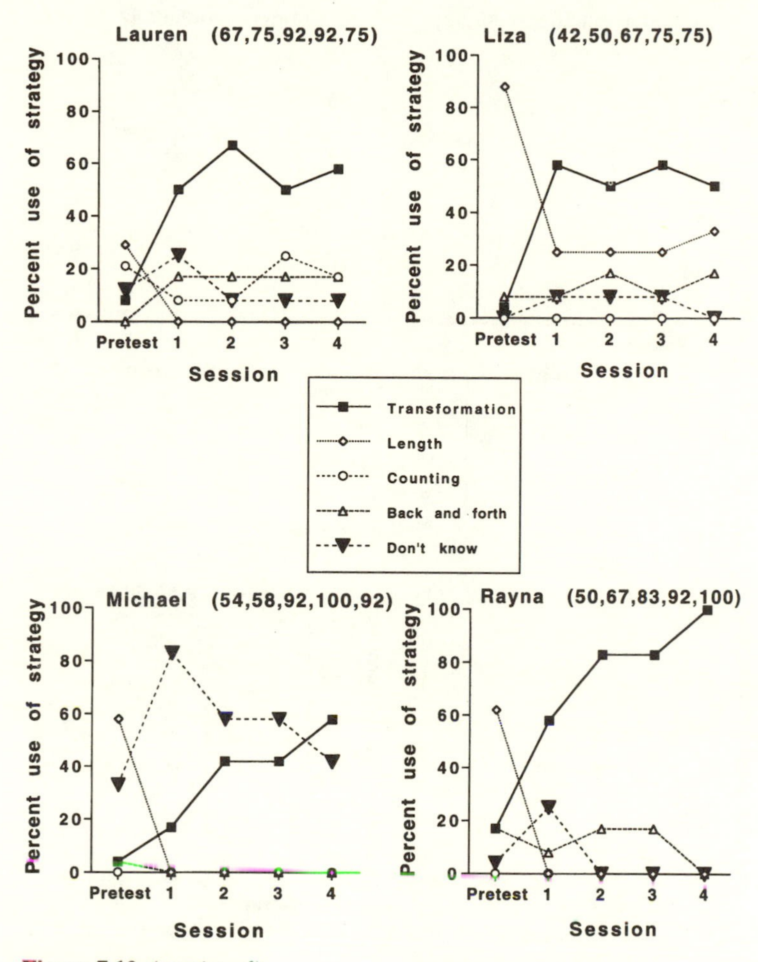

Figure 7.10 (*continued*)

explanations used on the pretest; the greater the number of distinct explanations a child advanced on the pretest, the more correct answers the child advanced during the training sessions. The second factor was whether the child ever advanced two or more explanations on a single pretest trial. Children who sometimes advanced multiple explanations on a given pretest trial learned more effectively during training. The third predictor was age; older children learned better. The three predictors accounted for 65% of the variance in children's percentage of correct answers during training.

It should be noted that the positive relation between number of distinct explanations used on the pretest and learning during the training period could not be reduced to some children already advancing transformational explanations on the pretest, and therefore being better able to learn. If this explanation were valid, the number of transformational explanations children advanced on the pretest should have predicted subsequent learning, but it did not. Nor could the relation

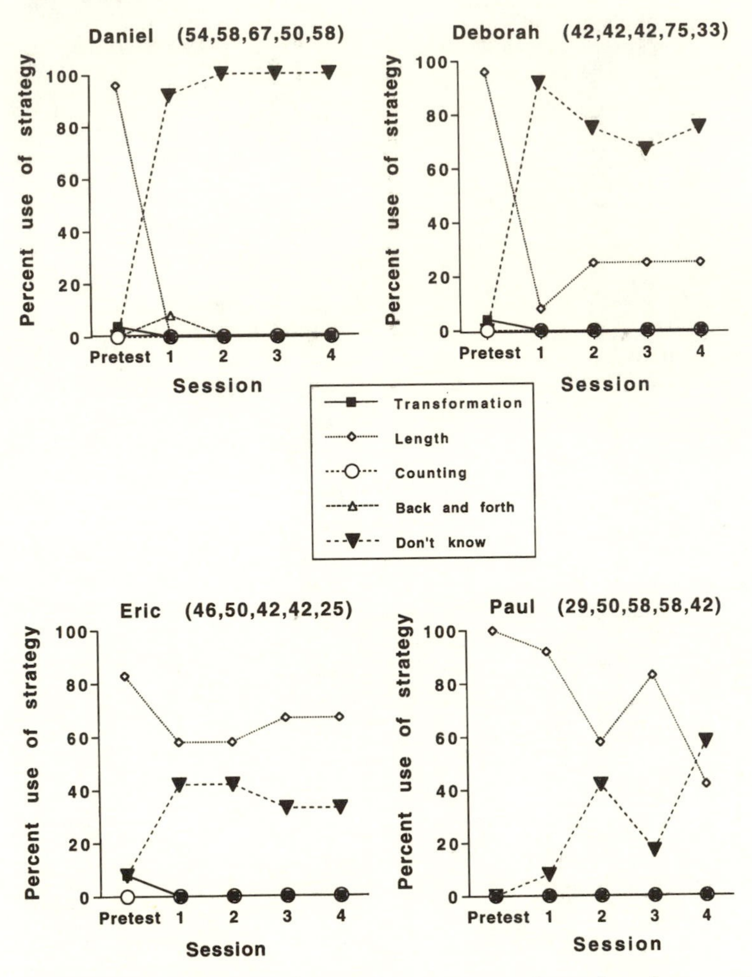

Figure 7.11. Changes over sessions in percentage of use of number conservation explanations by individual children asked to explain the experimenter's reasoning. These children are in the "decreasing length/increasing 'don't know'" subgroup.

be reduced to children who generated more correct answers during training having already been more accurate on the pretest. Had this been the case, percentage correct on the pretest should have predicted percentage correct during training. Again, however, it did not. Instead, the variability of reasoning per se, both across trials and within trials, seemed to be what predicted learning.[5]

Examination of which children generated multiple explanations within a single pretest trial revealed that the measure was related to the individual difference classifications described earlier. Among children who showed the pattern of increased-transformational-explanations/decreased-length-explanations, six of eight (75%) advanced two types of explanations on at least one pretest trial. Only

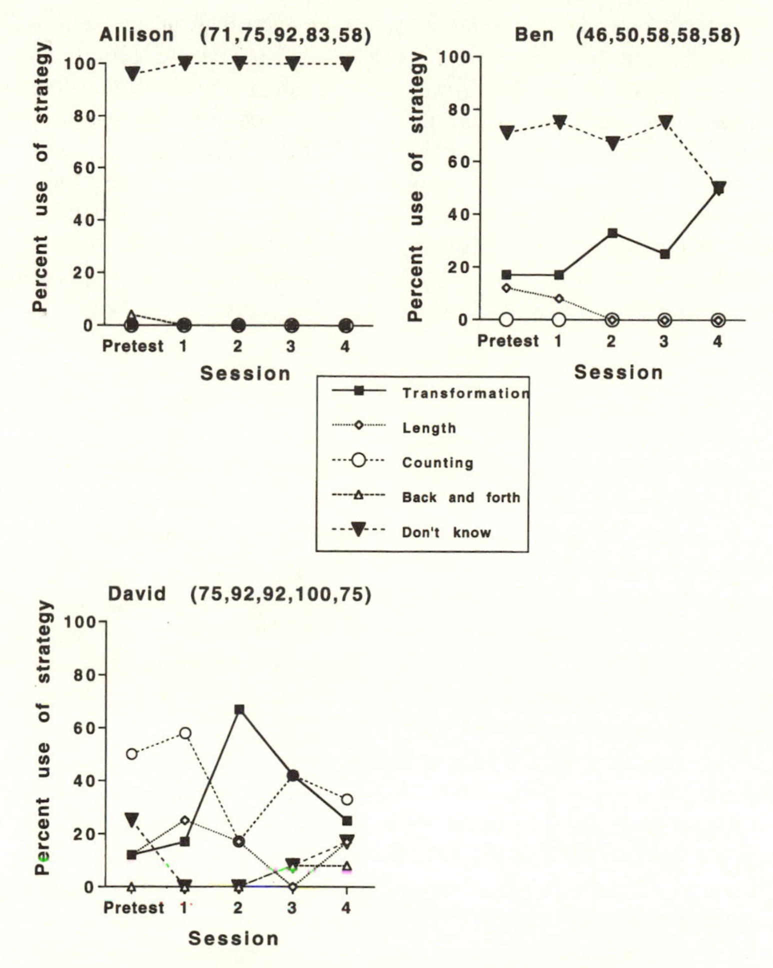

Figure 7.12. Changes over sessions in percentage of use of number conservation explanations by individual children asked to explain the experimenter's reasoning. These children are in the "idiosyncratic patterns" subgroup.

three of the other seven children (43%) did so. The difference became more striking when performance during the training sessions was included. All eight children who during training substantially increased their use of transformational explanations advanced multiple explanations on a single trial at some point during the study, versus three of seven of the other children. Over the course of the experiment, these eight children also advanced multiple explanations on considerably more trials than did the other seven children (means of 7.5 vs. 1.3 trials). In sum, generation of varied explanations on the pretest, both between and within trials, was positively related to subsequent learning.

The particular experience examined in the experiment, encouragement to explain another person's reasoning, may have general educational applications. Children as young as 5 years apparently can benefit from encouragement to understand another person's reasoning. Although they can generate useful explanations of other people's reasoning, they do not do so automatically. If they did, the request to explain the experimenter's reasoning would have been redundant with their spontaneous activity, and would not have aided learning. To the extent that young children are less likely than older individuals to generate such explanations spontaneously, but can derive similar benefits when they do so, it may prove especially worthwhile to encourage them to try to explain the reasoning underlying the behavior of more knowledgeable people, such as parents and teachers.

Collaborative Learning

Children construct new strategies not only while solving problems on their own, but also while working with others toward common goals. Some such problem solving involves scaffolding situations, in which a more knowledgeable person helps a less knowledgeable one to learn. Scaffolding occurs in the context of parents helping their children, teachers helping their students, coaches helping their players, and more advanced learners helping less advanced ones (Freund, 1990; Gauvain, 1992; Rogoff, Ellis, & Gardner, 1984; Wood, Bruner, & Ross, 1976). The goal of such interactions is for the less knowledgeable learner to construct strategies that the more advanced one already possesses.

In other situations, equally knowledgeable peers learn together. Such peer collaboration also often enhances problem solving and reasoning (Gauvain & Rogoff, 1989; Kruger, 1992; Teasley, 1995; Webb, 1991), though it does not always help (Russell, 1982; Russell, Mills, & Reiff-Musgrove, 1990; Tudge, 1992). Attempts to specify when collaboration helps learning have been hampered by lack of precise assessment of children's thinking before, during, and after the collaboration, and of the social interaction that went on during the collaboration.

To provide a more refined description of the process of change within a collaborative context, as well as to determine when collaboration aids problem solving, Ellis, Siegler, & Klahr (1993) examined children solving decimal fraction problems of the form: "Which is bigger, .239 or .47?" This task often causes fourth and fifth graders surprising difficulty.

The problem is that they often misapply mathematical rules acquired while learning previous content (Resnick, Nesher, Leonard, Magone, Omanson, & Peled, 1989). The two most common approaches are the *whole number rule* and the *fraction rule*. A child using the whole number rule would correctly judge .373 to be larger than .25, but would incorrectly judge .251 to be larger than .37. The children's explanations suggest that they are reasoning by analogy to whole numbers, where a longer chain of digits always does denote a larger number. In contrast, a fraction rule user would judge .37 to be larger than .251 but would also judge .25 to be larger than .373. This rule seems to reflect children trying to apply flawed understanding of fractional notation to the task. For example, they sometimes will say that .25 is larger than .373 because .25 involves hundredths, .373 involves thousandths, and hundredths are larger than thousandths. Alternatively, they sometimes say that .25 is larger because 1/25 > 1/373.

The Ellis et al. study involved a pretest, training, and a posttest. First, fifth graders took a pretest to identify the main way in which they initially solved such problems. On all problems, they were asked to choose the larger of two decimal fractions, each having one, two, or three digits.

The large majority of the children used one of the approaches identified by Resnick et al. on at least 80% of problems. The whole number rule was used by 63% of children, the fraction rule by 14%, and the correct rule by 15%.[6]

A few days after the pretest, the fifth graders were retested to see if they still used the same rule; about 80% did. These children were assigned to one of eight training groups. As illustrated in Figure 7.13, the groups varied in the children's initial approach (whole number rule or fraction rule), whether they received feedback, and whether they worked alone, worked with a partner who used the same initial rule, or worked with a partner who used a different initial rule.

During the training period, children received 12 problems, of the same form as on the pretest. Children who worked with a partner made an initial independent judgment on each trial, then compared their judgment to that of their partner, and then discussed the reasons underlying the judgments. At the end of the training period, all children were given a posttest, which was identical to the pretest; as on the pretest, they solved the posttest problems by themselves.

This design enabled us to address several issues:

1. Are children more likely to learn when they solve problems collaboratively than when they solve them on their own?

2. Is external feedback critical for learning in collaborative problem solving, or is the feedback produced through working with a partner sufficient to produce learning?

	Dyadic conditions			Alone conditions	
	Fraction/ whole	Fraction/ fraction	Whole/whole	Fraction	Whole
Feedback					
No feedback					

Figure 7.13. Experimental design in Ellis, Siegler, & Klahr (forthcoming). Shaded boxes indicate cells that were included in the design. The second row of the heading indicates the children's pretest rule(s). Thus, "fraction/whole" indicates that one child in the dyad used the fractions rule on the pretest and that the other used the whole number rule. Due to the relative scarcity of children using the fractions rule, and due "to zero of 55 children who were not given feedback adopting a correct rule on the posttest, no children were run in the conditions corresponding to the two unshaded rectangles.

3. Is collaboration more effective when children begin with different ways of thinking about the problem than when they begin with similar ways of thinking about it? Peers who think similarly might have an easier time seeing each other's point of view, but peers who initially think differently might more easily identify the flaws in the other person's reasoning, provide alternative ways of looking at the problem, and thus provide a basis for a solution different than either child's initial approach.

4. Do feedback and collaborative status interact so that feedback is essential for collaborators who begin with the same rule but not for ones who begin with different ways of thinking about the problem? When collaborators think differently about a problem, they may be able to detect and correct problems in the other person's thinking and thus render external feedback unnecessary.

Global Analysis

Results were analyzed at two levels: the global level of pretest-posttest changes, and the microgenetic level of how changes occurred during training. The global level analyses yielded answers to the four questions raised in the previous paragraph. With regard to the first, collaboration did prove to be helpful. Children more often answered consistently correctly on the posttest if they worked with a partner during training than if they worked alone.

The positive effects of collaboration, however, depended on external feedback also being present. Feedback was essential to learning the correct rule, both for children working in dyads and for children working alone. None of the 55 children who did not receive feedback during training used the correct rule on the posttest, whereas 49% of those who received feedback during training did. The criterion of at least 80% correct answers on the posttest problems was met by 58% of children who during training worked with a partner and received feedback, 21% of those who worked alone and received feedback, and 0% of those who did not receive feedback.

With regard to the third question, children who, during training, worked with a partner who used a different rule on the pretest did no better on the posttest than children who worked with a partner who used the same initial rule. Both did better than children who worked alone, but there was no differential effect of working with a partner who started with a different rule than one's own.

These findings imply the answer to the fourth question: External feedback was just as critical for partners who started with different rules as it was for those who started with the same rule in terms of likelihood of learning the correct rule. Partners who started with different rules were more likely to use a different rule on the posttest than on the pretest (often their partner's initial rule), but no more likely to adopt the correct rule than children who worked with a partner who started with the same rule as their own.

Microgenetic Analysis

To obtain a better understanding of how these outcomes came to be, Ellis et al. examined performance during the training session on a trial-by-trial basis. This analysis focused on the children who received feedback, because they learned more than the other children.

One striking finding, paralleling that in microgenetic analyses of learning over multiple sessions, was the variability within each child's thinking. Generation of the correct rule by no means insured its continued use. Only about one third of the children fit the prototypic patterns of generating the correct approach and then continuing to use it. Numerous other children generated it and then oscillated between it and other approaches (Figure 7.14).

Ellis et al. analyzed social aspects of the interaction as well as the answers and explanations that children generated. One factor that proved to be related to the amount of learning was the enthusiasm of the partner's reactions to the child's statements. In this context, enthusiasm meant strong interest in, rather than agreement with, the partner's ideas. Thus, the reactions that were coded as most enthusiastic were those in which a partner indicated strong agreement or strong disagreement with a child's statements, requested clarification of what the statements meant, or both.

Children whose partners reacted enthusiastically during the training session

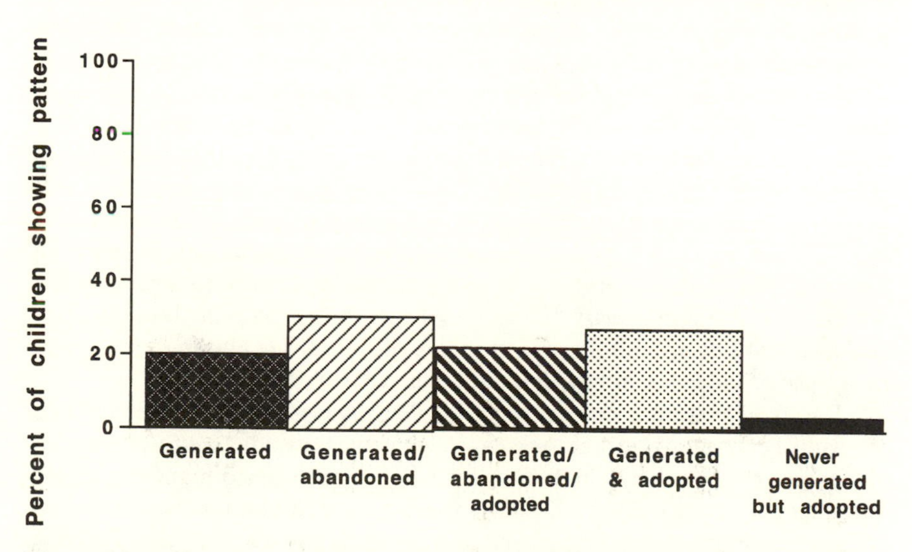

Figure 7.14. Percentage of fifth graders showing various patterns of generation, abandonment, and adoption of correct approaches for solving decimal-fractions comparison problems (Ellis et al., forthcoming). "Generate" means that child provided both a correct answer and a correct explanation at least once in the training session; "abandoned" means that the child subsequently used an incorrect explanation in the training session; "adopted" means that child used the correct rule on the posttest. Data are from children who worked in dyads and received feedback.

answered correctly more often on the posttest than did those whose partners showed less enthusiasm. Mean enthusiasm of the partner's reactions to the child's statements proved to be the single best predictor of the child's number correct on the posttest. Among the 66 children in dyads who received feedback, it accounted for 35% of the variance in individual children's number correct on the posttest. Total number of correct explanations advanced in the dyadic session added 16% to the variance that could be accounted for, mean clarity of the explanations added 3% more, and the partner's highest degree of enthusiasm on any single trial added 5% more. Together, the four variables accounted for 59% of the variance in posttest performance among these children. The example illustrates how examining cognitive and social variables concurrently within a microgenetic design can enhance understanding of learning.

Conclusions

Cognitive variability ultimately derives from construction of new ways of thinking. Despite children frequently generating new approaches, relatively little is known about the constructive process. Recognizing the prevalence of such innovations and studying them with microgenetic methods can considerably increase our understanding of cognitive change. In particular, such an approach can help us better understand the path, rate, breadth, variability, and sources of change.

One of the primary advantages of microgenetic methods is that they provide a more detailed depiction of the path of change than can standard cross-sectional or longitudinal methods. This was particularly evident in the Siegler and Jenkins (1989) study of discovery of the min strategy. The study revealed that the path of change was very different than that depicted in earlier models of development of addition strategies. One difference was that a previously hypothesized transition strategy, counting from the first addend, was not in fact used by any of the children prior to their use of the min strategy. Another difference was that a strategy that had not been hypothesized previously, the shortcut sum strategy, did appear to play a transitional role. It was used by 75% of the children, most of whom began using it shortly before they began using the min strategy, and it included features of both the sum strategy, that all of the children used previously, and of the min strategy, that most were soon to discover.

The study of number conservation (Siegler, 1995) revealed another aspect of the path of change. At least in some cases, logically more advanced strategies are sometimes employed by children at times when their performance is usually based on less sophisticated reasoning. Even though children in the study were chosen for rarely relying on the type of transformation, half of them advanced transformational explanations at least once during the pretest. Contrary to the implication of staircase conceptions, but consistent with the overlapping wave conception, the result suggests that even on tasks like conservation where the basic logic of more and less advanced strategies differ, the logics may coexist for protracted periods.

The microgenetic methods also revealed a considerable amount about what the experience of discovery was like. Some children's discoveries of the min strategy were accompanied by surprisingly articulate explanations of why the strategy was desirable. These children also tended to seem excited on the trial of discovery. Other children's discoveries were not accompanied by apparent insight, excitement, or even awareness that they had done anything different.

Rate and breadth of change correspond to two aspects of generalization: within-item and between-item. In the number conservation study (Siegler, 1995), which allowed clear distinction between them, the rates of both types of change were gradual. Children who advanced logically sophisticated explanations on a given pretest item quite often fell back on less advanced logics on the same item during training. Similarly, children who advanced logically sophisticated explanations early in the training period fairly often fell back on less advanced logics on the same item later in training. The same pattern emerged in the study of collaborative learning of decimal fractions and in the study of addition.

The breadth of change also increased gradually. In the number conservation study, even children who came to consistently explain the experimenter's reasoning in terms of transformations on items where her judgments were inconsistent with a length explanation continued to cite length on items on which her judgment, viewed in isolation, could be explained in that way. Thus, at first, children used the more advanced logic primarily on problems on which it was necessary, rather than on the full range of problems to which it applied. In the addition study, children used the min strategy far more often on challenge problems where it would do them the most good, even though it could have been beneficial on other problems as well.

Substantial individual differences in acquisition of new ways of thinking emerged on all of the tasks. On the addition task, preschoolers differed considerably in degree of awareness of having used a new strategy. Degree of awareness was positively related to generalization of the strategy. On the number conservation task, preschoolers who were asked to explain the experimenter's reasoning fell into three distinct groups: children who decreased their reliance on length and increased their reliance on the type of transformation, children who decreased their reliance on length but did not know what reasoning the experimenter used to generate her answers, and children who showed idiosyncratic patterns. Children in the first subgroup showed substantial increases in their own percentage of correct answers; children in the second and third subgroups did not.

Finally, the microgenetic designs allowed identification of numerous sources of change. In the study of preschoolers' addition, encountering challenge problems, problems that could easily be solved by the new strategy but not by previously discovered ones, led to greatly increased use of the new strategy. This increase was limited, however, to children who had already discovered the new approach. Children who had not already discovered it did not benefit from the challenge problems. The types of new strategies that were generated appear to have been influenced by conceptual understanding. In particular, children appeared to have goal sketches of the requirements of legitimate strategies in the domain, and these led to their generating legitimate new approaches without any trial and error.

In the number conservation study, being asked to explain the experimenter's reasoning emerged as a potent source of change. It considerably increased learning, relative to being asked to explain one's own reasoning or just being given feedback. Variability of reasoning also emerged as a potential source of cognitive change; children whose reasoning was more variable, both within a single pretest trial and over the entire pretest, subsequently learned more from training.

In the decimal fractions study, learning was facilitated by collaborating with a partner and receiving feedback. Among children who collaborated and received feedback, high degrees of learning were associated with active engagement of partners in each others' reasoning and with frequent exposure to correct reasoning by one's partner, as well as by clarity and correctness of one's own reasoning. Together, these findings illustrate how microgenetic studies can help us learn more about how children generate new ways of thinking.

Notes

1. In this analogy, the implied comparison case is a typical longitudinal design. With cross-sectional designs, the situation is even worse; what we get there is akin to a snapshot of Town A before a hurricane and a snapshot of a similar but not identical Town B after one.

2. Microgenetic methods are equally applicable for studying changes in social behavior as in studying changes in cognition. Studies of changes over the weeks or months just before and just after a child enters school or daycare illustrate opportunities to do naturalistic microgenetic studies of social (or cognitive) activity. All that is essential is observing changes as they occur with sufficiently dense sampling and sufficiently detailed analysis to reveal how the change is occuring.

3. The names of children have been changed to protect their privacy.

4. The fact that most discoveries did not occur on the first trial of the session suggests that the discoveries were not produced by parental intervention. If parents taught the min strategy, children presumably would have been likely to use it on the first trial of the next session. This argument does not rule out the possibility of outside instruction, because it is possible that parents taught the strategy to their children, that the children then forgot it, and that they remembered it later. However, the data, together with the literature showing that parents do not ordinarily teach this strategy to their children, made the possibility of outside instruction quite remote.

5. Whether this relation is due to all types of variability in thinking being useful, or only a subset, remains an open question. Breaking down the explanations advanced in Siegler (1995) into correct and incorrect ones indicated that number of types of correct explanations on the pretest was a significant predictor of learning, and number of types of incorrect explanations was not. However, both were positively correlated with subsequent learning ($r = .68$ for number of types of correct explanations and $r = .30$ for number of types of incorrect explanations). It seems likely that diverse correct ways of reasoning are more predictive of learning than diverse incorrect ways, but the incorrect ways could also be predictive if they signalled recognition of inadequacies of previous procedures or attempts to generate better ones.

6. Children's thinking about the decimal fractions problems was more variable than indicated by the consistent adherence of their judgments to these rules. It is telling that

about 20% of children who consistently used one rule on the pretest consistently used a different rule when retested a few days later. When children are asked to judge among discrete alternatives, their pattern of judgments is probably a good index of their dominant way of thinking, but it may understate the variability in their thinking (due to their desire to be consistent and to simplify the task).

8

A New Agenda for Cognitive Development

My goal in writing this book is to change the agenda of the field of cognitive development. In particular, I want to promote greater attention to the question that I believe is inherently at the core of the field: How do changes in children's thinking occur? Focusing on change may not sound like a radical departure from current practice, but I believe it is. It will require reformulation of our basic assumptions about children's thinking, the kinds of questions we ask about it, our methods for studying it, the mechanisms we propose to explain it, and the basic metaphors that underlie our thinking about it. That modifications of all of these types are being proposed as a package is no accident. Just as existing approaches have directed our attention away from the change process, so may new ones lead us to focus squarely on it. This concluding chapter summarizes the kinds of changes in assumptions, questions, methods, mechanisms, and metaphors that I think are needed.

Assumptions

My initial decision to write this book was motivated by a growing discomfort with the large gap between the inherent mission of the field—to understand changes in children's thinking—and most of what we actually have been studying. As I thought about the problem, I came to the conclusion that existing assumptions, methods, and theories acted in a mutually supportive way to make what we typically do seem essential, and to make doing otherwise—that is, studying change directly—seem impossible. Even approaches that proclaimed themselves to be radical departures from traditional theories maintained many fundamental assumptions of those theories. An increasing body of empirical evidence, however, indicates that some of the assumptions are wrong and that the way in which they are wrong has led us to ignore fundamental aspects of development. In this section, I describe prevailing assumptions regarding variability, choice, and change, and propose alternatives that seem more consistent with empirical data and more useful for increasing our understanding of how changes occur.

Assumptions Regarding Variability

Traditional stage theories, such as Piaget's, Werner's, and Kohlberg's, and newer alternatives, such as neo-Piagetian theories (Case, 1992; Halford, 1993), theory-theories (Carey, 1985; Wellman & Gelman, 1992), and many information-processing theories (e.g., Klahr, 1992; Siegler, 1983), share two basic assumptions. One is that a given child thinks about a given topic in a single way at most points in development. The other is that identifying *the* way of thinking that children use at particular ages is, and should be, a major goal of the field.

The theories vary in the level at which thinking is said to be monolithic. The traditional stage theories and some neo-Piagetian theories (e.g., Case, 1985) posit commonalities in reasoning across a very broad range of content. Thus, a preoperational child is believed to reason in preoperational ways across a great many problems. Other neo-Piagetian approaches (e.g., Case & Okamoto, 1996; Halford, 1993) and theory-theory approaches posit commonalities of reasoning across smaller, but still substantial, ranges of material. In the theory-theory approaches, the relevant material is defined by the domain, such as biology, mechanics, or mind; in the neo-Piagetian ones, it is defined by the applicability of a type of reasoning, such as a central conceptual structure or pragmatic reasoning scheme. Thus, a 3-year-old might have a relatively advanced belief-desire theory of mind (and be expected to use it on a broad range of theory-of-mind tasks), but a relatively primitive psychologically based theory of biology. Information-processing approaches tend to focus at the yet more specific level of *N*-year-olds' strategy for remembering a certain type of material, their rule for solving a particular kind of problem, or their understanding of a particular concept. However, information-processing approaches also maintain the assumption that a given child uses a single rule, strategy, or conceptualization. The difference is in how broadly the thinking is believed to be applied.

It is important to note that all of these theories recognize some types of variability: variability among age groups, among cultures, and among children with different intellectual and personality attributes. Some of them, especially Piaget's, also recognize variability within a child during brief transition periods. However, the prevailing assumption is that the large majority of the time, a given child thinks in one and only one way about a given task or concept.

I believe this prevailing assumption is wrong. As demonstrated throughout the book, especially in chapters 3 and 4, a very large body of evidence contradicts the view that children's (or adults') thinking is monolithic at any level. Regardless of whether we are talking about development of phonology (Ferguson, 1986), syntax (Kuczaj, 1977), or semantics (Merriman & Bowman, 1989); arithmetic (Geary & Burlingham-Dubree, 1989), reading (Goldman & Saul, 1990), or spelling (Siegler, 1986); scientific reasoning (Schauble, 1990) or moral reasoning (Turiel, 1983); map drawing (Feldman, 1980), block stacking (Wilkinson, 1982), or number conservation (Church & Goldin-Meadow, 1986), careful analyses have shown children's thinking to be anything but monolithic. Thinking is not monolithic within a given domain, nor within a given task, nor within a given item. Even when the same child is presented the identical problem on two successive days, the child quite often uses different approaches on the two occasions (Siegler & McGilly, 1989; Siegler & Shrager, 1984). Even within a single presentation of a single item, children often generate varying ways of thinking, as indicated by differences between their gestures and their speech (Alibali & Goldin-Meadow, 1993; Goldin-Meadow, Alibali, & Church, 1993) and their expressing multiple ways of thinking within speech (Graham & Perry, 1993; Siegler, 1995). Thus, children's thinking, even about narrowly delimited topics, is more akin to an ecology of ideas, coexisting and competing with each other for use, than like the monoliths depicted in our theories.

The classic Piagetian task of number conservation provides an excellent illustration of the difference between traditional assumptions and current evidence. How many developmental psychologists do not know that on the standard Piagetian task, 4- and 5-year-olds choose the row that has been spread out and that now is longer, whereas 7- and 8-year-olds realize that spreading or compressing does not change the number of objects? Yet research examining children's number conservation approaches on a trial-by-trial basis has revealed that children who do not generally conserve nonetheless sometimes advance correct answers and logically based explanations of them, that children who choose the longer row often show different reasoning in their gestures, and that children fairly often advance more and less sophisticated verbal explanations on the same trial (Church & Goldin-Meadow, 1986; Siegler, 1995). This variability seems to have important consequences; children whose initial thinking about number conservation is more variable have been found to learn more from training (Alibali & Goldin-Meadow, 1993; Graham & Perry, 1993; Siegler, 1995).

Other approaches that focus on change, such as dynamic systems and connectionist approaches, also have emphasized the pervasiveness and importance of variability. For example, Thelen (1992) noted the "rampant variability of development, both among contexts and among individuals . . . barely perceptible differences in the organism or the task environment may produce dramatic and sometimes nonpredictable outcomes" (p. 191). She also noted that variability was particularly high during periods of rapid change (Thelen & Urich, 1991). The fact that these observations involved the motor development of infants, rather than the cognitive activity of preschoolers or school-age children, suggests that both high variability and a positive relation between variability and change may be quite general characteristics of development.

Such observations raise the question: "Why would the most prominent developmental theories of the past 100 years have depicted children's thinking and action as less variable than it really is?" A number of factors seem to have contributed. There are philosophical reasons: Many developmentalists have believed that our goal as scientists is to identify and describe the essence of children's thinking at different ages (Oyama, 1985). There are historical reasons: The most venerable theories in the field have established the precedent of depicting development as a series of long stable states separated by brief transitional periods.

There are pragmatic reasons: It is simpler and more dramatic for us to talk about children as thinking in a certain way at a certain age, rather than acknowledging the great variability that is present. There are reasons of social perception: Given evidence of behavioral variability, people tend to overestimate the frequency of the most common types of behavior and to underestimate the frequency of less common types (Fiske & Taylor, 1991). There are methodological reasons: Until the advent of videotaping technology, it was difficult to obtain reliable data about many types of variability that were present in children's behavior. Yet the empirical evidence for large-scale variability in every area of cognition has become impossible to ignore. It must be incorporated into our basic assumptions about cognitive development.[1]

Assumptions Regarding Choice

Ignoring the variability in children's thinking renders moot issues regarding choice. If children can think in only one way, if they know only a single theory, rule, principle, or strategy, they have no need to choose. They are slaves to their cognitive structures.

Consistent with the lack of focus on variability, the processes through which children choose among alternative ways of thinking have received relatively little attention. The main exception was that for about a decade, roughly from the mid-1970s to the mid-1980s, a number of researchers interested in metacognition examined variables that were hypothesized to influence whether children would use strategies that they had been taught (e.g., A. L. Brown et al., 1983; Cavanaugh & Perlmutter, 1982; Flavell & Wellman, 1977). However, when conscious knowledge about cognitive capacities, strategies, and problems proved less predictive of strategy use than had been expected, this line of research dwindled.

Within the present approach, in contrast, choice occupies a central position. If children's thinking about many phenomena is fundamentally variable, then they must constantly choose which approach to use on a given occasion. The processes that generate these choices may not resemble those envisioned in accounts that emphasize conscious metacognitive knowledge, but they are choice processes nonetheless. This has long been realized in the area of animal learning, where choice is widely recognized as a central issue (e.g., Catania, 1980; Gallistel, 1990; Myerson & Miezin, 1980). Substantial attention has been devoted to how rats, pigeons, and other animals distribute their responses among available alternatives (e.g., Herrnstein, 1970; 1990; Rachlin & Green, 1972; Neuringer, 1967; 1993; Staddon, 1991; Stokes, 1995). Choice is also viewed as a central problem in rational analyses of adult cognition (e.g., Gigerenzer, Hoffrage, & Kleinbolting, 1991; Lovett & Anderson, in press; Oaksford & Chater, 1994), as well as within studies of adults' decision making (e.g., Hogarth, 1987; Tversky & Kahneman, 1974). Looking to social sciences other than psychology, choice has long been considered central in economics (e.g., Hirschleifer, 1982), political science (e.g., Coombs & Avrunin, 1988), and anthropology (e.g., Durham, 1991). Some of the most heavily studied topics in economics, for example, concern how people and societies choose among alternative purchases, alternative divisions of income between saving and consumption, alternative levels of risk in investment, alternative pricings of goods, and so on.

Underlying these approaches, as well as the present one, are two assumptions regarding choice. First, voluntary behavior implies choice; understanding any voluntary behavior implies understanding why it, rather than an alternative, was chosen. Second, the choices that people make are generally adaptive. Approaches vary in whether they posit that choices are governed by the type of optimization often posited in economics, the type of matching law often posited in studies of animal learning, the mixture of environmental contingencies and processing limits posited by rational analyses of cognition, or the heuristics and biases posited within studies of decision making. All of the approaches, however, assume that the choices are adaptive, at least when considered within a broad context.[2]

Examination of children's choices has indicated that they also are adaptive. As discussed in chapter 5, the adaptiveness takes a variety of forms. From at least age 4 years onward, children choose adaptively between retrieval and use of a back-up strategy (Siegler & Shrager, 1984). The harder the problem, the more often they use back-up strategies. For example, the harder an addition problem, the more likely preschoolers are to use back-up strategies, such as counting on their fingers. This pattern of choices enables them to use the fast and easy retrieval approach when it can yield correct answers (e.g., on 2 + 2), and to use back-up approaches when those slower and more effortful approaches are needed to produce accurate performance (e.g., on 2 + 5). Such adaptive choices have been found among typical children, gifted children, and children with learning disabilities; among children from low income urban backgrounds and from high income suburban backgrounds; and among Chinese, French, Swedish, and American children (Geary & Brown, 1991; Geary, Fan, et al., 1993; Kerkman & Siegler, 1993; Lemaire & Siegler, 1995; Svenson & Sjoberg, 1983).

Children also choose adaptively among alternative strategies other than retrieval. For example, when infants need to locomote down ramps, they adjust their strategies to the steepness of the descent (Adolph, 1993). On relatively shallow ramps, they tend to rely on their usual mode of locomotion (crawling or walking); on somewhat steeper ramps, they tend to resort to safer though slower techniques (backing or sliding down); on yet steeper ramps, they often refuse to descend at all.

A third way in which children's choices are adaptive involves trial-to-trial changes. In serial recall, for example, children switch strategies most often when two conditions are met: They were incorrect on the previous trial, and they used a low effort, low accuracy strategy on it (McGilly & Siegler, 1989). Again, such choices make sense. When the previous strategy succeeded, there is no immediate reason to switch; when they do not know strategies that would produce higher accuracy than the approach they tried, there also is little reason to switch.

A final sense in which children choose adaptively involves learning. With increasing experience in a domain, children calibrate their strategy choices increasingly finely to demands of the particular task. For example, as infants gain experience going down ramps, they choose increasingly aptly when to crawl down, when to slide or back down, and when to refuse to descend (Adolph, 1993). The adaptiveness of older children's choices shows similar gains. Even in the first two weeks of learning multiplication, 8-year-olds' strategy choices are fairly adaptive, but the degree of adaptiveness increases as they learn which strategies work best on which problems (Lemaire & Siegler, 1995).

In sum, over a wide range of ages and domains, adaptive choices seem to be the rule. It thus seems reasonable to assume that children's choices generally are adaptive and to focus on finer grain issues such as the roles of implicit and explicit knowledge in contributing to the adaptive choices, the way in which choices balance considerations of immediate performance and longer term learning, and how choices are made in novel situations.

Assumptions Regarding Change

Few if any developmentalists would disagree with the proposition that changes in children's thinking are both pervasive and important. However, an outsider looking at our theories and research would have to wonder about the depth of our belief. Both traditional and contemporary theories have surprisingly little to say about how change occurs. We speak about changes from this stage to that stage, from this theory to that theory, from this rule to that rule. Rarely, however, do we have much to say about how such changes occur. The standard labels for hypothesized transition processes—assimilation, accommodation, and equilibration; change in M-space; conceptual restructuring; differentiation and hierarchic integration—are more promissory notes, telling us that we really should work on this some time, than serious mechanistic accounts.

In addition to the vagueness of these accounts, most of them relegate the changes of interest to the status of brief, widely separated episodes. The interesting changes occur during a short transition period during which the child moves from one stage to another, one amount of M-space to another, or one theory to another. What sets this transition process in motion, after a long period of stability, is generally left unspecified. What stops the change, engendering another long period of stability, is also left unclear.

Part of the unsatisfying quality of these accounts reflects the inherent difficulty of the task of explaining change. However, two characteristics of our accounts of change have added to the problem. One involves the size of the changes that have been posited. It is difficult to envision in any detail how a new stage of reasoning, a new theory of physics or biology, or a new unit of M-space would emerge. Perhaps the failure to explain such profound changes simply reflects the failure of a great enough genius to appear. Another possibility, however, is that the failure lies in our trying to explain types of change that do not exist. In biological evolution, new species do not appear in a single generation; rather, they reflect the accretion of many changes over many generations. The same seems likely to be true in cognitive evolution; rather than new stages or theories emerging *sui generis*, they more likely are the composite effect of many smaller realizations and discoveries that have gradually accumulated. Thus, one reason for the lack of compelling explanations of change may be that we have wanted to explain changes more sudden, more profound, and more encompassing than any that actually occur.

A second likely reason for the failure to explain changes in children's thinking is that we have not tried hard enough to generate such explanations. This problem seems related to the first one, albeit indirectly. The goal of explaining the grand changes assumed by many theories tends to implicitly devalue the goal of explaining the more specific changes that we all know exist. It is not that traditional theories deny the existence of frequent small changes; they clearly recognize them. However, by placing such great emphasis on hypothesized prolonged periods of stability and on brief transition periods separating them, they relegate to the periphery the goal of explaining the less profound and dramatic changes that may in the end be all that exist.

The impact of this implicit devaluation of the goal of explaining specific changes is exacerbated by the difficulty of explaining any kind of change. It is very hard to generate rigorous, mechanistic explanations of even small changes in children's thinking, for example, acquisition of a new strategy. If generating such explanations is not accorded very high value within the field, few will go to the trouble of generating them. From personal experience, I can testify that it is easier to conduct five studies that demonstrate differences in the strategies of children of different ages than to formulate a single simulation that convincingly explains how any one of the changes occurs. Unless the field accords great value to rigorous explanations of particular changes in children's thinking, there simply will not be many such explanations.

Thus, along with the assumptions regarding the centrality of variability and choice in cognitive development, the third basic assumption of the present approach is that children's thinking is continuously changing, and that we should study the changes as directly as possible. Rather than waiting for some profound insight into how a preoperational child could become a concrete operational child, how a child with an M-space of 3 could become a child with an M-space of 4, or how a child with an Aristotelian theory of mechanics could become a child with a Newtonian theory of mechanics, we can focus right now on the many smaller changes that are constantly occurring and that generate much, maybe all, of cognitive growth.

It may turn out that understanding these smaller changes will be insufficient for a full understanding of cognitive development. There may be a macro-development, such as that envisioned within stage theories, that is produced by different mechanisms than micro-development. Regardless of whether micro-level changes totally account for macro-level change, however, they almost certainly are large contributors to it. As discussed in chapter 2, theorists of biological evolution disagree as to whether it is necessary to posit special macro-evolutionary mechanisms (cataclysmic events such as comets or asteroids hitting the Earth) to explain large-scale changes in species. All agree, however, that micro-evolutionary mechanisms (such as mutation and genetic recombination) make a large contribution to macro-evolution as well. As we gain better understanding of micro-level change mechanisms that contribute to cognitive development, a similar conclusion seems likely to emerge. Thus, it seems well worthwhile to focus a great deal of energy and attention on explaining changes as we find them: changes involving addition of new concepts, rules, principles, and strategies; increasing frequency of using advanced ways of thinking and decreasing frequency of using less advanced ones; increasingly effective execution of all approaches; and increasing constraints on discovery processes.

Questions

These assumptions about the roles of variability, choice, and change raise a number of new questions about cognitive development and suggest different ways of thinking about other longstanding questions.

Questions About Variability

Traditionally, cognitive developmentalists have asked "Through what sequence of stages, theories, rules, or strategies do children progress on their way to mature understanding?" Recognition of the variability of cognition suggests that this question should be differentiated into several more specific ones. What set of approaches is used at any given age or level of understanding? What are their relative frequencies, and under what conditions do children use each one most often? What leads to relatively ineffective approaches continuing to be used when more effective approaches are available? What leads to generation of new approaches when effective ones are already known?

A set of particularly intriguing questions regarding variability involves its causes and consequences. Why would we use a variety of approaches, even on a given problem, rather than always using the single best one? Studies of the learning of rats, pigeons, and adult humans suggest that past reinforcement history is one important determinant. Rats, pigeons, and adult humans all are responsive to direct reinforcement of variability (Neuringer, 1992; 1993). For example, when reinforcement depends on producing a sequence of four pecks that differs from the previous sequence of four pecks, pigeons increase the variability of their responses. Adult humans respond not only to such response contingencies but also to verbal instruction to do tasks in different ways. Such instructions increase their scores on test of divergent thinking (Baer, 1994).

It is unclear how frequently such direct reinforcement of variability occurs in the everyday environment. However, indirect reinforcers that are omnipresent in the everyday environment also influence the degree of variability (Stokes, Mechner, & Balsam, in press). In particular, intermittent schedules of reinforcement lead to more variable behavior than do continuous reinforcement schedules. Extinction of previously reinforced responses also heightens the degree of variability.

A particularly interesting proposal, made by Stokes (1995), is that along with learning particular skills, people and other animals also learn a target level of variability for that skill. For example, verbal instruction in rules for executing a behavior generally produces less variable responses than does learning the same behavior through unstated reinforcement contingencies. The differing degrees of variability persist even after the initial reinforcement contingency changes. In general, acquiring a skill under conditions that produce more variable initial behavior seems to produce more variable subsequent behavior, even when there was never any direct reinforcement of variability (Stokes et al., in press).

In addition to these determinants of relative variability of responses on different tasks, the existence of positive relations between initial variability and subsequent learning may maintain a degree of variability on tasks in general (Alibali & Goldin-Meadow, 1993; Church & Goldin-Meadow, 1986; Goldman & Saul, 1990; Graham & Perry, 1993; Siegler, 1995). Part of the reason for this relation is that children whose thinking is initially more variable are more likely to include useful ways of thinking within their repertoires. For example, in Siegler and Jenkins (1989), children who had used the min strategy at least once before they encountered the challenge problems more often learned to solve the challenge problems through heightened use of that strategy. However, this greater probability of inclusion of strategies that yield correct performance is not the only reason for the relation between cognitive variability and learning. In Siegler (1995), number of correct answers on the pretest, number of correct explanations on the pretest, and whether a child ever generated a correct explanation on the pretest did not predict learning. However, sheer number of different strategies on the pretest did.

This finding is unlikely to mean that all variants are equally useful, nor that all variants are useful at all. Illustratively, in Siegler (1995), number of pretest strategies that yielded correct performance was more closely related to subsequent learning than was number of pretest strategies that yielded incorrect performance (though both correlations were positive). Anyone who has been in a brainstorming session, or a faculty meeting, knows that some ideas add variability but do not elevate the quality of the discussion. Possessing several ways of thinking that reflect good understanding of the domain, even if that understanding is only partial, seems likely to be more conducive to learning than possessing several ways that reflect poor understanding. It remains an important challenge, though, to establish exactly which types of cognitive variability are helpful and which are not.

Findings of the positive relation between cognitive variability and learning raise numerous questions. How general is the relation? Do experiences that lead to increased variability also lead to greater learning? Is some children's thinking in general more variable than that of others, and are these children in general better learners? Further specifying causes and consequences of the variability in children's thinking seems an intriguing area for future investigation.

A related question involves whether younger individuals' thinking is generally more variable than that of older ones, and if so, whether this greater variability helps them learn some types of content more effectively. In several domains, notably language and motor activity, variability is especially high early in development. These also are domains in which very young children seem to be especially effective learners relative to older children and adults (e.g., Ferguson, 1986; Johnson & Newport, 1989). In the short run, the young children's greater variability seems disadvantageous in terms of generating correct pronunciations, grammar, and locomotor activity. However, in the longer run, the high variability may benefit their learning by leading to their trying many alternatives and learning how well each works. Infancy and early childhood seems a particularly appropriate time for high variability, because there is so much to learn and because the costs of non-optimal performance are not that great (see Bjorklund & Green, 1992, for a similar argument). It thus seems worthwhile to ask whether cognitive variability is especially high early in development, and if so, whether the high variability aids learning.

Questions About Choice

These questions about variability raise corresponding questions about children's choices among the varying ways of thinking. One set of questions concerns *which choices are made*: What dimensions of problems and situations influence children's choices among alternative ways of thinking? Are there age-related unities in the types of choices that children find most appealing at particular ages, and if so, why? Do individual children's choices differ only because of differing knowledge, or do temperamental and stylistic differences also influence the choices?

A second set of questions concerns the *adaptiveness of choices*. What are the different ways in which choices are adaptive? Do they maximize some kind of expected utility (and if so, how is that expected utility computed)? Do they conform to the type of matching law often used to describe animal behavior?

A third set of questions concerns *how choices are made*. What processes generate strategy choices? Do the processes used in novel domains differ from those in familiar ones? How do capacity constraints influence children's choices? Can one or two dramatic experiences change strategy choices in large ways, (and if so how does this occur)? How do children decide to use strategies that may not be beneficial immediately but that could yield benefits in the long run?

Asking such questions about choice not only suggests new areas for research, it also can improve understanding of well-established phenomena. Consider one of the best-known developmental findings: the 5 to 7 shift. In a classic article, White (1965) suggested that there was a fundamental change between ages 5 and 7 in children's thinking. A central type of evidence for this change was that on a large variety of tasks, 5-year-olds based their responses on a single stimulus dimension, whereas 7-year-olds and older children focused on multiple dimensions. For example, on liquid quantity conservation problems, 5-year-olds answered solely on the basis of the relative height of the liquid columns, whereas 7-year-olds considered cross-sectional area as well as height.

Since 1965, two facts have become evident. First, 5-year-olds have the capacity to consider multiple dimensions, and on many tasks they do. Second, despite the first fact, 5-year-olds do focus on a single dimension considerably more often than do older children or adults.

The pair of findings is difficult to explain within approaches that posit fixed stages, capacity constraints, or theories. If children can think in more advanced ways, why wouldn't they do so? Citing horizontal decalages merely labels the phenomenon. Citing inviolate capacity constraints does not explain why some of the tasks on which 5-year-olds reason unidimensionally are no more complex than ones on which they reason multidimensionally. Citing domain-specific theories as a basis for the advanced responses ignores the fact that many of the differences occur within a given domain, often within a single task framed in slightly different ways.

In contrast, assuming that 5-year-olds often have available both unidimensional and multidimensional ways of thinking about problems, and viewing the children as choosing which way of thinking to use in particular situations, suggests a more positive agenda. In particular, it suggests searching for the factors that determine the choices.

One such analysis (Siegler, 1996) suggested four characteristics of tasks that bias choices toward unidimensional reasoning: the problem is unfamiliar, it requires a quantitative comparison, it requires a choice between discrete response alternatives, and it includes a single perceptually or conceptually dominant stimulus dimension that points to an incorrect choice as the right one.

All of these conditions hold true on the classic problems on which 5-year-olds have been found to reason unidimensionally: conservation, class inclusion, time-speed-distance, balance scales, shadow projection, probability, temperature, sweetness, and so on. The unfamiliarity of such tasks means that young children will not have had prior opportunity to learn that there are multiple relevant dimensions. Questions that require a discrete choice along a single quantitative dimension (e.g., which glass has more water; which car went faster; which side will go down?) lead children to seek a single quantitative dimension on which to base choices. Differences among alternatives along a dimension more salient than the one asked about in the question bias children toward choosing on the basis of differences among the alternatives along the salient dimension.

Consider how these four characteristics apply to a single task, number conservation. Most 5-year-olds never have encountered a situation very much like this task; standard number conservation questions require children to make a discrete choice between the two rows; asking which row has more objects leads children to seek a single quantitative dimension on which to base answers; and the perceptual salience of one row being longer than the other results in children usually basing their choices on that dimension.

Do we benefit by thinking of such classic problems in terms of choices among alternative ways of thinking about the problem? I believe we do. Recall that even children who usually rely on length on number conservation problems sometimes explain their reasoning in terms of the type of transformation or the results of counting (Siegler, 1995). Recall also that even on an individual number conservation trial on which a child explains her reasoning in terms of length, her gestures often indicate attention to the density of objects within the row as well (Church & Goldin-Meadow, 1986). These observations probably would not have been made if the investigators had not suspected that 5-year-olds' behavior reflects choices among alternative ways in which they are capable of thinking about the problem. Thus, viewing children's thinking in terms of factors that influence choice processes can provide fresh ways of thinking about even thoroughly investigated tasks and issues in the field.

Questions About Change

These questions regarding variability and choice raise related questions regarding change. What experiences lead to shifts in the number and frequency of different ways of thinking? Do older individuals rely on conscious analyses more often in choosing among approaches (because they are generally more analytic and reflective), or do younger individuals more often rely on conscious analyses (because they do not have sufficient associative knowledge to choose without such analyses)? How do children's choices shape their further development: Does the formative influence differ with the particular strategy that was used to generate the choice? Is there any long-term benefit to having arrived at a choice through conscious, analytic processes rather than through unconscious, intuitive ones?

Another set of questions about change involves how children generate new approaches. What is the experience of discovery like? How does conceptual understanding constrain children's discoveries, and how do increases in this understanding lead to increasingly constrained new approaches? Are the same individuals consistently the first to add new strategies within a domain and across domains?

A set of questions of special interest concerns constraints on children's discovery processes. In chapter 7, the goal sketch construct was proposed to account for children's ability to discover useful new strategies without any trial and error. The idea was that understanding the basic hierarchy of goals and subgoals that must be met by legitimate strategies in a domain would both steer children toward useful new approaches that met the requirements and away from conceptually flawed alternatives that did not. Thus, goal sketches would serve a function similar to that postulated for constraints and principles by Gelman (1993), Keil (1989), Markman (1989), and Newport (1990) in such domains as counting, acquisition of vocabulary and syntax, and construction of naive theories of biology. Like these principles and constraints, goal sketches were hypothesized to be domain specific, to generally begin in implicit form, to lead children to focus selectively on relevant input, to guide learning, and to allow judgments of the legitimacy of unfamiliar procedures (Siegler & Crowley, 1994).

However, potentially important differences also distinguish goal sketches from constraints and principles. Constraints and principles have been invoked to explain the rapidity of learning in situations that have three characteristics: the domains seem evolutionarily important, learning is virtually universal, and the age of acquisition is similar for all children. None of these assumptions are made for goal sketches, because they are attempts to explain constraints on culturally contingent as well as noncontingent acquisitions.

But how similar are the mechanisms that underlie the operation of constraints and principles on one hand and goal sketches on the other? They clearly have similar effects; for example, both allow children to avoid trial and error, and both allow them to accurately judge the appropriateness of procedures that they do not use. However, it is unknown whether these effects are produced in the same way. It also is unknown whether the universality of the one and the particularity of the other reflects different mechanisms leading to their creation or simply differential availability of relevant input (all children encounter language, living things, and counting at early ages, but whether and when children encounter tick-tack-toe is highly variable). Explicit models of how both types of conceptual constraints on learning are created, and how they exercise their effects, are needed to indicate their degree of similarity.

Another question regarding cognitive change for which intriguing evidence is starting to emerge is: How broadly are new ways of thinking generalized once they have been discovered? We might imagine that new approaches initially would be overgeneralized (due to a desire to exercise the new skill), undergeneralized (due to habitual use of old approaches or to uncertainty regarding when the new approach is useful), or applied in the same way as when more is known about them.

In fact, undergeneralization of new ways of thinking seems to be the typical pattern. For example, when children discover the min strategy, even those who can articulate why it is better than the main alternative, counting from one, continue to rely more on the less advanced approach (Siegler & Jenkins, 1989). Similarly, when children begin to rely on the type of transformation to answer number conservation problems, they still often refer to the relative lengths of the rows when the longer row has more objects (Siegler, 1995). The finding parallels results in language development showing that newly discovered vocabulary words tend to be undergeneralized (Anglin, 1977; Dromi, 1987). Determining why new approaches are often generalized so slowly, and what kinds of experiences lead to more rapid generalization, is one of many ways in which asking questions about variability, choice, and change may deepen our understanding of cognitive development.

Methods

Addressing these questions will require supplementing typical methods for studying development with ones that yield finer grained data. Two methods that can provide such data are trial-by-trial assessments of thinking and microgenetic designs.

Trial-by-Trial Cognitive Assessments

The primary data in most studies of cognitive development, mean percentage correct and mean solution time, are averages of the performance of many children over many trials. This makes considerable sense if children of a given age think about the task in a single, consistent way. However, if cognitive activity varies from child to child, and from trial to trial for a given child, aggregating across children and trials inevitably conveys a distorted impression of the thinking that gave rise to the data.

Examples cited in chapter 3 illustrated the consequences of such data averaging when thinking is variable between and within individuals. In one case, a strategy that accurately predicted the mean solution time on each problem was actually used on less than 40% of trials (Siegler, 1987a). In another, a strategy that predicted the mean solution time on each problem was actually not used by anyone (Siegler, 1989b). In both cases, the fit of the strategy to the pattern of mean solution times was caused by a combination of the relative frequencies of different strategies, the variance on the dependent measure generated by each one, and positive correlations in performance generated by them.

In contrast, in these and other studies (e.g., Cooney et al., 1988; Ladd, 1987), the combination of videotaped records of ongoing behavior and self-reports immediately following each trial have proved capable of yielding valid assessments of children's thinking on a trial-by-trial basis. Both convergent and discriminant validation for the strategy classifications has been provided by solution time and error data. For example, in Siegler (1987a), the strategy that quite accurately predicted the mean solution time of each problem when that mean was based on times on all trials proved to be an even better predictor of the solution times on the subset of trials on which children were classified as using that strategy. In contrast, on the other trials, that strategy never predicted the data very well. Better predictions were provided by the predictors that followed logically from the particular strategies that children were classified as using on those trials.

When are immediately retrospective self-reports, such as those used in these studies, likely to provide valid indexes of thinking? Ericsson and Simon (1991) reviewed the literature on verbal protocols and concluded the crucial factors are that (a) Each trial takes at least a second or two, long enough to produce a symbol in working memory; (b) each trial should not take so long (more than a half minute or a minute) that the symbol is no longer in working memory when the report is given; (c) the question that subjects are asked concerns how they solved the problem, rather than the external variables that led them to think about it that way.

When trials take longer than can be accurately remembered at the end of the trial, verbal protocols given during performance often produce useful data. Providing such protocols often slows performance, and at times it changes the pattern of performance as well (Russo, Johnson, & Stephens, 1989). However, in many cases, such concurrent protocols yield insights into people's thinking on lengthy tasks and provide a moment-to-moment record of the thinking that occurs in solving a single problem.

Even when valid verbal self-reports cannot be obtained, either because the process of interest is too brief or because the population of interest is not sufficiently articulate, trial-by-trial assessments can still be useful. For example, Adolph (1993; 1995) videotaped infants descending ramps. From the tapes, she was able to identify the strategy each infant used on each trial. Preschoolers' and retarded children's addition strategies and older children's word identification and spelling strategies also have been assessed solely through videotapes of overt behavior during each trial (Geary & Brown, 1991; Siegler, 1986). When valid immediately retrospective verbal protocols can be obtained, they can enhance the quality of cognitive assessments beyond that possible through relying on videotapes of ongoing behavior alone (McGilly & Siegler, 1990). However, the more general point is that obtaining trial-by-trial assessments of cognitive activity, with or without verbal self-reports, generally will lead to more accurate assessments of children's thinking than making inferences on the basis of data averaged over trials.

Microgenetic Methods

Studying change requires methods that, unlike conventional cross-sectional and longitudinal approaches, yield information about the changes while they are occurring. As discussed in chapter 7, microgenetic methods offer one such approach. The key characteristics of such methods are observations that span as large a portion as possible of the period of rapid change, have a high density of observations within this period (relative to the rate at which the competence of interest is changing), and include intense analyses of both qualitative and quantitative aspects of the changes. This is what has led to their use by investigators interested in change, regardless of whether their theoretical allegiances are Piagetian, Vygotskyian, dynamical systems, or information processing.

Microgenetic methods offer a number of advantages for studying change. They can and have yielded information regarding what leads to new ways of thinking, what the experience of discovery is like, and how new ways of thinking are generalized once they begin to be used. They also have disconfirmed hypothesized transition strategies, led to discovery of other transitional strategies that had not been hypothesized, indicated experiences that sparked discoveries, and identified other types of experiences that facilitated generalization of already discovered approaches.

A very recent study (Stern & Siegler, 1996) illustrates how the combination of trial-by-trial analyses of strategy use and a microgenetic design can advance understanding of how change occurs. The study focused on an insight problem, the *$A + B - B$ problem.* This problem, first studied by Bisanz & LeFevre (1990), can be solved by first adding the value of *B* and then subtracting it. The problem also can be solved via the shortcut of realizing that the answer must be *A*, because adding and subtracting the same value must equal 0. After studying performance of 6-, 9-, and 11-year-olds on this task, Bisanz and LeFevre concluded that most 11-year-olds solved the problems by using the shortcut, and that most 6- to 9-year-olds did not.

Bisanz and LeFevre's conclusion was based on the finding that for most 6- to 9-year-olds, mean solution time on each problem increased linearly with the size of *B*, whereas after this age, the size of *B* had no effect on the times. The logic was reasonable: If children add and subtract *B*, solution times should increase with increases in the sizes of the numbers being added and subtracted. On the other hand, if children take the shortcut, the size of *B* should be irrelevant, because all that is necessary is to note that the numbers being added and subtracted are equal. As noted above, however, such chronometric analyses, which rely on data averaged over trials, underestimate the variability of strategy use. Thus, assessing thinking on a trial-by-trial basis seemed likely to reveal greater use of the insight than evident in the chronometric analysis.

To determine whether children younger than 10 actually do generate the insight, and how they come to do so, we presented 30 8-year-olds a pretest, seven practice sessions, and a posttest. The pretest included problems on which the insight was applicable ($A + B - B$ and $A + B - A$) and problems on which it was not ($A + B - C$). In each of the seven practice sessions, $A + B - B$ problems were presented either on all trials (the *blocked condition*) or scattered among $A + B - C$ problems, on which the shortcut was inapplicable (the *mixed condition*). Children in the two groups received the same total number of problems, but children in the blocked condition received more $A + B - B$ problems. The posttest was the same as the pretest for children in both groups.

Strategy use on each trial was assessed in two ways. One involved asking children immediately after each trial how they had solved the problem. The other was based on the solution time on the trial. Solution times on this task fell into a bimodal pattern, with many times below 2 seconds (presumably the trials on which children relied on the insight) and almost all other times above 4 seconds (presumably the trials on which they added and subtracted). Having the two measures of strategy use allowed examination of the relation of conscious strategy use (as measured by the self-reports) and unconscious use (trials of less than 2 seconds on which the child nonetheless claimed to have solved the problem by adding and subtracting the B term).

Under both blocked and mixed conditions, more than 80% of the second graders explicitly noted on at least one trial that two of the numbers were equal and said that they solved the problem without adding or subtracting. Solution time patterns lent converging evidence; average solution times on such trials were under 2 seconds, much faster than on other trials. Thus, most second graders did have the insight, at least sometimes. Children in the blocked condition generated it earlier in the practice sessions, used it more consistently after they generated it, and used it more often on the posttest in which both types of problems were included. On the other hand, children who were given the mixed-problem practice sessions less often overgeneralized the strategy to posttest problems where it was inappropriate (i.e., by answering "A" on $A + B - C$ problems). The percentage of children who performed ideally on the posttest—consistently using the shortcut when appropriate and not using it when inappropriate—was identical under blocked and mixed presentations. Thus, both blocked and mixed presentations had advantages and disadvantages for learning.

The results also shed light on the relation of consciousness to discovery and generalization of new strategies. On the first trials on which a given child produced solution times under two seconds, the child rarely reported using the shortcut strategy. Instead, children claimed to have added and subtracted the B term, despite the extremely rapid solution time making this almost impossible. The children also tended not to use the shortcut consistently following this first use. Consistency of use of the shortcut (as indicated by very short RTs) grew more rapidly after children first said they used it than before. This finding was consistent with the hypothesis that consciousness of using a new strategy promotes its generalization (Siegler & Jenkins, 1989).

The Stern and Siegler experiment illustrates the types of benefits that can be gained from combining trial-by-trial assessments of thinking and a microgenetic design. It showed that even at ages and under conditions in which children did not consistently solve problems via the insight, they still sometimes generated it. The study also showed that blocked and mixed problem presentations led to different paths of change, that unconscious use of new strategies preceded conscious use, and that becoming conscious of the new approach led to increased generalization. This type of detailed information about change simply could not be obtained within traditional cross-sectional or longitudinal designs.

Part of the reason for my enthusiasm about microgenetic methods is that they have yielded a set of consistent results regarding change. One consistent finding is that change is rarely a sudden event; old ways of thinking continue to be used for extended periods after superior alternatives have been generated (e.g., Dromi, 1987; Ellis, Siegler, & Klahr, 1993; Grannott, unpublished; Kuczaj, 1977; Kuhn, Garcia-Mila, Zohar, & Anderson, 1995; Schauble, 1990; Thelen & Ulrich, 1991). Another consistent finding is that children generate new ways of thinking not just after existing approaches fail, but also when existing approaches are succeeding (Adolph, 1993; Karmiloff-Smith, 1984; 1986; Metz, 1993). A third repeated finding is that generation of new approaches involves surprisingly little trial and error (Metz, 1985; Siegler & Jenkins, 1989; van Lehn, 1990). At least in the domains that have been studied, children rarely try illegitimate new approaches, instead limiting their attempts to approaches consistent with the central requirements for legitimate strategies in the domains. Such results regarding change have been obtained over a wide age range (infants to adults), a wide range of content areas (scientific reasoning, map drawing, locomoting up and down ramps, arithmetic, collaborative problem solving, and number conservation, among them), and by investigators with varying theoretical predispositions (Piagetian, Vygotskyian, dynamical systems, and information processing).

Although microgenetic methods have been used primarily to study cognitive, linguistic, and motor development, they have just as much potential for studying social development. Indeed, social development offers some especially exciting possibilities. Many important influences on social development occur at times that can be anticipated in advance. Birth of a sibling; entrance into daycare, preschool, or school; and moving to a new neighborhood are prominent examples. These predictable events offer the opportunity for intensely studying children in the period leading up to the event, at the time of the event, and after the event.

Even when the timing of changes is difficult to anticipate, microgenetic methods can still be useful in studying social development. For example, Steinberg (1981) followed adolescent boys and their mothers over a one-year period as the boys entered puberty. He found that the early part of the period brought increases in the frequency with which the boys and their mothers interrupted each other. As puberty progressed, the mothers' interruptions of their sons declined, though no corresponding decline in the sons' interruptions occurred. Steinberg noted that the observations could only have been made by following the adolescents both before and during each child's puberty; there were no comparable age-related regularities. Thus, microgenetic methods may prove just as useful for studying social development as they have for studying cognitive development.

Mechanisms

A major reason for using trial-by-trial assessments and microgenetic methods is to obtain data detailed enough to suggest specific hypotheses about the mechanisms that produce the changes. Many overviews of the field have noted that a lack of specificity about change mechanisms is a failing common to all major developmental theories (de Ribaupierre, 1989; Flavell, 1984; Klahr, 1995; Miller, 1993; Sternberg, 1984). The field is not lacking in high-level abstractions that are claimed to produce change: assimilation, accommodation, equilibration, zone of proximal development, conceptual restructuring, differentiation and hierarchic integration. However, concrete ideas about how such constructs produce their effects have been scarce.

A set of specific ideas about the workings of one change mechanism, self-modification through problem-solving experience, was presented in chapter 6. These ideas were embodied within Siegler and Shipley's (1995) Adaptive Strategy Choice Model (ASCM). Taken literally, ASCM is a computer simulation of the development of single-digit addition from 4 years onward. However, the model also provides a more general illustration of how self-modification can generate changes in children's thinking.

The core idea of ASCM is that cognitive change is often generated through experience gained while solving problems. This idea is embodied in the following way. Each time a strategy is used to solve a problem, the experience yields information regarding the strategy, the problem, and their interaction. This information is preserved in a database on each strategy's speed and accuracy for solving problems in general, problems with particular features, and specific problems. When a problem is encountered, the database for each strategy is used to compute a strength for that strategy. These strengths are the model's way of projecting how well the strategy is likely to do on that problem. The likelihood of any given strategy being chosen is determined by the strength of that strategy relative to the strengths of alternative strategies. Each problem-solving experience changes the database of the strategy that was used, and thus changes the probability of the strategy being chosen in the future.

Within ASCM, strategy selection is also influenced by each strategy's novelty. As in the Piagetian construct of functional assimilation, the basic idea is that children like to exercise new competencies. The model operationalizes this idea by assigning novelty points to each newly discovered strategy. At their initial level, these novelty points lead to the new approach being used occasionally. With each exercise of the new strategy, it loses a certain amount of novelty strength, but gains strength from its speed and accuracy in solving the problem. If the strength gained from using the new strategy exceeds the loss of novelty points, as happens when the new strategy is relatively successful, that strategy is used increasingly. If the strength gained does not offset the loss of novelty points, as happens when the new strategy is relatively unsuccessful, the new approach decreases in use. Thus, new strategies that seem promising are used increasingly, and ones that seem unpromising do not continue to be used indefinitely.

The novelty points construct is not an ad hoc mechanism, included to make the simulation run. Rather, its inclusion reflects a belief about the basic architecture of the human cognitive system. More than any other species, human beings are inclined to try novel approaches, approaches that are different than those they have used before and different than those used by others around them. This property must arise either from some specific mechanism that makes novel approaches attractive for use or as a by-product of the workings of other mechanisms. The microgenetic data on strategy discovery indicate that newly discovered approaches often are not used very often, thus indicating that the strength of newly discovered strategies often is not great. However, the microgenetic data also indicate that the strength of newly discovered strategies is sufficient for them to be used occasionally under ordinary circumstances and for their use to increase quickly if especially propitious circumstances arise. The novelty points mechanism, as implemented within ASCM, indicates one way in which the cognitive system could produce such behavior.

The output generated by ASCM indicated that its mechanisms yield performance and learning that resemble those of children in many ways. From quite early in learning, ASCM found the same problems easy, and the same problems difficult, as do children. It also generated fairly adaptive choices among strategies from early in learning. As it gained problem-solving experience, its speed, accuracy, and frequency of use of advanced strategies all increased. Choices among strategies, which were always reasonably adaptive, became more so. The best predictors of the model's speed and accuracy changed in the same ways as those of children. ASCM also generalized to novel problems increasingly reasonably, and generated the same types of individual difference patterns found among children. It explained such apparent paradoxes as why children who are best at using back-up strategies are the first to stop using those strategies and why children who are worst at using them continue to use them the longest. Especially striking, it led to novel predictions about children's performance that proved accurate, and to novel explanations of puzzling previous findings.

Simulation models of development are growing in number, albeit slowly. For example, a recent edited collection (Simon & Halford, 1995) includes simulations of a number of classic developmental phenomena, including transitive inference, analogical reasoning, number conservation, and proportional reasoning. Simulations well-grounded in data are also becoming increasingly prevalent in language development (e.g., MacWhinney & Leinbach, 1991; Plunkett & Sinha, 1991) and perceptual development (e.g., Aslin, 1993; Banks & Shannon, 1993).

These are important milestones in efforts to specify cognitive-developmental change mechanisms. Computer simulations do not change unless well-specified mechanisms make them change. The simulations also are important because they force the modeler to be specific about two other key aspects of the change process: the organism's initial knowledge and the kind of environment in which the changes occur.

The contribution of simulation models to understanding of developmental mechanisms is evident in their suggesting potential solutions to such longstanding questions as how continuous underlying changes in knowledge can give rise to relatively sudden changes in behavior (McClelland, 1995; Munakata, McClelland, Johnson, & Siegler, 1995; van der Maas & Molenaar, 1992; van Geert, 1991) The contribution is also reflected in the types of criticisms that can be leveled at such models. For example, Klahr (1995) criticized several of the simulations within the Simon and Halford collection for hypothesizing implausible numbers and types of input problems. At first glance, it might seem strange to view such a criticism as a point in favor of simulations. However, as Klahr noted, it is hard even to imagine similar criticisms being leveled at constructs such as equilibration, zone of proximal development, or differentiation and hierarchic integration. They and their hypothesized learning environments are not described in nearly enough detail to allow such specific criticisms to be raised.

As noted in chapter 2, a high-level commonality unites a wide variety of simulation models. They possess mechanisms for generating variability, for choosing nonrandomly among the variants, and for preserving the lessons of past experience so that they use the relatively successful variants increasingly often. This characterization holds true regardless of whether the models are phrased within production system, connectionist, or dynamical systems frameworks, and over a wide range of types of development being modeled. The pattern suggests that ability to fulfill these functions, the hallmarks of biological evolution, may be a unifying characteristic among otherwise diverse cognitive-developmental mechanisms. Satisfaction of these functions may also provide a standard to look to in generating new proposals regarding developmental mechanisms.

Metaphors

As noted by Lakoff and Johnson (1980), we organize much of our experience around metaphors. These metaphors are ordinarily unconscious, but they powerfully influence our thinking nonetheless.

The title of Case's (1992) book, *The Mind's Staircase*, points to a metaphor that I believe has organized most thinking about cognitive development for the past century: cognitive development as a staircase. Within this metaphor, children think at a certain level for a prolonged period of time (a tread on the staircase), then their thinking moves rapidly upward for a brief period (a riser), then it settles for an extended period at another, higher level (the next tread), then it increases rapidly to a yet higher level (the next riser), and so on. As discussed in chapter 4, the staircase metaphor characterizes descriptions generated by stage theorists and non-stage-theorists alike.

In the face of what we have learned in the past decade about children's thinking—the pervasive variability, the continuing changes in the conditions under which each way of thinking is chosen, and the frequency with which new approaches are generated—this venerable metaphor seems outdated. New metaphors, as well as new assumptions, questions, methods, and mechanisms, seem essential.

The overlapping-waves metaphor provides an alternative way of envisioning cognitive development that seems consistent with what we have learned about it. This metaphor involves thinking about each way of thinking as a wave approaching a seashore, with several waves (ways of thinking) overlapping at any given point in time, with the height of each wave (frequency of use of the ways of thinking) continuously changing, with different waves being most prominent at different times, and with some waves never being the most prominent but still influencing other waves and contributing to the tide. The metaphor is depicted schematically in the top panel of Figure 8.1.

This way of depicting change is flexible enough to depict staircase progres-

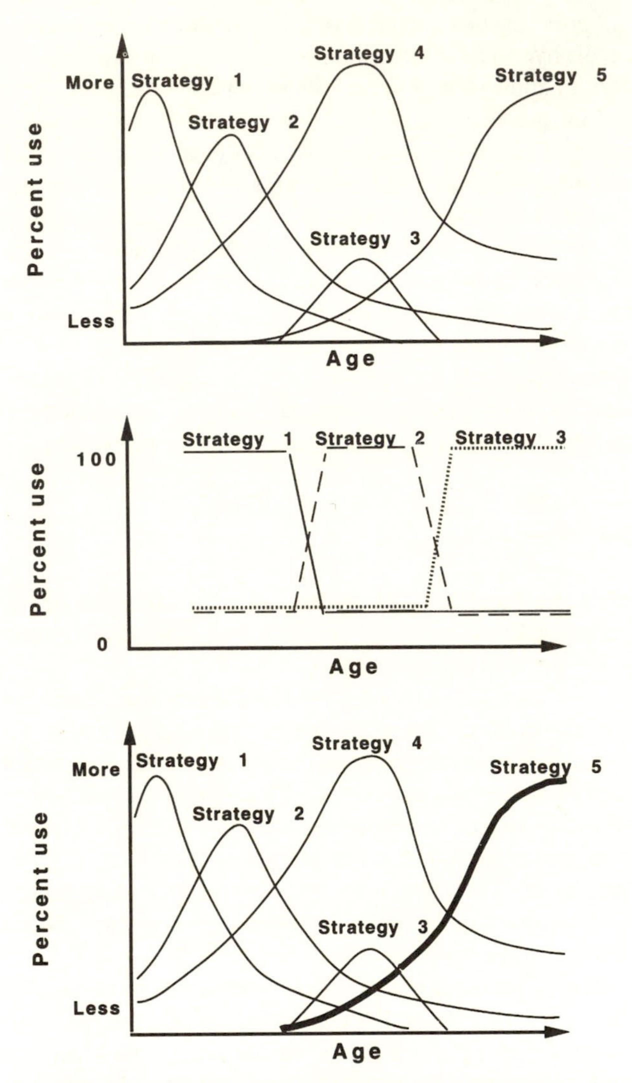

Figure 8.1. Top: An overlapping waves depiction of a typical pattern of cognitive development. Middle: An overlapping waves depiction of a staircase progression. Bottom: An overlapping waves depiction of a typical cognitive developmental pattern, with use of the most advanced strategy highlighted.

sions. As shown in the middle panel of Figure 8.1, they would look like a succession of waves with very steep rises and falls. It also allows us to focus on the frequency of the most advanced way of thinking (as in the bottom panel of Figure 8.1) without losing information about the prevalence of the other approaches.

The overlapping waves metaphor also has a more general virtue. Waves are constantly moving, changing, reconfiguring themselves. Each is different from the last and different from itself slightly earlier in time. Endessly variable, endlessly changing—a wave, like children's thinking, never stands still.

Notes

1. In this discussion of assumptions about variability, as in almost all of the book, the focus has been on variability in the thinking of children. This does not mean that such variability is limited to the thinking of children, or even that it is necessarily more prominent in their thinking than in that of adults. For example, substantial variability in adults' thinking has been documented in question answering (Reder, 1987), sentence-picture verification (Marquer & Pereira, 1990), scientific reasoning (Kuhn et al., 1995), addition (LeFevre, Sadesky, & Bisanz, 1996), multiplication (Reder & Ritter, 1992; Siegler, Adolph, & Lemaire, in press), and reading comprehension (Goldman & Saul, 1990). It doubtless is present in any number of other domains as well.

Regardless of whether we are talking about children or adults, this argument is not intended to imply that we should never describe thinking as less variable than it really is. For example, when teaching a basic undergraduate developmental psychology course, it seems entirely reasonable to focus on how children of given ages most often think and the types of changes with age that occur in these modal ways of thinking. However, we should not confuse our own understanding of children's thinking with what we can convey to undergraduates taking their first course in the field.

2. At first impression, heuristics and biases such as availability and anchoring might seem to constitute exceptions to the assumption that choices generally are adaptive. As noted by Kahnemann and Tversky (1972), however, although these heuristics may lead to faulty estimates in some situations, they are broadly adaptive in that they allow people to make reasonable estimates in many situations in which they lack specific knowledge.

References

Abrams, R. A., & Balota, D. A. (1991). Mental chronometry: Beyond reaction time. *Psychological Science, 2*, 153–157.

Acredolo, C., & Horobin, K. (1995). *The uncertainty theory of cognitive development: An uncertain theory resolutely embraced.* Manuscript submitted for publication, University of California at Davis.

Acredolo, C., & O'Connor, J. (1990, May–June). *Polanyi, Gibson, and Piaget: The role of uncertainty in cognitive development.* Paper presented at the 20th Annual Symposium of the Piaget Society, Philadelphia, PA.

Acredolo, C., & O'Connor, J. (1991). On the difficulty of detecting cognitive uncertainty. *Human Development, 34*, 204–223.

Ada, G. L., & Nissal, G. (1987). The clonal-selection theory. *Scientific American, 257*, 62–69.

Adolph, K. E. (1993). *Perceptual-motor development in infants' locomotion over slopes.* Unpublished doctoral dissertation, Emory University, Atlanta, GA.

Adolph, K. E. (1995). A psychophysical assessment of toddlers' ability to cope with slopes. *Journal of Experimental Psychology: Human Perception and Performance, 21*, 734–750.

Adolph, K. E., Eppler, M. A., & Gibson, E. J. (1993). Crawling versus walking: Infants' perception of affordances for locomotion over sloping surfaces. *Child Development, 64*, 1158–1174.

Alibali, M. W., & Goldin-Meadow, S. (1993). Gesture-speech mismatch and mechanisms of learning: What the hands reveal about a child's state of mind. *Cognitive Psychology, 25*, 468–573.

Anderson, J. H. (1983). *The architecture of cognition.* Cambridge, MA: Harvard University Press.

Anderson, J. R. (1990). *The adaptive character of thought.* Hillsdale, NJ: Lawrence Erlbaum Associates.

Anderson, J. R. (1991). Is human cognition adaptive? *The Behavioral and Brain Sciences, 14*, 471–484.

Anderson, J. R. (1993). *Rules of the mind.* Hillsdale, NJ: Lawrence Erlbaum Associates.

Anglin, J. M. (1977). *Word, object, and conceptual development.* New York: W. W. Norton.

Antell, S. E., & Keating, D. P. (1983). Perception of numerical invariance in neonates. *Child Development, 54*, 695–701.

Anumolu, V., Reilly, K. D., & Bray, N. W. (1992). A hybrid neural network system with serial learning and associative components. In *Proceedings of Workshop on*

Neural Networks and International Simulation Technology Conference, Society for Computer Simulation, San Diego, CA.

Appelbaum, M. I., & McCall, R. B. (1983). Design and analysis in developmental psychology. In P. H. Mussen (Ed.), *Handbook of child psychology: Vol. 1 History, theory and methods*. New York: Wiley.

Ashcraft, M. H. (1982). The development of mental arithmetic: A chronometric approach. *Developmental Review, 2*, 213–236.

Ashcraft, M. H. (1987). Children's knowledge of simple arithmetic: A developmental model and simulation. In J. Bisanz, C. J. Brainerd, & R. Kail (Eds.), *Formal methods in developmental psychology*. New York: Springer-Verlag.

Aslin, R. (1993). Perception of visual direction in human infants. In C. E. Granrud (Ed.), *Visual perception and cognition in infancy*. Hillsdale, NJ: Lawrence Erlbaum Associates.

Astington, J. W., Harris, P. L., & Olson, D. R. (1988). *Developing theories of mind*. Cambridge: Cambridge University Press.

Baer, J. (1994). Divergent thinking is not a general trait: A multidomain training experiment. *Creativity Research Journal, 17*, 35–46.

Baillargeon, R. (1987). Object permanence in 3 1/2- and 4 1/2-month-old infants. *Developmental Psychology, 23*, 655–664.

Baillargeon, R. (1993). The object concept revisited: New directions in the investigation of infants' physical knowledge. In C. E. Granrud (Ed.), *Visual perception and cognition in infancy*. Hillsdale, NJ: Lawrence Erlbaum Associates.

Baker, L., & Brown, A. L. (1984). Metacognitive skills and reading. In P. D. Pearson (Ed.), *Handbook of reading research Part 2*. New York: Longman.

Baldwin, J. M. (1895). *Mental development in the child and the race: Methods and processes*. New York: Macmillan.

Banks, M. S., & Shannon, E. (1993). Spatial and chromatic visual efficiency in human neonates. In C. E. Granrud (Ed.), *Visual perception and cognition in infancy*. Hillsdale, NJ: Lawrence Erlbaum Associates.

Barody, A. J. (1990). The development of kindergartners' mental-addition strategies. *Learning and Individual Differences, 2*, 73–86.

Baron, J., Treiman, R., Wilf, J. F., & Kellman, P. (1980). Spelling and reading by rules. In U. Frith (Ed.), *Cognitive Processes in Spelling*. London: Academic Press.

Bauer, P. J., & Mandler, J. M. (1989). Taxonomies and triads: Conceptual organization in 1- to 2-year-olds. *Cognitive Psychology, 21*, 156–184.

Beilin, H. (1977). Inducing conservation through training. In G. Steiner (Ed.), *Psychology of the 20th century* (Vol. 7, Piaget and beyond). Zurich: Kindler.

Bem, S. L. (1981). Gender schema theory: A cognitive account of sex typing. *Psychological Review, 88*, 354–364.

Berko, J. (1958). The child's learning of English morphology. *Word, 14*, 150–177.

Bisanz, J., & LeFevre, J.-A. (1990). Strategic and nonstrategic processing in the development of mathematical cognition. In D. F. Bjorklund (Ed.), *Children's strategies: Contemporay views of cognitive development*. Hillsdale, NJ: Lawrence Erlbaum Associates.

Bjorklund, D. F., & Coyle, T. R. (in press). Utilization deficiencies in the development of memory strategies. In F. E. Weinert & W. Schneider (Eds.), *Research on memory development: State of the art and future directions*. Hillsdale, NJ: Erlbaum.

Bjorklund, D. F., & Green, B. L. (1992). The adaptive nature of cognitive immaturity. *American Psychologist, 47*, 46–54.

Borkowski, J. M., & Krause, A. (1983). Racial differences in intelligence: The importance of the executive system. *Intelligence, 7*, 379–395.

Bowerman, M. (1982). Starting to talk worse: Clues to language acquisition from children's late speech errors. In S. Strauss (Ed.), *U-Shaped behavioral growth*. New York: Academic Press.

Bradley, R. A., & Terry, M. E. (1953). Rank analysis of incomplete block designs. I. The method of paired comparisons. *Biometrika, 39*, 324–345.

Braine, M. D. S. (1959). The ontogeny of certain logical operations: Piaget's formulation examined by nonverbal methods. *Psychological Monographs, 73* (Whole No. 475).

Brainerd, C. J. (1973). Judgments and explanations as criteria for the presence of cognitive structures. *Psychological Bulletin, 79*, 172–179.

Bray, N. W., Saarnio, D. A., Borges, L. M. & Hawk, L. W. (1993). Intellectual and developmental differences in external memory strategies. *American Journal on Mental Retardation, 99*, 19–31.

Brent, D. E., & Routh, R. K. (1978). Response cost and impulsive word recognition errors in reading-disabled children. *Journal of Abnormal Child Psychology, 6*, 211–219.

Brody, L. R. (1981). Visual short-term cued recall memory in infancy. *Child Development, 52*, 242–250.

Brown, A. L. (1976). The construction of temporal succession by pre-operational children. In A. D. Pick (Ed.), *Minnesota Symposium on Child Psychology: Vol. 10*. Minneapolis: University of Minnesota.

Brown, A. L. (1990). Domain-specific principles affect learning and transfer in children. *Cognitive Science, 14*, 107–133.

Brown, A. L., Bransford, J. D., Ferrara, R. A., & Campione, J. C. (1983). Learning, remembering, and understanding. In P. H. Mussen (Ed.), *Handbook of child psychology: Cognitive development* (Vol. 3). New York: Wiley.

Brown, A. L., & DeLoache, J. S. (1978). Skills, plans, and self-regulation. In R. S. Siegler (Ed.), *Children's thinking: What develops?*. Hillsdale, NJ: Erlbaum.

Brown, A. L., & Reeve, R. A. (1986). Reflections on the growth of reflection in children. *Cognitive Development, 1*, 405–416.

Brown, J. S., & Burton, R. B. (1978). Diagnostic models for procedural bugs in basic mathematical skills. *Cognitive Science, 2*, 155–192.

Brown, R., Cazden, D., & Bellugi, U. (1969). The child's grammar from I to III. In J. P. Hill (Ed.), *Minnesota Symposium on Child Psychology*. Minneapolis: University of Minnesota Press.

Brown, R. A. (1973). *A first language: The early stages*. Cambridge, MA: Harvard University Press.

Brownell, W. A., & Carper, D. V. (1943). Learning the multiplication combinations. *Duke University Research Studies in Education, 7*, 1–177.

Brownell, W. A., & Chazal, C. B. (1935). The effects of premature drill in third-grade arithmetic. *Journal of Educational Research, 29*, 17–28.

Bruner, J. S., Olver, R. R., & Greenfield, P. M. (1966). *Studies in cognitive growth*. New York: Wiley.

Brunswik, E. (1955). Representative design and probabilistic theory in a functional psychology. *Psychological Review, 62*, 193–217.

Bryant, P. E., & Trabasso, T. (1971). Transitive inferences and memory in young children. *Nature, 232*, 457–459.

Burnet, S. M. (1970). *Immunological surveillance*. Oxford: Pergamon Press.

Buss, D. M. (1991). Evolutionary personality psychology. *Annual Review of Psychology, 42*, 459–491.

Byrnes, J. P. & McClenny, B. (1994). Decision-making in young adolescents and adults. *Journal of Experimental Child Psychology, 58*, 359–388.

Butterfield, E. C., & Albertson, L. R. (1995). On making cognitive theory more general and developmentally pertinent. In W. Schneider & F. E. Weinert (Eds.), *Memory performance and competencies: Issues in growth and development*. Hillsdale, NJ: Erlbaum.

Butterfield, E. C., Siladi, D., & Belmont, J. M. (1980). Validating theories of intelligence. In H. Reese & L. P. Lipsitt (Eds.), *Advances in child development and child behavior* (Vol. 15). New York: Academic Press.

Campbell, N. A. (1991). *Biology*. Redwood City, CA: Benjamin/Cummings.

Campbell, D. T. (1960). Blind variation and selective retention in creative thought as in other knowledge processes. *Psychological Review, 67*, 380–400.

Campbell, D. T. (1974). Unjustified variation and selective retention in scientific discovery. In F. J. Ayala & T. Dobzhansky (Eds.), *Studies in the philosophy of biology*. London: Macmillan.

Carey, S. (1985). *Conceptual change in childhood*. Cambridge, MA: MIT Press.

Carey, S., & Gelman, R. (Eds.). (1991). *The epigenesis of mind: Essays on biology and cognition*. Hillsdale, NJ: Erlbaum.

Carpenter, P. A., & Just, M. A. (1975). Sentence comprehension: A psycholinguistic processing model of verification. *Psychological Review, 82*, 45–73.

Carpenter, T. P. (1986). Conceptual knowledge as a foundation for procedural knowledge: Implications from research on the initial learning of arithmetic. In J. Hiebert (Ed.), *Conceptual and procedural knowledge: The case of mathematics*. Hillsdale, NJ: Erlbaum.

Carpenter, T. P., & Moser, J. M. (1984). The acquisition of addition and subtraction concepts in grades one through three. *Journal for Research in Mathematics Education, 15*, 179–202.

Carver, C. S., & Scheier, M. F. (1992). *Perspectives on personality* (2nd ed.). Needham Heights, MA: Simon & Shuster.

Case, R. (1974). Structures and strictures: Some functional limitations on the course of cognitive growth. *Cognitive Psychology, 6*, 544–574.

Case, R. (1978). Intellectual development from birth to adulthood: A neo-Piagetian interpretation. In R. S. Siegler (Ed.), *Children's thinking: What develops?* Hillsdale, NJ: Erlbaum.

Case, R. (1985). *Intellectual development: A systematic reinterpretation*. New York: Academic Press.

Case, R. (1992). *The mind's staircase: Exploring the conceptual underpinnings of children's thought and knowledge*. Hillsdale, NJ: Erlbaum.

Case, R., & Okamoto, Y. (1996). The role of central conceptual structures in the development of children's thought. *Monographs of the Society for Research in Child Development* (Serial No. 246).

Catania, A. C. (1980). Freedom of choice: A behavioral analysis. In G. H. Bower (Ed.), *The psychology of learning and motivation* (Vol. 14). New York: Academic Press.

Cavanaugh, J. C., & Perlmutter, M. (1982). Metamemory: A critical examination. *Child Development, 53*, 11–28.

Chaiken, S. (1980). Heuristic versus systematic information processing and the use of source versus message cues in persuasion. *Journal of Personality and Social Psychology, 39*, 752–766.

Chang, F.-L., & Greenough, W. T. (1984). Transient and enduring morphological correlates of synaptic activity and efficacy change in the rat hippocampal slice. *Brain Research, 309*, 35–46.

Changeux, J.-P., & Dehaene, S. (1989). Neuronal models of cognitive functions. *Cognition, 33*, 63–109.

Charlesworth, W. R. (1986). Darwin and developmental psychology: 100 years later. *Human Development, 29*, 1–35.

Chi, M. T. H. (1978). Knowledge structures and memory development. In R. S. Siegler (Ed.), *Children's thinking: What develops?* Hillsdale, NJ: Erlbaum.

Chi, M. T. H., Bassok, M., Lewis, M., Reimann, P., & Glasser, R. (1989). Self-explanations: How students study and use examples in learning to solve problems. *Cognitive Science, 13*, 145–182.

Chi, M. T. H., Feltovich, P. J., & Glaser, R. (1981). Categorization and representation of physics problems by experts and novices. *Cognitive Science, 5*, 121–152.

Chi, M. T. H., & Koeske, R. D. (1983). Network representation of a child's dinosaur knowledge. *Developmental Psychology, 19*, 29–39.

Church, R. B., & Goldin-Meadow, S. (1986). The mismatch between gesture and speech as an index of transitional knowledge. *Cognition, 23*, 43–71.

Colby, A., Kohlberg, L., Gibbs, J., & Lieberman, M. (1983). A longitudinal study of moral judgement. *Monographs of the Society for Research in Child Development, 48* (Serial No. 200).

Coles, M. G. H., Gratton, G., Bashore, T. R., Eriksen, C. W., & Donchin, E. (1985). A psychophysiological investigation of the continuous flow model of human information processing. *Journal of Experimental Psychology: Human Perception and Performance, 11*, 529–533.

Collins, L. M. (1991). Measurement in longitudinal research. In L. M. Collins & J. L. Horn (Eds.), *Best methods for the analysis of change: Recent advances, unanswered questions, future directions*. Washington, DC: American Psychological Association.

Coombs, C. H., & Avrunin, G. S. (1988). *The structure of conflict*. Hillsdale, NJ: Erlbaum.

Cooney, J. B., & Ladd, S. F. (1992). The influence of verbal protocol methods on children's mental computation. *Learning and Individual Differences, 4*, 237–257.

Cooney, J. B., Swanson, H. L., & Ladd, S. F. (1988). Acquisition of mental multiplication skill: Evidence for the transition between counting and retrieval strategies. *Cognition and Instruction, 5*, 323–345.

Cooper, L. A., & Regan, D. (1982). Attention, perception and intelligence. In R. Sternberg (Ed.), *Handbook of human intelligence*. New York: Cambridge University Press.

Cooper, L. A., & Shepard, R. N. (1973). Chronometric studies of the rotation of mental images. In W. G. Chase (Ed.), *Visual information processing*. New York: Academic Press.

Cosmides, L., & Tooby, J. (1987). From evolution to behavior: Evolutionary psychology as the missing link. In J. Dupre (Ed.), *The latest on the best: Essays on evolution and optimality*. Cambridge, MA: MIT Press.

Crowder, R. G. (1976). *Principles of learning and memory*. Hillsdale, NJ: Erlbaum.

Crowley, K., & Siegler, R. S. (1993). Flexible strategy use in young children's tic-tac-toe. *Cognitive Science, 17*, 531–561.

Cziko, G. (1995). *Without miracles: Universal selection theory and the second Darwinian evolution*. Cambridge, MA: MIT Press.

Darwin, C. (1859). *On the origins of species by means of natural selection*.

Davidson, J. E. (1986). The role of insight in giftedness. In R. J. Sternberg & J. E. Davidson (Eds.), *Conceptions of giftedness*. New York: Cambridge University Press.

Davison, M., & McCarthy, D. (1988). *The matching law: A research review*. Hillsdale, NJ: Erlbaum.

Dawes, R. M. (1979). The robust beauty of improper linear models in decision making. *American Psychologist, 34*, 571–582.

Deary, I. J. (1988). Applying evolutionary epistomology: From immunity to intelligence. *Journal of Social Biological Structure, 11*, 399–408.

Dehaene, S., & Changeux, J.-P. (1989). A simple model of prefrontal cortex function in delayed-response tasks. *Journal of Cognitive Neuroscience, 1*, 244–261.

DeKay, W. T., & Buss, D. M. (1992). Human nature, individual differences, and the importance of context: Perspectives from evolutionary psychology. *Current Directions in Psychological Science, 1*, 184–189.

DeLoache, J. S. (1984). Oh where, oh where: Memory-based searching by very young children. In C. Sophian (Ed.), *Origins of cognitive skills*. Hillsdale, NJ: Erlbaum.

DeLoache, J. S. (1987). Rapid change in the symbolic functioning of young children. *Science, 238*, 1556–1557.

Dempster, F. N. (1981). Memory span: Sources of individual and developmental differences. *Psychological Bulletin, 89*, 63–100.

de Ribaupierre, A. (Ed.). (1989). *Transition mechanisms in child development: The longitudinal perspective*. New York: Cambridge University Press.

Diamond, A. (1985). Development of the ability to use recall to guide action, as indicated by infants' performance of AB. *Child Development, 56*, 868–883.

Dodge, K. A., Pettit, G. S., McCloskey, C. L., & Brown, M. M. (1986). Social competence in children. *Monographs of the Society for Research in Child Development, 51* (Whole No. 213).

Dromi, E. (1987). *Early lexical development*. London: Cambridge University Press.

Durham, W. D. (1991). *Coevolution*. Stanford, CA: Stanford University Press.

Dweck, C. S., & Leggett, E. L. (1988). A social-cognitive approach to motivation and personality. *Psychological Review, 95*, 256–273.

Eckerman, C. O., & Didow, S. M. (1989). Toddlers' social coordinations: Changing responses to another's invitation to play. *Developmental Psychology, 25*, 794–804.

Edelman, G. M. (1987). *Neural Darwinism: The theory of neuronal group selection*. New York: Basic Books, Inc.

Egan, D. E., & Grimes-Farrow, D. D. (1982). Differences in mental representations spontaneously adopted for reasoning. *Memory and Cognition, 10*, 297–307.

Eisenberg, N., Miller, P. A., Shell, R., McNally, S., & Shea, C. (1991). Prosocial development in adolescence: A longitudinal study. *Developmental Psychology, 27*, 849–857.

Ellis, S. A., & Siegler, R. S. (in press). Planning as a strategy choice. Why don't children plan when they should? In S. Friedman & E. Scholnick (Eds.), *Why, how, and when do we plan: The developmental psychology of planning*. Hillsdale, NJ: Erlbaum.

Ellis, S., Siegler, R. S., & Klahr, D. (1993, March). *Effects of feedback and collaboration on changes in children's use of mathematical rules*. Paper presented at the meeting of the Society for Research in Child Development, New Orleans, LA.

Ericsson, K. A., & Polson, P. G. (1988). A cognitive analysis of exceptional memory for restaurant orders. In M. T. H. Chi, R. Glaser, & M. J. Farr (Eds.), *The nature of expertise*. Hillsdale, NJ: Erlbaum.

Ericsson, K. A., & Simon, H. A. (1991). *Protocol analysis* (2nd ed.). Cambridge, MA: MIT Press.

Ervin, S. M. (1964). Imitation and structural change in children's language. In E. H. Lenneberg (Ed.), *New directions in the study of language*. Cambridge, MA: MIT Press.

Estes, W. K. (1956). The problem of inference from curves based on group data. *Psychological Bulletin, 53*, 134–140.

Fabricius, W. V., & Hagen, J. W. (1984). The use of causal attributions about recall performance to assess metamemory and predict strategic memory behavior in young children. *Developmental Psychology, 20*, 975–987.

Falkenhainer, B., Forbus, K. D., & Gentner, D. (1986). *The structure-mapping engine.* Paper presented at the American Association for Artifical Intelligence, Philadelphia, PA.

Farah, M. J., & Kosslyn, S. M. (1982). Concept development. In H. W. Reese & L. P. Lipsitt (Eds.), *Advances in child development and behavior*. New York: Academic Press.

Feldman, D. H. (1980). *Beyond universals in cognitive development*. Norwood, NJ: Ablex.

Feldman, D. H. (1986). *Nature's gambit: Child prodigies and the development of human potential*. New York: Basic Books.

Ferguson, C. A. (1986). Discovering sound units and constructing sound systems: It's child's play. In J. S. Perkell & D. H. Klatt (Eds.), *Invariance and variability in speech processes*. Hillsdale, NJ: Erlbaum.

Field, D. (1987). A review of preschool conservation training: An analysis of analyses. *Developmental Review, 7*, 210–251.

Fischer, K. W. (1987). Relations between brain and cognitive development. *Child Development, 58*, 623–632.

Fishbein, M., & Ajzen, I. (1975). *Belief, attitude, intention, and behavior: An introduction to theory and research*. Reading, MA: Addison-Wesley.

Fiske, S. T., & Taylor, S. E. (1991). *Social cognition* (2nd ed.). New York: McGraw Hill.

Flavell, J. H. (1971). Stage-related properties of cognitive development. *Cognitive Psychology, 2*, 421–453.

Flavell, J. H. (1979). Metacognition and cognitive monitoring: A new area of cognitive-developmental inquiry. *American Psychologist, 34*, 906–911.

Flavell, J. H. (1981). Cognitive monitoring. In P. Dickson (Ed.), *Children's oral communication skills*. New York: Academic Press.

Flavell, J. H. (1984). Discussion. In R. J. Sternberg (Ed.), *Mechanisms of cognitive development*. New York: Freeman.

Flavell, J. H. (1985). *Cognitive development* (2nd ed.). Englewood Cliffs, NJ: Prentice-Hall.

Flavell, J. H., Beach, D. R., & Chinsky, J. M. (1966). Spontaneous verbal rehearsal in a memory task as a function of age. *Child Development, 37*, 283–299.

Flavell, J. H., Green, F. L., & Flavell, E. R. (1986). Development of knowledge about the appearance-reality distinction. *Monographs of the Society for Research in Child Development, 51* (1, Serial No. 212).

Flavell, J. H., Miller, P. H., & Miller, S. A. (1993). *Cognitive development* (3rd ed.). Englewood Cliffs, NJ: Prentice Hall.

Flavell, J. H., & Wellman, H. M. (1977). Metamemory. In R. V. Kail, Jr. & J. W. Hagen (Eds.), *Perspectives on the development of memory and cognition*. Hillsdale, NJ: Erlbaum.

Fox, N., Kagan, J., & Weiskopf, S. (1979). The growth of memory during infancy. *Genetic Psychology Monographs, 99*, 91–130.

Freund, L. S. (1990). Maternal regulation of children's problem solving behavior and its impact on children's performance. *Child Development, 61*, 113–126.

Friedman, S. L., Scholnick, E. K., & Cocking, R. R. (1987). *Blueprints for thinking: The role of planning in cognitive development*. Cambridge, MA: Cambridge University Press.

Fuson, K. C. (1984). More complexities in subtraction. *Journal for Research in Mathematics Education, 15*, 214–225.

Fuson, K. C. (1988). *Children's counting and concepts of number*. New York: Springer-Verlag.

Fuson, K. C., Richards, J., & Briars, D. J. (1982). The acquisition and elaboration of the number word sequence. In C. Brainerd (Ed.), *Progress in cognitive development: Children's logical and mathematical cognition* (Vol. 1). New York: Springer-Verlag.

Gallistel, C. R. (1990). *The organization of learning*. Cambridge, MA: MIT Press.

Gardner, W. P., & Rogoff, B. (1990). Children's deliberateness of planning according to task circumstances. *Developmental Psychology, 26*, 480–487.

Gauvain, M. (1992). Social influences on the development of planning in advance and during action. *International Journal of Behavioral Development, 15*, 377–398.

Gauvain, M., & Rogoff, B. (1989). Collaborative problem solving and children's planning skills. *Developmental Psychology, 25*, 139–151.

Geary, D. C. (1990). A componential analysis of an early learning deficit in mathematics. *Journal of Experimental Child Psychology, 49*, 363–383.

Geary, D. C. (1995). *Children's mathematical development*. Washington, DC: American Psychological Association.

Geary, D. C., & Brown, S. C. (1991). Cognitive addition: Strategy choice and speed-of-processing differences in gifted, normal and mathematically disabled children. *Developmental Psychology, 27*, 398–406.

Geary, D. C., Brown, S. C., & Samaranayake, V. A. (1991). Cognitive addition: A short longitudinal study of strategy choice and speed-of-processing differences in normal and mathematically disabled children. *Developmental Psychology, 27*, 787–797.

Geary, D. C., & Burlingham-Dubree, M. (1989). External validation of the strategy choice model for addition. *Journal of Experimental Child Psychology, 47*, 175–192.

Geary, D. C., Fan, L., & Bow-Thomas, C. C. (1992). Numerical cognition: Loci of ability differences comparing children from China and the United States. *Psychological Science, 3*, 180–185.

Geary, D. C., Fan, L., Bow-Thomas, C. C., & Siegler, R. S. (1993). Even before formal instruction, Chinese children outperform American children in mental addition. *Cognitive Development, 8*, 517–529.

Geary, D. C., Widaman, K. F., & Little, T. D. (1986). Cognitive addition and multiplication: Evidence for a single memory network. *Memory and Cognition, 14*, 478–487.

Geary, D. C., Widaman, K. F., Little, T. D., & Cormier, P. (1987). Cognitive addition: Comparison of learning disabled and academically normal elementary school children. *Cognitive Development, 2*, 249–269.

Geary, D. C., & Wiley, J. G. (1991). Cognitive addition: Strategy choice and speed-of-processing differences in young and elderly adults. *Psychology and Aging, 6*, 474–483.

Gelman, R. (1972). The nature and development of early number concepts. In H. W. Reese & L. P. Lipsitt (Eds.), *Advances in child development and behavior*. New York: Academic Press.

Gelman, R. (1993). A rational-constructivist account of early learning about numbers and objects. In D. Medin (Ed.), *The psychology of learning and motivation* (Vol. 30). San Diego, CA: Academic Press.

Gelman, R., & Gallistel, C. R. (1978). *The child's understanding of number*. Cambridge, MA: Harvard University Press.

Gelman, R., Meck, E., & Merkin, S. (1986). Young children's numerical competence. *Cognitive Development, 1*, 1–29.

Gelman, S. (1988). The development of induction within natural kind and artifact categories. *Cognitive Psychology, 20*, 65–95.

Gentner, D. (1989). The mechanisms of analogical transfer. In S. Vosniadou & A. Ortony (Eds.), *Similarity and analogical reasoning*. London: Cambridge University Press.

Gentner, D., & Toupin, C. (1986). Systematicity and similarity in the development of an analogy. *Cognitive Science, 10*, 277–300.

Ghatala, E. S., Levin, J. R., Pressley, M., & Goodwin, D. (1986). A componential analysis of the effects of derived and supplied strategy-utility information on children's strategy selection. *Journal of Experimental Child Psychology, 41*, 76–92.

Gibson, E. J. (1994). Has psychology a future? *Psychological Science, 5*, 69–76.

Gick, M. L., & Holyoak, K. J. (1980). Schema induction and analogical transfer. *Cognitive Psychology, 15*, 1–38.

Gigerenzer, G., Hoffrage, U., & Kleinbolting, H. (1991). Probabilistic mental models: A Brunswikian theory of confidence. *Psychological Review, 98*, 506–528.

Gillilund, G., & Shiffrin, R. M. (1984). A retrieval model for both recognition and recall. *Psychological Review, 91*, 1–67.

Glucksberg, S., & Keysar, B. (1990). Understanding metaphorical comparisons: Beyond similarity. *Psychological Review, 97*, 3–18.

Goldberg, D. E. (1983). *Computer-aided gas pipeline operation using genetic algorithms and rule learning*. Unpublished doctoral dissertation, University of Michigan.

Goldin-Meadow, S., Alibali, M. W., & Church, R. B. (1993). Transitions in concept acquisition: Using the hand to read the mind. *Psychological Review, 100*, 279–297.

Goldman, S. R., Mertz, D. L., & Pelegrino, J. W. (1989). Individual differences in extended practice functions and solution strategies for basic addition facts. *Journal of Educational Psychology, 81*, 481–496.

Goldman, S. R., & Saul, E. U. (1990). Flexibility in text processing: A strategy competition model. *Learning and Individual Differences, 2*, 181–219.

Goldman-Rakic, P. S. (1987). Development of cortical circuitry and cognitive function. *Child Development, 58*, 601–622.

Gould, S. J. (1984). Relationship of individual and group change. Ontogeny and phylogeny in biology. *Human Development, 27*, 233–239.

Graham, T., & Perry, M. (1993). Indexing transitional knowledge. *Developmental Psychology, 29*, 779–788.

Granott, N. (1991). Puzzled minds and weird creatures: Phases in the spontaneous process of knowledge construction. In I. Harel & S. Papert (Eds.), *Constructionism. Research reports and essays, 1985–1990, by the Epistemology & Learning Research Group*. Norwood, NJ: Ablex Publishing Corporation.

Granott, N. (1993). Patterns of interaction in the co-construction of knowledge: Separate minds, joint effort, and weird creatures. In R. Wozniak & K. W. Fischer (Eds.),

Development in context: Acting and thinking in specific environments (Vol. 2). Hillsdale, NJ: Lawrence Erlbaum.

Granott, N. (1995). *From macro to micro and back: An analysis and explanation of microdevelopment.* Unpublished manuscript.

Greenfield, P. M., & Lave, J. (1982). Cognitive aspects of informal education. In D. A. Wagner & H. W. Stevenson (Eds.), *Cultural perspectives on child development.* San Francisco, CA: Freeman.

Greenough, W. T., Black, J. E., & Wallace, C. S. (1987). Experience and brain development. *Child Development, 58*, 539–559.

Grene, M. (1987). Hierarchies in biology. *American Scientist, 75*, 504–510.

Groen, G. J., & Parkman, J. M. (1972). A chronometric analysis of simple addition. *Psychological Review, 79*, 329–343.

Groen, G. J., & Poll, M. (1973). Subtraction and the solution of open sentence problems. *Journal of Experimental Child Psychology, 16*, 292–302.

Groen, G. J., & Resnick, L. B. (1977). Can preschool children invent addition algorithms? *Journal of Educational Psychology, 69*, 645–652.

Guttentag, R. E. (1984). The mental effort requirement of cumulative rehearsal: A developmental study. *Journal of Experimental Child Psychology, 37*, 92–106.

Guyote, M. J., & Sternberg, R. J. (1981). A transitive-chain theory of syllogistic reasoning. *Cognitive Psychology, 13*, 461–525.

Halford, G. (1993). *Children's understanding: The development of mental models.* Hillsdale, NJ: Lawrence Erlbaum Associates.

Halford, G. (1995). Modeling the development of reasoning strategies: The roles of analogy, knowledge, and capacity. In T. Simon & G. Halford (Eds.), *Developing cognitive competence: New approaches to process modeling.* Hillsdale, NJ: Erlbaum.

Hamann, M. S., & Ashcraft, M. H. (1985). Textbook presentations of the basic addition facts. *Cognition and Instruction, 3*, 173–192.

Hare, M. L. (1990). *The role of similarity in Hungarian vowel harmony: A connectionist account.* University of California at San Diego.

Hebbeler, K. (1976). *The development of children's problem-solving skills in addition.* Unpublished doctoral dissertation, Cornell University.

Herrnstein, R. J. (1970). On the law of effect. *Journal of the Experimental Analysis of Behavior, 13*, 243–266.

Herrnstein, R. J. (1990). Rational choice theory: Necessary but not sufficient. *American Psychologist, 45*, 356–367.

Hindle, D. (1978). Approaches to vowel normalization in the study of natural speech. In D. Sankoff (Ed.), *Linguistic variation: Models and methods.* New York: Academic Press.

Hirschleifer, J. (1982). Evolutionary models in economics and law: Cooperation versus conflict strategies. *Research in Law and Economics, 4*, 1–60.

Hogarth, R. M. (1987). *Judgment and choice* (2nd ed.). New York: Wiley.

Holland, J. H., Holyoak, K. J., Nisbett, R. E., & Thagard, P. R. (1986). *Induction: Processes of inference, learning, and discovery.* Cambridge, MA: MIT Press.

Holyoak, K. J., Koh, K., & Nisbett, R. E. (1989). A theory of conditioning: Inductive learning within rule-based default hierarchies. *Psychological Review, 96*, 315–340.

Houlihan, D. M., & Ginsburg, H. P. (1981). The addition methods of first- and second-grade children. *Journal for Research in Mathematics Education, 12*, 95–106.

Hubbard, K. E., LeFevre, J., & Greenham, S. L. (1994, June). *Procedure use in multipli-*

cation by adolescents. Paper presented at the Annual meeting of the Canadian Society for Brain, Behavior, and Cognitive Science, Vancouver.

Huttenlocher, J., & Burke, D. (1976). Why does memory span increase with age? *Cognitive Psychology, 8*, 1–31.

Huttenlocher, P. R. (1979). Synaptic density in human frontal-cortex-developmental changes and effects of aging. *Brain Research, 63*, 195–205.

Inhelder, B., Ackerman-Vallado, E., Blanchet, A., Karmiloff-Smith, A., Kilcher-Hagedorn, H., Montagero, J., & Robert, M. (1976). The process of invention in cognitive development: A report of research in progress. *Archives de Psychologie, 171*, 57–72.

Inhelder, B., & Piaget, J. (1958). *The growth of logical thinking from childhood to adolescence*. New York: Basic Books.

Jakobson, R. (1968). *Child lanugage, aphasia and phonological universals* (A. R. Keiler, Trans.). The Hague: Mouton. (Original work published in 1941)

Jerne, N. K. (1955). *Proceedings of the National Academy of Science USA, 41*, 849.

Johnson, J. S., & Newport, E. L. (1989). Critical period effects in second language learning: The influence of maturational state on the acquisition of English as a second language. *Cognitive Psychology, 21*, 60–99.

Johnson-Laird, P. N., Byrne, R. M. J., & Tabossi, P. (1989). Reasoning by model: The case of multiple quantification. *Psychological Review, 96*, 658–673.

Jones, R. M., & Van Lehn, K. (1991). Strategy shifts without impasses: A computational model of the sum-to-min transition. In *Proceedings of the Thirteenth Annual Conference of the Cognitive Science Society*. Hillsdale, NJ: Lawrence Erlbaum Associates.

Just, M. A., & Carpenter, P. A. (1985). Cognitive coordinate systems: Accounts of mental rotation and individual differences in spatial ability. *Psychological Review, 92*, 137–172.

Justice, E. M. (1985). Categorization as a preferred memory strategy: Developmental changes during elementary school. *Developmental Psychology, 21*, 1105–1110.

Kagan, J., Rosman, B. L., Day, D., Albert, J., & Phillips, W. (1964). Significance of analytic and reflective attitudes. *Psychological Monographs, 78* (Whole No. 578).

Kahneman, D., & Tversky, A. (1972). Subjective probability: A judgment of representativeness. *Cognitive Psychology, 3*, 430–454.

Kahneman, D., & Tversky, A. (1982). The simulation heuristic. In D. Kaheman, P. Slovic, & A. Tversky (Eds.), *Judgment under uncertainty: Heuristics and biases*. New York: Cambridge University Press.

Karmiloff-Smith, A. (1984). Children's problem solving. In M. Lamb, A. L. Brown, & B. Rogoff (Eds.), *Advances in developmental psychology*, (Vol. 3, pp. 39–89). Hillsdale, NJ: Erlbaum.

Karmiloff-Smith, A. (1986). Stage/structure versus phase/process in modelling linguistic and cognitive development. In I. Levin (Ed.), *Stage and structure: Reopening the debate*. Norwood, NJ: Ablex.

Karmiloff-Smith, A. (1992). *Beyond modularity: A developmental perspective of cognitive science*. Cambridge, MA: MIT Press.

Karmiloff-Smith, A., & Inhelder, B. (1977). If you want to get ahead, get a theory. *Cognition, 3*, 195–212.

Kaye, D. B., Post, T. A., Hall, V. C., & Dineen, J. T. (1986). The emergence of information retrieval strategies in numerical cognition: A developmental study. *Cognition and Instruction, 3*, 137–166.

Kearins, J. M. (1981). Visual spatial memory in Australian aboriginal children of desert regions. *Cognitive Psychology, 13*, 434–460.

Keeney, F. J., Cannizzo, S. R., & Flavell, J. H. (1967). Spontaneous and induced verbal rehearsal in a recall task. *Child Development, 38*, 953–966.

Keeney, R. L., & Raiffa, H. (1976). *Decisions with multiple objectives: Preferences and value tradeoffs*. New York: Wiley.

Keil, F. C. (1989). *Concepts, kinds, and cognitive development*. Cambridge, MA: MIT Press.

Keil, F. C. (1992). The origins of an autonomous biology. In M. R. Gunnar & M. Maratsos (Eds.), *Modularity and constraints in language and cognition: The Minnesota Symposia on Child Psychology, Volume 25*. Hillsdale, NJ: Erlbaum.

Kerkman, D. D., & Siegler, R. S. (1993). Individual differences and adaptive flexibility in lower-income children's strategy choices. *Learning and Individual Differences, 5*, 113–136.

Klahr, D. (1982). Nonmonotone assessment of monotone development: An information processing analysis. In S. Strauss (Ed.), *U-shaped behavioral growth*. New York: Academic Press.

Klahr, D. (1984). Transition processes in quantitative development. In R. J. Sternberg (Ed.), *Mechanisms of cognitive development*. New York: Freeman.

Klahr, D. (1992). Information processing approaches to cognitive development. In M. H. Bornstein & M. E. Lamb (Eds.), *Developmental psychology: An advanced textbook* (3rd ed.). Hillsdale, NJ: Lawrence Erlbaum Associates.

Klahr, D. (1995). Computational models of cognitive change: The state of the art. In T. J. Simon & G. S. Halford (Eds.), *Developing cognitive competence: New approaches to process modeling*. Hillsdale, NJ: Lawrence Erlbaum Associates.

Klahr, D., & Siegler, R. S. (1978). The representation of children's knowledge. In H. W. Reese & L. P. Lipsitt (Eds.), *Advances in child development* (Vol. 12). New York: Academic Press.

Klayman, J. (1985). Children's decision strategies and their adaptation to task characteristics. *Organizational Behavior and Human Decision Processes, 35*, 179–201.

Kluwe, R. H. (1982). Cognitive knowledge and executive control: Metacognition. In D. Griffin (Ed.), *Animal mind-human mind*. New York: Springer.

Kogan, N. (1983). Stylistic variation in childhood and adolescence: Creativity, metaphor, and cognitive styles. In P. H. Mussen (Ed.), *Handbook of child psychology, Vol. III, Cognitive development*. New York: Wiley.

Kohlberg, L. (1969). Stage and sequence: The cognitive-developmental approach to socialization. In D. A. Goslin (Ed.), *Handbook of socialization theory and research*. Chicago: Rand McNally.

Kreutzer, M. A., Leonard, C., & Flavell, J. H. (1975). An interview study of children's knowledge about memory. *Monographs of the Society for Research in Child Development, 40* (Serial No. 159).

Krueger, J., Rothbart, M., & Siriam, N. (1989). Category learning and change: Differences in sensitivity to information that enhances or reduces intercategory distinctions. *Journal of Personality and Social Psychology, 56*, 866–875.

Kruger, A. (1992). The effects of peer and adult-child transactive discussions with peers and adults. *Merrill-Palmer Quarterly, 38*, 191–211.

Kuczaj, S. A. (1976). *"-ing," "-s," & "-ed": A study of the acquisition of certain verb inflections*. Unpublished doctoral dissertation, University of Minnesota.

Kuczaj, S. A. (1977). The acquisition of regular and irregular past tense forms. *Journal of Verbal Learning and Verbal Behavior, 16*, 589–600.

Kuhn, D. (1984). Cognitive development. In M. H. Bornstein & M. E. Lamb (Eds.), *Developmental psychology: An advanced textbook*. Hillsdale, NJ: Erlbaum.

Kuhn, D. (1988). Cognitive development. In M. H. Bornstein & M. E. Lamb (Eds.), *Developmental psychology: An advanced textbook* (2nd ed.). Hillsdale, NJ: Erlbaum.

Kuhn, D. (1989). Children and adults as intuitive scientists. *Psychological Review, 96*, 674–689.

Kuhn, D. (1995). Microgenetic study of change: What has it told us? *Psychological Science, 6*, 133–139.

Kuhn, D., Amsel, E., & O'Laughlin, M. (1988). *The development of scientific thinking skills*. San Diego, CA: Academic Press.

Kuhn, D., Garcia-Mila, M., Zohar, A., & Anderson, C. (1995). Strategies of knowledge acquisition. *Monographs of the Society for Research in Child Development* (Serial No. 245).

Kuhn, D., & Phelps, E. (1982). The development of problem-solving strategies. In H. Reese (Ed.), *Advances in child development and behavior, Vol. 17*. New York: Academic Press.

Kuhn, D., Schauble, L., & Garcia-Mila, M. (1992). Cross-domain development of scientific reasoning. *Cognition and Instruction, 9*, 285–327.

Kyllonen, P. C., Lohman, D. F., & Snow, R. E. (1984). Effects of aptitudes, strategy training, and task facets on spatial task performance. *Journal of Educational Psychology, 76*, 130–145.

Kyllonen, P. C., Lohman, D. F., & Woltz, D. J. (1984). Componential modeling of alternative strategies for performing spatial tasks. *Journal of Educational Psychology, 76*, 1325–1345.

Labov, W. (1969). Contraction, deletion, and inherent variability of the English copula. *Language, 45*, 715–762.

Labov, W., Yaeger, M., & Steiner, R. A. (1972). *A quantitative study of sound change in progress*. Report on NSF Contract GS-3287. Philadelphia: U. S. Regional Survey.

Ladd, S. F. (1987). *Mental addition in children and adults using chronometric and interview paradigms*. Unpublished doctoral dissertation, University of Northern Colorado, Greeley.

Lakoff, G., & Johnson, M. (1980). *Metaphors we live by*. Chicago: University of Chicago Press.

Lamarck, J. B. (1809). *Zoological Philosophy*. London: Macmillan.

Langer, E. J. (1989). *Mindfulness*. Reading, MA: Addison-Wesley.

Langley, P. (1987). A general theory of discrimination in learning. In D. Klahr, P. Langley, & R. Neches (Eds.), *Production system models of learning and development*. Cambridge, MA: MIT Press.

Larkin, J., McDermott, J., Simon, D., & Simon, H. (1980). Expert and novice performance in solving physics problems. *Science, 208*, 140–156.

Lawler, R. W. (1985). *Computer experience and cognitive development: A child's learning in a computer culture*. New York: Wiley.

LeFevre, J., & Kulak, A. G. (1994). Individual differences in the obligatory activation of addition facts. *Memory and Cognition, 22*, 188–200.

LeFevre, J. A., Bisanz, J., Hubbard, K. E., Buffone, L., Greenham, S. L., & Sadesky, G. S. (in press). Multiple routes to solution of single-digit multiplication problems. *Journal of Experimental Psychology: General*.

LeFevre, J. A., Bisanz, J., & Mrkonjic, L. (1988). Cognitive arithmetic: Evidence for obligatory activation of arithmetic facts. *Memory and Cognition, 16*, 45–53.

LeFevre, J. A., Kulak, A. G., & Bisanz, J. (1991). Individual differences and developmental change in the associative relations among numbers. *Journal of Experimental Child Psychology, 52*, 256–274.

LeFevre, J. A., Sadesky, G. S., & Bisanz, J. (1996). Selection of procedures in mental addition: Reassessing the problem-size effect in adults. *Journal of Experimental Psychology: Learning, Memory, and Cognition, 22*, 216–230.

Lemaire, P., Barret, S. E., Fayol, M., & Abdi, H. (1994). Automatic activation of addition and multiplication facts in elementary school children. *Journal of Experimental Child Psychology, 57*, 224–258.

Lemaire, P., & Siegler, R. S. (1995). Four aspects of strategic change: Contributions to children's learning of multiplication. *Journal of Experimental Psychology: General, 124*, 83–97.

Leonard, L. B., Rowan, L. E., Morris, M., & Fey, M. E. (1982). Intra-word phonological variablilty in young children. *Journal of Child Language, 9*, 55–69.

Leslie, A. M. (1987). Pretense and representation: The origins of "theory of mind." *Psychological Review, 94*, 412–426.

LeVay, S., Wiesel, T. N., & Hubel, D. H. (1980). The development of ocular dominance columns in normal and visually deprived monkeys. *Journal of Comparative Neurology, 191*, 1–51.

Levin, I., Wilkening, F., & Dembo, Y. (1984). Development of time quantification: Integration and nonintegration of beginnings and endings in comparing durations. *Child Development, 55*, 2160–2172.

Levine, S. C., Jordan, N. C., & Huttenlocher, J. (1992). Development of calculation abilities in young children. *Journal of Experimental Child Psychology, 53*, 72–103.

Lewis, L. P. (1980). *Strategies children use in spelling*. Unpublished doctoral dissertation, University of Denver.

Lewontin, R. C. (1978). Adaptation. *Scientific American, 239*, 212–230.

Liben, L. S. (1987). *Development and learning: Conflict or congruence?* Hillsdale, NJ: Erlbaum.

Lichtenstein, S., & Slovic, P. (1971). Reversals of preference between bids and choices in gambling decisions. *Journal of Experimental Psychology, 89*, 46–55.

Lichtenstein, S., & Slovic, P. (1973). Response-induced reversals of preference in gambling: An extended replication in Las Vegas. *Journal of Experimental Psychology, 101*, 16–20.

Lorsbach, T. C., & Gray, J. W. (1985). The development of encoding processes in learning disabled children. *Journal of Learning Disabilities, 18*, 222–227.

Lovett, M. C., & Anderson, J. R. (in press). History of success and current context in problem solving: Combined influences on operator selection. Manuscript submitted for publication.

Luce, R. D. (1959). *Individual choice behavior: A theoretical anlaysis*. New York: Wiley.

Lumsden, C. J., & Wilson, E. O. (1981). *Genes, mind, and culture: The coevolutionary process*. Cambridge, MA: Harvard University Press.

MacLeod, C. M., Hunt, E. B., & Mathews, N. N. (1978). Individual differences in the verification of sentence-picture relationships. *Journal of Verbal Learning and Verbal Behavior, 17*, 493–507.

MacWhinney, B., & Chang, F. (in press). Connectionism and language learning. In C. Nelson (Ed.), *The Minnesota Symposium on Child Psychology*.

MacWhinney, B., & Leinbach, J. (1991). Implementations are not conceptualizations: Revising the verb learning model. *Cognition, 40*, 121–157.

MacWhinney, B., Leinbach, J., Taraban, R., & McDonald, J. (1989). Language learning: Cues or rules? *Journal of Memory and Language, 28*, 255–277.

Maloney, D. P., & Siegler, R. S. (1993). Conceptual competition in physics learning. *International Journal of Science Education, 15*, 283–295.

Mandler, J. M., Bauer, P. J., & McDonough, L. (1991). Separating the sheep from the goats: Differentiating global categories. *Cognitive Psychology, 23*, 263–298.

Maratsos, M. P. (1982). The child's construction of grammatical categories. In E. Wanner & L. Gleitman (Eds.), *Language acquisition: The state of the art* (pp. 240–266). New York: Cambridge University Press.

Marchman, V. A., & Callan, D. E. (1995). Multiple determinants of the productive use of the regular past tense suffix. *Proceedings of the 17th Annual Cognitive Science Society*. Hillsdale, NJ: Erlbaum.

Marcus, G. F., Pinker, S., Ullman, M., Hollander, M., Rosen, T. J., & Xu, F. (1992). Overregularization in language acquisition. *Monographs of the Society for Research in Child Development, 57* (Serial No. 228).

Markman, E. M. (1989). *Categorization and naming in children: Problems of induction*. Cambridge, MA: MIT Press.

Markman, E. M., & Seibert, J. (1976). Classes and collections: Internal organization and resulting holistic properties. *Cognitive Psychology, 8*, 561–577.

Marquer, J., & Pereira, M. (1990). Reaction time in the study of strategies in sentence-picture verification: A reconsideration. *The Quarterly Journal of Experimental Psychology, 42A*, 147–168.

Marsh, G., Friedman, M., Welch, V., & Desberg, P. (1980). The development of strategies in spelling. In U. Frith (Ed.), *Cognitive processes in spelling*. London: Academic Press.

Mathews, N. N., Hunt, E. B., & McCleod, C. M. (1980). Strategy choice and strategy training in sentence-picture verification. *Journal of Verbal Learning and Verbal Behavior, 19*, 531–548.

Mayr, E. (1982). *The growth of biological thought*. Cambridge, MA: Belknap Press of Harvard University Press.

Mayr, E. (1988). *Toward a new philosophy of biology: Observations of an evolutionist*. Cambridge, MA: Harvard University Press.

McCall, R. B., Applebaum, M. I., & Hogarty, P. S. (1973). Developmental changes in mental performance. *Monographs of the Society for Research in Child Development, 38* (Serial No. 150).

McCarthy, D. A. (1954). Language development in children. In L. Carmichael (Ed.), *Manual of child psychology* (2nd ed.). New York: Wiley.

McClelland, J. L. (1995). A connectionist perspective on knowledge and development. In T. Simon & G. Halford (Eds.), *Developing cognitive competence: New approaches to process modeling*. Hillsdale, NJ: Erlbaum.

McCloskey, M. (1983). Intuitive physics. *Scientific American, 248*, 122–130.

McCloskey, M., Washburn, A., & Felch, L. (1983). Intuitive physics: The straight-down belief and its origin. *Journal of Experimental Psychology: Learning, Memory, and Cognition, 9*, 636–649.

McGarrigle, J., & Donaldson, M. (1974). Conservation accidents. *Cognition, 3*, 341–350.

McGilly, K., & Siegler, R. S. (1989). How children choose among serial recall strategies. *Child Development, 60*, 172–182.

McGilly, K., & Siegler, R. S. (1990). The influence of encoding and strategic knowledge on children's choices among serial recall strategies. *Developmental Psychology, 26*, 931–941.

McGraw, M. (1935). *Growth: A study of Johnny and Jimmy*. New York: Appleton-Century Co.

Mehler, J. (1982). Studies in the development of cognitive processes. In S. Strauss (Ed.), *U-Shaped behavioral growth*. New York: Academic Press.

Menyuk, P. (1969). *Sentences children use*. Cambridge, MA: MIT Press.

Merriman, W. E., & Bowman, L. L. (1989). The mutual exclusivity bias in children's word learning. *Monographs of the Society for Research in Child Development, 54* (3–4, Serial No. 220).

Metz, K. (1985). The development of children's problem solving in a gears task: A problem space perspective. *Cognitive Science, 9*, 431–472.

Metz, K. (1993). From number to weight: Transformation of preschoolers' knowledge of the pan balance. *Cognition and Instruction, 11*, 31–93.

Miller, G. A., Galanter, E., & Pribram, K. H. (1960). *Plans and the structure of behavior*. New York: Holt.

Miller, K. (1989). Measurement as a tool for thought: The role of measuring procedures in children's understanding of quantitative invariance. *Developmental Psychology, 25*, 589–600.

Miller, K., Perlmutter, M., & Keating, D. (1984). Cognitive arithmetic: Comparison of operations. *Journal of Experimental Psychology: Learning, Memory, and Cognition, 10*, 46–60.

Miller, K. F., & Paredes, D. R. (1990). Starting to add worse: Effects of learning to multiply on children's addition. *Cognition, 37*, 213–242.

Miller, P. H. (1993). *Theories of developmental psychology* (3rd ed.). New York: W. H. Freeman and Company.

Miller, P. H., & Seier, W. L. (1994). Strategy utilization deficiencies in children: When, where, and why. In H. W. Reese (Ed.), *Advances in child development and behavior* (Vol. 25). New York: Academic Press.

Morss, J. R. (1990). *The biologising of childhood: Developmental psychology and the Darwinian myth*. Hillsdale, NJ: Erlbaum.

Munakata, Y., McClelland, J. L., Johnson, M. H., & Siegler, R. S. (1995). *Now you see it, now you don't: A gradualistic framework for understanding infants' successes and failures in object permanence tasks* (Technical Report PDP.CNS.94.2). Pittsburgh, PA: Carnegie Mellon University, Parallel Distributed Processing and Cognitive Neuroscience.

Myerson, J., & Miezin, F. M. (1980). The kinetics of choice: An operant systems analysis. *Psychological Review, 87*, 160–174.

Naus, M. J., & Ornstein, P. A. (1983). Development of memory strategies: Analysis, questions, and issues. In M. T. Chi (Ed.), *Trends in memory development research*. New York: Karger.

Neches, R. (1987). Learning through incremental refinement procedures. In D. Klahr, P. Langley, & R. Neches (Eds.), *Production system models of learning and development*. Cambridge, MA: MIT Press.

Nesselroade, J. R. (1990). The warp and the woof of the developmental fabric. In R. Downs, L. Liben, & D. S. Palermo (Eds.), *Visions of development, the environment, and aesthetics: The legacy of Joachim F. Wohlwill*. Hillsdale, NJ: Lawrence Erlbaum.

Neuringer, A. (1992). Choosing to vary and repeat. *Psychological Science, 3*, 246–250.

Neuringer, A. (1993). Reinforced variation and selection. *Animal Learning & Behavior, 21*, 83–91.

Neuringer, A. J. (1967). Effects of reinforcement magnitude on choice and rate of responding. *Journal of the Experimental Analysis of Behavior, 10*, 417–424.

Newell, A. (1973). You can't play 20 questions with nature and win: Projective com-

ments on the papers of this symposium. In W. G. Chase (Ed.), *Visual information processing*. San Diego, CA: Academic Press.
Newell, A. (1990). *Unified theories of cognition*. Cambridge, MA: Harvard University Press.
Newell, A., Shaw, J. C., & Simon, H. A. (1958). Elements of a theory of human problem solving. *Psychological Review, 65*, 151–166.
Newell, A., & Simon, H. A. (1972). *Human problem solving*. Englewood Cliffs, NJ: Prentice-Hall.
Newport, E. L. (1990). Maturational constraints on language learning. *Cognitive Science, 14*, 11–28.
Nisbett, R. E., & Wilson, T. D. (1977). Telling more than we can know: Verbal reports on mental processes. *Psychological Review, 84*, 231–259.
Oaksford, M., & Chater, N. (1994). A rational analysis of the selection task as optimal data selection. *Psychological Review, 101*, 608–631.
Oyama, S. (1985). *The ontogeny of information: Developmental systems and evolution*. New York: Cambridge University Press.
Paley. (1822). *Natural Theology*. London.
Palincsar, A. S., & Brown, A. L. (1984). Reciprocal teaching of comprehension-monitoring activities. *Cognition and Instruction, 1*, 117–175.
Paris, S. G. (1988). Models and metaphors of learning strategies. In C. E. Weinstein, E. T. Goetz, & P. A. Alexander (Eds.), *Learning and study strategies: Issues in assessment, instruction, and evaluation*. San Diego: Academic Press.
Paris, S. G., & Lindauer, B. K. (1982). The development of cognitive skills during childhood. In B. Wolman (Ed.), *Handbook of developmental psychology*. Englewood Cliffs, NJ: Prentice-Hall.
Park, B., & Hastie, R. (1987). Perception of variability in category development: Instance- versus abstraction-based stereotypes. *Journal of Personality and Social Psychology, 53*, 621–635.
Payne, J. W., Bettman, J. R., & Johnson, E. J. (1988). Adaptive strategy selection in decision making. *Journal of Experimental Psychology: Learning, Memory, and Cognition, 14*, 534–552.
Payne, J. W., Bettman, J. R., & Johnson, E. J. (1993). *The adaptive decision maker*. Cambridge: Cambridge University Press.
Pellegrino, J. W., & Goldman, S. R. (1989). Mental chronometry and individual differences in cognitive processes: Common pitfalls and their solutions. *Learning and Individual Differences, 1*, 203–225.
Perkins, D. A. (1994). Creativity: Beyond the Darwinian paradigm. In M. A. Boden (Ed.), *Dimensions of creativity*. Cambridge, MA: The MIT Press.
Perner, J. (1991). *Understanding the representational mind*. Cambridge, MA: Bradford Books.
Perner, J., & Mansbridge, D. G. (1983). Developmental differences in encoding length series. *Child Development, 54*, 710–719.
Perry, M., Church, R. B., & Goldin-Meadow, S. (1988). Transitional knowledge in the acquisition of concepts. *Cognitive Development, 3*, 359–400.
Peterson, G., & Barney, H. (1952). Control methods used in a study of vowels. *Journal of the Acoustical Society of America, 24*, 175–184.
Piaget, J. (1952a). *The child's concept of number*. New York: W. W. Norton.
Piaget, J. (1952b). *The origins of intelligence in children*. New York: International University Press.

Piaget, J. (1969a). *The child's conception of physical causality*. Totowa, NJ: Littlefield, Adams, & Co.

Piaget, J. (1969b). *The child's concept of time*. New York: Ballantine.

Piaget, J. (1970). *Psychology and epistemology*. New York: Viking Press.

Piaget, J. (1971). *Biology and knowledge*. (B. Walsh, Trans.) Chicago: University of Chicago Press. (Original work published 1967)

Piaget, J. (1975). Phenocopy in biology and the psychological development of knowledge. In H. E. Gruber & J. J. Voneche (Eds.), *The essential Piaget: An interpretive reference and guide*. New York: Basic Books, Inc.

Piaget, J. (1976). *The grasp of consciousness: Action and concept in the young child*. Cambridge, MA: Harvard University Press.

Plomin, R. (1986). *Development, genetics, and psychology*. Hillsdale, NJ: Lawrence Erlbaum Associates.

Plunkett, K., & Sinha, C. (1991). Connectionism and developmental theory. *Psykologisk Skriftserie Aarhus, 16*, 1–34.

Premack, D. (1965). Reinforcement theory. In D. Levine (Ed.), *Nebraska symposium on motivation*. Lincoln: University of Nebraska Press.

Pressley, M., Borkowski, J. G., & O'Sullivan, J. T. (1984). Memory strategy instruction is made of this: Metamemory and durable strategy use. *Educational Psychology, 19*, 94–107.

Pressley, M., & Levin, J. R. (1987). Elaborative learning strategies for the inefficient learner. In S. J. Ceci (Ed.), *Handbook of cognitive, social, and neuropsychological aspects of learning disabilities*, (Vol. 2). Hillsdale, NJ: Erlbaum & Associates.

Proffitt, D. R., Kaiser, M. K., & Whelan, S. M. (1990). Understanding wheel dynamics. *Cognitive Psychology, 22*, 342–373.

Rachlin, H. C., & Green, L. (1972). Commitment, choice, and self-control. *Journal of the Experimental Analysis of Behavior, 17*, 15–22.

Rakic, P., Bourgeois, J.-P., Eckenhoff, M. F., Zecevic, N., & Goldman-Rakic, P. S. (1986). Concurrent overproduction of synapses in diverse regions of the primate cerebral cortex. *Science, 232*, 232–235.

Ravn, K. E., & Gelman, S. A. (1984). Rule usage in children's understanding of "big" and "little". *Child Development, 55*, 2141–2150.

Reder, L. M. (1982). Plausibility judgments versus fact retrieval: Alternative strategies for sentence verification. *Psychological Review, 89*, 250–280.

Reder, L. M. (1987). Strategy selection in question answering. *Cognitive Psychology, 19*, 90–138.

Reder, L. M., & Ritter, F. E. (1992). What determines initial feeling of knowing? Familiarity with question terms, not with the answer. *Journal of Experimental Psychology: Learning, Memory, and Cognition, 18*, 435–451.

Reese, H. W. (1962). Verbal mediation as a function of age level. *Psychological Bulletin, 59*, 502–509.

Resnick, L. B., & Neches, R. (1984). Factors affecting individual differences in learning ability. In R. J. Sternberg (Ed.), *Advances in the psychology of human intelligence*. Hillsdale, NJ: Erlbaum.

Resnick, L. B., Nesher, P., Leonard, F., Magone, M., Omanson, S., & Peled, I. (1989). Conceptual bases of arithmetic errors: The case of decimal fractions. *Journal of Research in Mathematics Education, 20*, 8–27.

Rogoff, B., Ellis, S., & Gardner, W. P. (1984). Adjustment of adult-child instruction according to child's age and task. *Child Development, 20*, 193–199.

Rovee-Collier, C. (1989). *The "memory system" of prelinguistic infants*. Paper presented at the Conference on the Development of Neural Bases of Higher Cognitive Functions, Chestnut Hill, PA.

Russell, J. (1982). Cognitive conflict, transmission, and justification: Conservation attainment through dyadic interaction. *Journal of Genetic Psychology, 140*, 283–297.

Russell, J., Mills, I., & Reiff-Musgrove, P. (1990). The role of symmetrical and asymmetrical social conflict in cognitive change. *Journal of Experimental Child Psychology, 49*, 58–78.

Russo, J. E., & Dosher, B. A. (1983). Strategies for multiattribute binary choice. *Journal of Experimental Psychology: Learning, Memory, and Cognition, 9*, 676–696.

Russo, J. E., Johnson, E. J., & Stephens, D. L. (1989). The validity of verbal protocols. *Memory and Cognition, 17*, 759–769.

Scarr, S. (1992). Developmental theories for the 1990s: Development and individual differences. *Child Development, 63*, 1–19.

Schauble, L. (1990). Belief revision in children: The role of prior knowledge and strategies for generating evidence. *Journal of Experimental Child Psychology, 49*, 31–57.

Schliemann, A. D. (1992). Mathematical concepts in and out of school in Brazil: From developmental psychology to better teaching. *Newsletter of the International Society for the Study of Behavioral Development* (Serial No. 22, No. 2), 1–3.

Schneider, W. (1985). Developmental trends in the metamemory-memory behavior relationship: An integrative review. In D. L. Forrest-Pressley, G. E. MacKinnon, & T. G. Waller (Eds.), *Cognition, metacognition, and human performance*. New York: Academic Press.

Schneider, W., & Pressley, M. (1989). *Memory development between 2 and 20*. New York: Springer-Verlag.

Scollon, R. (1976). *Conversations with a one-year old*. Honolulu: University Press of Hawaii.

Secada, W. G., Fuson, K. C., & Hall, J. W. (1983). The transition from counting-all to counting-on in addition. *Journal for Research in Mathematics Education, 14*, 47–57.

Seidenberg, M. S., & McClelland, J. L. (1989). A distributed developmental model of word recognition and naming. *Psychological Review, 96*, 523–568.

Seidenberg, M. S., & McClelland, J. L. (1990). More words but still no lexicon: Reply to Besner, et. al. (1990). *Psychological Review, 97*, 447–452.

Shafir, E., & Tversky, A. (1992). Thinking through uncertainty: Nonconsequential reasoning and choice. *Cognitive Psychology, 24*, 449–474.

Shultz, T. R., Schmidt, W. C., Buckingham, D., & Mareschal, D. (1995). Modeling cognitive development with a generative connectionist algorithm. In T. Simon & G. Halford (Eds.), *Developing cognitive competence: New approaches to process modeling* (pp. 205–261). Hillsdale, NJ: Erlbaum.

Shultz, T. R., Fisher, G. W., Pratt, C. C., & Rulf, S. (1986). Selection of causal rules. *Child Development, 57*, 143–152.

Sidman, M. (1952). A note on functional relations obtained from group data. *Psychological Bulletin, 49*, 263–269.

Siegler, R. S. (1976). Three aspects of cognitive development. *Cognitive Psychology, 8*, 481–520.

Siegler, R. S. (1978). The origins of scientific reasoning. In R. S. Siegler (Ed.), *Children's thinking: What develops?* Hillsdale, NJ: Erlbaum.

Siegler, R. S. (1981). Developmental sequences within and between concepts. *Monographs of the Society for Research in Child Development, 46* (Whole No. 189).

Siegler, R. S. (1983). Five generalizations about cognitive development. *American Psychologist, 38*, 263–277.
Siegler, R. S. (1986). Unities across domains in children's strategy choices. In M. Perlmutter (Ed.), *Perspectives on intellectual development: The Minnesota symposia on child psychology, Vol. 19*. Hillsdale, NJ: Erlbaum.
Siegler, R. S. (1987a). The perils of averaging data over strategies: An example from children's addition. *Journal of Experimental Psychology: General, 116*, 250–264.
Siegler, R. S. (1987b). Strategy choices in subtraction. In J. A. Sloboda & D. Rogers (Eds.), *Cognitive processes in mathematics*. Oxford: Oxford University Press.
Siegler, R. S. (1988a). Strategy choice procedures and the development of multiplication skill. *Journal of Experimental Psychology: General, 117*, 258–275.
Siegler, R. S. (1988b). Individual differences in strategy choices: Good students, not-so-good students, and perfectionists. *Child Development, 59*, 833–851.
Siegler, R. S. (1989a). Hazards of mental chronometry: An example from children's subtraction. *Journal of Educational Psychology, 81*, 497–506.
Siegler, R. S. (1989b). Mechanisms of cognitive development. *Annual Review of Psychology, 40*, 353–379.
Siegler, R. S. (1995). How does change occur: A microgenetic study of number conservation. *Cognitive Psychology, 25*, 225–273.
Siegler, R. S. (1996). Unidimensional thinking, multidimensional thinking, and characteristic tendencies of thought. In A. J. Sameroff and M. Haith (Eds.), *Reason and responsibility: The passage through childhood*. Chicago: University of Chicago Press.
Siegler, R. S., Adolph, K. E., & Lemaire, P. (in press). Strategy choices across the life-span. In L. Reder (Ed.), *Implicit learning and metacognition: The 27th Carnegie Mellon Cognition Symposium*. Hillsdale, NJ: Erlbaum.
Siegler, R. S., & Ashcraft, M. H. (1995). Strategy choices in adults' multi-digit multiplication. Manuscript in preparation.
Siegler, R. S., & Campbell, J. (1989). Individual differences in children's strategy choices. In P. L. Ackerman, R. J. Sternberg, & R. Glaser (Eds.), *Learning and individual differences: Advances in theory and research*. New York: W. H. Freeman and Company.
Siegler, R. S., & Crowley, K. (1991). The microgenetic method: A direct means for studying cognitive development. *American Psychologist, 46*, 606–620.
Siegler, R. S., & Crowley, K. (1994). Constraints on learning in nonprivileged domains. *Cognitive Psychology, 27*, 194–226.
Siegler, R. S., & Jenkins, E. (1989). *How children discover new strategies*. Hillsdale, NJ: Erlbaum.
Siegler, R. S., & McGilly, K. (1989). Strategy choices in children's time-telling. In I. Levin & D. Zakay (Eds.), *Time and human cognition: A life span perspective*. The Netherlands: Elsevier.
Siegler, R. S., & Richards, D. (1979). Development of time, speed, and distance concepts. *Developmental Psychology, 15*, 288–298.
Siegler, R. S., & Robinson, M. (1982). The development of numerical understandings. In H. W. Reese & L. P. Lipsitt (Eds.), *Advances in child development and behavior (Vol. 16)*. New York: Academic Press.
Siegler, R. S., & Shipley, C. (1995). Variation, selection, and cognitive change. In T. Simon & G. Halford (Eds.), *Developing cognitive competence: New approaches to process modeling*. Hillsdale, NJ: Erlbaum.
Siegler, R. S., & Shrager, J. (1984). Strategy choices in addition and subtraction: How do

children know what to do? In C. Sophian (Ed.), *Origins of cognitive skills*. Hillsdale, NJ: Erlbaum.

Siegler, R. S., & Taraban, R. (1986). Conditions of applicability of a strategy choice model. *Cognitive Development, 1*, 31–51.

Siegler, R. S., & Vago, S. (1978). The development of a proportionality concept: Judging relative fullness. *Journal of Experimental Child Psychology, 25*, 371–395.

Simon, H. A. (1955). A behavioral model of rational choice. *Quarterly Journal of Economics, 69*, 99–118.

Simon, H. A. (1957). *Administrative behavior*. New York: Macmillan.

Simon, H. A. (1981). *The sciences of the artificial*. Cambridge, MA: MIT Press.

Simon, T., & Klahr, D. (1995). A computational theory of children's learning about number conservation. In T. Simon & G. Halford (Eds.), *Developing cognitive competence: New approaches to process modeling*. Hillsdale, NJ: Erlbaum

Simon, T., & Halford, G. (Eds.). (1995). *Developing cognitive competence: New approaches to process modeling*. Hillsdale, NJ: Erlbaum.

Smetana, J. G. (1981). Preschool children's concepts of moral and social rules. *Child Development, 52*, 1333–1336.

Smiley, S. S., & Brown, A. L. (1979). Conceptual preference for thematic or taxonomic relations: A nonmonotonic age trend from preschool to old age. *Journal of Child Psychology, 28*, 249–257.

Smith, N. V. (1973). *The acquisition of phonology: A case study*. Cambridge: Cambridge University Press.

Staddon, J. E. R. (1991). Selective choice: A commentary on Herrnstein (1990). *American Psychologist, 46*, 793–797.

Starkey, P. (1992). The early development of numerical reasoning. *Cognition, 43*, 93–126.

Staszewski, J. J. (1988). Skilled memory and expert mental calculation. In M. T. H. Chi, R. Glaser, & M. J. Farr (Eds.), *The nature of expertise*. Hillsdale, NJ: Erlbaum.

Stavy, R., Strauss, S., Orpaz, N., & Carmi, G. (1982). U-Shaped behavioral growth in ratio comparisons. In S. Strauss (Ed.), *U-Shaped behavioral growth*. New York: Academic Press.

Steinberg, L. D. (1981). Transformations in family relations at puberty. *Developmental Psychology, 17*, 833–840.

Steinberg, R. (1983). *A teaching experiment on the learning of addition and subtraction facts*. Unpublished doctoral dissertation, University of Wisconsin, Madison.

Stern, E. & Siegler, R. S. (1996). *A microgenetic study of children's use of arithmetic shortcut strategies*. Manuscript in preparation.

Sternberg, R. J. (1984). Introduction. In R. J. Sternberg (Ed.), *Mechanisms of cognitive development*. New York: Freeman.

Sternberg, R. J. (1985). *Beyond IQ: A triarchic theory of human intelligence*. New York: Cambridge University Press.

Sternberg, R. J., & Ketron, J. L. (1982). Selection and implementation of strategies in reasoning by analogy. *Journal of Educational Psychology, 74*, 399–413.

Sternberg, R. J., & Rifkin, B. (1979). The development of analogical reasoning processes. *Journal of Experimental Child Psychology, 27*, 195–232.

Sternberg, R. J., & Weil, E. M. (1980). An aptitude x strategy interaction in linear syllogistic reasoning. *Journal of Educational Psychology, 72*, 226–239.

Stigler, J. W., & Perry, M. (1988). Mathematics learning in Japanese, Chinese, and American classrooms. In G. B. Saxe & M. Gearhart (Eds.), *Children's mathematics*. San Francisco: Jossey-Bass.

Stipek, D. (1984). Young children's performance expectations: Logical analysis or wishful thinking? In J.G. Nicholls (Ed.), *Advances in motivation and achievement: Vol. 3, The development of achievement motivation*. Greenwich, CT: JAI Press.

Stokes, P. D. (1995). Learned variability. *Animal Learning and Behavior, 23*, 164–176.

Stokes, P., Mechner, F., & Balsam, P. (in press). Indirect selection of variability: Effects of different teaching procedures on task variability and topography.

Strauss, M. S., & Cohen, L. P. (1978). *Infant immediate and delayed memory for perceptual dimensions*. Unpublished manuscript, University of Illinois, Urbana.

Strauss, S. (1982). *U-shaped behavioral growth*. New York: Academic Press.

Svenson, O. (1975). Analysis of time required by children for simple additions. *Acta Psychologica, 39*, 289–302.

Svenson, O. (1985). Memory retrieval of answers of simple additions as reflected in response latencies. *Acta Psychologica, 59*, 285–304.

Svenson, O., & Broquist, S. (1975). Strategies for solving simple addition problems: A comparison of normal and subnormal children. *Scandinavian Journal of Psychology, 16*, 143–151.

Svenson, O., & Hedenborg, M. L. (1979). Strategies used by children when solving simple subtractions. *Acta Psychologica, 43*, 477–489.

Svenson, O., & Sjoberg, K. (1983). Evolution of cognitive processes for solving simple additions during the first three school years. *Scandinavian Journal of Psychology, 24*, 117–124.

Symons, D. (1992). On the use and misuse of Darwinism in the study of human behavior. In J. H. Barkow, L. Cosmides, & J. Tooby (Eds.), *The adapted mind: Evolutionary psychology and the generation of culture*. New York: Oxford University Press.

Teasley, S. D. (1995). The role of talk in children's peer collaborations. *Developmental Psychology, 31*, 207–220.

Thelen, E. (1992). Development as a dynamic system. *Current Directions in Psychological Science, 1*, 189–193.

Thelen, E., & Smith, L. B. (1994). *A dynamic systems approach to the development of cognition and action*. Cambridge, MA: MIT Press/Bradford Books.

Thelen, E., & Ulrich, B. D. (1991). Hidden skills. *Monographs of the Society for Research in Child Development, 56* (Serial No. 223).

Tudge, J. R. H. (1992). Processes and consequences of peer collaboration: A Vygotskian analysis. *Child Development, 63*, 1364–1379.

Turiel, E. (1983). *The development of social knowledge: Morality and convention*. Cambridge: Cambridge University Press.

Turiel, E. (1989). Domain-specific social judgments and domain ambiguities. *Merrill-Palmer Quarterly, 35*, 89–114.

Turiel, E., & Davidson, P. (1986). Heterogeneity, inconsistency, and asynchrony in the development of cognitive structures. In I. Levin (Ed.), *Stage and structure: Reopening the debate*. Norwood, NJ: Ablex Publishing Corporation.

Turner, A. M., & Greenough, W. T. (1985). Differential rearing effects on rat visual cortex synapses. I. Synaptic and neuronal density and synapses per neuron. *Brain Research, 329*, 195–203.

Tversky, A. (1969). Intransitivity of preferences. *Psychological Review, 76*, 31–48.

Tversky, A., & Kahneman, D. (1973). Availability: A heuristic for judging frequency and probability. *Cognitive Psychology, 4*, 207–232.

Tversky, A., & Kahneman, D. (1974). Judgment under uncertainty: Heuristics and biases. *Science, 185*, 1124–1131.

Tversky, A., Sattath, S., & Slovic, P. (1988). Contingent weighting in judgment and choice. *Psychological Review, 95*, 371–384.

van der Maas, H. L. J., & Molenaar, P. C. M. (1992). Stagewise cognitive development: An application of catastrophe theory. *Psychological Review, 99*, 395–417.

van Geert, P. (1991). A dynamic systems model of cognitive and language growth. *Psychological Review, 98*, 3–53.

Van Lehn, K. (1986). Arithmetic procedures are induced from examples. In J. Hiebert (Ed.), *Conceptual and procedural knowledge: The case of mathematics*. Hillsdale, NJ: Erlbaum.

Van Lehn, K. (1990). *Mind bugs: The origins of procedural misconceptions*. Cambridge, MA: MIT Press.

Vygotsky, L. S. (1978). *Mind and society: The development of higher mental processes*. Cambridge, MA: Harvard University Press.

Wagner, D. A. (1978). Memories of Morocco: The influence of age, schooling and environment on memory. *Cognitive Psychology, 10*, 1–28.

Webb, N. (1991). Task-related verbal interaction and mathematics learning in small groups. *Journal for Research in Mathematics Education, 22*, 366–389.

Wellman, H. M. (1983). Metamemory revisited. In M. T. H. Chi (Ed.), *Trends in memory development research*. Basel: Karger.

Wellman, H. M. (1990). *The child's theory of mind*. Cambridge, MA: MIT Press.

Wellman, H. M., & Gelman, S. A. (1992). Cognitive development: Foundational theories of core domains. *Annual Review of Psychology, 43*, 337–375.

Wechsler, M. A., & Adolph, K. E. (1995, April). *Learning new ways of moving: Variability in infants' discovery and selection of motor strategies*. Poster presented at the meeting of the Society for Research in Child Development, Indianapolis, IN.

Werner, H. (1925). Uber mikromelodik und microharmonik [Musical micromelodies and microscales]. *Zeitschrift Psychologie, 98*.

Werner, H. (1948). *Comparative psychology of mental development*. New York: International Universities Press.

Wertsch, J. V., & Stone, C. A. (1978). Microgenesis as a tool for developmental analysis. *Laboratory of Comparative Human Cognition, 1*, 8–10.

White, S. H. (1965). Evidence for a hierarchical arrangement of learning processes. In L. P. Lipsitt & C. C. Spiker (Eds.), *Advances in child behavior and development* (Vol. 2). New York: Academic Press.

Widaman, K. F., Geary, D. C., Cormier, P., & Little, T. D. (1989). A componential model for mental addition. *Journal of Experimental Psychology: Learning, Memory, and Cognition, 15*, 898–919.

Wiesel, T. N., & Hubel, D. H. (1965). Comparison of the effects of unilateral and bilateral eye closure on cortical unit responses in kittens. *Journal of Neurophysiology, 28*, 1029–1040.

Wilkinson, A. C. (1982). Partial knowledge and self-correction: Developmental studies of a quantitative concept. *Developmental Psychology, 18*, 876–893.

Wilkinson, A. C. (1984). Children's partial knowledge of the cognitive skill of counting. *Cognitive Psychology, 16*, 28–64.

Williams, K. G., & Goulet, L. R. (1975). The effects of cuing and constraint instructions on children's free recall performance. *Journal of Experimental Child Psychology, 19*, 464–475.

Wilson, T. D., & Stone, J. I. (1985). Limitations of self-knowledge: More on telling more than we can know. In P. Shaver (Ed.), *Review of personality and social psychology* (Vol. 6). Beverly Hills, CA: Sage.

Winer, G. A. (1974). Conservation of different quantities among preschool children. *Child Development, 45*, 839–842.

Wolters, G., Beishizen, M., Broers, G., & Knoppert, W. (1990). Mental arithmetic: Effects of calculation procedure and problem difficulty on solution latency. *Journal of Experimental Child Psychology, 49*, 20–30.

Wood, D., Bruner, J., & Ross, G. (1976). The role of tutoring in problem solving. *Journal of Child Psychology and Psychiatry, 17*, 89–100.

Woods, S. S., Resnick, L. B., & Groen, G. J. (1975). Experimental test of five process models for subtraction. *Journal of Educational Psychology, 67*, 17–21.

Wynn, K. (1992). Addition and subtraction by human infants. *Nature, 358*, 749–750.

Yoshimura, T. (1974). *Strategies for addition among young children*. Paper presented at the 16th Annual Convention of the Japanese Association of Educational Psychology, Tokyo.

Yussen, S. R., & Levy, V. M. (1977). Developmental changes in knowledge about different retrieval problems. *Developmental Psychology, 13*, 114–120.

Author Index

Subject Index